WOMEN, MARRIAGE, AND FAMILY

IN MEDIEVAL CHRISTENDOM

Photograph courtesy of the Pontifical Institute of Mediaeval Studies

WOMEN, MARRIAGE, AND FAMILY

IN MEDIEVAL CHRISTENDOM

ESSAYS IN MEMORY

OF

MICHAEL M. SHEEHAN, C.S.B.

Edited by

CONSTANCE M. ROUSSEAU

and

JOEL T. ROSENTHAL

1998

Studies in Medieval Culture XXXVII

Medieval Institute Publications

WESTERN MICHIGAN UNIVERSITY

Kalamazoo, Michigan, USA 49008-3801

© Copyright 1998 by the Board of The Medieval Institute
Kalamazoo, Michigan 49008-3801

Library of Congress Cataloging-in-Publication Data

Women, marriage, and family in medieval Christendom : essays in memory
  of Michael M. Sheehan, C.S.B. / edited by Constance M. Rousseau and
  Joel T. Rosenthal.
      p.   cm. -- (Studies in medieval culture ; 37)
    Includes bibliographical references and index.
    ISBN 1-879288-65-6 (alk. paper). -- ISBN 1-879288-66-4 (pbk. :
  alk. paper)
      1. Women--History--Middle Ages, 500-1500. 2. Marriage--History.
    3. Family--History. 4. Social history--Medieval, 500-1500.
    5. Civilization, Medieval.   I. Sheehan, Michael M. (Michael
    McMahon), 1925-   . II. Rousseau, Constance M. III. Rosenthal,
    Joel Thomas, 1934-   . IV. Series.
    CB351.S83 vol. 37
    [HQ1143]
    306.8'09'02--dc21   97-47782
                                                                CIP

Cover design by Linda K. Judy
Printed in the United States of America

CONTENTS

PREFACE

hen Michael Sheehan died suddenly it left his wide circle of students and colleagues bereft of an opportunity to say a proper thank you or farewell. This volume of papers represents, on the part of the authors and editors, an attempt at both personal and professional closure. The volume was suggested by Constance M. Rousseau, and I am flattered that she sought me as a co-editor.

In addition to Michael Sheehan's former doctoral and licentiate students who have made the volume a reality by presenting essays, we wish to acknowledge the support of many others who encouraged us to go ahead with this project. Leslie Abrams, Conrad Harkins, and Marion Hollinger are Sheehan students who were not able to contribute but who were supportive of the volume from its inception. James K. Farge, C.S.B., of Saint Michael's College, University of Toronto, and Sue Sheridan Walker of Northeastern Illinois University endorsed our efforts and supported the idea that the "Sheehan legacy" should be shown as extending to the next generation of scholars. At various stages between the early planning and the semi-final word editing we have had useful help and generous advice from Phyllis Cardullo, Christopher Kennedy, Francine Mancini, Cynthia Messenger, Nancy Kovacs, Caroline Suma, Grace Desa, Jean Murtrie, Karen Kinsdale, Virginia Brown, Sheila D. Campbell, Reverend Martin Dimnick, C.S.B., Joseph W. Goering, John Leyerle, Roger E. Reynolds, George Rigg, Jill R. Webster, Norma Kroll, Mary Ann E. Rousseau, Esq., Marcia Stenz, and Georges Whalen. And among our contributors, the advice of Dyan Elliott, Jacqueline Murray, John Carmi Parsons, Frederik Pedersen, David A. E. Pelteret, and Kathryn Ann Taglia contributed to the shape and focus of the collection. To those who knew and worked with Michael Sheehan it seems fitting that a volume in his memory is the collective and collaborative product of so many different people and viewpoints.

We also want to note a special mark of gratitude for the more personal contributions of †Walter H. Principe and J. Ambrose Raftis, scholars and teachers who knew Michael as a friend and colleague and whose reflections here add a touch that none of his doctoral students was comfortable about providing. The staff of Providence College (especially of the History Department), of the Centre for Medieval Studies of the University of Toronto, and of the Pontifical Institute of Mediaeval Studies all made important contributions. Finally, the staff of Medieval Institute Publications at the Medieval Institute of Western Michigan University assured us, from the beginning, that this was a volume they would be pleased to publish; their early and strong endorsement has been vital.

Michael Sheehan would have been uncomfortable at any display of sentiment concerning his role as a teacher, particularly at one that even hinted at how much respect and affection he commanded from those who knew him. But a volume that he inspired by his own work and by his personal dedication to the world of scholarship would have been, I think, well received. Our only regret is that this has come so very late.

—Joel T. Rosenthal

CONTRIBUTORS

Audrey Douglas

Researcher for the Records of Early English Drama. She studied at Saint Anne's College, Oxford, and Queen's University in Kingston before coming to Toronto. She was the research editor for the *Cumberland, Westmorland, and Gloucestershire* volume in the REED series.

Dyan Elliott

Associate Professor of History and Adjunct in Religious Studies, Indiana University. Author of *Spiritual Marriage: Sexual Abstinence in Medieval Wedlock* and *Fallen Bodies: Pollution, Sexuality & Demonology in the Middle Ages* (forthcoming, 1998), she is presently working on female mysticism and inquisitional practice.

Timothy S. Haskett

Assistant Professor of History, University of Victoria. He has written on Chancery and testamentary material as well as on canon and common law and diplomatic editing.

Margaret H. Kerr

A lawyer in Toronto, with her degrees from the University of Toronto. She has published on medieval criminal law including the ordeal and the appeal of felony. Her recent books include *Canadian Tort Law in a Nutshell, The Complete Guide to Buying, Owning and Selling a Home in Canada*, and *Make It Legal: What Every Canadian Entrepreneur Needs to Know About Business Law.*

Shannon McSheffrey

Associate Professor at Concordia University, she studied at Carleton University before coming to Toronto. She has published *Gender and Heresy: Women, Men, and Lollard Communities, 1420–1530*, and *Love and Marriage in Late Medieval London.*

Jacqueline Murray

Associate Professor of History and Director of the Humanities Research Groups, University of Windsor. She has published on family, gender, and sexuality, and compiled, with Michael Sheehan, *Domestic Society in Medieval Europe: A Select Bibliography*. She is co-editor with Konrad Eisenbichler of *Desire and Discipline: Sex and Sexuality in the Premodern West.*

John Carmi Parsons

Assistant Professor, Department of History, University of Toronto. He is the author of *The Court and Household of Eleanor of Castile in 1290, Eleanor of Castile: Queen and Society in Thirteenth-Century England*, editor of *Medieval Queenship*, and co-editor with Bonnie Wheeler of *Medieval Mothering.*

Frederik Pedersen

Lecturer in History at the University of Aberdeen and member of the executive committee of the Scottish Society for Northern Studies. He has published on the Hanse and Danish family law, and is the author of *Romeo and Juliet of Stonegate: A Medieval Marriage in Crisis* and of a forthcoming book on marriage cases in the fourteenth-century York Cause Papers.

David A. E. Pelteret

Director of Administration at New College, University of Toronto, and Adjunct Associate Professor at the Centre for

Medieval Studies. He studied at Cape Town and Oxford before coming to work with Michael Sheehan, and he has published the *Catalogue of English Post-Conquest Vernacular Documents* and *Slavery in Early Mediaeval England.*

†*Walter H. Principe, C.S.B.*

Late Professor of the University of Toronto and Fellow of the Pontifical Institute of Mediaeval Studies. He published widely in the areas of historical theology and the history of medieval theology.

J. Ambrose Raftis, C.S.B.

Professor Emeritus, University of Toronto, and formerly President of the Pontifical Institute of Mediaeval Studies. He studied at Cambridge (where he played ice hockey) in addition to Toronto and has published many books and articles on English agricultural, village, and economic and social history.

Joel T. Rosenthal

Professor of History, State University of New York at Stony Brook. He works on late medieval social history and co-edits *Medieval Prosopography.*

Constance M. Rousseau

Associate Professor of History at Providence College. She studied at Notre Dame before coming to the University of Toronto. She has published several articles on Innocent III and social relationships.

Kathryn Ann Taglia

Instructor in the Women's Studies Program at the University of North British Columbia. She is completing her doctoral dissertation at the University of Toronto on the history of childhood in late medieval France.

INTRODUCTION

When, in the twelfth century, Bernard of Chartres described his contemporaries "as standing on the shoulders of giants" he was not merely expressing intellectual modesty but was also recognizing the tradition and continuum of knowledge. The grammarian was implying that thinkers of his era could transcend their own abilities by expanding upon the rich inheritance left them by the ancients.

Indeed, Bernard's intellectual forebears in the monasteries of Europe had preserved the Greco-Roman and Judeo-Christian heritages to be handed down from generation to generation by scholar to scholar and teacher to student. This process has continued into the present—exemplified in the life and work of Michael M. Sheehan of the order of Saint Basil, professor of history at the Pontifical Institute of Mediaeval Studies in Toronto, Canada.

When Michael M. Sheehan passed away unexpectedly on 23 August 1992, he bequeathed a rich and lasting legacy for those remaining behind. His legacy consisted of his own writings in medieval social history, his pastoral work, his scholarly relationships, and personal friendships with many individuals in Canada and abroad. The culminating part of his legacy, however, extended far beyond this.

Sheehan was a highly gifted mentor, teacher, and scholar whose instruction inspired generations of students to pursue the study of history and to do academic research so as to become further links in the ever-expanding web of culture. By his careful guidance, he trained his students in the methodology of approaching and interpreting texts that enabled them to read history "forwards rather than backwards." In this way, they saw historical events and cultural attitudes through the eyes of the medievals themselves rather than through a twentieth-century perspective. Students consequently explored the various avenues of choice open to medieval people. These options, as Sheehan himself was accustomed to say, were like the many veins and arteries extending from the heart and finally branching into countless fine capillaries. Historical development offered several vital paths that could be followed, and an historian had to be fully aware of all of them, not just the ones that ultimately prevailed. Thus, emphasizing the free choice of humans in reaching solutions rather than merely focusing on the predetermined route of what finally happened, Sheehan showed his students the nuances and the complexity of history and of all human life.

Sheehan not only introduced his students to the intricacies of human life but also sensitized them to the subtleties of language and the need for accurate expression. His interest in words—their etymologies and shades of meaning—caused his students to be more mindful about their exact choices of terms in order to frame their ideas with clarity and precision.

Students were also taught to let the sources provide the historical questions to be posed. They came to work inductively, reading "out of" rather than "into" the evidence. This research method engaged his students intimately and thoroughly with their sources, which were supplemented with evidence from other disciplines but which still remained the focus of the extended thesis research. This methodology prevented the student from practicing an impressionistic form of scholarship where much could be argued on the support of little evidence. Sheehan, a man of enormous integrity, was careful not to claim more in his own writings than his sources permitted, an example of *honestas* that profoundly influenced the work of his students.

Historical accuracy was and is certainly of great import. Yet ideas—sophisticated, critical, but most significantly, original—were vital to Father Sheehan. His way of looking at history—organic and dynamic—and his encouragement of creativity engendered in his students the need to pose new questions and find new answers. Thus, these younger historians brought their own individual voices and fresh insights to the texts.

The eleven essays offered here in Father Sheehan's memory reflect his imprint and spirit as well as the originality of his former students. These essays consider three thematic categories that were dominant in most of Sheehan's own scholarly work. These are the role, position, and contributions of medieval women; the development of Christian marriage, especially in the High Middle Ages; and the secular family with its legal and emotional relationships. A close reading of the papers, particularly those concerned with the mainstream themes of marriage and the family, reveal what we can designate as the Sheehan school of social history. The collection expands on several of Sheehan's research areas; it shows a considerable interest in medieval England but does not disregard the Continent.

In seven of the studies, those by Murray, McSheffrey, Pedersen, Kerr, Taglia, Rousseau, and Haskett, we see the overarching Sheehanesque vision, in which legal sources are used to discern the truths of medieval society. The legal sources are varied—secular and ecclesiastical court records, pastoral manuals, conciliar decrees, papal letters, and testaments. While these contributors continue their research from this primarily legal perspective, others, such as Parsons, have gone farther afield, taking a more prosopographical approach. Still others, such as Pelteret, Elliot, and Douglas, are inclined to a third interest of Sheehan's—the study of women from Anglo-Saxon times to the late medieval period. Their essays use chronicles, hagiography, and account records. They sound, at first instance, least like the Sheehan voice; and yet, we can also say that his scholarly interest in the lives of medieval women resonates in all of his academic work. His fascination with the development of marriage and the family could hardly leave the situation of women untouched, although he did not always specifically express its implications.

Father Sheehan, whose love of learning was only superseded by his desire for God, challenged his students, demanding of them an ability far beyond what they themselves sometimes believed they possessed. A seminal influence in their intellectual odyssey, he recognized their potential before many of them had gained the confidence to perceive it in themselves. Like the best of dedicated scholar-teachers, he lifted his students up and bore them aloft on his shoulders. They stood on the shoulders of a giant.

—*Constance M. Rousseau*

In Memoriam

MICHAEL SHEEHAN—
A PERSONAL PROFILE
BY A FRIEND

†Walter H. Principe, C.S.B.

As Michael Sheehan and I sat reading the morning newspaper, we heard Father Dwyer, by far the most loquacious of all our Basilian confreres and a great raconteur, coming down the hall talking to someone else or simply declaiming without an audience—we weren't sure which! As he entered the room, Father Dwyer declared in his stentorian tones, "Gentlemen, I have nothing to say." To which Michael, looking up from his papers, grinningly responded: "Please be brief." We all broke into laughter, including Father Dwyer, who as an admirer of Churchill's quick-witted responses recognized a reply worthy of his oratorical hero.

Michael's quick wit—gentle, humorous, and never cutting—was one of his most endearing qualities, something that made him an appreciated member of many different social groups. Also welcome were his evident intelligence, competence, and extensive interests, the sources of many a contribution to wide-ranging discussions among his confreres, colleagues, and other friends. Oh, he could be irritating at times, as when he adopted a paternalistic and somewhat condescending manner towards others, even his peers (women colleagues sometimes found this

1

hard to take), or when, in a meeting that had deliberated long on some topic and voted its decision, he would stubbornly start to go back over the discussion with views from his own perspective. But everyone recognized that his exceptional kindness and concern for others were the basic qualities that modified such characteristics. And what might have looked like paternalism for peers came across to students as a fatherly concern that carried many of them through difficult times on the way to completing their studies.

I first met Michael when we were fellow students in our freshman year at the University of Toronto. I remember his confiding to me, as we met in the university library one day, of his dream of becoming an aviator. Although he never fulfilled that dream, it was typical of a certain romanticism and derring-do that he showed in different ways all his life. Indeed, I wonder if his sad death was not the result of that same spirit. For on the morning of his death, at breakfast, he kept rubbing his leg either to ease pain or increase circulation, but instead of resting or having it looked after, he countered the problem head-on, mounting his bicycle and speeding off on what was to be his last journey. I shall never forget my last sad view of him in the hospital emergency room, the last signs of life ebbing from his injured body after the life-support systems were withdrawn because his head had been so badly damaged by his fall and his heart had been stricken in the ambulance taking him to the hospital.

I had often seen this energetic response to different circumstances during our college and theology years together and even more during the two years we spent together in Paris at L'École Pratique des Hautes Études. To see Michael, with his soutane tucked up so as to avoid the gears or spokes of the bicycle, wheeling through Parisian traffic on the way to the Sorbonne, was to catch a glimpse of a Celtic spirit not unlike that of those great travelers of ancient times.

Coming from a milk-drinking Canadian background, he quickly noticed the aversion of the French to that beverage and had fun teasing those wine-drinking, liqueur-sipping *citoyens*. At a banquet celebrating the ordination of a newly ordained priest I had known from correspondence, we were regaled with course after course, each one interrupted by short speeches or songs sung together; the speeches became more eloquent, the singing more vigorous as the wine lubricated the food and the vocal chords. At one point the mother of the new priest asked Michael, "What do you drink on occasions like this?" When he replied with a slight smile, "Milk," the poor woman almost became sick on the spot. He used the same ploy with the waiters at a French restaurant when they asked what beverage we would like at the end of the meal—his request for milk led them to gather in a corner, laughing and pointing at the table where this strange North American was eating. Of course, the laugh was really his, at their reaction.

In his personality I always thought that Michael was a remarkable mix of the fine qualities of his mother and father. I met his mother, together with several of the McMahon clan women, first, and saw in them the refined, courteous, intelligent, precise, somewhat precious yet forceful manner of speaking and acting that was typical of Michael. Then when I met his father, a hearty, good-humored, practical man full of chuckles and stories, I saw the other aspects of Michael's personality, the rambunctious, daring, laughing adventurer ready to try anything that challenged or interested him.

The love of the outdoors and adventuresome spirit he inherited from his father endured in Michael's love of rock-hunting on the pre-Cambrian shield in Canada and in archaeological digs in Turkey. He prepared for one of these digs by driving a Land Rover across Europe, following the route of one of the crusades. He was no bookbound historian—he wanted to get some "feel" of past events by experiencing landscapes and travel situations and even by fingering remains of the past in his digs. And in our two years together in Europe, he regularly organized our travel plans so that we could see and appreciate the great monuments and smaller witnesses to the life and achievements of people in the past.

Michael had the advantage of an exceptionally good education. One could see in his freshman year at university how effective his schools in Renfrew were. Then at the University of Toronto he took the difficult honors course in Philosophy, English, and History; the breadth and depth of this undergraduate course showed itself in a corresponding breadth and depth in everything he approached. This was furthered by his studies in theology preparatory to his ordination to the priesthood in 1950. It was increased even further when, while studying theology, he also began the multidisciplinary program of the Pontifical Institute of Mediaeval Studies. In those days, the first-year program included nine different courses of two hours each, covering a very wide range of topics necessary to understand medieval culture (we old-timers regret the loss of this breadth for present-day students). Michael spread out this first-year program and much of the upper years' requirements over several years as he did his theology at the same time—a grueling regimen indeed. The result, however, was that in Paris he was far better equipped for research than most of the highly intelligent but too narrowly focused graduate students and senior researchers in Paris.

It was from 1951 to 1953 that he and I studied in France, living practically as roommates and traveling about Europe together. During those years he expanded his already brilliant intellectual achievements. He soaked up in his extraordinary visual memory and good aesthetic sense all the artistic beauties that we saw on our travels. (I did tease him, though, that while living in Paris he only went to the Louvre on the last day of our stay there! In this and in other matters he could sometimes procrastinate.) These memories and insights became an important part of his courses in the Faculty of Theology of Saint Michael's, the Pontifical Institute of Mediaeval Studies, and the University of Toronto.

From 1953 on Michael taught church history in the theology faculty: the year of his death would have been his fortieth year of teaching there. From his very first year of teaching he was one of the prime movers in the reorganization of the theology program at Saint Basil's Seminary, and this paved the way for the development of the full-blown Faculty of Theology of Saint Michael's, which is now an important component of the Toronto School of Theology as well as a major participant in theological education in North America. In recent years Michael was being urged to withdraw gradually from that work for the sake of his health and for the important writing he was doing, but he persisted because he saw the need for church history among future ministers of the Gospel. Since my office was situated opposite his for many years, I was always aware of how many students, professors, friends, and other people seeking help came to his door and found a warm, ready welcome. He would give oral examinations in his office to history students from the Saint Michael's Faculty of Theology, a plodding, wearying process that sometimes took him three days to complete, so many were his students and so great his care.

I cannot resist telling a story about his kindly humorous attempts to help a student. The student in question was a chronic hypochondriac and, of course, found in Michael a sympathetic ear for his endless tales of woe. One day he came to complain to Michael about the pain he had suffered by having had some kidney stones removed. Michael replied very sympathetically: "Yes, I know what that pain is like. I've had the same problem; in fact, here in my desk I have one of the stones they removed from me." Upon which he drew from the drawer a large stone he had gathered on a rock-gathering field

trip and showed it to the student! What Michael found especially amusing about the incident was that the overly serious
and worried student didn't catch on to the joke until he applied
his considerable scientific knowledge to the stone and concluded that its chemical composition prevented it from being a
kidney stone. Only then did he have a good laugh at himself
and relax a bit.

It was, of course, not only theology students but also many
graduate students in the licentiate programs of the Institute and
the doctoral programs in the Centre for Medieval Studies and
the Department of History of the University of Toronto who
benefited from his teaching and direction of their research.
Again, I could see them constantly coming to his office for
advice or see him in the room at the end of our floor engaged
in the tedious work of discussing with them and correcting the
written work of his students. I might add that this devotion to
students was at the cost not only of his personal health but
also of many important publications he had started or had in
mind—publications that would have satisfied his personal bent
for sharing his insights and research with others, that would
have made great contributions to learning, and that would have
enhanced his reputation even further. He did not have the
narrowly restricted office hours of some professors who prefer
their research and writing to helping students. This charitable
service to students was in a sense a dying to self of the kind
that Michael heard urged upon him by Jesus in the Gospel and
that he always strove to accomplish with the help of grace.

In all his historical work Michael was no backward-looking
scholar. Everything he did in his historical work seeded his
fertile mind and produced rich fruits for present-day discussions, whether in the university community, the secular world,
or the Church. For those who think scholarship, especially
historical scholarship, an impractical waste of time and talent,
he stands as a counter-witness. His studies in legal history

made him a valuable helper in writing statutes for several corporate groups; his work on the family and in art history made him an important consultant for archdiocesan administrators or committees and for the university community. The aged were one of his chief concerns and interests, poignantly so as he went every other day to help feed his mother at the Saint Joseph's Health Centre and visit all the sick and the aged around his mother, and he applied his historical knowledge of social and family life in a practical way in conferences for the aged in our day. He was one of the chief planners and organizers for the yearly Michaelmas Conference, which draws together leaders in the professions, business, and politics for serious discussions about modern problems in the light of the Gospel, of history, and of theology. Michael Sheehan's historical knowledge and the insights it gave him and those whose lives he touched made him a beacon in the sometimes gloomy morass of contemporary problems.

I have referred to Michael's sense of dedication to others as a part of his dying to self. Indeed, Michael cannot be understood or appreciated if we fail to recognize this dynamic in his life. He viewed all his work as a ministry like the ministry Paul spoke of in words used at Michael's funeral Eucharist:

> Because we possess this ministry through God's mercy, we do not give in to discouragement. . . . It is not ourselves we preach but Christ Jesus as Lord, and ourselves as your servants for Jesus' sake. . . . We possess this treasure [of ministry] in earthen vessels, to make it clear that its surpassing power comes from God and not from us. (2 Corinthians 4: 1.5.7)

Thus Michael fit in well with the teaching of the Vatican Council (1962–65) recalling that each baptized Christian shares in the priestly, prophetic, and servant leadership rôles of Christ and that the ordained presbyter is called to exercise these rôles full-time for the Christian community and indeed for the whole world needing evangelization. As an ordained presbyter Michael exercised these three rôles admirably: he delighted in his *priestly* rôle, whether he was preaching or hearing confessions or celebrating the Eucharist in parishes or concelebrating with a group of us each morning, or counseling those many persons who came to him with their troubles. His *prophetic or teaching* rôle as presbyter was so evidently a ministry—both by his attitudes and interests but also by another important contribution some would not realize. In university circles there is still plenty of prejudice against Catholics, so that Michael's witness as an outstanding scholar equal or superior to the top rung of university scholars was one of his most important contributions, a true exercise of the prophetic teaching rôle of a presbyter. In fact, his election as Vice-President of the prestigious Medieval Academy of America, which would have led to his being President, recognized his scholarship but, I am sure, also his personal qualities flowing from his rôle as presbyter. He exercised that third rôle of a presbyter, being a *servant leader*, by endlessly sharing meetings and planning sessions for the good of the institutions he worked in, or for the archdiocese.

One of Michael's traits was important to me personally and to our community relationships; it is a trait that I think is a model for all of us today, whether in civil society or religious life. With his profound sense of history and institutions, and his knowledge of law, Michael sometimes found himself in disagreement with his confreres or colleagues over what he considered shallowly thought-out ideas or decisions; he tended to be intelligently conservative in his views even if it meant standing somewhat alone. But this never stood in the way of his being at one with others in charity and friendship. He knew what Thomas Aquinas taught, that we can have differences of opinion all the while remaining in concord, being one at heart in love and affection, or at least in mutual respect and civility. He knew from his study of the Middle Ages that it was by disputed questions and lively discussion that truth emerged, and he did not confuse differences of opinion or outlook with rejection, much less hatred, of the person with whom he disagreed. In this he has something to say today, when too frequently different views of how to address social and political problems, or how to live the Gospel in our day, can degenerate into discord, backbiting, rash judgment about the good intentions or faith of others, and even hatred and calumny. His example of concord, of unity in love despite differences of opinions, is a light set on high for all.

This quality, plus his total dedication as a presbyter and religious, had deep roots in Michael's life of prayer. In addition to his daily prayer of the Liturgy of the Hours and his daily celebration of the Eucharist, he spent long periods in prayer in the presence of Our Lord in the Blessed Sacrament. He frequently referred to spiritual readings that fed his prayer life, and his spiritual outlook often gave our conversations a deeper perspective on things. Thus, a short time before his death, he remarked to another Basilian how sad it is that we spend so much time trying to prolong our lives and so little time preparing to meet the Lord at the moment of death. I think that is why he cared less for self-preservation, why he took chances with his health and kept on in spite of melanoma and other ills, why he gave of himself so generously, knowing that prayer and service of Christ in others was the way to seek God. The psalm recited at his funeral, "O God, you are my God whom I seek," with its attendant verses, would be a fitting motto for his life.

The energy with which Michael Sheehan dedicated himself to so many projects had a source in his character that many did not know. Like Saint Francis de Sales, on whose feast he was born and whose example he cherished, he had a strong and, by his own admission, irascible temperament that only rarely showed itself. Like that saint, he gracefully channeled this strong temperament into a loving active concern for each person he met. Together with his intellectual and aesthetic endowments, this outgoing care for others is the trait most people recognized in him. What was especially striking about his concern was that he not only responded to the needs of others, he often intuited their needs, sometimes before they even realized themselves, and he acted generously to help them.

A reviewer of Michael Sheehan's book on the will in medieval England, after summarizing the great significance of this work for lawyers and others, concluded with this tribute:

> So complete and thorough an account, to 1300, of testamentary law and its application inevitably produced facts and conclusions that dictate corrections and revisions of earlier historians. Sheehan makes them, and, with a modesty not too common among revisionists, he neither flaunts his findings nor pillories his predecessors. Justly, he may take pride in the quality of his book, but he may take a greater pride in having written it with the humility that so becomes both his callings, the priest and the historian.—William Huse Dunham, *American Historical Review* (January 1964): 426–27

This tribute, written in the early years of Michael Sheehan's career, presaged both his subsequent academic achievements and his continually edifying personal spirituality.

THE INTERDISCIPLINARY CONTEXT
OF A CAREER

J. Ambrose Raftis, C.S.B.

he career of Michael Sheehan straddled a period of fundamental change in the structure of academic research and teaching at North American universities. It cannot be the purpose of these few paragraphs to assess the general success or failure of such change since scholars have devoted little attention to analysis of the question. Yet the remarkable growth over the past few decades in the fields designated by the title of this volume derives in no small part from such change. So, an attempt will be made to present the career of Michael Sheehan as a case study suggestive of an introductory approach to the topic of academic restructuring.

Tracing the history of the word *interdisciplinary* has been suggested as a useful place at which to begin. The Social Science Research Council of New York approached the topic in this fashion and discovered that the term *interdisciplinary* came into vogue only in the 1930s although the realities were immediately apparent after World War I in the founding of the ACLS in 1918, in this same Council in 1924, and the New School for Social Research in 1925.[1]

---

[1] *Items*, Social Science Research Council, 40 (1986): 17.

Limiting oneself to the history of the term in this fashion does provide a useful indicator of the degree to which the social sciences had lost ground from, or perhaps never had been accepted into, the nineteenth-century view of the humanities. But it is useful to recall that at the very time when so many departments were being formed in modern universities there was a very open view. John Henry Newman seemed to be speaking of a common opinion when he stated in *The Idea of a University*, "I say, then, that the systematic omission of any one science from the catalogue prejudices the accuracy and completeness of our knowledge altogether, and that, in proportion to its importance."[2] And again:

> It [the university] teaches all knowledge by teaching all branches of knowledge, and in no other way . . . in a university he will just know where he and his science stands . . . he is kept from extravagance by the very rivalry of other studies.[3]

Michael Sheehan pursued his undergraduate program at the University of Toronto under this vision of the humanities. Much attention was given to various means by which the student could obtain a mix of different disciplines. That is to say, departments supported a wide variety of interdepartmental programs even for those students in the demanding special disciplines called honors courses. Michael Sheehan followed such a course entitled "Philosophy, English and History." In our current viewpoint, such a program would be called "elitist" not only because it was adapted to brilliant students but also because the more prominent senior professors taught first-year candidates. This latter practice encouraged a further mix of professors. For example, one of the courses taken by Michael

---

[2] *The Idea of a University Defined and Illustrated* (London, 1912), p. 51.

[3] Newman, *Idea*, pp. 166–67.

Sheehan from the Department of English entitled "Nineteenth-Century Thought" included lectures from professors of philosophy and political science as well as English.

This proximity of professors occurred in other traditions as well. Significant for Medieval Studies was the experience at the University of Strasbourg after World War I. As Lucien Febvre recalled,

> At the university, our seminar rooms [that is, Marc Bloch and Febvre] were close. Our doors faced each other. And they were open. There was no question of medievalists feeling in conscience bound to ignore modern times; nor, inversely, of moderns to deal at arms' length with the Middle Ages. In fact, our students moved from one room to the other—and their teachers with them. [4]

In more private memoirs Marc Bloch and Étienne Gilson spoke of the same experience. Others, no doubt, such as Gabriel LeBras were similarly involved.

When Michael Sheehan turned to graduate studies at the Pontifical Institute of Mediaeval Studies he was fortunate in having an institution inspired by the blend of these two traditions. The principle of openness to various disciplines lay behind the stress upon the establishing of the Institute on the campus of a large modern university; and the effort to maintain a proper community of scholars was expected to be maintained by making medieval culture rather than any one or group of disciplines the common purpose of the program.

By the 1960s, when Michael Sheehan became a full-fledged professor, the academic scene had become radically transformed. Specialization within departmental fields had become too intense and varied for inclusion within older broad interdepartmental courses. The rapid increase in numbers of students

---

[4] *Combats pour l'histoire* (Paris, 1953), p. 393 (trans. by J. Ambrose Raftis).

no longer made possible the luxury of having the most prominent professors available for first-year undergraduates. Departments quickly lost their vision of the humanities as administrative issues replaced academic priorities. For example, the old course in nineteenth-century thought was dissolved because the Department of Philosophy argued that such a course was an intrusion upon the territory of philosophy.

Perhaps because graduate programs were not funded separately from the undergraduate departmental organization, the University of Toronto offered greater freedom for re-organization of graduate programming. In any case, there emerged a large number of new centers and institutes. Among these was the Centre for Medieval Studies, and with his work in this Centre from the 1960s Michael Sheehan literally did not have to break stride in the interdisciplinary pattern of his career. Of course, centers and institutes in the humanities can be mere paper umbrellas for the new organizational types of the time. But there are several characteristics that distinguish vital centers, and the work of Michael Sheehan serves to isolate some of the more important of these.

Gifted with imaginative curiosity and a prodigious memory, Sheehan became involved in the School of Theology, the Department of History, and the Department of Fine Art as well as the Centre for Medieval Studies and the Pontifical Institute of Mediaeval Studies. Such a range of endeavors could have easily degenerated into academic dilettantism were it not for two significant factors. The first of these was the dedicated respect held for others working in various fields related to his own. He did not try to do work that was better done by others. Especially was this noticeable when scholars were virtually specialists in his "own" area of research. In this age when so many scholars treat their specialization as a piece of real estate, Michael Sheehan never showed the slightest petty jealousy over the work of James A. Brundage or Richard H.

Helmholz, to take but two examples. He expected well-trained scholars to be able to make their own individual contributions to the one field. In short, this was a quality of the genuine humanist as well as of a scientific scholar.

Second, this same quality surfaced in the structural program of the Pontifical Institute. But it was often more required by the organizational dynamics of the Centre for Medieval Studies. The formation of an individualized program for a student required equal respect for each discipline in the program. Even more, the major field and Ph.D. committees implied acknowledgment of the fact that others would make contributions to the thesis topic, although the latter had been largely determined by the supervisor. Indeed, it was possible that other staff members could introduce modifications to one or other of the disciplines involved. The extraordinary number of committees and theses boards upon which Michael Sheehan served are as much a tribute to this quality as to his generosity.

Not surprisingly, these openly co-operative characteristics generated project development upon a tertiary level above and beyond teaching programs and thesis research. Several of these were able to be mounted at the University of Toronto itself owing to the availability of considerable staff groupings in some areas and the support of the federal Social Science and Humanities research grants. Less spectacular and less acknowledged but at least equal in significance was the rapid growth of international co-operation and the financial support given to this co-operation by granting agencies. It seems proper to designate this international development as a genuine academic institution. For these extensive communication-based group studies could never have taken place within a department nor even within a large university. In a real sense these are independent disciplines in their own right. Such, indeed, were the "family studies" of which Michael Sheehan became a part and that are so much the genesis of this volume. It is finally beginning to be argued that such processes should in fact *find* the most important areas for academic development in the future. On this point, David L. Featherman is of interest as he asks the question "What Does Society Need from Higher Education?"[5]

Michael Sheehan did not take time to reflect on his career, but as a long-time colleague I feel competent to make the observations presented here. In doing so I have become impressed by the need for such retrospective analysis. The Allan Blooms and Lawrence Stones who would have us return to some idyllic world do not in fact properly represent the vision of the traditional humanities. Increasing concern about the fact that more and more history conferences differ little from social science conferences might be somewhat defused by more reflection upon how Marc Bloch considered himself to be a humanist. Furthermore, those who remain mired in the administrative reorganization of the ever-growing number of specializations have not looked at the lessons to be learned from the careers of such as Michael Sheehan. There is a tried and proven possibility of a new collegiality. There is a formula for harnessing wisdom of the past with the ever-changing dynamics of our society.

---

[5] *Items*, 47 (1993): 40.

WOMEN

BEDE'S WOMEN

David A. E. Pelteret

Countless are the traps which the scheming enemy has set throughout the world's paths and plains: but among them the greatest—and the one scarcely anybody can evade—is woman. Woman the unhappy source, evil root, and corrupt offshoot, who brings to birth every sort of outrage throughout the world. For she instigates quarrels, conflicts, dire dissensions; she provokes fighting between old friends, divides affections, shatters families. But these are trivia I speak of: she dislodges kings and princes from the throne, makes nations clash, convulses towns, destroys cities, multiplies slaughters, brews deadly poisons. She hurls conflagration as she rampages through farmsteads and fields. In sum, there lurks in the universe no manifestation of evil in which woman does not claim some part for herself.

So wrote Marbod of Rennes in the first few decades of the twelfth century in his essay on "The Whore" ("De meretrice") or, as some manuscripts entitle it, "The Evil Woman" ("De muliere mala"), in his *Liber decem capitulorum*.[1] (To bend over backwards to

---

[1] "Innumeros inter laqueos, quos callidus hostis / Omnes per mundi calles camposque tetendit, / Maximus est et quem uix quisquam fallere possit / Femina, triste caput, mala stirps, uitiosa propago, / Plurima quae totum per mundum scandala gignit, / Quae lites, rixas et diras seditiones / Excitat et ueteres bello committit amicos, / Separat affectus, natos ciet atque parentes / (Parua loquor), reges solio mouet atque tetrarchas, / Gentes collidit, quatit oppida, diruit urbes, / Caedes multiplicat, letalia pocula miscet, / Per uillas

be fair to him, one should mention that he does follow this chapter with a slightly longer one praising women.) This sort of misogynistic claptrap was not unusual in the Middle Ages, but it was seemingly not the outlook of the first historian of the English people, Bede. Here are his comments in his *Ecclesiastical History of the English People* on the abbess Hild:

> In . . . the year of our Lord 680, Hild who . . . was abbess at the monastery called Whitby and a most devoted servant of Christ, departed on 17 November, after having done many heavenly deeds on earth, to receive the rewards of the heavenly life, at the age of sixty-six. Her career falls into two equal parts, for she spent her first thirty-three years very nobly in the secular habit, while she dedicated an equal number of years still more nobly to the Lord, in the monastic life. She was of noble birth, being the daughter of Hereric, King Edwin's nephew. It was in company with Edwin that she received the faith and the mysteries of Christ through the teaching of Paulinus of blessed memory, the first bishop of the Northumbrians, and she preserved that faith inviolate until she was counted worthy to behold Him.[2]

---

agrosque furens incendia iactat; / Denique nulla mali species grassatur in orbe, / In qua non aliquam sumat sibi femina partem" (*Marbodi Liber decem capitulorum* 3.1–14, ed. Rosario Leotta [Rome, 1984], pp. 97–99; trans. in *Woman Defamed and Woman Defended: An Anthology of Medieval Texts*, ed. and trans. Alcuin Blamires with Karen Pratt and C. W. Marx [Oxford, 1992], pp. 100–01. The extract comes from chap. 3; his praise of women, chap. 4, is entitled "De muliere bona" or, as in one MS, "De matrona").

[2]". . . anno dominicae incarnationis DCLXXX, religiosissima Christi famula Hild, abbatissa monasterii quod dicitur Streanaeshalch . . . , post multa quae fecit in terris opera caelestia, ad percipienda praemia uitae caelestis de terris ablata transiuit die XV kalendarum Decembrium, cum esset annorum LXVI; quibus aequa partione diuisis, XXXIII primos in saeculari habitu nobilissime conuersata conpleuit, et totidem sequentes nobilius in monachica uita Domino consecrauit. Nam et nobilis natu erat, hoc est filia nepotis Eduini regis, uocabulo Heririci; cum quo etiam rege ad praedicationem beatae memoriae Paulini primi Nordanhymbrorum episcopi fidem et sacramenta Christi

The differences in tone between these two passages are striking, and this prompts the question as to what Bede's attitude was towards women. In this paper we shall explore how he portrayed them in his writings, especially in his most famous and accessible work, the *Ecclesiastical History*.[3]

The passage on Hild immediately reveals two facts that must be firmly borne in mind. The first is obvious once one has noticed it, namely, the women in Bede's writings are *his* creations. No writings *by women* are included in his dossier of evidence about the establishment of the early English church, although he quotes *in extenso* from the letters of such figures as Pope Gregory the Great[4] and Abbot Ceolfrith.[5] Nor do women speak directly to us in his work, and so the possessive case employed in the title of this essay was not flippantly chosen: Hild exists for us because of what *Bede* chose to tell us about her.

Furthermore, as we can see from the tone and presentation of the extract just quoted, Bede's vision was shaped by pre-existing literary forms and their interpretation. We shall concentrate on the influence of hagiography, which is the genre

---

suscepit, atque haec, usquedum ad eius uisionem peruenire meruit, intemerata seruauit" (*Bede's Ecclesiastical History of the English People* 4.23[21], ed. and trans. Bertram Colgrave and R. A. B. Mynors [Oxford, 1969; repr. with corrections, 1991], pp. 404–07 [text and trans.]). (Unless otherwise specified, book, chapter, and page references will be to this edition of the *Historia ecclesiastica*, hereafter HE.)

[3] For a discussion of Bede's writings see *Baedae Opera historica*, ed. Charles Plummer, 2 vols. (Oxford, 1896), 1: xxxvii–lvi, and for a list of the MSS in which they appear see M. L. W. Laistner, collab. H. H. King, *A Hand-List of Bede Manuscripts* (Ithaca, N.Y., 1943).

[4] Aside from the responses to Augustine's questions (HE 1.27, pp. 78–102), the authenticity of which has been a matter of some scholarly controversy, Bede provides transcripts of Gregory's letters in HE 1.28–32, pp. 102–14.

[5] HE 5.21, pp. 534–50.

most obviously relevant in this portrayal of Hild. We should not forget, however, that Bede was a prolific biblical commentator and his literary imagination was thus likely also to have been profoundly imbued with the principles of contemporary biblical exegesis. In this instance, for example, he may have portrayed Hild's lifespan as falling into two segments of thirty-three years each because Christ was believed to have died at the age of thirty-three.[6] This association with Christ serves to enhance the reader's impression of her sanctity.

The ways in which women are depicted in Bede's works will be viewed from three perspectives. First, since the women are Bede's creations, paradoxically we have to spend some time looking at Bede himself as an individual: the man who was born about 673; who was put into the care of Abbot Benedict Biscop of Wearmouth at the age of seven; who does not seem to have traveled beyond his monastery of Jarrow except to its organizational twin, Wearmouth, a few miles away, and to York, destined to become in 735 (the year of Bede's death) the archiepiscopal see of the Roman church in northern England. Then, we must turn to matters literary. A consideration of his motivation for composing the writings of his maturity, the *History of the Abbots*, his version of the *Life of Saint Cuthbert*, and, pre-eminently, his *Ecclesiastical History*, will surely shape our evaluation of the contents of these works, as will the recognition of the dominant literary genre employed by Bede in his portrayal of women, namely, the Saint's Life. And finally, we shall have to relate Bede's women to the wider Anglo-Saxon world, both in order to evaluate in what ways his society shaped his views and to assess how far his portrayals will permit us to describe the reality of the position of women within that society.

---

[6]Nicholas J. Higham, "King Cearl, the Battle of Chester and the Origins of the Mercian 'Overkingship,'" *Midland History* 17 (1992): 1–15, at p. 3.

To compose a psychohistory of a person who lived over 1,250 years ago would seem to be an act of *hubris*. There are a few aspects of Bede's personality, however, about which comments may plausibly be made. The first is a general characteristic: Bede's sense of discretion. He is inclined to keep quiet or, at worst, when condemning others, to proceed obliquely and by allusion. One example must suffice. Only if we have read his *Life of Saint Cuthbert* would we know that affairs at Lindisfarne had gone badly awry in the year after Cuthbert's death. When we read in the *Ecclesiastical History*, therefore, the seemingly innocuous statement that Bishop Wilfrid was responsible for the monastery in that year, we could easily miss the implied criticism.[7]

Bede proceeds by such indirection, in fact, that it has often been assumed that he composed his *Ecclesiastical History* in a state of detached monastic objectivity. His early works should have signalled long ago that he was hardly a detached scholar. His sense of outrage both at the imputations of heresy laid against him by the otherwise unknown cleric David and the failure of Wilfrid to defend him at this time are palpable in his letter to Plegwine, composed in 708, some five years after his entering the priesthood;[8] the hurt feelings are still evident in the preface to his *De temporum ratione*, published nearly twenty years later in 725.[9] But age encouraged greater

---

[7] HE 4.29(27), p. 442; cf. *Bedae Vita sancti Cuthberti* 40, in *Two Lives of Saint Cuthbert: A Life by an Anonymous Monk of Lindisfarne and Bede's Prose Life*, ed. and trans. Bertram Colgrave (Cambridge, 1940; repr. 1985), p. 286. Stability was restored once Eadberht had been consecrated bishop of the see.

[8] "Exhorrui, fateor, et pallens percunctabar, cuius hereseos arguerer" ("I trembled, I confess, and, pale-faced, was interrogated, being accused of this heresy"): *Epistola ad Pleguinam* 1, in *Bedae Opera de temporibus*, ed. Charles W. Jones (Cambridge, Mass., 1943), p. 307, lines 6–7.

[9] *De temporum ratione, Praefatio*, in Jones, *Bedae Opera de temporibus*, p. 176, lines 37ff.

discretion: Bede learned, as many a wise person does, to bridle his tongue, and some modern investigators, misled perhaps by the chimera of scholarly objectivity, have been eager to see in his later work their own ideal of scholarly detachment.

Another aspect of Bede's personality may be deduced from his personal circumstances. He had what most psychologists would regard as a deprived childhood.[10] When he was seven years old, kinsmen placed him in the all-male environment of Jarrow, where he lived out the rest of his life. I think we can discern some consequences of this in his writings. When he describes abbesses he frequently refers to them as "mothers" of the virgins under their care: no less than four of them are so described.[11] In two places he goes further. In his *Life of Saint Cuthbert* he tells how the saint was accustomed to call his nurse "mother" and, indeed, as the story progresses he slips into using this sobriquet quite naturally: on being begged by her to pray for help when flames start to engulf a house in her village, Cuthbert assures her: "Do not be afraid, mother, be calmer; for this fire, however fierce, will not harm you and yours."[12] Elsewhere he describes Æthelburh, abbess of Barking, as a "mother and nurse [*nutrix*] of a company of women devoted to God."[13] Though we can but conjecture here,

---

[10]Bede provides a brief autobiography in HE 5.24, p. 566.

[11]Æthelburh of Barking, Æbbe, Hild, and Æthelthryth. See further below, nn. 13, 25. It must be acknowledged that by the 7th century the practice was widespread of referring to an abbess as a "mother" (*mater* as opposed to *genetrix*), so this evidence is not significant of itself. See further, Jo Ann McNamara and John E. Halborg, with E. Gordon Whatley, *Sainted Women of the Dark Ages* (Durham, N.C., 1992), p. 11.

[12]"Ne timeas . . . mater, animaequior esto, non enim tibi tuisue haec quamlibet ferox flamma nocebit": Colgrave, *Bedae Vita sancti Cuthberti* 14, pp. 200 (text), 201 (trans.).

[13]"Deo deuotarum mater ac nutrix . . . feminarum": HE 4.6, pp. 356 (text), 357 (trans.).

I suspect that Bede never knew his mother and was perhaps brought up by a nurse. Why else would he have mentioned at the end of the *Ecclesiastical History* that he was given into the hands of the monastery at Jarrow by his "kinsmen"?[14] The responses of human beings to deprivation are infinite: some will rise above it; others succumb emotionally; yet others become destructive of themselves or those around them. Certainly one possible response would be to idealize motherhood while ignoring its reality: the pain and messiness of childbirth; the "mewling and puking" of infants; the subtle interplay of anger, love, fear, and power between mother and child. We shall return to motherhood in another connection later.

Finally, we must note the social rôle that Bede chose to play as one dedicated to the monastic life from a tender age, namely, to learn, to teach, and to write. How many monks in fact chose such a rôle? Implicit in the monastic life was the ideal of virginity, and from his writings this was clearly an ideal to which Bede was devoted. This made him oblivious of the emotional comforts of the marital bond. He sounds quite peeved, for instance, when he relates that King Sebbi of the East Saxons had to defer his entry into a monastery because his wife obstinately refused to be separated from him—and only reluctantly permitted it late in their life![15] Implicit in the search for healing for spouses and children is the concept of family, but Bede does not dwell on it, and the familial ties exist in these stories in order to permit the saint to work a miracle.[16] In spite of the generally laudatory tone of the

---

[14]"cura propinquorum": HE 5.24, pp. 566 (text), 567 (trans.).

[15]HE 4.11, pp. 364–66.

[16]See Colgrave, *Bedae Vita sancti Cuthberti* 15 (Cuthbert heals the wife of a reeve [*praefectus*]), 29 (Cuthbert sends holy water to heal the wife of a *gesith* [*comes*]), and 33 (Cuthbert restores a boy dying of the plague to his mother), pp. 202–06, 252–54, and 258–60.

comments quoted about Hild, we should not be surprised to find in one whose life was spent in a celibate male environment that he does display occasional misogyny, as can be seen twice in his *Life of Saint Cuthbert*: Ælfflæd's expressions of surprise at the confirmation of a prophecy of Cuthbert's is described as "woman-like," and her request of Cuthbert that he prophesy who was to be the heir of her brother Ecgfrith, destined to die in an ill-judged attack on the Picts, is described as "feminine audacity."[17] It is easy to miss these slurs, since they are just passing remarks—but they are ones that are highly revelatory.

What we read in Bede's writings was shaped not only by his personality but also by his literary purposes and the literary forms he employed. There is no consensus as yet as to Bede's literary purposes behind the works of his more mature years such as the *History of the Abbots*, the *Life of Saint Cuthbert*, and the *Ecclesiastical History*. I am persuaded by Walter A. Goffart and others that Bede was prompted to compose these works by far from disinterested motives.[18] The shadow of Bishop Wilfrid lies dark across his pages. Essentially what we see in these works are numerous human counterweights to the massive presence in the early history of the English church of Saint Wilfrid, a presence that Bede was eager to downplay.

In Bede's *Ecclesiastical History* we are all familiar with several prominent abbesses on whom the spotlight falls at scattered points in his narrative, notably Hild, Ælfflæd,

---

[17]"stupore femineo" and "audacia feminea": Colgrave, *Bedae Vita sancti Cuthberti* 34 and 24, pp. 264–65 (text and trans.) and 236. The second quotation is from J. F. Webb's translation in *The Age of Bede*, ed. D. H. Farmer (Harmondsworth, 1965; repr., rev. and new introd., 1983), p. 74.

[18]Goffart, *The Narrators of Barbarian History (A.D. 550–800): Jordanes, Gregory of Tours, Bede, and Paul the Deacon* (Princeton, 1988); chap. 4 is entitled "Bede and the Ghost of Bishop Wilfrid."

Æthelburh, and Æthelthryth.[19] These four will be the focus of attention in the ensuing discussion.

We should note that Bede selected these women because they could assist him in the political case he was trying to argue. It was not an easy one. Wilfrid, and subsequently his biographer in the *Life of Bishop Wilfrid*,[20] had presented a powerful argument that the strength of Roman Christianity in England derived not from the mission of Augustine, which by the fifth decade of the seventh century had appeared to be petering out, but from the intellectual power, physical energy, administrative skill, oratorical prowess, political influence, and spirituality of Wilfrid. Wilfrid's claims had been opposed by, amongst others, Hild, an abbess whose outlook had been shaped by Celtic Christianity. In spite of the limitations of the hagiographic genre, we can still perceive Hild's redoubtable personality. Yet she was on the wrong side when it came to

---

[19]For Hild see HE 3.24, p. 292, 4.23(21), pp. 404–14, and 5.24, p. 564, s.a. 680; for Ælfflæd: HE 3.24, pp. 290–92, and 4.26(24), pp. 428–30. Æthelburh, sister of Eorcenwald, bishop of London, and abbess of Barking, is of unknown parentage (HE 4.6, pp. 354–56, and 4.9–10, pp. 360–62), as is recognized by C. R. Hart in *The Early Charters of Eastern England* (Leicester, 1966), p. 117 and n. 6, and by E. Gordon Whatley in *The Saint of London: The Life and Miracles of St. Erkenwald* (Binghamton, 1989), p. 57. She should not to be confused with her namesake, the daughter of Anna, king of the East Angles, and abbess of Faremoûtier-en-Brie (HE 3.8, p. 238), or with Æthelburh Tate, daughter of King Æthelberht of Kent and wife of King Edwin of Northumbria (HE 2.9, pp. 162–66, 2.11, pp. 172–74, 2.14, pp. 186–88, and 2.20, p. 204), a confusion that has a long history. This error has been perpetuated by the indexer of HE, p. 597, who has merged Æthelburh of Barking and Æthelburh, daughter of Anna, under the same heading, a mistake still overlooked in the most recent reprinting (one of many reasons why Plummer's superb edition retains its utility.) For Æthelthryth see HE 4.3, p. 338, 4.19(17)–20(18), pp. 390–400, and 4.22(20), p. 404.

[20][Stephen of Ripon], *The Life of Bishop Wilfrid by Eddius Stephanus*, ed. and trans. Bertram Colgrave (Cambridge, 1927; repr. 1985).

the matter of Easter. Bede's strategy is a fascinating one. By means of careful selection and placement, he is able to reduce Wilfrid's stature while largely ignoring Hild's misguided ways.

Hild's position as putative host of the Synod of Whitby held in 664 to resolve the dating of Easter is not discussed by Bede, and in the third book of the *Ecclesiastical History* the floor is given to the young Wilfrid. Bede must have made a conscious choice to deny Hild any part in the proceedings, since even Stephen of Ripon, whom we might have expected not to have been a sympathetic reporter because of Hild's opposition to his hero, Wilfrid, had felt constrained to mention that the Synod was held "in the presence of the holy mother and most pious . . . Hild"; Bede masks her presence by reporting that when the synod was held at Whitby, "at this time Hild, a woman devoted to God, was abbess."[21] Perhaps Bede balked here at the notion that a woman could help shape ecclesiastical doctrine. Nevertheless, he always appears to be trying to be an honest historian and, given the importance he accorded to Roman ways such as the calculation of Easter and the form of the tonsure, he could hardly deny Wilfrid a place in his story. Instead he uses literary means to reduce Wilfrid's impact on us, the readers. Rather than presenting us with a biography of Wilfrid first, Bede relates the story of the Whitby synod in chapter 25 and only three chapters later does he present us with some rather ambiguous biographical tidbits about Wilfrid.[22] Since we do not know Wilfrid at the point

---

[21]"praesente sanctimoniale matre piissima Hilde": [Stephen of Ripon], *Life of Wilfrid* 10, pp. 20 (text) and 21 (trans.), and "cui tunc Hild abbatissa Deo deuota femina praefuit": HE 3.25, pp. 298 (text), 299 (trans.). For the full account of the synod see ibid., pp. 298–308.

[22]HE 4.28, pp. 314–16, provides a curious description of Wilfrid's episcopal consecration. The opening lines of the chapter record his visit to Paris, where he was consecrated "with great splendour" ("magno cum honore") and where

when we hear him presenting the Romanist case at Whitby, he personally has less impact on us at first reading than does the case that he was making at the synod.

Hild's opportunity to gain the spotlight comes later, in Book 4, where her sanctity, her death, and the miracles that took place after her demise are given full attention by Bede.[23] In this fourth book she stands as an autonomous person, one of a number of noteworthy rivals to Wilfrid presented to us in the *Ecclesiastical History*.

The rôle of Ælfflæd, Hild's successor at Whitby, can also been seen as offsetting Wilfrid. Initially she entered the monastery of Hartlepool, later transferred to Whitby, and then became abbess there. Unlike Hild, she helps Wilfrid regain his episcopal see—but this is an incident that does not receive much attention. Her relationship with Wilfrid is matched by her friendship with Cuthbert. Like Hild, therefore, she counterbalances an overweighty Wilfrid, who is portrayed as being dependent on her favor.[24]

---

he "lingered abroad for his consecration" ("Quo adhuc in transmarinis partibus propter ordinationem demorante": Colgrave's trans. fails to record the subtle dig present in *adhuc* [still]). But most of the chapter is devoted to Chad, who is introduced to us as "a holy man, modest in his ways" ("uirum sanctum, modestum moribus"); only at the end of the chapter is Wilfrid reintroduced, not as the humble itinerant pastor that Chad is seen to have been but as one who introduced Catholic principles to the churches of the English through his teaching. This is consistent with his advocacy of the Catholic cause at the Synod of Whitby, which is presumably why Bede feels constrained to mention this: Wilfrid had followed appropriate Catholic practice in his episcopal consecration, whereas Chad had not—but Wilfrid's personality is less fully realized and less attractively presented in this chapter than is Chad's.

[23] HE 4.23(21), pp. 404–14.

[24] Ælfflæd's support of Wilfrid leads to her getting significantly more attention in Stephen of Ripon's *Life* of Wilfrid: see [Stephen of Ripon], *Life of Wilfrid* 43, 59, and 60, pp. 88, 128, and 130–32.

Literary form obviously also played a major part in many of Bede's female portraits, especially those of abbesses, which are shaped according to the dictates of the conventions of the Saint's Life. I do not propose to devote much attention to this literary form, which is well-known to most medievalists, other than to observe at this point that as far as Bede's saintly women are concerned the word *Life* is something of a misnomer: rather, there is a concentration on their deaths and the miracles associated therewith.

For Bede, two words seem frequently to epitomize the sanctity of these women: *motherhood* and *virginity*. Æthelburh, sister of the bishop of London, Saint Eorcenwald, is the "mater congregationis," the mother of her Barking monastic congregation. The same words are used to describe Æbbe, the abbess of Coldingham. Of Hild we are told, "All who knew Hild, the handmaiden of Christ and abbess, used to call her mother because of her outstanding devotion and grace." In the case of Æthelthryth the two concepts of motherhood and virginity are combined in one phrase: when she built her abbey near Ely she became "the virgin mother of many virgins dedicated to God."[25] This combination of motherhood and virginity can be explained if we move beyond the possibly autobiographical aspects of Bede's life to ecclesiastical ideas that were then current.

Though we are well aware of the importance of the links between the Anglo-Saxon church and Rome, Anglo-Saxon scholars have not spent a great deal of time examining the political and religious cross-currents flowing in the Mediterranean world and their possible impact on the Anglo-

---

[25] Æthelburh: "sollicita mater congregationis" (HE 4.7, p. 356), and see also n. 13 above; Æbbe: "matri congregationis" (HE 4.25[23], p. 424); Hild: "omnes qui nouerant ob insigne pietatis et gratiae matrem uocare consuerant" (HE 4.23[21], p. 410); Æthelthryth: "uirginum Deo deuotarum perplurium mater uirgo" (HE 4.19[17], p. 392).

Saxon church, such as the recrudescence of the Monophysite heresy in Constantinople that so exercised Theodore shortly after he arrived in England.[26] In this regard I want to emphasize the slow accretion of the Marian cult in Rome in the latter part of the seventh century and (especially) the beginning of the eighth.

Mary does not play a prominent part in the Gospels and, though she is mentioned by Tertullian, her cult really only starts with the Council of Ephesus in 431, after which it rapidly gained prominence.[27] In 609, Pope Boniface IV broke with tradition by consecrating a pagan temple, the Pantheon, as a Christian church. It was dedicated to the Virgin Mary and all the martyrs.[28] Perhaps this dramatic event influenced the young Roman mission in faraway Canterbury, because the first monastery there, dedicated to Peter and Paul, was later supplemented by a chapel just east of the main church dedicated to the Virgin Mary. Another seventh-century church dedicated to Mary was to be found at Reculver in Kent, and she was also the patron of a number of female monastic houses, such as Minster-in-Thanet (also in Kent), Barking in Essex, and Tynemouth in Northumbria.[29]

---

[26]For a discussion of Monophysite doctrine and the related Monothelite heresy, see D. W. Johnson, "Monophysitism," and Linda C. Rose, "Monothelitism," in *Dictionary of the Middle Ages*, ed. Joseph R. Strayer, 13 vols. (New York, 1982–89), 8: 476–79 and 479–80.

[27]See Marina Warner, *Alone of All Her Sex: The Myth and the Cult of the Virgin Mary* (London, 1976).

[28]Richard Krautheimer, *Rome: Profile of a City, 312–1308* (Princeton, 1980), p. 72.

[29]HE 2.6, p. 156. As Colgrave and Mynors point out in HE, p. 157, n. 1, all that remains of the Church of St. Mary, Canterbury, is the base of the west wall, the church having been partially demolished in the 11th century to enable Abbot Wulfric to build his rotunda. See further H. M. Taylor and Joan

The cult of Mary offered a peculiar attraction to the newly-recognized church in the late Antique world. The female principle had been widely acknowledged in the religions of the eastern Mediterranean: everyone will recall the famous statue of Diana of the Ephesians. Mary presented a figure to which men could offer devotion and we should not be surprised that it was at Ephesus that she was accorded her title of "Theotokos." In Constantinople she was to became so important that she even took on a protective function for the city,[30] thus becoming not unlike Athena in her martial attributes. This latter aspect seems not to have found favor in the West, where a more passive and demure Mary became popular.

For women her rôle was more problematic, for she was the embodiment of one of the paradoxes that so characterize the theology of Christianity. She was the perfect Mother, a position to which no celibate nun devoted to the service of God could attain. And she was the ever-perfect Virgin, a state no mother could claim.

When Benedict Biscop, the founder of the monasteries at Wearmouth and Jarrow, visited Rome for the fourth time in 679–80, there were a number of major churches dedicated to her, notably Santa Maria Maggiore, whose fifth-century mosaic of the Annunciation and Epiphany is still to be seen over the chancel arch.[31] Benedict returned from Rome laden with

---

Taylor, *Anglo-Saxon Architecture*, 3 vols. (Cambridge, 1965–78), 1: 134–43; A. W. Clapham, *English Romanesque Architecture: Before the Conquest* (Oxford, 1930), p. 19 and Fig. 49 opposite p. 151. For other Marian dedications in England see Mary Clayton, *The Cult of the Virgin Mary in Anglo-Saxon England* (Cambridge, 1990), pp. 125–29.

[30] Averil Cameron, "The Theotokos in Sixth-Century Constantinople: A City Finds Its Symbol," *Journal of Theological Studies*, n.s., 29 (1978): 79–108, esp. p. 97.

[31] See Émile Mâle, *The Early Churches of Rome*, trans. David Buxton (London, 1960): Santa Maria Maggiore, Pl. 37, the 5th-century mosaic of the

ecclesiastical treasures, amongst which was a series of paintings, including one of Mary and others of the twelve apostles.[32] We can understand why the picture of Mary might have appealed to him, for as abbot of the Monastery of Saints Peter and Paul in Canterbury he must have worshiped at the chapel of Saint Mary there.[33] The paintings he arranged over the arch leading to the apse in his new church at Wearmouth. Quite which iconographic form of the Virgin he brought with him from Rome is unclear.[34] It is unlikely to be the *Maria lactans*[35] or *orans*,[36] both rather rare images. *Maria regina* was already known in the fifth century,[37] and it is an image to which we shall briefly return later, but this also is unlikely to

---

Annunciation and Epiphany, Pl. 38 (pp. 192–93). See also Walther Buchowiecki, *Handbuch der Kirchen Roms: Der römische Sakralbau in Geschichte und Kunst von der altchristlichen Zeit bis zur Gegenwart*, 3 vols. (Vienna, 1967–74), 1: 237–76 and 2: 818–23; Guglielmo Matthiae, *Le chiese di Roma dal IV al X secolo* (Rome, 1962).

[32] *Historia abbatum* 6, in Plummer, *Baedae Opera historica*, 1: 369–71, convenient trans. in Farmer, *Age of Bede*, pp. 190–91.

[33] *Historia abbatum* 3, in Plummer, *Baedae Opera historica*, 1: 367, trans. in Farmer, *Age of Bede*, p. 188.

[34] For an introduction to the iconography of the Virgin see Gertrud Schiller, *Ikonographie der christlichen Kunst*, 5 vols. in 7 (Gütersloh, 1966–91), 4.2: *Maria*.

[35] For representations see Schiller, *Ikonographie* 4.2, Pls. 418–20; its inspiration may have come from Isis breast-feeding Harpocrates; for an example see André Grabar, *The Golden Age of Justinian: From the Death of Theodosius to the Rise of Islam*, trans. Stuart Gilbert and James Emmons (New York, 1967), p. 177, Pl. 190. This depiction first appears in Coptic art of the 6th–7th centuries: Ioli Kalavrezou, "Images of the Mother: When the Virgin Mary Became *Meter Theou*," *Dumbarton Oaks Papers*, no. 44 (1990): 165–72 and Figs. 1–18, at p. 166.

[36] Grabar, *Golden Age*, p. 176, Pl. 189 (Orant Virgin surrounded by apostles, from the Monastery of St. Apollo in Bawit, Egypt).

[37] Mâle, *Early Churches of Rome*, p. 193, Pl. 38 (Santa Maria Maggiore).

be the way in which she was portrayed, as Bede in describing the paintings in his *Lives of the Abbots* calls her "genetrix."[38] This use of the word *mother* indicates that the icon most likely took the form of Mary best known today, namely, Mary with the Christ child.[39] Thus the sister church of Wearmouth almost certainly had as its central image on the chancel arch the figure of Mary as Mother. It must have been an image that Bede carried with him throughout his life.

In the pontificate of Pope Sergius I (687–701), a man of Syrian origin, the cult underwent a major series of liturgical developments. The *Liber pontificalis* tells us that he instituted the feasts of the Annunciation, Nativity, and Dormition of Saint Mary, as well as the Greek feast of Saint Simeon.[40] I

---

[38]"imaginem uidelicet beatae Dei genetricis semperque uirginis Mariae" ("a painting of the Mother of God, the Blessed Mary Ever-Virgin"): *Historia abbatum* 6, in Plummer, *Baedae Opera historica*, 1: 369, trans. in Farmer, *Age of Bede*, p. 190. Professor Rosemary Cramp has suggested to me that the iconography of these paintings may be preserved on the coffin of St. Cuthbert, which, *inter alia*, bears representations of the Virgin and Child and the 12 apostles, a suggestion that supports my conjecture. See further, Ernst Kitzinger, "The Coffin-Reliquary," in *The Relics of Saint Cuthbert*, ed. C. F. Battiscombe (Oxford, 1956), pp. 202–304 and Pls. 4–14.

[39]Grabar, *Golden Age*, pp. 166, 170–71, Pls. 176, 180, 182, and Schiller, *Ikonographie* 4.2, Pl. 426. See also the Dewsbury Cross fragments, illustrated in G. Baldwin Brown, *The Arts in Early England*, 2nd ed., 6 vols. in 7 (London, 1926–37), 6.2, Pl. 54 (opposite p. 187).

[40]"Constituit autem ut diebus Adnuntiationis Domini, Dormitionis et Natiuitatis sanctae Dei genetricis semperque uirginis Mariae ac sancti Symeonis, quod Ypapanti Greci appellant, letania exeat a sancto Hadriano et ad sanctam Mariam populus occurrat" ("He decreed that on the days of the Lord's Annunciation, of the Falling-asleep and Nativity of St Mary the ever-virgin mother of God, and of St Simeon [which the Greeks call *Hypapante*], a litany should go out from St Hadrian's and the people should meet up at St Mary's") (*Le Liber pontificalis: texte, introduction et commentaire*, ed. Louis Duchesne, 2 vols. [Paris 1886–92; repr. with supp. vol. of additions and corrections of L. Duchesne, ed. Cyrille Vogel, Paris, 1955–57], 1: 376, lines 4–6 [text]; *The*

find it significant that when Wilfrid was returning from his last trip to Rome, undertaken just four years after Sergius's pontificate ended, he had an angelic vision while he was seriously ill in Meaux. The central theme in this dream was Wilfrid's failure to foster the cult of the Virgin. Stephen of Ripon tells us how Wilfrid was commanded by the angel Michael to dedicate a church in her honor, which he duly did on his return to Northumbria.[41]

We do not have to assume the influence of Wilfrid on Bede here, however, for he was in possession of a recension of the *Liber pontificalis* that included the Life of Sergius.[42] As he was a priest who was scrupulous about his orthodoxy, we can be sure that he took note of these liturgical developments. I would suggest that in consequence Bede strove to elevate the women who were central to the establishment of the Roman

---

Book of Pontiffs [Liber Pontificalis]: *The Ancient Biographies of the First Ninety Roman Bishops to AD 715*, trans. with introd. Raymond Davis [Liverpool, 1989], p. 87 [trans.]). A successor of his, John VII (1 Mar. 705–18 Oct. 707) built an oratory of the "holy mother of God" ("sanctae Dei genetricis") inside St. Peter's; he also "adorned with painting the basilica of the holy mother of God which is called *Antiqua*, and he there built a new ambo, and above the same church an Episcopium which he wanted to build for his own use. . ." ("Basilicam itaque sanctae Dei genetricis qui Antiqua uocatur pictura decorauit, illicque ambonem nouiter fecit et super eandem ecclesiam episcopium quantum ad se construere maluit") (text: Duchesne, *Le Liber pontificalis*, 1: 385, lines 2 and 6–8; trans. Davis, *Book of Pontiffs*, p. 88. For a translation of the lives of later popes see *The Lives of the Eighth-Century Popes* [Liber Pontificalis]: *The Ancient Biographies of Nine Popes from AD 715 to AD 817*, trans., introd., and commentary Raymond Davis [Liverpool, 1992]).

[41] [Stephen of Ripon], *Life of Wilfrid* 56, p. 122, and cf. ibid. 63, p. 136. The cult of the archangel Michael was also strong in 7th-century Italy, as Henry Mayr-Harting points out in *The Coming of Christianity to Anglo-Saxon England*, 3rd ed. (University Park, Pa., 1991), p. 297, n. 65.

[42] In fact, he had a recension that went up to the time of his writing in 731: see Davis, *Book of Pontiffs*, p. iii.

church in Britain by bestowing on them attributes of Mary. Present in his portraits is the same ambivalence that lay within the cult of Mary, which encouraged both the empowerment and the disempowerment of women. His abbesses are all depicted as morally and spiritually admirable people whose conduct was to be emulated—even Æbbe, whose mixed monastic house at Coldingham Bede found morally dubious.[43] Yet when we examine Bede's literary presentation of these lives, they are oddly disempowering of women.

A few examples will illustrate this point. We might begin with Æthelburh of Barking, the third of the four great abbesses mentioned earlier. Here is a clear instance where Bede employs a source now lost to us,[44] a Life of a founding abbess of a monastic house of a kind familiar to us from Merovingian sources[45] that the misfortunes of history have largely denied us from Anglo-Saxon sources (except in the notable case of the Mildred legends).[46] Because we lack the source, we do not know what Bede chose to omit. What I find striking about what he chose to *include* is that everything in his portrait conveys images of illness and death. It is as if Bede subconsciously wanted to reduce Æthelburh's impact on others as a living woman and was only ready to acknowledge her spiritual significance by physically disabling her. We cannot say that this is just chance, because Bede also depicts Hild at her physical weakest.[47] This is not to say that for Bede and for many of his contemporary readers, including perhaps even

---

[43]HE 4.25(23), pp. 424–26.

[44]See HE, pp. xxxii and 356, n. 2.

[45]See, e.g, the *Vita sanctae Balthildis*, in MGH SS rer. Merov. 2: 475–508.

[46]See D. W. Rollason, *The Mildrith Legend: A Study in Early Medieval Hagiography in England* (Leicester, 1982).

[47]HE 4.23(21), pp. 410–14.

women, these portrayals of physical suffering would have been perceived as other than complimentary. The dominance of body imagery in the rhetoric of early Christian discourse[48] had elevated the status of dying in a way quite alien to the literary traditions of the pagan Greco-Roman world. The early accounts of the tortures of martyrdom had modulated into the travails of the dying saint. Bede was following a well-developed literary tradition in this; but with the advantage of the perspective of history, we can see that Bede's portrayal of Æthelburh did not encourage his readers to think of her as a person actively involved in the management and control of everyday affairs.

A rather different way of reducing the stature of a significant female personality is to be found in his portrait of the abbess Æthelthryth,[49] who married twice and yet was able to preserve her virginity. Clearly she was a major figure in the early Church. After a year spent at the monastery of Coldingham she became abbess of a monastery in the vicinity of Ely (where she became known as Audrey, from whose fair the word "tawdry" derives). Having described her, Bede feels it appropriate to obtrude himself into the story in the form of a complex abecedarian poem that he was ostensibly inspired to write because of Æthelthryth's regal virginity.[50] The Marian influence is again evident: not the maternal Mary this time but

---

[48] For the importance of bodily imagery and the notion of rhetoric here I am indebted to Averil Cameron's Sather Classical Lectures, *Christianity and the Rhetoric of Empire: The Development of Christian Discourse* (Berkeley, 1991), esp. pp. 68–71. On the troubled relationship between early Christian thinkers and the human body, Peter Brown, as always, has many insightful comments to make: see his *The Body and Society: Men, Women and Sexual Renunciation in Early Christianity* (New York, 1988).

[49] HE 4.3, p. 338, 4.19(17)–20(18), pp. 390–400, 4.22(20), p. 404.

[50] HE 4.20(18), pp. 396–400.

Maria regina, the Queen of Heaven, a concept that was to undergo considerable development in late Anglo-Saxon England.[51] But the literary virtuosity of Bede's composition serves only to distract us from Æthelthryth's physical presence and her accomplishments by shifting our focus away from her to the abstraction celebrated by the poem, Virginity.

Absent from these portraits of female saints are the depictions of them as vigorous and spontaneous girls. Bede was not absolutely constrained by the hagiographic genre here; we do get a brief glimpse of the young Cuthbert, engaging in pranks and playing games. Admittedly, according to Bede in Cuthbert's eighth year, when Bede himself had been placed in monastic care,[52] Cuthbert was brought up short by a three-year-old who reminded him of his spiritual duties. (In North America today, we would probably send them both off to child psychiatrists!) Even the youthful Wilfrid is permitted some individuality: we are told something of his childhood personality, his entry into the monastery of Lindisfarne at the age of fourteen, and how he subsequently goes off on the grand tour with Benedict Biscop. He dallies in Lyons while Benedict impatiently proceeds to Rome, and he spends more time in Lyons on his return, where he is tonsured.[53] The tone of Bede's

---

[51] See Clayton, *Cult of the Virgin Mary*, and Philippe Verdier, *Le couronnement de la Vierge: les origines et les premiers développements d'un thème iconographique* (Montreal, 1980).

[52] Colgrave, *Bedae Vita sancti Cuthberti* 1, p. 154. Note the fascinating amendment that Bede makes to the text of the *Vita sancti Cuthberti auctore anonymo* 1.3, in ibid., p. 64, which says that Cuthbert was eight when this happened ("puer esset annorum octo"); Bede changes this to "ad octauum aetatis annum" ("the eighth year of his age").

[53] HE 5.19, pp. 516–20. Professor Cramp has observed to me that Bede does not give physical descriptions of women but occasionally mentions the physical appearance of men, presumably another consequence of living in an all-male environment.

descriptions of his men and his women is thus very different.

It is apparent that women played an important mediating rôle in early Anglo-Saxon society. The most famous example of this in early English literary sources is to be found in the description of Wealhtheow, Hygelac's consort, in the Old English epic poem, *Beowulf*, where her position as the cupbearer affords her the opportunity to act as a mediator. First she serves her husband, then the *duguð* (veterans) and *geogoð* (young warriors) in the hall, and finally the guest, Beowulf. Michael J. Enright's analysis of the part played by the wife of the leader has sensitized us to how important Wealhtheow's function was in retaining peace amongst the competing egos of the males of the warrior-band desirous of the lord's attention and favor.[54] We might think today of the personal secretary (usually female) to the company director (usually male) who manages accessibility to the boss's timetable and attention. It is a duty that many women justifiably are profoundly dissatisfied at performing—but it must not blind us to the fact that such a position carries power of a kind. Bede twice mentions a woman bearing a cup[55] but undercuts any power this function might imply by likening it to the action of the apostle Peter's mother-in-law, who ministered to Christ and the apostles after she had been healed by Jesus (Matthew 8: 14–15). Here Peter's mother was in humble gratitude undertaking the duties of a servant rather than acting as a mediator. (Bede's two stories may, in fact, be

---

[54]See "Lady with a Mead-Cup: Ritual, Group Cohesion and Hierarchy in the Germanic Warband," *Frühmittelalterliche Studien* 22 (1988): 170–203, repr. with revisions in *Lady with a Mead Cup: Ritual, Prophecy and Lordship in the European Warband from La Tène to the Viking Age* (Blackrock, co. Dublin, 1996). The passage under discussion is in *Beowulf*, lines 612–29, in *Beowulf and The Fight at Finnsburg*, ed. Friedrich Klaeber, 3rd ed. (Boston, 1950), pp. 23–24, available in numerous translations.

[55]Colgrave, *Bedae Vita sancti Cuthberti* 29, p. 254, and HE 5.4, p. 462.

a doublet.) On two other occasions women play a similar serving rôle: an offer of food by a "religious housewife" to Cuthbert, which he rejects, and an offer of "devoted service" to Cuthbert by the wife of a *gesith* whom he had healed.[56]

Bede also enables us to gain an insight into a woman's position as a marriage partner, whereby her union with a male leader permitted the extension of the power interests of a ruler or the pacifying of two *gentes* who had been at war with each other. A case in point is the marriage of Bertha, daughter of the king of Paris, to Æthelberht of Kent.[57] We must not underrate the potential power exercised by the women who were the center of these transactions. Bertha was accompanied by a Christian bishop and retained her religion in the midst of the pagan Kentishmen. When Eanflæd went back to Northumbria, she did not allow herself to succumb to the liturgical practices of the Northumbrian king whom she had married. He still followed the outdated mode of calculating Easter while she, her priest, and her entourage kept to the Roman ways that she had brought from Kent. The consequence was that while her husband, King Oswiu, was celebrating Easter, she was still in the midst of Lent, observing Palm Sunday.[58]

Bede acknowledged this rôle, and we can find several examples of queens who were the agents or channels of conversion to Roman Christianity of their spouses.[59] But Bede's

---

[56]"religiosae matris familias" and "deuotum . . . ministerium": Colgrave, *Bedae Vita sancti Cuthberti* 5 and 15, pp. 168 and 206.

[57]On the hegemonic implications of this marriage see Ian N. Wood, *The Merovingian North Sea* (Alingsås, 1983), and idem, "Frankish Hegemony in England," in *The Age of Sutton Hoo: The Seventh Century in North-Western Europe*, ed. M. O. H. Carver (Woodbridge, Suff., 1992), pp. 235–41.

[58]HE 3.25, p. 296.

[59]The marriages of Æthelburh Tate, daughter of Æthelberht of Kent, who married Edwin of Northumbria (HE 2.9, p. 162), and Alhflæd of Northumbria,

acknowledgment is not overt: we have to seek these examples out, and they do not linger on the memory because, as Stephanie Hollis has pointed out, none is permitted to bring about direct conversion of a people.[60] We are more likely to remember those wives who influenced their husbands *against* Christianity, such as Rædwald's wife,[61] and Peada, who was murdered "by the treachery, or so it is said, of his wife."[62]

In scrutinizing Bede's women at close quarters it is easy to lose our sense of perspective. If we stand back, we cannot but deny that they are rarely brought into prominence. To offset Wilfrid's importance, Bede devotes five chapters at the beginning of Book 5 of the *Ecclesiastical History* to Cuthbert, but in telling of the saintly Eorcengota in Book 3 he decides to limit himself to describing "her departure from this world," leaving the miracles that occurred on the night of her death "to be related by her own people."[63] Even the leading women whom he discusses in any degree of detail are disempowered

---

who married Peada of the Middle Angles (HE 3.21, p. 278), were both conditional on the conversion of their husbands-to-be; and we may suspect that Bertha with her Merovingian bishop, Liudhard, in Canterbury (HE 1.25, p. 74) and Eafe of the Hwicce, married to the pagan king of the South Saxons (HE 4.13, p. 372), played their parts in preparing their spouses for accepting Christianity.

[60] *Anglo-Saxon Women and the Church: Sharing a Common Fate* (Woodbridge, Suff., 1992), esp. pp. 226–27.

[61] "nam rediens domum ab uxore sua et quibusdam peruersis doctoribus seductus est, atque a sinceritate fidei deprauatus habuit posteriora peiora prioribus" ("for on his return home, he was seduced by his wife and by certain evil teachers and perverted from the sincerity of his faith, so that his last state was worse than his first"): HE 2.15, pp. 190 (text), 191 (trans.).

[62] "proditione, ut dicunt, coniugis suae": HE 4.24, pp. 294 (text), 295 (trans.).

[63] "de transitu tantum illius . . . suis narrare permittimus": HE 3.8, pp. 238 (text), 239 (trans.).

by the hagiographic genre in which Bede presents them. We have to deduce their power through casual details that Bede happens to mention. When Cædmon discovers his talent for composing poetry and goes to his reeve, the latter presents him to the head of the monastery, Hild.[64] When a guest at a now-unknown monastery in Lindsey headed by Abbess Æthelhild is overcome at night by an evil spirit, "a servant ran and knocked at the abbess's gate and told her."[65]

As already mentioned, Rædwald is turned away from Christianity by a strong-minded wife,[66] and King Oswiu of Northumbria is constrained to celebrate Easter on his own because his wife Eanflæd will not budge from her Roman liturgical calendar, which she had learned in Kent.[67] Commenting on the Book of Ezra, Bede acknowledges the possibility of women as preachers.[68] And implicit in their position as

---

[64]HE 4.24(22), pp. 414–20, at p. 416. The story has stimulated a vast amount of scholarly commentary; for an introduction see Jeff Opland, *Anglo-Saxon Oral Poetry: A Study of the Traditions* (New Haven, 1980), esp. pp. 106–20.

[65]"cucurrit minister et pulsans ad ostium nuntiauit abbatissae": HE 3.11, pp. 248 (text), 249 (trans.).

[66]HE 2.15, p. 190.

[67]HE 3.25, p. 296.

[68]*In Ezram et Neemiam* 1.650–55, on Ezr 2: 65, in *Bedae Venerabilis Opera* 2.2A, ed. David Hurst, CCSL 119A (Turnhout, 1969), p. 257: "Bene autem cantoribus etiam cantrices iunguntur propter sexum uidelicet femineum in quo plurimae repperiuntur personae quae non solum uiuendo uerum etiam praedicando corda proximorum ad laudem sui creatoris accendant et quasi suauitate sanctae uocis aedificantium templum domini adiuuent laborem." ("It is good indeed that to the male cantors are joined female cantors on account of their sex, whereby are found very many people who, not only by their life but by their words, inflame the hearts of their neighbours, not only by living but indeed by preaching, and assist the labour of those building the temple of the Lord as though by the pleasing quality of their holy voices," trans. in Hollis, *Anglo-Saxon Women*, p. 269, n. 136, at p. 270.)

abbesses was the comfortable exercise of power, administrative, intellectual, and spiritual, over mixed communities of men and women dependent on substantial landholdings. Hild's intellectual importance is acknowledged indirectly when Bede mentions various bishops who studied at her monastery before attaining their episcopal sees—but even here Bede's motivation is suspect, since two of the five were given bishoprics at the expense of Wilfrid's claim to episcopal jurisdiction over the whole of Northumbria.[69] About the double monasteries in which women like Hild lived he tells us frustratingly little, but from a lost Life of Saint Æthelburh of Barking he vouchsafes us a little snippet of evidence about a three-year-old boy, Æsica, who was cared for by nuns and who, in his death-throes from the plague, cried out to one of them. Some kind of family life within the Barking community is implied here. And since monasteries like Barking were endowed with property from wealthy families, we should not fly to hasty conclusions as to the social interactions within these early monastic *familiae*, the relationships between its members and the wider society, and the part that women played in these interactions.[70]

---

[69] Of the men, Bosa, Ætla, Oftfor, John of Beverley, and Wilfrid II, Bosa was given the see of York and John, Hexham: HE 4.23(21), pp. 408–10. See Goffart, *Narrators*, pp. 261–62 and n. 131, and HE, pp. 408–09, n. 2.

[70] HE 4.8, p. 358. There has been a revival of interest in the phenomenon of double monasteries; a new sensitivity to issues of gender might encourage archaeologists to increase their efforts to learn more about these foundations. Roberta Gilchrist has pointed the way in *Gender and Material Culture: The Archaeology of Religious Women* (London, 1994), esp. pp. 22–36, containing a valuable map of double houses and a table listing the primary literary sources that mention such houses. See also Dagmar Beate Baltrusch-Schneider, "Die angelsächsischen Doppelklöster," in *Doppelklöster und andere Formen der Symbiose männlicher und weiblicher Religiosen im Mittelalter*, ed. Kaspar Elm and Michel Parisse (Berlin, 1992), pp. 57–79, with a résumé in French.

Perhaps the most striking aspect of Bede's control over his women is that they are never allowed to speak for themselves other than in the most constrained of circumstances. In this Bede was following a long tradition in early male Christian literature of silencing women.[71] We briefly hear Seaxburh, the sister of Æthelthryth, cry out, "Glory be to the name of the Lord!" when she discovers that the incision made by the surgeon Cynefrith to try to remove the tumor on Æthelthryth's neck—an operation that probably led to her demise—had been healed after her death. But the story is Cynefrith's and he is merely quoting her words.[72] The account of Hild's death is preceded by the story of Imma, the Northumbrian thegn who was captured on the battlefield and sold to a Frisian slaver before being redeemed by the Kentish king.[73] The chapter following her death is devoted to Caedmon.[74] Both men are permitted to speak to us in their own words. Hild speaks to us only in the third person.

My recollection of how Bede portrayed women had been a favorable one, but as I re-read his writings my views became less positive. To be sure, he does not display the flagrant misogyny of Marbod of Rennes, but his misogyny is of a more

---

[71] Averil Cameron, "Virginity as Metaphor: Women and the Rhetoric of Early Christianity," in *History as Text: The Writing of Ancient History*, ed. A. Cameron (London, 1989), pp. 184–205, at p. 193, n. 56. Augustine found it possible to compose his *Confessions* without mentioning by name the woman who bore his child: he tells of his pain and sense of loss, but her desire not to live with another man thereafter is used merely as a moral *exemplum* rather than as an expression of her feelings. The silencing of women is now a subject of active feminist analysis: see Dale Spender, *Man Made Language*, 2nd ed. (London, 1985), esp. chap. 2.

[72] " 'Sit gloria nomini Domini' ": HE 4.19, pp. 394 (text), 395 (trans.).

[73] HE 4.22(20), pp. 400–04.

[74] HE 4.24(22), pp. 414–20.

covert and insidious kind. My suggestions about Bede's literary purposes in writing the *Ecclesiastical History* lead me to conclude that women in this work were a tool of his polemical endeavors, described because they represented interests antithetical to those of Wilfrid. Hild was wrong about Easter—but she had opposed Wilfrid before the pope himself[75] and so is worthy of extended treatment. Admittedly, we do see women in action, but mostly in extremely limited circumstances: in sickness and death, or at best, as mediators whereby Christianity could be introduced to pagans. Even in the latter rôle they could serve evil purposes, as Rædwald's wife did in leading him back to pagan ways. And we cannot get away from the fact that women are minor actors in Bede's dramas; in works such as the *History of the Abbots* and *Life of Saint Cuthbert* they receive hardly a walk-on part. In spite of this, Bede could not hide the power that women were able to wield in early Anglo-Saxon society: Abbess Ælfflæd's unself-conscious summoning of Cuthbert to sail over from Farne in order to discuss "matters of importance" with her;[76] the very hosting of the Synod of Whitby by Hild, who is only obliquely mentioned by Bede; the opportunities presented to women to introduce new religious perceptions to peoples who were often not of their own tribe; their considerable learning, acknowledged by Bede when he describes Hild's successor at Whitby as "a teacher";[77] and their ability to attain the highest levels of sanctity. His

---

[75] See [Stephen of Ripon], *Life of Wilfrid* 54, p. 116.

[76] "de necessariis": Colgrave, *Bedae Vita sancti Cuthberti* 24, p. 234. She met him not at Whitby, the house where she had succeeded Hild, but on an island in the mouth of the River Coquet "famous for its companies of monks" ("monachorum coetibus insignis"), which implies that she had considerable freedom of movement.

[77] "doctrix": HE 4.26(24), p. 430.

portrayal of women may in general be positive; but we have to screen out much misogyny that is Bede's inheritance from the patristic writers and theologians of late Antiquity and the early Middle Ages.[78]

---

[78]The original version of this paper was delivered at the Sixth Meeting of the International Society of Anglo-Saxonists at Wadham College, Oxford, in August 1993. I wish to thank the Humanities and Social Sciences Research Committee of the University of Toronto for a grant that covered the costs of attending this conference.

DOMINAE OR DOMINATAE?
FEMALE MYSTICISM
AND THE TRAUMA OF TEXTUALITY[1]

Dyan Elliott

n November of 1430, Francesca Bussa dei Ponziani, later affectionately known as Francesca Romana or Frances of Rome, had a remarkable vision. While she was immersed in prayer, her confessor, John Mattiotti, seemingly entered her oratory, equipped with pen, parchment, and other writing implements. " 'I want to record the very great visions and revelations, which God has revealed to you,' " he said. He even urged that *she* should learn to write and thus " 'compose great books from so many and such great divine visions.' " Frances immediately recognized that the devil had assumed her confessor's form and was attempting to seduce her by appealing to her vanity. When she denounced him, he at first feigned surprise that she could speak so disrespectfully of one who handled the Body of Christ. He further defended himself by drawing attention to both her privilege and her mortality: " 'I came here to write the very profound things shown to you so that when you die (because you are mortal) I will be able to preach and announce the

---

[1]An earlier version of this paper was presented at the 28th International Congress on Medieval Studies, Kalamazoo, Mich., May 1993.

marvellous things God revealed in you.' " The sermon in question, preached by the confessor of a recently deceased individual, would be standard posthumous procedure in the inauguration of a new saint's cult. Thus John's last comment, an inflected promise of public sanctity, was the ultimate temptation for self-aware piety. Frances's redoubled efforts at denunciation unsettled the pseudo-confessor sufficiently that he shifted shape, thus assuming forms better suited to his nature. After a brief stint as a dragon (which struck her, threw her into the air, and then hung her over the balcony), he then became an aggressive but otherwise nondescript man, who threatened to kill Frances's son and then Frances (in that order, as it would inflict more suffering on Frances). When she calmly answered that he could do nothing without God's permission, the man hurled a sharp and seemingly lethal dart at Frances. She caught it and removed the iron tip, which was about the span of two palms in length—not unlike the pen that constituted the initial threat. The life-threatening dart is further likened to the soul-threatening writing materials, in that its lengthy iron tip, once removed, "fluttered like the frailest kind of parchment."[2]

This vision was said to have occurred a year after John became Frances's confessor. Her earlier confessor, Father Anthony of Monte Savello, had never attempted to record her visions or to chronicle her virtues. That Frances, already forty-six years old compared with John's thirty-four years and presumably accustomed to her own spiritual habits, is presented as construing the process of redaction as aggressive, intrusive, and spiritually lethal is suggested by her reciprocal

---

[2]*Acta sanctorum*, new ed., 67 vols. (Paris, 1863–1983), Mar., 2: 156 (henceforth AA SS). Unless otherwise indicated, my discussion of Frances's life and revelations is based on John Mattiotti's *vita*, the earliest written.

aggression—tantamount to a visionary castration of the demonic scribe.[3] That the pen and weapon, symbols of masculine privilege and aggressivity, are ultimately reducible to the flimsiest parchment may even hint at the transcendent superiority of the spoken, female *parole* over the authority of written history.[4] And yet there is another sense, impossible to ignore, in which Frances's apparent hostility is simply a trope required as a precondition of her entry into the process of inscription. For a female mystic's authenticity was proportionate to her degree of aversion to publicity in general and to the writing process in particular. It is the process by which visionary word becomes text, and the ramifications of this process for female agency, that I wish to examine in this paper.[5]

---

[3] On Frances and her confessors, see the 17th-century life of Maria Magdalena Anguillaria, in AA SS, Mar., 2: 186, 190; also, the Bollandist preface, pp. 90–91.

[4] On this distinction see Michel de Certeau, *The Mystic Fable*, 1: *The Sixteenth and Seventeenth Centuries*, trans. Michael B. Smith (Chicago, 1992), pp. 192–93.

[5] Insofar as this area concerns the collaborative relationship of confessor and mystic, my discussion builds on available reconstructions of their shifting power dynamics, as described in the important work of Caroline Walker Bynum, John Coakley, and Aviad M. Kleinburg (Bynum, *Holy Feast and Holy Fast: The Religious Significance of Food to Medieval Women* [Berkeley, 1987], pp. 227–37; Coakley, "Gender and the Authority of the Friars: The Significance of Holy Women for Thirteenth-Century Franciscans and Dominicans," *Church History* 60 [1991]: 445–60, and idem, "Friars as Confidants of Holy Women in Medieval Dominican Hagiography," in *Images of Sainthood in Medieval Europe*, ed. Renate Blumenfeld-Kosinski and Timea K. Szell [Ithaca, N.Y., 1991], pp. 222–46; Kleinberg, *Prophets in Their Own Country: Living Saints and the Making of Sainthood in the Later Middle Ages* [Chicago, 1992], esp. chap. 4). My particular emphasis on the redaction of a female visionary's revelation and how this affects female agency is also indebted to contemporary feminist analyses of mysticism as a mechanism for female empowerment and the subversion of patriarchy. See, e.g., Elizabeth

I will be exploring this issue with special attention to the problems of the female lay mystic of the later Middle Ages—a figure whose uncloistered status made the source of her mystical inspiration particularly suspect, thus causing certain patterns in female spirituality to be "writ large." The following considerations will shape my inquiry: What are some of the ideological factors that impede the textualization of mystic utterance? What impact do these impediments have on the relationship between the confessor and his penitent? What strategies are necessary to validate mystic speech, and how did these, in turn, yield to repressive strategies of containment?

IMPEDIMENTS TO TEXTUALIZATION

Before even confronting the problems posed by redaction, the female saint must overcome formidable inhibitions to any form of self-expression. Not the least of these pretextual obstacles is the saint's theoretical resistance to her implied singularity as a recipient of visions, as well as her sensitivity to the possibility of diabolic illusion. The proper attitude for the prospective mystic/saint is one of deep refusal. Jean Gerson

---

Petroff, *Consolation of the Blessed* (New York, 1979), pp. 39–82; eadem, *Body and Soul: Essays on Medieval Women and Mysticism* (New York, 1994), esp. pt. 3, pp. 139–224; Karma Lochrie, "The Language of Transgression: Body, Flesh, and Word in Mystical Discourse," in *Speaking Two Languages: Traditional Disciplines and Contemporary Theory in Medieval Studies*, ed. Allen J. Frantzen (Albany, N.Y., 1991), pp. 115–40, 253–59; eadem, *Margery Kempe and Translations of the Flesh* (Philadelphia, 1991), esp. chaps. 3–4, pp. 97–166; Laurie A. Finke, *Feminist Theory, Women's Writing* (Ithaca, N.Y., 1992), esp. chap. 3, pp. 75–107. For a reasoned critique of the unequivocal association of mysticism with female empowerment, see Sarah Beckwith's "A Very Material Mysticism: The Medieval Mysticism of Margery Kempe," in *Medieval Literature: Criticism, Ideology, and History*, ed. David Aers (Brighton, Suss., 1986), pp. 34–57.

cites with approval several classic examples of this kind of pious demurral. For instance, Bonaventure requested three months of demonic possession to rid him of a desire for visions. An ascetic from the *Vitae patrum* covered his eyes before an ostensible vision of Christ, saying, "'I don't want to see Christ now: it is enough if I see him in heaven.'" (As it happened, the vision was a demonic illusion, so little harm was done.)[6] This message is also internalized by female mystics. Bridget of Sweden (died 1373) allegedly proved her pious reticence by attempting to flee from the visionary Christ the first three times that he appeared. After each of these occasions, moreover, she immediately sought an opportunity to confess and receive Communion—presumably to purge herself of possible demonic contamination.[7]

But even if the visionary is finally prepared to credit the divine inspiration of her revelations, disclosure is still a vexed issue. In fact, reluctance to have revelations made public is the most powerful testimony to "good faith." Thus the twelfth-century Elisabeth of Schönau, who, along with her more famous contemporary Hildegard of Bingen, is associated with the reawakening of mysticism in the West, is reported by her brother and amanuensis, Ekbert, as reasoning thus:

---

[6]*De probatione spirituum* c. 9, in Gerson, *Oeuvres complètes*, ed. Palémon Glorieux, vol. 9 (Paris, 1973), p. 182; trans. Paschal Boland in *The Concept of "discretio spirituum" in John Gerson's "De probatione spirituum" and "De distinctione verarum visionum a falsis"* (Washington, D.C., 1959), p. 33. Gerson's scepticism regarding female spirituality is discussed below.

[7]See the Life by Prior Peter Olavsson from Alvastra and by Master Peter Olavsson from Skänninge that was included in Bridget's process of canonization (Isak Collijn, ed., *Acta et processus canonizacionis beate Birgitte* [Uppsala, 1924–31], pp. 80–81; trans. Albert Ryle Kezel, *Birgitta of Sweden: Life and Selected Revelations*, ed. Marguerite Tjader Harris [New York, 1990], pp. 77–78).

"You ask me, brother, and for this reason you came, to narrate to you the mercies of the Lord which, according to the good purpose of his grace, he deemed to work in me. I am ready in all ways, brother, to satisfy your love, for my soul also desired for a long time that it should be given to me to confer with you concerning all those things and to hear your opinion; but, I pray, defer and attend a little, my beloved, to the multiple perplexities of my heart, which confine me more than can be believed. If that word, which you hear, were to go forth into the community, just as through certain incautious brothers (God knows) against my will it already went forth in part, what talk would there be amongst the people about me, do you suppose? Some perhaps will say that I am of considerable sanctity, and will attribute my merits to the grace of God, judging that I am something, although I may be nothing. But others will think within themselves, saying: If this were the servant of God, she would certainly remain quiet, and would not permit her name to be made much of in the land—these ones not knowing by what stimuli (*qualibus stimulis*) I was urged to speak. Nor will people be wanting who say that the things they hear from me are all female figments, or perhaps they will judge me ridiculed by Satan. In these and other ways, dearest, it will be necessary that I be aired in the mouths of the people. And whence should this happen to me, that I may be made conspicuous to some, I who chose to be in hiding, and who certainly does not judge myself worthy, that whosoever should raise up their eyes to gaze at me? It also increases my perplexities not a little that it pleased the lord abbot that my words be commended to writing. For what am I that those things which are from me should be handed down to memory? Could this not also be ascribed to arrogance?"[8]

Ekbert's representations of Elisabeth's qualms were more than mere formulae. Her correspondence with Hildegard of Bingen

---

[8]F. W. E. Roth, ed., *Die Visionen der hl. Elisabeth und die Schriften der Aebte Ekbert und Emecho von Schönau* (Brünn, 1884), p. 2. On Ekbert and Elisabeth's collaboration, with special emphasis on Ekbert's influence, see Anne L. Clark, *Elisabeth of Schönau: A Twelfth-Century Visionary* (Philadelphia, 1992), pp. 50–67, 130–31.

showed a painful preoccupation with her own reputation. In Elisabeth's first letter to Hildegard, she complains that detractors unjustly blame her for setting a precise date for the end of the world—a charge she vigorously denies. She then attempts, rather obsessively, to set the record straight. Hildegard offers consolation—albeit in a stern form. She reminds Elisabeth that a prophet has no voice of her own and, thus by implication, urges her personal disinvestment.[9]

THE GROWING ASCENDANCY OF THE CONFESSOR/SCRIBE

Elisabeth and Hildegard also inaugurate the familiar pattern of a poorly educated or even illiterate female mystic giving dictation to a more learned cleric—a dynamic that will become so omnipresent and predictable that it may as well be called compulsory hetero-textuality.[10] Although the limited education of the average female mystic and her consequent dependence on a male scribe are regrettable from the point of view of efforts to reconstruct a distinct female voice, the scribe's initiative generally safeguards the woman against the imputation

---

[9]For Elisabeth's letter see Roth, *Die Visionen*, pp. 70–74; for Hildegard's response see PL 197: 216–18. For translation see Kathryn Kerby-Fulton and Dyan Elliott, "Self-Image and the Visionary Role in Two Letters from the Correspondence of Elizabeth of Schönau and Hildegard of Bingen," *Vox Benedictina* 2 (1985): 204–23. Also see Barbara Newman's "Hildegard of Bingen: Visions and Validation," *Church History* 54 (1985): 163–75.

[10]There are, of course, significant deviations from this pattern, such as Mechtild of Hackeborn, whose scribe was none other than Gertrude the Great. But even this celebrated exception is reinscribed to fit the gendered norm I have outlined when the Middle English translator renders Mechtild's reference to her scribe in the masculine (see Theresa A. Halligan, ed., *The Booke of Gostlye Grace of Mechtild of Hackeborn* [Toronto, 1979], lines 14–18, p. 589; cf. *Liber specialis gratiae* 5.24 [Poitiers, 1877], pp. 356–57). I am grateful to Kathryn Kerby-Fulton for drawing this example to my attention.

that she has collaborated to an unflattering degree in the production of her own *fama*. Hence, by articulating Elisabeth's multiple apprehensions over redaction, Ekbert underscores the external pressures that both he and her abbot brought to bear in favor of textuality—pressures that eventually overcame her own judicious misgivings.

Female mystics tended to become more dependent on their confessor/scribes as the Middle Ages progressed.[11] Such a dependence was grounded in the soundest of self-protective reflexes. The number of female mystics accelerated at a steady rate over the course of the Middle Ages, particularly lay mystics, whose uncloistered status was regarded with alarm.[12] The clergy's sceptical response can in part be gauged by the proliferation of the genre directed to the discernment of spirits, since Satan can transform himself into an angel of light (2 Corinthians 11: 14).[13] The female mystic's scribe/confessor by necessity became something of an ad hoc expert in this kind of discernment, guarding her, and by association himself, from

---

[11] See Dyan Elliott, *Spiritual Marriage: Sexual Abstinence in Medieval Wedlock* (Princeton, 1993), pp. 261–63. Note that Bynum suggests that female Italian saints both dominate and are dominated by their confessors, compared with their Northern counterparts (*Holy Feast*, p. 140).

[12] See André Vauchez, *La sainteté en Occident aux derniers siècles du Moyen Âge: d'apres le proces de canonisation et les documents hagiographiques* (Rome, 1981), pp. 472–78.

[13] On the discernment of spirits, see François Vandenbroucke, "Discernement des esprits au moyen âge," *Dictionnaire de spiritualité ascetique et mystique: doctrine et histoire*, vol. 3 (Paris, 1957), cols. 1254–66; William A. Christian, *Apparitions in Late Medieval and Renaissance Spain* (Princeton, 1981), pp. 188–203; Kathryn Kerby-Fulton, "'Who has Written this Book?': Visionary Autobiography in Langland's C Text," in *The Medieval Mystical Tradition in England: Exeter Symposium V*, ed. Marion Glasscoe (Cambridge, 1992), pp. 101–16. The various treatises of discernment of Alphonse of Pecha and Jean Gerson, written in response to Bridget of Sweden's visions, are discussed below.

the shallows of heterodoxy. The fates of "heresiarchs"—women such as Marguerite Porete or Guglielma of Milan—demonstrate the dangers of inadequate or incompetent mediation.[14]

Many of the confessors of the more successful mystics were, not surprisingly, skilled theologians who were better equipped to address the heightened criteria generated within a critical climate. Bridget of Sweden, for instance, was the beneficiary of massive clerical support. Her first book of revelations was preceded by an elaborate preface by her confessor Mathias of Linköping—a trained canonist and theologian whom Bridget's visionary Christ had characterized as having "experience in discerning the two types of spirits."[15] The prologue's dramatic incipit, "Stupor et mirabilia audita sunt in terra nostra," sets the stage for Mathias's claim that Christ's contemporary communications with the humble (Bridget) were more stupendous than God's conversations with Moses.[16] Mathias does not miss the opportunity to allay possible

---

[14]On Guglielma, see Barbara Newman, "WomanSpirit, Woman Pope," in *From Virile Woman to WomanChrist: Studies in Medieval Religion and Literature* (Philadelphia, 1995), pp. 182–223, 295–304; and Stephen Wessley, "The Thirteenth-Century Guglielmites: Salvation Through Women," in *Medieval Women*, ed. Derek Baker (Oxford, 1978), pp. 289–303. Note that despite Cistercian efforts to have Guglielma recognized as a saint, her first and most influential interpreter was another woman, the visionary Mayfreda de Pirovano. Marguerite Porete made the mistake of writing her revelations herself. This task might have been better left to Guiart de Cressonsacq, the humble cleric who argued unsuccessfully for her life, only to find himself degraded and perpetually imprisoned (see Robert E. Lerner, *The Heresy of the Free Spirit in the Later Middle Ages* [Berkeley, 1972], pp. 71–78; H. C. Lea, *A History of the Inquisition of the Middle Ages*, 3 vols. [New York, 1887], 2: 123–24, and see the appendix, pp. 575–78, for Marguerite's sentencing).

[15]*Vita*, in Collijn, *Acta et processus*, p. 81; trans. Kezel, *Birgitta of Sweden*, p. 78.

[16]Bridget of Sweden, *Revelaciones: Book 1*, ed. Carl-Gustaf Undhagen (Stockholm, 1977), *Prol.*, p. 229.

objections to Bridget, a noble and ostensibly worldly matron, by stressing that she separated herself from the flesh and the world as soon as opportunity permitted through the transition to a spiritual marriage.[17] Bridget's official *vita* was written by the "two Peters," one a theologian and the other the prior of a Cistercian monastery, both of whom had attended her as confessors and companions in Rome.[18] In addition, the theologian Alphonse of Pecha, former bishop of Jaén and one of Bridget's confessors in her later years, was not only responsible for arranging Bridget's visions in their final form but also wrote an elaborate defense of her visions—itself a treatise on the discernment of spirits. Alphonse demonstrates Bridget's own adeptness in spiritual discernment and emphasizes the careful submission of all her revelations to her confessors.[19] The theologian John of Marienwerder, confessor to the Prussian mystic Dorothea of Montau (died 1394), who was herself Bridget of Sweden's spiritual client, also directly tackles the question of mystical discernment.[20] In the longest of the four *vitae* he

---

[17]Bridget of Sweden, *Revelaciones: Book 1, Prol.*, p. 233. On Bridget's spiritual marriage see Elliott, *Spiritual Marriage*, pp. 226, 238–39, 245–46.

[18]See Eric Colledge, "*Epistola solitarii ad reges:* Alphonse of Pecha as Organizer of Birgittine and Urbanist Propaganda," *Mediaeval Studies* 18 (1956): 23–24.

[19]Alphonse of Pecha, *Epistola solitarii ad reges* c. 6 and 4, in *Alfonso of Jaén: His Life and Works*, ed. Arne Jönsson (Lund, 1989), pp. 152–53, 135–36. Also see Colledge's discussion, "*Epistola solitarii ad reges*," esp. pp. 25–42.

[20]Dorothea's mystical pregnancy, described in the *Septililium* (a series of visions on divine love), reveals the extent of her indebtedness to Bridget. The Lord, moreover, explicitly uses the parallel to reassure Dorothea (and hence the reader) that her visionary experience is free from suspect novelty (see Franz Hipler, *Septililium B. Dorothea* 1.17, *Analecta Bollandiana* 2 [1883]: 437; cf. 1.9, 420–21. Note that Gerson isolates gratuitous novelty as one of the telltale signs of a spurious vision [see *De probatione spirituum* c. 8, in *Oeuvres complètes* 9: 181; trans. Boland, *Concept*, pp. 31–32; cf. Gerson's

wrote on his saintly penitent's behalf, he includes a section with the rubric "True testimonies that she was not deceived about the revelations" in direct response to the Johannine exhortation to prove the spirits to see whether they are from God (1 John 4: 1). This section is immediately followed by an elaborate twenty-four point proof providing a more systematic analysis of the same issue.[21] John also wisely shared some of the responsibility for Dorothea's spiritual direction with the celebrated canonist John Reyman.[22]

Many of the tensions in the relationship between Dorothea and John are illuminated by the minutiae of their intimate collaboration. Again, in John's longest and most ambitious *vita*, the section entitled "How the writing of the revelations was done and approved by God" details both the practical obstacles of redaction as well as possible ideological difficulties. The most apparent stumbling-block was a predictable, but hardly innocuous, one. At the age of forty-four Dorothea was still an attractive widow and, prior to her entrance into the *reclusorium* where she would end her life, John (himself forty-eight) dared not work with her anywhere except out in the open area of the church itself:

De examinatione doctrinarum 2.4, *Oeuvres complètes* 9: 470]). The Lord also compares the nature of Dorothea's revelations with those of Bridget, by way of validation, while Bridget herself appears to Dorothea. See Hans Westpfahl, ed., *Vita Dorotheae Montoviensis Magistri Johannis Marienwerder* 6.8, 7.19 (Cologne and Graz, 1964), pp. 300, 355. For John, see Franz Hipler, "Johannes Marienwerder, der Beichvater der seligen Dorothea von Montau," *Zeitschrift für die Geschichte und Altertumskunde Ermlands*, 29.1 (1956): 1–92, esp. pp. 7–26 on his education and theological writings; on his various *vitae* of Dorothea see pp. 62–73.

[21] Westpfahl, *Vita Dorotheae* 1.5–6, pp. 40–49. Cf. John's 24 proofs with Alphonse of Pecha's seven in *Epistola solitarii* c. 6, in Jönsson, *Alfonso of Jaén*, pp. 154–66.

[22] See Hipler, "Johannes Marienwerder," p. 42.

> not in a home, or a bedroom, or some corner of the church, lest
> sinister opinion or suspicion concerning them arise, whence the odor
> of good reputation is infected. The Confessor anxiously dreaded
> this. . . . He knew that the reputation of spiritual men was slippery.[23]

Moreover, the actual process of redaction was in itself arduous. In the beginning, John worked on wax tablets and then recopied this text onto papyrus with a reed pen and ink. But eventually, worn out by this cumbersome two-fold process, John began recording directly onto the papyrus.

The task was complicated by the fact that both John and Dorothea felt compelled to conceal their activity from passersby. This precaution, which seems to have originated with John, speaks volumes. If the occupation of writing were detected, John would have been cleared from any appearance of unchastity. Yet writing appears to have been regarded as even more dangerous than the suspicion of dalliance with an attractive widow. The open avowal that John was recording Dorothea's revelations would have been tantamount to endorsing them and, perhaps by extension, endorsing her claims to sanctity. That John perceived this disclosure as precocious and even dangerous is made clear by his anger when Dorothea "through a slip of the tongue" revealed their occupation to an inquisitive layperson.[24]

In view of John's apprehensions it is not surprising that writing itself becomes a matter for mystic commentary and even intervention. A number of Dorothea's revelations seek explicitly to reassure John, in particular, and vindicate the writing process generally. In response to Dorothea's inadvertent disclosure, for example, Christ says, " 'Have no fear! I want to

---

[23]Westpfahl, *Vita Dorotheae* 1.7, p. 50.

[24]Westpfahl, *Vita Dorotheae* 1.7, p. 50.

preserve you both unharmed and guard you well.' "[25] When John was still exhausting himself in copying out the revelations in duplicate, the Lord intervenes: " 'Say to your Confessor: I will not die soon! On that account I do not want you to fatigue yourself so. For I fear that you will harm yourself excessively.' " On other occasions, however, revelation acted as a goad to writing: " 'Write strongly! Do not waste time! Nor is it necessary for your Confessor to implicate himself in outer things! For I wish to give him ample writing and reading.' "[26]

But perhaps more important than these directives on pacing was the supernatural commentary, communicated to John by Dorothea, that construed his writing not simply as ancillary but as integral to the visionary process—an explicit assurance that he was not simply witness to but actually was participating in mystical charisma.[27] Thus the Lord attempted to dispel John's fear of the potential dangers of writing by underscoring his privilege as a partaker ("particeps") of Dorothea's revelation. On one occasion, for example, our furtive collaborators found themselves in the grip of writers' block:

> On a certain day, the Spouse and her Confessor wrote with great difficulty in the work—afflicting themselves indeed, but for a long time not finding the right words for expressing the revealed things to be written then. That evening the Lord from his innate affection, deigned to approve this small amount of writing and difficulty in

---

[25]Westpfahl, *Vita Dorotheae* 1.7, p. 51.

[26]Westpfahl, *Vita Dorotheae* 1.7, p. 51.

[27]Cf. Coakley's remark regarding the friars' relations with holy women: "The assumption seems to have been . . . that these women possessed supernatural contacts which the friars lacked. . . . The friars were therefore beneficiaries of extraordinary contact with the divine, although they specifically lacked the ability to make the contact themselves" ("Gender and the Authority of Friars," p. 456). Dorothea's revelation may have advanced John a notch beyond this usual level of privilege.

work, saying thus to his Spouse: "Among all the other sweet conversations over honey and honeycombs, today's was the best and especially acceptable to me, because you afflicted yourselves together through your labor. . . . Through afflicting yourselves in this way you worked better than if you had written many more things without affliction."

The Lord singles John out for special praise: " 'the hands with which your Confessor wrote about the revelations serve me and show those reading the paths to salvation.' "[28]

Yet, too successful a literary production would be self-defeating, since the hallmark of the divine alterity of the original experience resides in the impossibility of its complete written communication, an implicit principle that is often emphasized by the mystic's protestations of inexpressibility.[29] Angela of Foligno (died 1309) punctuated her confessor/scribe's work with startled misrecognitions and disavowals: " 'You have written what is bland, inferior, and amounts to nothing; but concerning what is precious in what my soul feels you have written nothing.' "[30] The celebrated incompetence of the various scribes of Margery Kempe (died after 1438) was, in itself, a surety against too suspiciously satisfying a written record.[31]

---

[28]Westpfahl, *Vita Dorotheae* 1.7, p. 52.

[29]Michel de Certeau characterizes mysticism as "an object that escapes" and a "language of the unsayable" ("Mysticism," *Diacritics* 22 [1992]: 17). Also see Sarah Beckwith, "Problems of Authority in Late Medieval Mysticism: Language, Agency, and Authority in the *Book of Margery Kempe*," *Exemplaria* 4 (1992): 180–82.

[30]*The Book of Angela (Memorial)* 1.2, in *Angela of Foligno: Complete Works*, trans. Paul Lachance (New York, 1993), pp. 137–38; cf. *The Book of Angela (Instructions)* 4, pp. 247–48.

[31]See Sanford Brown Meech and Hope Emily Allen, *The Book of Margery Kempe*, EETS, o.s., no. 212 (1940), pp. 3–6, 216, 220–21. For other essential ways in which Margery's incompetent scribes help to authorize her text, see

Thus, despite supernatural reassurances that Dorothea and John's collaboration was divinely endorsed, what they revealed was in many ways a record of what remained concealed. Indeed, the sixteenth proof of the authenticity of Dorothea's visions turned on the question of their inexpressibility. The Lord ordered Dorothea to tell her confessor,

> "It is impossible that my action, my state, and my life will ever be totally expressed to you. Indeed God said to me that not only is it impossible for me to express it totally, but even impossible for me to comprehend it. I could not express all the wonderful things even if I had many tongues."[32]

STRATEGIES FOR CONTAINMENT

Thus far, I have emphasized those aspects in which the relation of the mystic and her scribe can be seen as corroborative of her authenticity and facilitative of her self-expression. Yet, the indispensability of the priestly presence is not only an acknowledgment of clerical responsibility to aid and abet the mystical process but also it creates a matrix from which to stage interference. Jean Gerson's *De probatione spirituum* of 1415 is a case in point. The most famous of the various treatises on spiritual discretion written in this period, this essay crystallized many of the inchoate apprehensions of the clerical

---

Lynn Staley Johnson, "The Trope of the Scribe and the Question of Literary Authority in the Works of Julian of Norwich and Margery Kempe," *Speculum* 66 (1991): 833–38.

[32]Westpfahl, *Vita Dorotheae* 1.6, p. 46; cf. 2.18–19, pp. 80–81. There were also certain things that God forbade Dorothea from revealing altogether (2.15, p. 77). The inadequacy of the written text corresponds with Dorothea's anti-intellectual spiritual "work ethic." Thus in the first chapter of the *vita* she deprecates the book-learning extolled by a local preacher in favor of knowledge acquired directly from God (1.1, p. 31).

hierarchy concerning female mysticism and presented a blueprint for its containment. Addressed to the Fathers of Constance assembled to end the papal schism, it challenged Bridget of Sweden's canonization.[33] By extension, the treatise adopts a skeptical attitude towards the many mystical women of the age, powerfully restating what for our purposes is the "ur" question: "Why was the communication of such visions made to another person?"[34] This clerical anxiety, acting with and upon the *topos* of saintly humility, was responsible for shaping the mystical experience of the later Middle Ages within a progressively punitive framework.

Supernatural persuasion (ratified by priestly pressure) generally provided the best alibi for the publication of visions. But such persuasion can easily shift from benign prompting to a more coercive, and hence disciplinary, regime that ultimately compromises (rather than facilitates or "stages") female autonomy. Much of the prescient John of Marienwerder's twenty-four point system had accordingly been oriented towards protecting Dorothea from aspersions surrounding female arrogance and loquacity, while simultaneously protecting himself against

---

[33]See Colledge, "*Epistola solitarii ad reges*," p. 45. Note that Gerson's first treatise on this subject, *De distinctione revelationum visionum a falsis*, was completed in late 1401. Gerson later implies that it was occasioned by his near spiritual seduction through the revelations of a holy laywoman, Ermine de Reims: "Fui pridem, fateor, per relationes aliquorum magnae merito reputationis, proximus seductioni de quadam Hermina, Remensi, nisi modum responsionis propriae, Deo volente, temperassem. Circa quod tempus opusculum compilavi, seu lectionem unam de distinctione revelationum verarum a falsis" (*De examinatione doctrinarum* 2.6, in *Oeuvres complètes* 9: 474). His earlier endorsement of Ermine appears in his letter to Jean Morel, which the editor Glorieux tentatively dates 1408. If Gerson is to be taken at his word there is good reason to date this letter earlier.

[34]Gerson, *De probatione spirituum* c. 10 (*Oeuvres complètes* 9: 183, trans. Boland, *Concept*, p. 35).

charges of gullibility. Thus divine compulsion is enlisted to overcome pious reticence. In number 11 the Lord asserts to Dorothea: "'Were you to omit to speak of the effects of my goodness, your heart would be torn out and you would soon expire.'" Number 12 registers Dorothea's observation that she was never divinely punished for these "pronouncings" (the word she used to characterize her dictation to John) as she was for other gratuitous speech. Moreover, the Divine Presence looms vigilantly over the entire collaboration like an anxious editor: number 18 notes that Dorothea was miraculously wounded for all errors and omissions in her "pronouncings."[35]

Generally such pressures were brought to bear on the mystic directly, but there are exceptions. After Bridget of Sweden had proved her pious reticence by attempting physical flight from the source of the vision, she was then ordered to tell Peter, subprior of the monastery of Alvastra, to take down her revelations in Latin. While Bridget complied without demurral, it was Peter who "in the end decided from humility that he would not undertake to write the said divine revelations, judging himself unworthy for such things and being uncertain about illusion from the devil." He paid for his scrupulosity: his ruminations were resolved by a divine blow that made him fall to the ground as if dead.[36]

A divinely induced malady was frequently enlisted to vanquish saintly reticence. Indeed, Michel de Certeau has identified sickness itself with a kind of currency in mystical discourse: "a pathos of the body inscribes its authenticating mark upon the will and pays for the scriptorial production."[37]

---

[35]Westpfahl, *Vita Dorotheae* 1.6, pp. 44, 45, 47.

[36]Bridget of Sweden, *Revelaciones extravagantes* c. 48, ed. Lennart Hollman (Uppsala, 1956), p. 163.

[37]*Mystic Fable*, p. 191.

This transactional pattern is already present in the lives of Hildegard of Bingen and Elisabeth of Schönau. In the famous *Protestificatio* of *Scivias*, Hildegard reports that when she refused to heed the divine mandate to record and publicize her visions, out of humility, her compliance was nevertheless achieved through a prolonged illness. Elisabeth was also no stranger to celestial pressures. She quickly overcame her face-saving reticence when an angel appeared and gave her a sound thrashing that left her wracked with pain for three days.[38] Indeed, illness is doubly catalytic in these cases, since their sickly dispositions seemingly made such women susceptible to visions in the first place. Variants of this pattern would continue to be a celebrated feature of female spirituality. Julian of Norwich's vision of Christ's passion is intrinsically linked with her divinely solicited illness; Lidwine of Schiedam's debilitated body is the condition of her entry into divine favor.[39] Moreover, much of Certeau's analysis focuses on the frail Theresa of Avila, thus indicating that this pattern extends beyond the medieval period. On each side of revelation is pain that is frequently resolved in redaction.

But supernatural coercion did not always authorize mystic speech—quite the contrary. The priest as privileged reader and

---

[38]Hildegard of Bingen, *Scivias*, ed. Adelgundis Führkötter and Angela Carlevaris, CCCM 43 (Turnhout, 1978), 1: 5–6; Roth, *Die Visionen*, p. 71; trans. Kerby-Fulton and Elliott, "Self-Image and the Visionary Role," p. 215.

[39]Edmund Colledge and James Walsh, eds., *A Book of Showings to the Anchoress Julian of Norwich*, 2 vols. (Toronto, 1978), shorter text, c. 1–3, 1: 201–10; longer text, c. 2–3, 2: 285–93. For Lidwine see AA SS, Apr., 2: 307–16. On female mysticism and its relation to illness, see Bynum, "'. . . And Woman His Humanity': Female Imagery in the Religious Writing of the Later Middle Ages" and "The Female Body and Religious Practice in the Later Middle Ages," in eadem, *Fragmentation and Redemption: Essays on Gender and the Human Body in Medieval Religion* (New York, 1991), pp. 173–75, 188–90.

ultimate interpreter of these supernatural persuasions (even, or perhaps especially, when they were enacted on the woman's body) could also read to the opposite purpose. He could take what have hitherto been construed as authorizing strategies and, by turning them on their heads, reapply them to enforce de-authorization and silence. And so Gerson ironically appropriated Alphonse of Pecha's defense of Bridget of Sweden and reshaped it into a critique.

While Alphonse criticizes those who are inclined to dismiss the revelations of "simple spiritual unlearned people and those of the female sex," it is precisely these interest groups that Gerson's *De probatione spirituum* stigmatizes.[40] Arguing from the "inside," his hostile characterizations of female spirituality go right to the heart of some of the mystic's most important authorizing strategies, which had been developed over the course of the Middle Ages. Gerson's quasi-medicalized discourse implicates female raptures in what he perceives as a degenerative syndrome:

> Since the judgment of the intellect is affected by an injured brain, if anyone who has been thus injured is subject to strange fancies, we do not have to inquire further to discover from what spirit those neurotic and illusory visions come, as is evident in cases of insanity and in various other illness.[41]

For Gerson, brain damage does not only signify the kind of injury that would result from a sharp rap on the head: one might just as easily become imbalanced by severe penitential practices. In his companion treatise *De distinctione verarum*

---

[40] Alphonse of Pecha, *Epistola solitarii* c. 1, in Jönsson, *Alfonso of Jaén*, p. 120; Gerson, *De probatione spirituum*, esp. c. 7, 11 (*Oeuvres complètes* 9: 180, 184; trans. Boland, *Concept*, pp. 30, 36–37).

[41] *De probatione spirituum* c. 7 (*Oeuvres complètes* 9: 180; trans. Boland, *Concept*, p. 30).

revelationum a falsis, Gerson tells of a married woman from Arras who was senselessly starving herself to death, thus associating heroic feats of fasting, perhaps the signature mark of female spirituality, with exhibitionism, suicidal tendencies, and derangement.[42] Elsewhere he ridicules these women's male supporters, who misdiagnose their visionary singularity:

> Jerome blames those men who, for shame, learn from women. What if one of this sex was judged to walk in great and marvelous things above herself, to add visions to visions daily, to report lesions of the brain, epilepsy, congelation, or some melancholy as a miracle?[43]

Such characterizations would necessarily undercut the efficacy of sickness as an enabling factor.

Gerson queries the necessity and, implicitly, the credibility of a plethora of visions through his characterization of a terse Godhead: " 'God speaketh once, and repeateth not the self-same thing the second time (Job 33: 14).' In fact, it would be tiresome, not to say foolish, to have to accept a multiplicity of visions as having been revealed from the mouth of God."[44] The economy of divine locutions naturally heightens the equation between sanctity and taciturnity. But Gerson also more explicitly attacks female publication—in the broadest sense from spoken word to written text—as it runs counter to apostolic authority. He glosses the apostolic prohibition of female teaching, arguing that Eve lied twice in her first utterance.

---

[42]*De distinctione verarum revelationum a falsis* (*Oeuvres complètes* 3: 43–44; trans. Boland, *Concept*, pp. 87–89).

[43]Gerson, *De examinatione doctrinarum* 2.2 (*Oeuvres complètes* 9: 467).

[44]*De probatione spirituum* c. 8 (*Oeuvres complètes* 9: 181; trans. Boland, *Concept*, pp. 32–33). This seems to have been a favorite passage of Gerson's: cf. *De examinatione doctrinarum* 2.6 (*Oeuvres complètes* 9: 474) and *De passionibus animae* c. 4 (ibid., 9: 13).

(Specifically, in her relation of the divine interdiction, she said that God ordered them not to eat or touch the forbidden fruit lest perhaps they die—gratuitously adding "touch" and making the certain uncertain.) This point is buttressed by an exemplary argument from silence highlighting Jerome's illustrious female circle: "Where are the things written by so many of the most erudite women: Paula, Eustochium, and the like? Certainly nothing remains because no one presumed."[45] The dire consequences of such presumption are only too apparent in the calamity of the papal schism, which he attributes to the visionary intervention of two unnamed women—clearly Catherine of Siena and Bridget of Sweden.[46] Gerson also stigmatizes women who seek endless conversations under the pretext of frequent confession—an aspect of female piety that had traditionally argued for spiritual scrupulosity.[47] But, perhaps most damaging, he strikes at the heart of the confessional relationship through the predictable argument that "for even the most deeply religious men, no matter how great their sanctity, a common life and familiarity with women are not safe." What begins as spiritual love is all too easily transformed into carnal love.[48] He also impugns the fatuousness of

---

[45] Gerson, *De examinatione doctrinarum* 2.2 (*Oeuvres complètes* 9: 468). Regarding the ambivalence to female speech, see Sharon Farmer, "Softening the Hearts of Men: Women, Embodiment and Persuasion in the Thirteenth Century," in *Embodied Love: Sensuality and Relationship as Feminist Values*, ed. Paula M. Cooey, Sharon A. Farmer, and Mary Ellen Ross (San Francisco, 1987), pp. 115–22; eadem, "Persuasive Voices: Clerical Images of Medieval Wives," *Speculum* 61 (1986): 538–40; R. Howard Bloch, *Medieval Misogyny and the Invention of Western Romantic Love* (Chicago, 1991), pp. 54–58.

[46] Gerson, *De examinatione doctrinarum* 2.4 (*Oeuvres complètes* 9: 470).

[47] Gerson, *De probatione spirituum* c. 11 (*Oeuvres complètes* 9: 184; trans. Boland, *Concept*, p. 36).

[48] Gerson, *De distinctione verarum revelationum a falsis* (*Oeuvres complètes* 3: 51; trans. Boland, *Concept*, p. 98).

confessors who, in over-praising the purity of a few, encourage concealment and lies in the confessional of the many. This kind of irresponsible partiality causes him to call into question the testimony of the confessor in a process of canonization—thus undercutting a prospective lay saint's chief ally.[49]

FRANCES OF ROME AND JOHN MATTIOTTI

In the age of Gerson and the wake of the schism, when mistrust of female mysticism ran high, any collaboration between priest and female client that resulted in the production of a mystical text was a kind of triumph. I would argue that it was a costly triumph that both absorbed and reshaped the woman's mystical gifts as textual production left a deep impression on her spirituality. In returning to the relationship between Frances of Rome and John Mattiotti, one is struck by the degree to which their spiritual collaboration was oriented toward the vindication of the mystical text. Their complex strategies of authentication for this text not only were shaped by but also shaped Frances's celebrated virtues of taciturnity and obedience. These virtues, while clearly enabling channels for her ecstatic rapture—the conduit for contact with divine alterity—were also manipulated to function as ultimate guarantees of Frances's disinvolvement with textual production. And the proofs of this disinvolvement forcefully reinscribe an exceptionally passive role for female spirituality.

Saintly taciturnity and obedience exist on a continuum with secular conceptions of idealized womanhood in this period. Moreover, the powerful symbiosis of these two virtues is suggested by popular literature. Thus in the Griselda legend, to cite the most obvious example, her marriage is premised on

---

[49]Gerson, *De examinatione doctrinarum* 2.3 (*Oeuvres complètes* 9: 469).

her agreement to obey her husband's commands instantaneously and silently.[50] With respect to Frances, the familiar pairing of obedience and taciturnity operated as a mechanism of verification. Frances's own mobilization of these virtues enable her to avoid the stigmatized role of the virago-saint who distinguished herself by transcending gender boundaries, hence achieving a suspect singularity. In fact, one of her triumphs over a diabolical adversary turned on the rejection of her childhood ambition to live the life of a solitary in a desert hermitage.[51] Her submission to appropriate authority is instead demonstrated in her marriage of forty years and her ready compliance with ensuing domestic responsibilities. Demonic torment, moreover, frequently took the form of forestalling Frances's ready compliance with her husband's wishes.[52]

John Mattiotti was careful to establish Frances's freedom from the self-indulgence of loquacity. Not only does she punish herself for any gratuitous word, allegedly through blows that sometimes drew blood,[53] but John himself initiates all discussion of her inner life. Consistent with her propensity

---

[50]See Elaine Tuttle Hansen's reading of Chaucer's *Clerk's Tale*, which points out how such virtues invite male aggression (thus enforcing female submission), as well as open up a possibility for subversion of patriarchal authority —one which is quickly contained by the narrative ("The Powers of Silence: The Case of the Clerk's Griselda," in *Women and Power in the Middle Ages*, ed. Mary C. Erler and Maryanne Kowaleski [Athens, Ga., 1988], pp. 230–49). For the continuing emphasis on taciturnity and obedience as the quintessential female virtues in the early modern period, see Suzanne W. Hull, *Chaste, Silent, and Obedient: English Books for Women, 1475–1640* (San Marino, Calif., 1982).

[51]AA SS, Mar., 2: 161; see Elliott, *Spiritual Marriage*, p. 242.

[52]AA SS, Mar., 2: 156, 163; Elliott, *Spiritual Marriage*, p. 259.

[53]AA SS, Mar., 2: 95; also see Placido Tommaso Lugano, ed., *I Processi inediti per Francesca Bussa dei Ponziani (Santa Francesca Romana) 1440–1453* (Vatican City, 1945), process of 1451, p. 251.

for silence is a total aversion to discussing her mystical experiences—a reticence that would have been unpropitious for perpetuity had it not been for her exemplary obedience.

Through the mechanism of holy obedience, Frances was constrained to speak about her many raptures. The following pattern emerges in the selected series of visions that Mattiotti recorded. Frances first experiences what John called her "immovable ecstasy"; then she enters into a "moveable ecstasy"; finally she returns to her "natural senses" ("in naturalibus")—after which point John would ask what she saw.[54] When John was absent, Frances's spiritual daughters would report whether or not she had experienced a rapture, and then John would constrain her to reveal the visions later.[55] John's role in these proceedings is, of course, crucial: on the feast of Christmas in 1433, for example, Frances received the Christ child to hold and began to sing with joy. John informs us that her song unfortunately went unrecorded, owing to his illness.[56] Their mystical collaboration is premised on Frances's reluctance. On one occasion the habitual guardian angel, who accompanied Frances everywhere but was visible only to her, administered a blow to the neck that brought her to her knees before the priest. The offense resided in her unwillingness to reveal the

---

[54]See, e.g., AA SS, Mar., 2: 108, vis. 8; 2: 118, vis. 20). Sometimes after Communion she went into rapture "in extasi mobili" and her spiritual joy would be revealed through her singing and through her hand movements—likened to the gestures that professional singers use (AA SS, Mar., 2: 109, vis. 10). In dialogue with Christ, she alternated between immobile ecstasy when he spoke and the more mobile ecstasy when she joyously responded (AA SS, Mar., 2: 113, vis. 15).

[55]See, e.g., AA SS, Mar., 2: 117, vis. 19.

[56]AA SS, Mar., 2: 144, vis. 57. Cf. a similar omission mentioned in Anguillaria's later *vita* (AA SS, Mar., 2: 185).

contents of a vision to John.[57] It is no accident that the last
revelation that John chose to record is Frances's vision of holy
obedience—the virtue that operated as presiding muse or,
better still, as "ghost writer" for the entire corpus.[58]

Thus far we have explored aspects of what I would distinguish as a primary level of obedience, in which Frances en-
gages in after-the-fact divulgence of mystical communications.
These communications operate as a mirror reflecting a mirror:
the revelation of revelation. In fact, this image often emerges
in Frances's visionary lexicon—frequently she sees writing
that affirms the mysteries of the faith in the depth of a splendid mirror.[59] Yet in these retrospective accounts, even as the
divine presence has receded from Frances, it necessarily eludes
John and the reader more completely. Although her relative
passivity in the reluctant *dictatio* authenticates the experience
she is recounting, her moment has passed. By the time Frances
has returned *in naturalibus* and begins to dictate, the ultimate
authentication, the Spirit that raptured her, has departed.

John anticipates this problem by pressuring Frances into
providing additional documentation. In other words, he orders
Frances to speak during her raptures—again enlisting holy
obedience. In this way, John strives to communicate at least a
trace of the alterity of Frances's original experience.[60] There
are certain subjects, for example, that Frances would only
discuss while she was in ecstasy—thus distinguishing them as
privileged sites of alterity and hence advancing a special claim

---

[57]See Lugano, *I Processi*, process of 1440, p. 98.

[58]AA SS, Mar., 2: 154, vis. 97; see Elliott, *Spiritual Marriage*, pp. 241–42.

[59]AA SS, Mar., 2: 106, vis. 5; cf. 2: 115, vis. 17.

[60]See, e.g., Lugnano, *I Processi*, process of 1440, p. 65. Her process also
notes her willingness to take other orders in the course of her raptures. Hence
she would stand, sit, etc., on command (pp. 27, 31).

for their authenticity. The various shapes in which demons appeared to her was seemingly one such subject.[61]

John thus seems to exemplify the positive strategies discussed earlier in this essay, in which a confessor can serve as a vital facilitator. But the ease with which facilitation can shift to coercion and even repression is suggested by the successive stages of John's involvement. The success of John's experiment with Frances's ecstatic speech spawned as many problems as rewards. Anticipating possible doubts and objections from his audience, he directed most of his precious moments of contact with alterity to attempted verifications of the premise behind the experiment itself. For example, when Frances was in ecstasy, John inquired under holy obedience how she spoke in this state. She answered that this is all done under obedience when she is outside of her senses. She neither hears nor feels; nor does she remember what things she said in ecstasy after she has returned to her normal state.[62] Supernatural intervention was required to allay John's concern as to why Frances could respond to orders and speak while enraptured but not control the twitching of her hands. Thus Saint Paul, speaking through Frances after she went into ecstasy, told John that supernal truths cause mutations in the body, while the faculties themselves are bound and alienated. A name cannot be placed on this state: it does not correspond to either sleep or wakefulness.[63]

In addition to John's efforts to sustain the presumption of "otherness" through internal proofs (namely by the testimony of one still enraptured), he also staged proofs from the outside. These experiments often entailed public demonstrations of

---

[61] AA SS, Mar., 2: 158–59.

[62] AA SS, Mar., 2: 147, vis. 64.

[63] AA SS, Mar., 2: 147, vis. 65.

Frances's visionary obedience. For example, once when she was in ecstasy, John ordered her to adore the Sacrament, which was at that moment being consecrated in the adjoining chapel. Much to the amazement of bystanders, she instantly obeyed, though never departing from her ecstasy.[64]

We know from the process of canonization that John also staged less dignified and sometimes rather brutal experiments—experiments that might be considered extra-textual, since they do not appear in his work but would nevertheless reflect favorably on his writings. Saint Paul, in the course of his explication of Frances's trance, had said that the individual "can suffer torments and feel nothing."[65] John instituted some modest experiments to vindicate these claims. On a number of occasions, wishing to probe and demonstrate the extent of his holy charge's ecstatic passivity, John told her spiritual daughter Rita "to torture her harshly." Rita used all the force she could muster in an effort to separate Frances's hands, which were habitually joined when she was in this state. Frances remained marble-like until John ordered her to move. In another instance, John caused several of the sisters to poke her in the face, which still elicited no response.[66] John, ever the obliging impresario, even invited the bishop to touch Frances while she was in ecstasy. The bishop refused, thinking himself unworthy.[67] Though insensible in the ecstasy proper, Frances does mention in the course of one of her conversant raptures that she often felt the ill-effects of these experiments after the fact.[68] By a comparative standard, Frances would seem to have

---

[64] AA SS, Mar., 2: 149, vis. 72.

[65] AA SS, Mar., 2: 147, vis. 65.

[66] Lugnano, *I Processi*, process of 1440, pp. 29, 61–62.

[67] Lugnano, *I Processi*, process of 1440, p. 64.

[68] AA SS, Mar., 2: 147, vis. 64.

gotten off exceptionally lightly. Skeptics stabbed the enrapt Christine of Stommeln with scissors, while Charles of Anjou poured molten lead over the feet of the immobilized Douceline of Marseilles.[69]

Only on very rare occasions does Frances actually interrupt the otherwise smooth textualization of her visionary life. Our opening account of the vision in which she challenged the demonic scribe was one such occasion. Since this vision was an excellent demonstration of her own ability to distinguish between true and false spirits, it could of course be rechanneled into the vindication of the text itself. On several occasions male prophets appear with messages for John— messages that likewise authenticate Frances's mystical experience. Thus the prophet David says,

> ". . . do not doubt further in these matters that are permitted to be manifested to you by God; you can only doubt as long as God permits [Frances] to remain [in this world]; but afterwards when she will be called to God, then your understanding will be evident and you will understand the mystery and you will satisfy your mind. Do not try any more after you have tried so many times."[70]

A similar message was sent via John the Baptist.[71] Such interventions were, on the one hand, warrants for the necessary opacity appropriate to visions professing contact with the divinity. Similar statements had issued from Dorothea of Montau concerning the essentially hidden nature of her life. But on the other hand, in Frances's case it is tempting to construe these celestial visitors as advocates on her behalf, urging John to abandon his puerile experiments.

---

[69]Kleinberg, *Prophets*, pp. 94, 123.

[70]AA SS, Mar., 2: 124, vis. 29.

[71]AA SS, Mar., 2: 128, vis. 35.

Occasionally, Frances attempted to position herself more closely to the centers of textual production. Once she forgot what the Virgin and her attendant saints said to her in a vision, and her confessor ordered her under holy obedience to think carefully over the forgotten words. Later, when she was at prayer in her private oratory, her mind raised "in fear of obedience," her familiar angel appeared, holding the forgotten words on a page.[72] As time progressed, her efforts to intervene textually became bolder. Two years later, in October 1434, she received mystical notice of the imminent destruction of Rome but was simultaneously provided with an antidote in the form of a celestial text. Frances had the privilege of seeing just how this text was produced. The Virgin Mary, stipulating the number of Masses, processions, and the like necessary to save the sinful city, dictated to Saint Paul, who recorded her words on parchment. After some time, Mary Magdalene took over from the Virgin Mary, with Paul still acting as scribe. Finally, Paul gave this parchment to Frances's personal angel, who held it for Frances, who read what was on this page to her confessor, who recorded what she said. The procedure lasted far into the night and was continued into the next day. As soon as John entered an item, it was deleted from the angel's parchment.[73] There is an optimistic side to this vision, in that

---

[72] AA SS, Mar., 2: 128, vis. 36. Cf. the time John arrived and asked Frances if there was anything new ("si aliquid novi sentiret"). She answered that her angel was holding a letter written by St. Paul, which turned out to contain a string of flowery compliments to the *anima* and a discussion of her spiritual strengths. After Frances read the letter to her confessor, the script disappeared from the *charta* in the angel's hand (vis. 67, 2: 147–48).

[73] AA SS, Mar., 2: 156, vis. 63. According to another source, Frances actually convinced John to seek the pope (then in Pisa), to alert him to this potential catastrophe (see n. e, pp. 146–47). The episode of the heavenly text is also reported in the process for canonization, which adds that when night came John was so tired that he could barely see and asked if he could

Frances's situation is comparable to that of the two Marys—dictating to the plodding Paul. This reading affirms the widespread view that the charismatic mystic who dictates to her more learned, but less enlightened, scribe occupies the position of power. Frances's visionary texts also bespeak her efforts to resist John's domination of the textual process, figuratively reasserting her own centrality to textual production; yet she remains the reader, rather than actual producer, of the mystical script. The celestial but ephemeral text, supported by an angelic hand, disappears the moment that John records her words.

MYSTICAL AGENCY?

Even in the most auspicious cases, the apparent autonomy enjoyed by the female mystic in the recital of her visions is deeply compromised by the involvement of an amanuensis—no matter how discreet or benignly intended the role. Already requiring the ventriloquizing of the voice of a greater (usually male) spirit, revelation is in addition filtered through the pen of an institutionally authorized (and almost invariably male) scribe. In Frances's case, which I take to be representative, exaggerated passivity is the precondition of participation in the textualization of her life. Moreover, by the early fifteenth century this is what the mystical medium seemed to require. In her celebrated letter to Guibert of Gembloux, Hildegard had insisted on her own wakeful lucidity throughout the reception of her own visions, but three hundred years later such a claim

---

continue his transcription the following day. When he returned, Frances completed reading the items that remained on the *charta*. John heard what she read but could not see the page (Lugnano, *I Processi*, process of 1440, pp. 85–87).

was untenable.[74] One might further speculate that Margery Kempe's defeated bid for sanctity or even Julian of Norwich's limited influence were consequences of their unabashed involvement in the recording of their revelations. A successful saint, such as Frances, is less an actor than one acted upon. Stretched like parchment, she is suspended between two sharp instruments of revelation—the one belonging to God and the other to her confessor. The more demonstrably passive she is, the truer her text. It was up to the confessor to test the extent of her passivity, and he did this by demonstrating her unflinching obedience. By establishing his own control he was simultaneously establishing God's control.

Freud found certain parallels between the psychoanalyst and his client and the priest and his possessed subject. But John Mattiotti's "tests" of the insensible Frances evoke an even less dignified interim phase: the stage hypnotist/magician displaying his power over his lovely supine victim. Immobile, and helpless, her anaesthetized form hovers somewhere between the saintly visionary and Freud's tremulous hysteric.

---

[74]See Peter Dronke's translation of Hildegard's letter to Guibert in *Women Writers of the Middle Ages: A Critical Study of Texts from Perpetua (†203) to Marguerite Porete (†1310)* (Cambridge, 1984), p. 168. Also see Kerby-Fulton and Elliott, "Self-Image and the Visionary Role," p. 206.

SALISBURY WOMEN
AND THE PRE-ELIZABETHAN PARISH

Audrey Douglas

ntil the later sixteenth century, when Elizabethan
Salisbury's economy was in serious decline, more
than half the city's work force was engaged in the
woolen industry; leather and metal work, and
victualing, occupied most of the remainder.[1] During this period,
municipal and guild books have little to say about women,
though ecclesiastical court records afford copious detail of
their lives, albeit usually resulting from a disciplinary and even
punitive approach to matters social, familial, and sexual. In the
early seventeenth century, female apprentices first appear in
Salisbury's records, almost contemporaneously with the incorporation in 1612 of its municipal government and the establishment of thirty-five chartered trade companies.[2]

---

[1] John H. Chandler, *Endless Street: A History of Salisbury and Its People*
(Salisbury, 1983), pp. 11–20, and 67–71; Salisbury's population is reckoned
at 6,000–8,000. This essay stems from research on Salisbury intended for
publication in the REED series (Records of Early English Drama [University
of Toronto Press]), carried out with funding from the Social Sciences and
Humanities Research Council, Canada, and the British Academy.

[2] Women are mentioned in, e.g., Wiltshire Record Office (hereafter WRO),
G23/1/1, Salisbury Corporation, Ledger Book A, fol. 158r (1451), an order
concerning prostitutes; and in G23/1/251, Tailors' Guild Book, fol. 147v
(1561), an order concerning attendance of members and wives at the annual

For the pre-Elizabethan period, however, that is, from the fifteenth century to about 1560 (when changes in English church life were substantially and irreversibly established), it is possible to fill out and balance this patchy, even distorted, picture of women's lives, largely from records of two city parishes: Saint Edmund's, dating from 1269, served by a college of priests; and Saint Thomas's, founded early in the thirteenth century and appropriated in 1399 to the fabric of the cathedral.[3] These records, examined in detail below, have a three-fold significance. First, with regard to Saint Thomas's, they allow rudimentary demographic analysis of the communicant body, both women and men. Second, more generally, they affirm the role of women, whether as individuals interacting with their parish church or collectively within the local community, often in a festive or practical context. Third, and equally important

---

supper; see also Edmund R. Nevill, "Salisbury in 1455," *Wiltshire Archaeological and Natural History Magazine* 37 (1911–12): 87–91, for a 15th-century bishop's rental that includes a number of female tenants. Martin Ingram, *Church Courts, Sex and Marriage in England, 1570–1640* (Cambridge, 1987), deals with Salisbury and Wiltshire material. See also below, n. 20.

[3]Oblations books for St. Thomas's, two of four pieces collectively numbered WRO, 1900/98: [2], paper booklet, three restored folios, n.d., partial list of Lent oblations; [3], paper booklet, four restored folios headed "liber quadragesimalis dni' Iohannis Clarke anno dni' mcxxxij" (i.e., Lent 1533, modern chronology). For churchwardens' accounts: WRO, 1900/78 and 1900/68–76, St. Thomas's (1546–1600); WRO, 1901/66–71, St. Edmund's (1443–1570). Reference here is to transcriptions in Henry J. F. Swayne, ed., *Churchwardens' Accounts of S. Edmund and S. Thomas, Sarum, 1448–1702* (Salisbury, 1896) (hereafter Swayne), with corrections from the MSS. Until 1539 St. Thomas's accounts were kept by proctors acting for the cathedral chapter. The oldest parish, St. Martin's, has no accounts for the period under discussion. My thanks to the WRO staff, esp. to Steven Hobbs, County Archivist, for help in reassembling fragmented churchwardens' rolls for St. Edmund's, subsequently renumbered (Apr. 1994); and to Suzanne Eward, Archivist and Librarian, Salisbury cathedral.

in this respect, they point to the process of sixteenth-century church reformation, together with economic change, as ultimately responsible for the removal of customary or ritual opportunities that had hitherto given women visibility as a group and allowed them, individually or collectively, to share certain parish activities in partnership with men.

Thanks to the list of offerings preserved for Saint Thomas's in Lent 1533, we can catch a glimpse of the parish community on the eve of the Reformation. In that year 244 intended communicants, recorded alphabetically by baptismal name, came to confession in preparation for the Easter Communion: a typical entry in the oblations book reads, "Cornelyus Iohnson pro de[cim]is & obla[cionibus] xvj d."[4] Attendance at Easter Communion constituted an obligatory act; D. M. Palliser suggests, however, that in practice it was acceptable for each household to be represented at Easter by one or more—and not necessarily all—of its individual members. This may well explain the relatively small proportion of parishioners listed.[5]

---

[4]WRO, 1900/98 [3]; marginal crosses confirm receipt of payments, which total £8 13s. 8d. The parish priest received oblations at Easter and other feasts, in theory from all over 18 years, of independent means; also at weddings, purifications, and funerals (Peter Heath, *Medieval Clerical Accounts* [York, 1964], p. 22).

[5]"Introduction: The Parish in Perspective," in *Parish, Church and People: Local Studies in Lay Religion, 1350–1750*, ed. S. J. Wright (London, 1988), p. 21; other (unlisted and unshriven) persons may have attended at Easter. The total population of St. Thomas's is generally reckoned to be 2,000 or more—returns to chantry commissioners (1548) claim a total of 1,652 "whiche receyve the blessyd communion" (Dora H. Robertson, "Notes on Some Buildings in the City and Close of Salisbury Connected with the Education and Maintenance of the Cathedral Choristers," *Wilts. Arch. and Nat. Hist. Mag.* 48 [Dec. 1937]: 18); this figure must refer to all parishioners of communicable age—i.e., a parish census rather than a record of active communicants. The 1551–52 churchwardens received £8 16s. 8¼d. for Easter offerings and tithes from "the hoole parysshe" (Swayne, p. 278), which suggests ca. 250

The communicants listed may be broken down by gender and social category (Figure 1). The latter term here refers to the record's limited indications of life-cycle stage and marital status. (Details of occupation, at this period, are irrelevant to the cure of souls.) There is an almost even split between females (51 percent) and males (49 percent). A woman may be described as widow (*vidua*), wife (*vxor*), female servant (*famula*), or girl (*puella* or *filia*). A few women are uncategorized; they are here referred to as single females. Men fall into two categories: those described, singly, as male servant (*famulus*), and a larger number unidentified by life-cycle stage or marital status, most of whom give both tithe and oblations. These adult males must mainly comprise householders, though they possibly include boarders (journeymen employees) or "career" servants with a degree of independence (those living outside the employer's household, for example).[6]

Almost all the parishioners listed make oblations. Married women, of whom only ten offer oblations, are an exception; as dependents they presumably own nothing and therefore, customarily, are expected to offer nothing. Eight of nine parishioners described as paupers are women—four single females, two widows, a wife, and a servant. The ninth, a male adult, and three of the women (a wife and two single females) make

---

communicants. Cf. WRO, 1900/98 [2], a list of 118 parishioners, entered by baptismal name under E to W—about 30 or $^1/_5$ of the entries [= 1 fol.] are lost; comparison with the 1533 list indicates that most (as names under A to D) would have been women, for an overall total of ca. 150 communicants.

[6]WRO, 1900/98 [3]. For signs of servants' economic independence see references to the tenement of "John Gatecombe, servant," and the will of "William Hulman, servant," with probate granted to his employer (T. C. B. Timmins, ed., *The Register of John Chandler, Dean of Salisbury, 1404–17* Wiltshire Record Society, 39 [1984] [hereafter *Chandler Reg.*], nos. 499 and 507 [1407]).

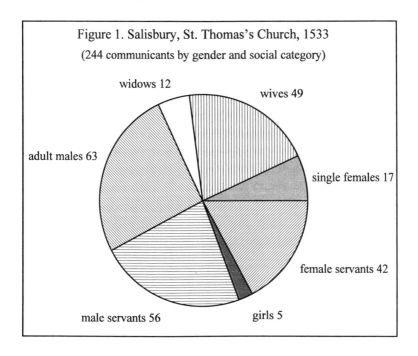

Figure 1. Salisbury, St. Thomas's Church, 1533
(244 communicants by gender and social category)

widows 12

wives 49

adult males 63

single females 17

female servants 42

male servants 56

girls 5

customary offerings. Payment in this situation, normally excused on the basis of poverty rather than dependence, was possibly subsidized by third parties as an act of charity. Similarly, servants' offerings were probably subsidized by employers where cash wages were not included in service contracts.[7]

There appears to be no fixed definition for tithes paid in Lent, which in any case are normally recorded with oblations as a composite sum, probably reflecting a payment dictated by

[7]The majority of legible entries for oblations only (including those with sums deliberately left blank) record sums of twopence: i.e., for male servants, 37 sums for 2d. out of 48 entries (plus one illegible sum); for wives, 10/42 (plus four illegible sums); for single females, 11/14 (plus one illegible sum); for widows, 8/11 (one with an additional 7d. for wax); for female servants, 34/38 (plus one illegible sum); for girls, 4/5. Totals in each category are made up from those paying tithe—see below.

custom or conscience rather than by a regulatory code.[8] Interestingly enough, a small group of women pays tithe: three wives, two single females and one widow, and three servants, each employed in a prominent Salisbury household.[9] Women's tithe payments may reflect profits from casual earnings (for example, from the scouring, mending, or washing noted below), as well as from brewing, retailing, or participation in a craft trade. Tithe-paying servants are perhaps long-term or senior retainers whose contracts include wages over and above their subsistence allowance.[10]

As was suggested earlier, parishioners probably communicated at Easter not only on their own account but as

---

[8]Easter offerings may include "confession pennies" and the "secret tithe," which seem to be what is in question at St. Thomas's in 1533 (Heath, *Medieval Clerical Accounts*, p. 22). A. G. Little, "Personal Tithes," *English Historical Review* 6 (Jan. 1945): 71, discusses two early tithe agreements that refer to collection in Lent—Tadcaster (1290) and Adlingfleet, Yorks. (1306); the vicar of Tadcaster is to have Lent tithes of "working men (*seruiencium*) . . . namely hired men (*mercenariorum*), tradesmen, bakers, carpenters" and other locally based tradesmen, as well as carters and female brewers.

[9]"Alys Powell famula M[r] Kellwey": Robert Kayleway was mayor, 1515–16 (WRO, G23/1/1, Corp. Ledger B, fol. 236r); "Elyzabeth Wykes famula Heyl[. .]": an inventory (1542) of the goods of Thomas Hele, merchant, lists goods valued at £98 2s. 10d.—his premises include house, warehouses, stable, tavern, and shop (Angela Conyers, ed., *Wiltshire Extents for Debts, Edward I to Elizabeth I*, Wilts. Rec. Soc., 28 [1973], no. 73); "Alys Blakborne famula M[r] Davy": either John Davey, who pays 13s. 4d. in the benevolence of 1545 (G. D. Ramsay, ed., *Two Sixteenth-Century Taxation Lists 1545 and 1576*, Wiltshire Records Branch, 10 [1954], p. 39), or William Davey, mayor, 1572–73 (WRO, G23/1/3, Corp. Ledger C, fol. 26v). Seven male servants pay tithe; three are members of named (and probably more prominent) households.

[10]Cf. also testamentary provision for "tithes forgotten" made by Salisbury women for St. Thomas's in 1407: Alice, wife of Richard Gele, "iremonger," 20d.; Maud Marschal, 6s. 8d. (*Chandler Reg.*, nos. 470, 497). Heath, *Medieval Clerical Accounts*, p. 18, notes an instance of 2d. or 3d. tithe paid on servants' wages of 16s., and 1d. or 2d. on 6s. 8d. "cum panno."

representatives of their respective households. Information contained in the 1533 list for Saint Thomas's may thus be used as evidence for the varying role of male heads of household, wives, and dependent servants or offspring in the pattern of communicant attendance. The focus here is on the *communicant household*, with the assumption that one or more household members, having come to confession in Lent, presumably attend at Easter. Here, *household* means a unit of two or more persons. In the discussion that follows it is posited (1) where the list of communicants offers evidence (a) of last name, linking husband and wife, or parent and child; or (b) for a servant, of employer's last name (for instance, "famulus Cuffe") linking him (or her) to a listed adult male. In either case two or more such persons named in the document are presumed to be members of one household, with husband or employer deemed "householder." A household is also posited (2) where (a) a servant is qualified by an employer's last name, as above, or (b) a woman is termed, for example, "Alys Cutler vxor," but no last-name evidence exists for a listed adult male to whom either servant or wife can be linked. Again, a household of at least two is assumed (servant and employer, wife and husband), even though only one member (servant or wife) is named in the document. On this basis two groups are singled out from the 244 listed parishioners. Group 1 consists of 104 persons, representing fifty-four households constructed on the basis of (1a–b) and (2a) above; Group 2 consists of thirty-six wives, each representing one household—see (2b) above.[11]

---

[11]The remainder, for whom there is no significant attribution, comprises 104 persons (44 male adults, 17 single women, 20 male servants, 12 widows, 7 female servants, 4 girls). The average number of those attending per household in Group 1 is 1.9 persons. On this basis, with 244 parishioners listed, ca. 127 communicant households are represented in this document. Parishioners under age 18 may be omitted from this list (see above, n. 4). WRO,

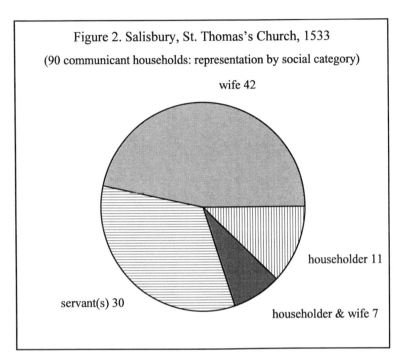

Figure 2. Salisbury, St. Thomas's Church, 1533

(90 communicant households: representation by social category)

wife 42

householder 11

householder & wife 7

servant(s) 30

Data ascertainable for Groups 1 and 2 (Figure 2) show a limited breakdown of household representation by social category, based on ninety households. Whether or not accompanied by dependents, wives represent almost half these households, male householders roughly one-eighth; well under 10 percent of households are represented by householder and wife attending together. For Group 1 (see table below), more complex data for fifty-four households show attendance in some detail, based on gender and social category. Only two households are represented by male head, wife, and servants. Less than half of the households include representation by householders and/or

---

1900/98 [2] (n.d.), with categories of *puer* and apprentice, in fact suggests a *lower* minimal age limit; in the 1533 list, however, the small number of girls and absence of male juvenile categories suggest assuming an age limit close to 18 years.

SALISBURY, SAINT THOMAS'S CHURCH, 1533
Representation of Fifty-Four Communicant Households by Gender and Social Category

Persons Representing Households	Number of Households	% of Total Households
1 male servant	12	22.2
1 female servant	9	16.7
Householder and servant(s)	9	16.7
Wife and servant(s)	6	11.1
Householder and wife	5	9.3
2 or more servants (male and female)	4	7.4
2 or more servants (female)	3	5.6
2 or more servants (male)	2	3.7
Householder, wife and servant(s)	2	3.7
Householder and son[a]	1	1.9
Householder, daughter, and servant	1	1.9
Total households	*54*	*102.2[b]*

[a]Thomas Chaffin the younger (who pays 2d.), entered with Thomas Chaffin the elder (who pays 40s.), is presumed here to be a dependent son rather than an adult male.
[b]Total exceeds 100% due to rounding.

wives, the majority being represented by one or more servants. Most commonly a household is represented either by one servant (male or female, twenty-one households), or by the householder or his wife attending with servant(s) (fifteen households). Among households represented only by servants, those sending both male and female (four) are outnumbered by the sum of those sending, singly or in groups of two or more, only males (fourteen) and only females (twelve). Finally, if matching couples are removed from the list, the remaining figures show that a large proportion of adult males (55/62 or

88.7 percent) and of wives (42/49 or 85.7 percent) attended without spouses. (Since distinctions of status are not recorded for males, there is no way of knowing how many of the men were widowed or single.)

Representation of the fifty-four households includes thirty-six male and thirty-seven female servants, with a median of two servants per household. Consideration of the median payment of tithe and oblation relative to four groups of adult males indicates that it is the most prosperous (or generous) adult males (attending with or without wives) who represent their households together with one or more servants. The figures, even allowing for the limited number of households involved, do not highlight an obvious elite relative to household representation by employer with servant(s). This situation seems to echo that in municipal government, where a recent study finds no obvious or self-perpetuating oligarchy of officeholders defined by rank, family connections, wealth, or economic interest.[12]

Thus, behind the contemporary alphabetical organization of the 1533 list lies an ordering of the parish relative to gender,

---

[12]The median sum (1) for 49 adult males paying tithe and oblation is 12d.; (2) for male heads in 18 of 54 households in Group 1, where each is included in the household representation, 18d.; (3) for male heads in 12 of these 18 households where servant(s) are included in household representation, 22d.; (4) for the remaining six households, where servants are not part of the representation, 16d. David C. Carr analyzes municipal government in "The Problem of Urban Patriciates: Office Holders in Fifteenth-Century Salisbury," *Wilts. Arch. and Nat. Hist. Mag.* 83 (1990): 118–35. In the later 16th century the Chaffin family—the 1533 list refers to the elder and younger Thomas, and servants of Christopher and George—evidently attended church as a household: in 1559–60 "Mr Hooper" gained for himself, wife, children, and servants those pews which his father-in-law, Thomas Chaffin, lately had (Swayne, p. 280); these were in the north chapel, named in 1608 as "Mr Chaffyns chapel," where the then Mr. Chaffin and his wife sat together in the front pew (WRO, 1900/92, Pew Book, paper booklet, 26 pp., p. [18])—a rare circumstance (see below, n. 53).

life-cycle stage, and marital status, apparent not only in the terminology of the document itself but also in the representation of households at the high point of the church year. The pattern of attendance tends to reinforce not so much the household as the consciousness and boundaries of each peer group, with, in general, householders and wives attending without partners and female and male servants acting as gender-distinct representatives of their households.[13]

For the communicant group as a whole there is a sharp contrast between the anonymity of over one-half of all males in the 1533 list (each his own man, so to speak) and the Church's four-fold classification of women, a system that clearly relates to the several female life-cycle stages that found visible and controlled sanction within the parish community. A woman's rites of passage from single life (as girl or servant) to wife, mother, and possibly widow were marked by appropriate ceremonies: wedding, purification (or churching, following childbirth), husband's funeral. Remarriage of course touched off a second round of one or more of these observances.[14]

---

[13]Short-term service contracts, enabling frequent change of employment or intermittent return to families (Peter Laslett, "The Institution of Service," *Local Population Studies*, no. 40 [Spring 1988]: 56), acted to distance servants from employing households. At St. Thomas's six male servants and one female share the last name of other parishioners listed outside the servant group, which indicates that family ties might easily be maintained locally. At the same time, affective bonds could develop between employers and servants, as exemplified in legacies: see below for wills of Dorothy Chaffin and Sybil Payne.

[14]In St. Martin's parish, Salisbury, 1577–99, one-third of all widows remarried; the interval between marriages was slightly shorter for men than for women (S. J. Wright, "'Churmaids, Huswyfes and Hucksters': The Employment of Women in Tudor and Stuart Salisbury," in *Women and Work in Pre-Industrial England*, ed. Lindsey Charles and Lorna Duffin [London, 1985], p. 111); in 1557–58 Simon Yate of St. Thomas's confidently paid 2s. 8d. for "his wyfes pewe beyng Ded & his wyves to come" (Swayne, p. 279).

The twilight zone in which single females existed, for whom no ritual affirmation existed in the parish community, is indicated by the lack of a term descriptive of their status at this period. Reference in the 1533 list to Margaret (who pays 12d. in tithe) as "soror Iohannis bonar" offers a clue to the position that a single woman might hold, dependent on a relative (often male) and possibly resident within his household; Margaret's brother was evidently a prosperous man—a "John Bonner" contributes 23s. 4d. to the royal benevolence of 1545.[15] Her circumstances were privileged—of seventeen single females listed in 1533 four are paupers, a poverty rate that in this instance appears to exceed that among the widows (see below). Entries for two of these women are extended, perhaps to distinguish them from each other, with references to "Isabell pauper iuxta ecclesia" and "Isabell pauper sub domo vest'" (that is, Saint Thomas's vestry, built early in the sixteenth century). Both women lived close to the church, but in the latter's case shelter may have been extended as an act of parochial charity.

The distinction between the unmarried groups of girls and female servants is uncertain. Girls, at 2 percent of the overall total, are the smallest subgroup. While forming perhaps a privileged few, exempt from the life-cycle stage of service, it is also possible that they comprise a slightly younger group, not yet of an age to be placed in service, or that they are employed as dependents in domestic industry. Young children are not, of course, listed in the record, even though they may have accompanied their parents to Mass.[16]

---

[15]The 17 single females include one illegible entry among 38 entries under A, of which 36 are female (WRO, 1900/98 [3]). Ramsay, *Two Taxation Lists*, p. 9; cf. below, a female relative of Dorothy Chaffin's first husband, Thomas Newman, living with Dorothy.

[16]In six English cities, 1599–1756, 5% of males and 4% of females aged 10–14 years were in service (Richard Wall, Jean Robin, and Peter Laslett,

Studies of preindustrial urban populations indicate that the peak employment years in service for both sexes were between the ages of fifteen and twenty-four. While Salisbury testators set the age of maturity in the early twenties, research in general suggests that marriage and childbearing were normally postponed among both sexes to the mid-twenties, the age when the maintenance of such responsibilities became economically feasible for young men.[17]

The important part played by service in early sixteenth-century Salisbury is reflected in Saint Thomas's communicant group, where female and male servants together form about 40 percent of the total (Figure 1 above). A good proportion of male servants were probably apprentices or other youthful workers employed in the domestic economy of the household.[18] Among

---

eds., *Family Forms in Historic Europe* [Cambridge, 1983], p. 94). The age of first Communion is debatable: e.g., Julian Cornwall, "English Population in the Sixteenth Century," *Economic History Review*, 2nd ser., no. 23 (1970): 32 and n. 5, cites ages of 14 or 10 years. Natalie Zemon Davis, "The Study of Popular Religion," in *The Pursuit of Holiness in Late Medieval and Renaissance Religion*, ed. C. E. Trinkaus and H. A. Oberman (Leiden, 1974), p. 320, cites varying ages (7, 12, 14 years) when children were thought capable of confession. In Stanford, Berks., "young youthes" aged 10 to 13 years, who helped buy platters and potingers in 1583, were obviously seen as a responsible sector of the parish (J. Charles Cox, *Churchwardens' Accounts from the Fourteenth Century to the Close of the Seventeenth Century* [London, 1913] [hereafter Cox], p. 288).

[17]Wall, Robin, and Laslett, *Family Forms*, p. 94: of the given population, 35% of males aged 15–19 and 30% of those aged 20–24 were in service; within the same age groups, 27% and 40% of females. For a summary of "suggestive assertions" about service see Laslett, "Institution of Service," pp. 55–60. Salisbury testators order the substance of bequests to be kept from females until age 20 (wills of Percival Stonax and Alice Holmes: WRO, Consistory Court, Register of Wills, vol. 2, fol. 132 [1561]); from a male until age 22 (*Chandler Reg.*, no. 454 [1407]).

[18]Comparison with undated WRO, 1900/98 [2], which includes five male servants, 11 apprentices, and 12 boys, indicates that the latter two groups are

women the term *famula*, at least in the context of Saint Thomas's communicants, has a triple connotation: of service; of unmarried status, since it is distinguished from *vxor* (wife); and hence, predominately, of youth, since the age of marriage was normally in the mid-twenties. It must also be added that marriage did not preclude a woman's being in service—for her it simply took precedence over occupation, so that whether she was employed at home, in an outside trade, or as an out-servant she remained primarily a "wife."[19] There is no evidence at this period to suggest that young women in Salisbury were employed as apprentices in housewifery, or other crafts, or in any way other than as domestic servants. Some probably found employment with relatives: among those listed in 1533, for example, Agnes Gerves, "famula Gerves," was probably servant to John Gerves and his wife, Agnes. "Isabell famula Cookes pauper," lacking her own last name as well as the wherewithal to make oblation, may have been taken into service, perhaps by relatives, as a minimal act of charity.[20]

Female servants comprise one-third of the women listed, and male servants slightly less than one-half of the men (Figure 1). No hard-and-fast conclusions can be drawn as to the ratio of age to maturity (evidence relative to age is discussed

---

hidden in the 1533 category of *famuli*, for a combined total of ca. 40%; an entry for "Robert Denis puer weuer" suggests non-apprenticeship labor.

[19]Michael Roberts, "'Words they are Women, and Deeds they are Men': Images of Work and Gender in Early Modern England," in Charles and Duffin, *Women and Work*, pp. 137–39, examines the role of occupations in conferring on males "a legal and fiscal identity as much as an economic one."

[20]Even in the 17th century, only five out of 138 service agreements in Salisbury (1603–14) concerned girls (Wright, "'Churmaids,'" p. 103); indentures mention housewifery with skills such as flax dressing or knitting (WRO, G23/1/128, Register of Apprenticeships 1612–14: Elizabeth Deacon and Mary Gunter). In his will (1562) John Gough names "Rose, my kinswoman and servant" (WRO, Consistory Court, Reg. Wills, vol. 2, fol. 130v).

in notes 4 and 16–18, above); nevertheless, the relative size of gender groups suggests a slight balance overall towards maturity, more so among females, enough perhaps to maintain and transmit traditional norms of behavior and belief though not to constitute a significant factor in repression of youthful energies. Also, if those listed are presumed to reflect the parish as a whole, then at least in this year the relative numbers of female and male servants afford a comfortable and confident setting for members of either sex, as well as a fair chance of achieving marriage within the group and—for women—passing into the predominant female subgroup of *vxores*.

A modicum of information relative to the life-cycle stage of marriage and childbearing may be gleaned from another source. Before 1538, when parishes were first required to keep registers of baptisms, weddings, and burials, such events were only indirectly recorded, again in oblations books. For Saint Thomas's two such books are extant, for 1523–24 and 1532–33, detailing sums offered at weddings, purifications, and funerals (that is, for "corpses") and on certain feast days.[21]

Receipts show that weddings were the most profitable of all these occasions, with sums usually offered in terms of one or more shillings rather than (as was usual with purifications

---

[21]WRO, 1900/98 [1] and [4], two paper booklets, 8 and 6 restored folios; sums are entered under month and day, Oct.–Sept. Figures for funerals suggest an abnormally high death rate for the latter year: 1523–24, 47 funerals; 1532–33, 97 funerals—mortality peaks in Oct. (32 funerals), Nov. (16), Apr. (8) and June (9). For evidence of plague in 1532 see J. F. D. Shrewsbury, *A History of Bubonic Plague in the British Isles* (London, 1970), pp. 168–69. Figures for weddings and purifications seem abnormally low in the latter year: WRO, 1900/98 [1], 1523–24: 26 weddings, 70 purifications; [4], 1532–33: 19 weddings, 59 purifications. Less informative *annual* totals of oblation receipts are found for St. Thomas's in proctors' receipts 1486–1539 (Salisbury, Dean and Chapter Archive, Press II, Boxes 1–2) and in churchwardens' accounts from 1545 (Swayne, p. 273).

and funerals) in pence. Celebration of marriage in the parish was regulated by the customary church prohibition in the seasons of Advent, Christmas, and Lent (roughly December, and February–March), when no offerings were recorded in either year. The peak months for weddings in 1523–24 were October and January (five each) and June (nine); in 1532–33 weddings were celebrated only in seven months, with a more even distribution.[22]

The record of purifications or churchings, a thanksgiving and cleansing ritual for women after childbirth, is subject to the same statistical drawback as a baptismal record, namely, the difficulty of estimating the customary interval between birth and the ritual act and the possibility of gaps or unrecorded information. In addition, it is impossible to establish from the number of churchings an accurate statistic for live births or infant survival.[23]

Evidence for purifications is presented in Figure 3. The low point in December for both years may owe as much to the liturgical season as to any matching rate of conception. The midwife's importance to the community as a whole is emphasized in Saint Thomas's churchwardens' accounts, where an entry for the grave of "mother mydwyfe" in 1545–46 is followed in 1547–48 by an entry for the grave of "mother

---

[22]Entries for various occasions may be grouped under one sum, making exact assessment impossible; but, e.g., WRO, 1900/98 [1], 1523: in Oct. oblations for weddings roughly average 2s. 5d.; funerals, 6d.; purifications, 4d. WRO, 1900/98 [4], 1532–33: Apr. (4 weddings), Oct., Jan., and Aug. (3), and June, July, and Sept. (2).

[23]At her churching a woman returned the chrysom cloth used at her child's baptism (Eamon Duffy, *The Stripping of the Altars: Traditional Religion in England, c.1400–c.1580* [New Haven, 1992], p. 280); payment for the cloth, recorded separately in St. Thomas's quarterly record of weddings, churchings, and chrysoms 1569–92 (WRO, 1900/96, Chrysom Book) is not detailed in earlier books.

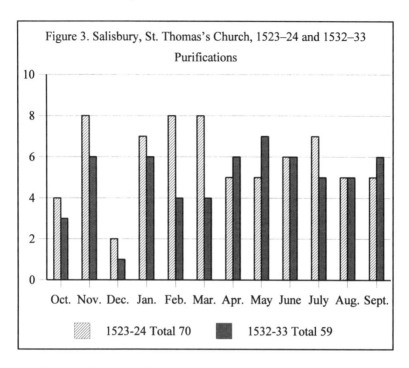

Figure 3. Salisbury, St. Thomas's Church, 1523–24 and 1532–33
Purifications

1523-24 Total 70   1532-33 Total 59

mydwyfe's husbande"—the only occasion in the accounts on which a husband is referred to in the context of his wife's profession. A seventeenth-century reference to the midwife's pew, by the font, suggests that at Saint Thomas's, as in other churches, special seating was assigned to women who came to be churched, usually accompanied by the midwife.[24]

Not surprisingly then, judged by volume of receipts, the best attended of the six annual feast days recorded in the oblation books was the Purification of the Blessed Virgin Mary, celebrated as the chief festival of the Virgin on 2 February. Focusing on an act of particular significance to wives and

---

[24]Swayne, pp. 273, 275; Cox, pp. 154, 193–94; see also Wright, " 'Chur-maids,'" p. 108, for a midwife's husband, admitted freeman of Southampton in 1601 on the strength of his wife's reputation.

mothers, the Candlemas celebration in fact gave full play to the intergenerational context of the gospel story—the infant Jesus, his parents, and the aging Simeon and Anna. Candles blessed at this feast might be placed close to women in labor or lit in times of storm or other danger. The occasion was universally marked by elaborate parish processions, each participant customarily offering a candle with one penny. At Saint Thomas's, in 1524, fifty-eight pounds of wax were purchased for candle-making, and money offerings amounted to 24s.; 22s. 4d. was given in 1533 (the next largest amount over both years is 16d. for 25 December 1532). If one penny is assumed to be the standard offering, then close to three hundred people came to church on 2 February 1524 (slightly more than in 1533), including, we may assume, a large proportion of female parishioners of every age.[25]

A wife's passage to widowhood was marked not only at her husband's death and funeral—for example, in her payments for his forthfare (passing bell) and knell, and for candles and hire of the bier—but also in the proving of his will, when she frequently acted as executor and under its terms emerged as a beneficiary of the estate. Where a business was involved, she might elect to carry it on herself, though many circumstances combined to make remarriage an easier option.[26] At Saint

---

[25]Duffy, *Stripping of the Altars*, pp. 15–22, discusses the significance of Candlemas. A much fuller calendar of *festa ferianda* was laid out in 1257 for the diocese of Salisbury and confirmed in 1330 (C. R. Cheney, "Rules for the Observance of Feast-days in Medieval England," *Bulletin of the Institute of Historical Research*, 34/90 [Nov. 1961]: 126–27, 137–38).

[26]Wright " 'Churmaids,' " pp. 112–16, summarizes obstacles offered to widows trying to carry on their husbands' trade, including desertion by employees; cf. the will of John Steer, Salisbury mercer, leaving a gown to John Carpenter who is to stay with Steer's wife until released from his contract at Christmas (*Chandler Reg.*, no. 466 [1407]). See below for widow Sybil Payne's possession of a shop with "small wares" (haberdashery), suggestive

Thomas's in 1533, the twelve widows named form slightly less than 10 percent of the female total (Figure 1); two are paupers.

At the end of our period two widows, both in the parish of Saint Thomas, made their wills. One was Dorothy Chaffin, whose second husband, a merchant, left her in comfortable circumstances; the other, Sybil Payne, whose shop brought her only a meager living. Dorothy's second marriage, to Christopher Chaffin, brought her into Salisbury's pre-eminent family, but she chose burial beside John Newman, her first husband, the father of offspring named in her will. Most of her money, clothing, and furnishings were left to a recently widowed daughter, Alice Gough (apparently without children). Other gifts went to two sons and their families and to children of Thomas Newman, possibly a deceased son. Also mentioned are five cousins (three female); through her first husband, a sister-in-law, and another of his kinswomen who lived with Dorothy; a female godchild, a former male servant, a female neighbor, and three others (one male). A comfortable widowed life of twelve years is exemplified in the number and quality of possessions to be distributed; careful planning of the will, with provision for possible dispute, reveals an extended network of relatives and friends. Dorothy died assured of widespread remembrance, as well as of her will's responsible execution in the hands of William, her son, and Richard Merivale, a cousin.[27]

---

of continuation in business with the help of the female servant to whom Sybil bequeathes the stock.

[27]WRO, Consistory Court, Reg. Wills, vol. 2, fols. 119r–120v (16 Apr. 1562); Dorothy died soon after making her will—her executors are mentioned in St. Thomas's churchwardens' accounts 1561–62 (Swayne, p. 282); Alice Gough's pew was paid for in 1545–46, Christopher Chaffin's bequests acknowledged 1551–52 (Swayne, pp. 273, 178). Probate for the will of John Gough was granted to Alice, his wife, 24 Feb. 1562 (Consistory Court, as above, fols. 130v–131r). See also above, at n. 12, "Mr Chaffyns chapel."

Not so Sybil Payne, at the opposite end of the social and economic scale, to judge by the history of her will, disputed by rival executors in the court of the subdean of Salisbury.[28] The dispute was rooted in Sybil's decision (July 1555) to change her executors, replacing John Harward and his colleague with two others (folio 45v). According to Sir Bertram Bylling, parish priest, the change was connected with the fact that there were insufficient goods to support the bequests (folio 38v), an opinion perhaps bluntly voiced to Sybil by the original executors. In any case, Sybil ordered the wife of Henry Lee, her cousin and one of the new executors, to make an inventory, "that ye shall not be deceauid" (folio 46r). The will presented for probate, after Sybil's death early on 9 September, named as executors John Harward and John Mylbryge rather than Lee and his colleague; Sir Bertram was appointed as one of the overseers (folios 38v–39r). Two explanations emerge from the record. Briefly, the first alleges that Sir Bertram visited the sick woman two days before she died, urging her to change her will (presumably to restore the original executors); Sybil answered that "hir will should stand." She then asked

> that she might receaue the Sacrament of the aulter, to which the said
> Sir Bertram answeryd that it is not past fortnight that she did receaue
> it and therfore ye mete not to haue it agayne, but ye may haue the
> holly oyle yf ye will. (folio 45r)

---

[28]WRO D4/3/1, Subdean's Act Book 1, fols. 38r–49v, passim, for answers to the court's interrogatories; the decision is not recorded. "Sibilla Paine vxor" occurs in St. Thomas's undated list of communicants, as does "Iohanna Payne virgo" (WRO 1900/98 [2]), possibly Sybil's daughter but deceased at the time the will was made. John Harward, a party to the dispute, paid 16s. 8d. in the benevolence of 1545 and was churchwarden at St. Thomas's 1550–52 (Ramsay, *Two Taxation Lists*, p. 9; Swayne, p. 278).

At twelve o'clock on the night of the following day, the story continues (folio 45v), Harward, Mylbryge, and Sir Bertram altered the will, reinserting their own names as executors and overseer. The second explanation, outlined by Sir Bertram and supported by Sybil's maid and another witness (a widow, perhaps a neighbor), is that on the day between the priest's visit and the morning of her death Sybil herself, throwing the most recent testament into the fire, restored Harward and Mylbryge as executors; they rewrote the will and called witnesses (folios 38v, 48r). The drama enacted here as a confrontation between the strong-willed Sybil (all agreed that she was of sound mind) and a determined group of men reveals the plight of a sick and aging woman who lacked the support and advice of trusted offspring or close male kin. Sybil's will shows that her nearest living relatives were a sister, nieces, and a nephew, while a close relationship with her maidservant is revealed in several bequests of personal possessions and "all the small wares within the shopp" (folio 39r). Much of the dispute probably stemmed from Sybil's insistence on the distribution of clothing to the poor (below, note 31), and the lack of substance to support it. It remains in question whether the priest's alleged refusal to administer the last sacrament was instrumental in any fiery consumption of the old will, though nothing suggests that Harward, Mylbryge, or Sir Bertram had any motive other than the need (as they saw it) to establish a sound testament.

While oblation records, examined above, facilitate a limited exploration of parish demography, especially in relation to household representation and gender grouping, churchwardens' accounts afford a quite different perspective. Churchwardens were responsible for maintenance of church fabric and provision of public worship, with income secured from gifts, offerings, fees, profits from property or "stock" (such as sheep or cattle), and money from special fund-raising events. Their payments and receipts present an intimate, less categoric picture of day-to-day life within the parish.

At Saint Thomas's and Saint Edmund's, for instance, payments collected by churchwardens for pews initially reinforce the concept of gender grouping: they indicate that most seats, though paid for by husbands or other male relatives, were occupied by women.[29] Yet details preserved in the earliest account for Saint Thomas's (1545–46) soften this apparent rigidity. Seating within pews, though visibly marking out wives and widows as a group, also served to mix and match female parishioners, providing in a random fashion or by choice an arena for social intercourse. Those who found seats that year included wives of a currier, butcher, dyer, shearman, and shoemaker, the proprietor's wife at the Angel Inn, and the sexton's wife. The shearman's wife lived at Fisherton Bridge; a widow, in Castle Street; a third woman, from Maddington, northwest of Salisbury, now lived in New Street. Other women are related, or named as if friends: a daughter and mother, a wife's sister, Elizabeth Nicholas and Edith Holte (perhaps servants), and Richard Godfrey's wife and Mylls's wife.[30]

---

[29]Occasional sums are paid for a husband and wife, or a man only. Servants were occasionally seated in the pre-Elizabethan Salisbury parish—the small number of women not designated as wives or other relatives may have been in this category: see also Swayne, p. 39 (1491–92), sums for "the seruant of John Daniell for a Sette . . . to her assigned" and "Cristiane Norys for a like sete." At St. Edmund's a woman's seat is first assigned in 1456–57 (Swayne, p. 359), with steady receipts for pews over the next 150 years; see Cox, pp. 67–69, for the history of St. Edmund's pews to the mid-17th century. St. Lawrence's, Reading, had special seating—near the mayor's wife and pulpit— for women whose husbands had either been mayors (1515–16) or brethren of the Jesus Mass (1545); by 1573 women's pews were graded at 4d. and 6d. At St. Oswald's, Durham, seating kept male and female youth apart and—except for a gentlewoman with servant—younger from older women (Cox, p. 191).

[30]Swayne, p. 273.

Churchwardens' accounts continually stress individual ties between women and the parish church, as exemplified in the record of numerous acts of charitable giving. These may consist of a few pence offered for wax or seasonal oblations, money or gifts in kind contributed to annual collections for church maintenance and special projects, or material bequests made to the church and those in need.[31] The wide range of possible giving—both as to destination and to amount— allowed all but the poorest women to perform personal and independent acts of piety, which at the same time bound them into the wider community of parish and city.

Such ties are further revealed in the pattern of female bequests, based on ten wills from the Salisbury area, all proved in 1407: six from Saint Thomas's parish, two from Saint Edmund's, one from Saint Martin's, and one from Saint Peter's, Old Sarum (the site of the original city of Salisbury). Except that most of these female testators, lacking real property, have only goods and chattels to dispose of—and hence fewer resources to support charitable gifts—their wills follow much the same pattern as those made by men. Thus all ten women leave small sums to their respective parish churches, two also providing sums for lights, respectively within the churches of Saint Thomas and Saint Martin. Alice

---

[31]See above, e.g., n. 7, for oblations; women often—and men occasionally— bequeathed brass or pewter goods to their church to be sold for profit. See also Charles Cotton, ed., *Churchwardens' Accounts of the Parish of St. Andrew, Canterbury. 1485–1625*, 1 vol. in 5 pts. (London, 1916) (hereafter *Canterbury*), pt. 3, p. 7 (1524–25), Dorothy Laurance's bequest of three sheets, two pillows, pillow cases "etc," given "unto thuse powr women beryng children dwelling [within] the precyncte of the parysshe"—presumably to be lent out at the time of their delivery. Sybil Payne (St. Thomas's, Salisbury) leaves "the poor people one doz sheets and one doz smocks . . . if theare lack canvas to make the said shirtes and smockes then I will that theare shalbe bought so much canvas to make them with all" (see ref. above, n. 28).

Porter of Old Sarum, the only single woman, assigns her house to the upkeep of her anniversary and numbers a chaplain among her executors. The other nine women include spouses as executors—one also names her mother. Eight are buried in their respective parishes; in Saint Edmund's one is to lie next to the font and another next to her father, being described as his "heiress" and—with no children of her own, it seems—leaving one tenement and her claim to three others to her husband and his heirs. Two women are buried in the cathedral, one next to her first husband. Eight leave bequests to the fabric of the cathedral (as encouraged by diocesan statute), and one her wedding ring to its statue of the Blessed Virgin Mary. Clothing and in one case a ring are left to daughters, a sister, a mother, and a number of other women. Bequests of jewelry, especially of rings, are the distinguishing mark of women's wills: five other rings (including two wedding rings) are included in gifts to parish and cathedral churches, while one testator orders her husband to dispose of all her jewelry and clothing in aid of the poor.[32]

Payments made by churchwardens to various individual women also reveal a profitable link between parish church and domestic economy. Liturgical needs afforded female parishioners opportunities to supplement household income: making, mending, and washing of surplices, vestments, cloths, and napery, together with cleaning of candlesticks, vessels, and ornaments, drew on a range of skills established as part of a woman's housewifery. Sewing and washing provided work at

---

[32]"De testamentis ordinandis" (ca. 1223), in *Charters and Documents Illustrating the History of the Cathedral, City, and Diocese of Salisbury, in the Twelfth and Thirteenth Centuries*, ed. W. H. R. Jones and W. D. Macray (London, 1891), p. 158. *Chandler Reg.*, nos. 468, 470, 472, 476, 478, 488, 493, 497, 499, 505. Cf. Cox, p. 148 (1488), for women's gifts (clothing and jewelry), used to adorn the statue of Our Lady of the Bridge, Derby.

home, sometimes steady, while cleaning of ornaments was more likely to be seasonal, centering on particular festivals. For instance, at Saint Edmund's, Alice Frye (or Fryer) made a vestment and for a year washed cloths for the high altar as well as ratchets (surplices) for the boys serving in the choir. Fourteen pence was due to "Edingdons wif for wesshing of lynyne ornamentes . . . and for sewynge ayene of the same to the Awbes." Elsewhere, frequent use was made of women's labor in the sixteenth century: at Saint Andrew's, Canterbury, Annes Reade was paid 4s. for mending eight surplices, making six small towels for altars and four cloths for side altars, and Hartt's wife, 3s. for a year's washing of church goods. "Bysschops wife" scoured a lamp for Christmas; "against Easter," two women cleaned the four great candlesticks, two for the high altar, and bowls in the rood loft, receiving, as male workers often did, meat and drink as well as wages. A husband's status was helpful in finding work: the sexton of Boxford, in Suffolk, scoured the church and his wife sewed albs, and over several years the clerk's wife washed surplices.[33]

Another source of women's income was the lodging or feeding of craftsmen and laborers employed in building or maintenance work on the parish church, whose daily expenses

---

[33]Swayne, p. 35 (WRO 1901/68/1 [?1493–94]), p. 42 (1500–01), p. 40 (1491–92); see also p. 27 (1481–82), p. 30 (1482–83), p. 69 (1527–28), mending vestments; p. 11 (1468–69), p. 42 (1494–95), washing or cleaning vestments. *Canterbury*, pt. 2, p. 60 (1522–23); pt. 3, pp. 21–22 (1527–28), p. 37 (1546–47); see also pt. 1, p. 18 (1493), p. 32 (1504–05), p. 40 (1504–07); pt. 2, p. 54 (1521–22)—mending or making of surplices; pt. 3, p. 31 (1545–46), mending albs when washed; pt. 3, p. 5 (1524–25), washing surplices and altarcloths; pt. 4, p. 14 (1561–62), cleaning the church. Peter Northeast, ed., *Boxford Churchwardens' Accounts, 1530–1561*, Suffolk Records Society, 23 (1982) (hereafter *Boxford*), p. 21 (1536); pp. 24, 26, 40, 45, 47–48 (1537–46); see also p. 39 (1542), making surplices; p. 45 (1545), making towels.

were met by the churchwardens. In Boxford parish, Piper's wife (later his widow) sold drink for steeplejacks and boarded carpenters working on the bells, perhaps helped here by her relationship to a Piper who himself worked on the bells. The wife of Robert Bonys, in Canterbury, also boarded bell carpenters, before and after the death of her husband. Such women may have run small alehouses or inns: "the wyfe of the Sarsens hedd" provided for George Poyning when he worked at Saint Thomas's, Salisbury, in 1549 and 1550, charging the churchwardens 35s. for twenty-one weeks in the latter year.[34]

The parish church served the economic needs of women in other less obvious ways. At Boxford two small payments are made for loads of ashes, each to an older or widowed woman, such waste thereby turned into a frugal source of income. A woman in Marston was employed to keep stray beasts off church property. In the middle decades of the sixteenth century Canterbury churchwardens leased gardens to four women for whom such small plots of land probably yielded vegetables or herbs for consumption or sale.[35]

Some of the most interesting entries occur for Saint Edmund's, Salisbury, where payments are made to women for various kinds of craft work. Margery Ingram, goldsmith, is paid for mending a lamp, a thurible, cruse, and paten, and for burnishing candelabra (all of silver), adding metal as necessary; later John Cammell's wife is paid for the repair of

---

[34]*Boxford*, p. 59 (1551), p. 66 (1556); see also p. 8 (1532), Benet's wife, for meat and drink to the carter; *Canterbury*, pt. 1, pp. 36, 40 (1504–07); Swayne (St. Thomas's), pp. 276–77.

[35]*Boxford*, pp. 50–51 (1547), Widow Sugge and Mother Raynowld; F. W. Weaver and G. N. Clark, *Churchwardens' Accounts of Marston, Spelsbury, Pyrton*, Oxford Record Society, 6 (1925), p. 22 (1559); *Canterbury*, pt. 3, p. 27 (1545–46), Winter's widow; p. 44 (1551–52), Mistress King; pt. 4, p. 12 (1560–62), Mr. King's daughter; pp. 29–31 (1573–74), widow Tondiex.

various ornaments. Ingler's wife is mentioned between 1481 and 1484, in connection with chandlery business (provision of wax and making of candles, tapers, and torches). In the sixteenth century Staunton's wife is paid for the making of "lights" for the church, Roger Smith's wife for the font taper and the Paschal candle, and Dorothy Wulfe for four baldrics (leather belts used in bell-hanging).[36]

Other records reveal female involvement in Salisbury's craft trades. A vicar at the cathedral bequeathes silver spoons and an ornamented silk belt to "Edith Wykham, weaver," in 1407; "Margery Sylkewoman" pays for a pew at Saint Thomas's in 1545–46. Additional evidence of leather-working comes from a rental of 1455 listing the bishop's tenants in Salisbury, among them "Johanna Parson tanner," paying 7d. for a tenement in Winchester Street; and from an obligation or bond of 1531 given by William Thornborough, described (verso) as a cordwainer, concerning the purchase of goods after due appraisal. Thornborough is to buy goods "as well lether vn<?made> as Botys or shoes redy made with all other necessaries made of lether . . . pertaining or belonging to the occupation or mystery of Cordweyners crafte . . . within the mansion house or shoppe late of one Martha Pope situate in Carternestrete" (Catherine Street, in Saint Thomas's parish).[37]

---

[36]Swayne, p. 13 (1469–70), p. 31 (1483–84), p. 27 (1481–82), p. 30 (1482–83), p. 32 (1483–84), p. 66 (1521–22), p. 62 (= WRO, 1901/69/6 [ca. 1530]), p. 69 (1527–28). See also p. 39 (1491–92), payment to Awuncelle Pouchemaker for six baldrics; Swayne's transcription of a further entry for Auncelle Purser (probably the same person), concerning a lantern "to her sold," depends on a difficult MS reading of "her" (WRO 1901/67/7). In the early 16th century a woman goldsmith in Bristol took apprentices (Ilana Krausman Ben-Amos, *Adolescence and Youth in Early Modern England* [New Haven, 1994], p. 145).

[37]*Chandler Reg.*, no. 404; Swayne, p. 273; Nevill, "Salisbury," p. 87; WRO, G23/1/63, parchment sheet, 170 x 265 mm, sealed, labeled "3/Box 6," contained in one of several bundles.

Those women designated as wives may have simply collected debts, having some responsibility for the financial side of a business. This seems to have been the case at Saint Edmund's with goodwife Wyndover's collection of money owing for timber and Mistress Coryett's for Easter wine. Designation by occupation, however, and/or omission of marital status—especially in church sources where spousal links are customarily noted—points to a woman's regular and independent means of livelihood, as opposed to occasional work undertaken to supplement household income or employment within a male relative's business. Studies indicate that while a woman could obtain craft skills through her husband, she might also receive an early training in her father's household, which enabled her to set up an independent business as a femme sole, notwithstanding subsequent marriage.[38]

Given the limits of our source material, the fact that three women—Dorothy Wulfe, Joanna Parson, and Martha Pope—are singled out in connection with leather working, three others

---

[38]Swayne, p. 93 (1551), a building account; p. 280 (1559–60)—"Jane Coryatt vxor" with two female servants (one named as "famula I[ohn] Coryat") appears in St. Thomas's 1533 list (WRO, 1900/98 [3]), while John "Coryet" pays 20s. in the 1545 benevolence (Ramsay, *Two Taxation Lists*, p. 39). Cf. *Canterbury*, pt. 1, p. 14 (1485), payment to Golesmith's widow for lamp oil. Ben-Amos, *Adolescence and Youth*, pp. 147, 149, suggests that minimal shop size and number of apprentices meant reliance on female household members or kin, who thus learned skills without formal apprenticeship or marriage; similarly, Wright " 'Churmaids,' " p. 106, finds that women commonly participated in weaving, tailoring, and shoemaking, trades where low numbers of household servants are recorded. See also Derek Keene, "Tanners' Widows," in *Medieval London Widows, 1300–1500*, ed. Caroline M. Barron and Anne F. Sutton (London, 1994), pp. 3–5: independent single women were prominent in London's silk and linen trades, with silkwomen, especially, able to carry on a business after marriage; in comparison, women leather workers were less likely to be independent and their skills more likely to be learned in their fathers' unpaid employment, in which (if tanners) they might continue into adulthood.

with chandlery, and two with smith work (the repair of church ornaments) is strong indication of active female participation in Salisbury's craft trades. Saint Edmund's employment of women raises other questions. Did the church's special liturgical needs attract trades in which women also readily found employment elsewhere? Or did the parish church provide an environment more tolerant of women who wished to practice a trade? The parish community encompassed a host of kindred, friendship, and neighborhood ties; at the same time, an informal network of "getting things done," and at the best price, into which churchwardens tapped as best they could, may well have facilitated craft opportunities for women.

Thus far we have explored churchwardens' accounts for the kinds of links—spiritual, social, and economic—that bound individual women to the local community of church and parish. Discussion of women's collective role within this arena, however, cannot be divorced from broader consideration of the purpose and functioning of the kind of peer groups, both male and female, examined earlier for Saint Thomas's. Such peer groups were not unique to Salisbury. Material from other parishes, chiefly in the south and west of England, reveals similar groups variously distinguished by age, marital status, and occupation (for instance, at Croscombe, below, note 46). A study of young males in Italy and France shows that in the fourteenth and fifteenth centuries traditional secular groupings, as well as religious confraternities, functioned as a means of social control at the threshold adolescent stage, when neither family nor marriage imposed an inherent discipline. A marked characteristic of such groups was mocking or festive play, which addressed "one of the central and perennial issues of adolescence in the West: the conflict between the upsurge of passions, sexual and other, and the increasing demands of conscience."[39]

---

[39]Davis, "Study of Popular Religion," p. 323.

What we know of preindustrial England suggests that similar socioeconomic factors (youthful service, late marriage, adolescent tensions) were present. Nevertheless, the structured emphasis given to adolescent confraternities in Europe has not yet been systematically demonstrated for England: for example, while evidence for seasonal and holiday activity seems to emphasize the role of youth, these were not in fact occasions reserved exclusively to the young; similarly, "play" in the mocking sense (with participants deriding those who flouted community mores, or themselves actively inverting the social order) cannot for the moment be attributed primarily to organized youthful male activity.[40] Rather, it seems to have been within the parish and its church—characteristically and perpetually familiar, whatever the location—that peer ties were best established, especially among an urban and mobile servant population, of local and immigrant origin, prone to short periods of unemployment. Moreover, as we shall see, peer group organization based on the local church afforded a practical means of dealing with the critical tension between passion and conscience.

Certainly the adolescent male—balanced between childhood and responsible maturity—ubiquitously hovers on the edge of society, presenting a potential threat and a challenge. But surely this is also true of young females, especially those placed in service outside the family and still awaiting marriage. In fact, we may extend this notion of marginality to

---

[40]Ben-Amos, *Adolescence and Youth*, chap. 8, "Spirituality, Leisure, Sexuality: Was There a Youth Culture?" pp. 183–207. But see Alun Howkins, *Reshaping Rural England: A Social History, 1850–1925* (London, 1991), p. 22: the life-cycle stage of boys working on Yorkshire farms was "based on a masculine community defined by living in with other lads and represented through the rough culture of the ploughplays and the notorious carnival of the annual hirings."

women in general, whether maidservant, wife, or widow. Within the Judeo-Christian heritage a woman was *sui generis* the subject of male distrust and unease, so that for her, as for children, certain limits and controls were deemed necessary.[41]

Broadly speaking then, parish peer groups operated partly as a means of social control, emphasizing gender boundaries and limiting a measure of approved activity to a single sex. Linked to this function, however—and just as important—they afforded a means of enlisting energies in the practical service of conscience. For such groups, both male and female, chiefly emerge from churchwardens' accounts as fund-raisers; women, for instance, contribute to general revenues or to the fabric, decoration, or furnishing of the parish church—even, as at Saint Edmund's, Salisbury, coming forward with a loan for the churchwardens from their own funds.[42] In some cases gender groups organize by street or locality, or themselves undertake special projects in order to raise money. In the eastern counties

---

[41]Eleanor Commo McLaughlin, "Equality of Souls, Inequality of Sexes: Women in Medieval Theology," in *Religion and Sexism: Images of Woman in the Jewish and Christian Traditions*, ed. Rosemary Radford Ruether (New York, 1974), pp. 213–66: "The physical, intellectual, and moral weakness of the woman required male dominance for her own spiritual and moral direction as well as that of her children" (p. 224).

[42]Cox, p. 34, wives contribute to costs of quickliming the church (Peterborough, 1476); p. 167, maidens and bachelors each deliver nine tapers for the Easter sepulcher (Heybridge, Essex, 1508); W. E. Daniel, ed., *St. John the Baptist, Glastonbury: Churchwardens' Accounts 1366–1587* (n.p., n.d; "printed in Somerset and Dorset Notes and Queries, 1895"), pp. 44–45 (1500), wives (*mulieres*) and girls contribute one-third the cost of re-gilding St. George's image; *Canterbury*, pt. 1, p. 26, pt. 2, pp. 10 and 15, women give money towards building of pews (1504–06, 1511–12) and purchase of a font cover (1514–15). For St. Edmund's: Swayne, p. 29 (1482–83), "de xiiij s ij d mutuatis et perquisitis vxorum parochie vz de antiquo Thesauro vj li & de nouo thesauro iiij li xiiij s ij d"; see also p. 267 (stewards' accounts of the Jesus Mass guild, 1539–40), wives' gift of £6 12s.

the performance of parish plays was organized on a wide terri-
torial scale over several townships; for a play in aid of a new
image of Saint George at Bassingbourn a group of thirteen
wives and one widow prepared refreshments, all but one brewing malt (partly as "gefftes") and seven also "baking wheetes."[43]

Mainly, however, the focus of each peer group's energy is
the maintenance of church "lights," the candles or tapers that
were placed before the images of saints within the parish
church. Here their activity approaches that of the regular parish
guilds or confraternities, and it is sometimes difficult to
discern a distinct boundary between such a peer group and an
organized guild. Money for the purchase of lights is variously
raised—for example, by active "gatherings" (collections), the
provision of a box before the saint's image, or like churchwardens (above, page 99) maintaining profitable administration
of stock. Excess annual profits, after payments for the light,
are usually handed over to the churchwardens for the use of
the whole church.[44] Again, which of these or other fiscal practices is in use is not always spelt out in the record. Clearly,
though, it was through this particular function that each peer
group, together with other more formal guilds, was drawn into
the community of the parish, its existence validated by direct
involvement in the approved and customary practice of the

---

[43]Cox, pp. 82–83 (1469–72, Bodmin), a women's collection for rebuilding
the church includes contributions from "maidenys yn Forstret" and "maidenys
of the borestret"; p. 38 (1510 and 1516, Wimborne Minster), "wyve of the
cuntrey" and "wyfe of the towne" (i.e., "wives") make and sell cakes for the
church's benefit; pp. 271, 273 (1510–12), accounts for Bassingbourn play.

[44]Duffy, *Stripping of Altars*, pp. 147–49; Cox, pp. 36–37. The system was
open to abuse: Margery Cotterell and Juliana Farman of Hungerford, Wilts.,
were probably stewards of St. Katherine's light when they took from it a
chalice, a missal, vestments, three altar cloths, a superaltar, 16 sheep and 10
marks; when cited in 1409, neither had (understandably) attended church for
five years (*Chandler Reg.*, p. 91, n. 1, and p. 247).

maintenance of lights—which, incidentally, constituted a major budget item in every church—and its energies thereby controlled and shaped towards a "conscientious" end.

Churchwardens' receipts and expenditures point to the role of women in this and other areas of church activity. At Saint Edmund's, John Cristian's wife delivers money for Saint Katherine's light in 1491–92. Sporadic reference is made to various women's lights up to 1557, at first in receipts for excess profits. In 1497–98, two stewards of the girls' light are named and two women for the light of the Blessed Virgin Mary; lights of daughters, wives, and servants are mentioned in 1517–18 and the servants' light in 1523–24. In later years sums are paid out for bearing into the church, and making and tending, of the wives' light, ca. 1530 and 1556–57. No mention of the festival's date is made in the accounts though it is almost certainly a feast of the Virgin. At Saint Thomas's, nine proctors' accounts, from the late fifteenth and early sixteenth centuries, note receipts for oblations from the wives' light on the feast of the Nativity of the Virgin (8 September); after 1520, however, these are dated 15 August ("pausatio," or final rest, of the Virgin). In this parish also, in 1546–47, church-wardens' accounts record payments for wives', daughters', and servants' lights, and for bearing, making, and lighting of wives' and maidens' lights (and cleaning of candlesticks) in 1547–48.

The relationship of the several peer groups in the ritual entry of the light is open to conjecture. The context and phrasing of account items seem to suggest that all three groups entered on the same occasion, each with its own light; in this case, if male confraternity example were followed, the servants and girls (as the least ranked) would have preceded the wives whose light, according to the accounts, was accompanied by minstrels or waits. Alternatively, female servants and girls may have brought in their lights close to 27 April, the feast of Saint Sytha (Zita of Lucca), patron saint of domestic servants, whose

cult was evidently established in the parish.[45] No peer groups
of young males seem to have been organized in Salisbury for
the maintenance of specific church lights, probably because of
the dominant position of craft guilds, which themselves supported lights in the parish churches.[46]

The patently practical purpose served by such parish
groups, however, must not be emphasized at the expense of an
accompanying less palpable role, provision of peer solidarity,
which for women was of particular significance. The wives of

---

[45]WRO 1901/67/7 (1491–92), under "Increments of Lights" (not in Swayne);
Swayne, pp. 47–48, 58, 66, 80 (= WRO 1901/69/7, ca. 1530), and p. 101; the
introduction, p. xv, gives Candlemas as the date for the women's light at St.
Edmund's (not supported in the accounts); Salisbury, Dean and Chapter Archive, Press II, Boxes 1–2, 27 proctors' accounts for St. Thomas's, noting
oblations *de lumine mulier'* or similar: for 8 Sept., 5 (1499–1500), 14 (n.d.,
?1512–13), 15 (1513–14), 20 (n.d., ?1514–20), 23 (n.d., ?1496–97 or
?1501–04), 24 (n.d.), 27 (n.d.), and accounts for 1488–90 and 1490–91
(formerly WRO, 1900/65 and 1900/67—now deposited in the Dean and
Chapter Archive); for 15 Aug., 21 (1537–38), and WRO, 1900/98 [1], oblations book, 1523–24, fol. 2v; Swayne, pp. 274–75 (1546–47 and 1547–48).
Salisbury tailors' midsummer entry into St. Thomas's church comprised journeymen and their stewards, then the light with masters' stewards, followed by
minstrels and masters with mayor and corporation members (Audrey Douglas,
"Midsummer in Salisbury: The Tailors' Guild and Confraternity 1444–1642,"
Renaissance and Reformation, n.s., 13/1 [1989]: 37; WRO, 1900/98 [1],
(1523–24), fol. 4r, for a short account headed "the box of seynt sythe and
seynt looye," with occasional sums noted).

[46]But see WRO, 1900/98 [1], above, n. 45: the feast of St. Loy, patron saint
of smiths, was celebrated on 25 June; journeymen (i.e., younger) smiths
brought their light into St. Thomas's at the end of June in 1524 and 1533
(WRO, 1900/98 [1], and [4]); journeymen tailors took their light to St. John
the Baptist's chapel on Ayleswade bridge (Douglas, "Midsummer in
Salisbury," p. 37). Cf. Croscombe, Somerset, where peer and craft groups co-
existed: from 1547, "younglyngs" (young men), maidens, archers (profiting
from Robin Hood plays), hogglers (laborers), webbers, and tuckers each
maintained a stock and also held special collections (Cox, pp. 336–37, 282).

Saint Edmund's not only maintained a particular light, bringing it into the church accompanied by city waits, but engaged in some form of associated dance (1538–39 and 1541–42). In the accounts the wives' dance occurs as an item of receipt and was presumably performed as a means of gathering money towards their light, possibly in association with their entry into the church. Saint Edmund's wives also had their own cross. At Saint Thomas's, apart from the bringing in of the women's lights, there was a Whitsun dance in which wives, daughters, and servants, together with young boys (*pueri* or *scolares*), took part, rewarded by a matching scale of cash payments and a lavish outpouring of wine and confectionery charged to the cathedral fabric masters. All these occasions, linked as they were with the liturgical round of the parish, not only reinforced the female hierarchy, basically that of the household, but also affirmed women collectively and visibly within the parish community at a time of festive rejoicing.[47]

It is important to stress that not all women's activity was restricted by gender boundaries. From the fifteenth century an increasingly regular source of income was found in collections made at Hocktide, when women and men exploited a traditional form of play for customary money forfeits, which were then given to the use of the parish church. Sometimes devoted to particular needs of the church fabric, the money was normally accounted for as a general item of revenue. Occasionally, as at Saint Edmund's, a meal was also held, apparently funded by part of the proceeds, or forming—as at Saint

---

[47]St. Edmund's: Swayne, pp. 83, 87; WRO, 1901/65, Ancient Account and Memoranda Book, p. 39 (1477–78). St. Thomas's: Audrey Douglas, "'Owre Thanssynge Day': Parish Dance and Procession in Salisbury," *Folk Music Journal* 6/5 (1994): 606–07.

Andrew's, Canterbury, where it was held in the Cornmarket—
an extension of the fund-raising process.[48]

Each of Salisbury's three parishes, like other parishes in the
south of England, also had a dancing day, when money was
collected as parishioners danced through city streets. In its
earlier stages, and certainly from the middle of the sixteenth
century, this was evidently an occasion for young adults of
both sexes to meet and mingle—again with the avowed
purpose of parish fund-raising—though evidence from Saint
Thomas's suggests that participation was eventually limited to
children by the 1580s, with first the exclusion of all males and
then of adult women. The demonstrable role of women in
these forms of parish fund-raising should not be underesti-
mated. An uninterrupted run of six churchwardens' accounts
for Saint Andrew's Canterbury between 1514 and 1520, for
example, shows that 10 percent of annual revenues, or one-
third of all casual revenues (as opposed to profits from rents
and farms), came from Hocktide activity.[49]

Even more significant, the organization of Hocktide revelry
and of special activities broke through the controls inherent in
the ordering of parish peer groups. Such customary means of
fund-raising, validated by tradition and the purpose for which

---

[48]In general men and women gathered money on Hock Monday and Tuesday
(second week after Easter Sunday), each group on its own day; in Salisbury
parishes the Hock gathering disappears after 1582. Swayne (for St.
Edmund's), pp. 87–88 (1543–44), 23s. received, 5s. spent on women and men
who gathered; p. 102 (1556–57), Hock receipts not itemized, but 7s. spent on
gatherers; *Canterbury*, pt. 3, p. 24 (1538–39), 17s. gathered, on two days and
at supper; p. 39 (1547–48), 8s. 8d. similarly gathered; see also Cox, p. 261
(St. Mary-at-Hill, 1497), wardens provide beef, ale, and bread for the wives;
p. 262 (St. Mary's, Reading, 1556), 3s. 4d. spent on women's supper.

[49]Douglas, " 'Owre Thanssynge Day,' " pp. 604–05, 608–09; *Canterbury*,
pt. 1, pp. 14, 20, 24, 29, 36, 41.

they were undertaken, enabled women to partake in "extraordinary" activities where both sexes, according to circumstance, freely associated, or bore equivalent or associated responsibilities. Hocktide receipts show married couples sharing responsibility for collection of money or churchwardens' wives accounting for the women's contribution. In the 1460s male and female parishioners at Saint Edmund's together organized and presided over church ales—in this case the so-called "king" and "queen" were married, but not to each other. At a play performed in Boxford, in aid of the church steeple, a widow, Joan Laughlyn, accounted for a portion of profits, as did Katherine Lyon (probably kin to a contemporary churchwarden) in connection with the Bassingbourn play (above, note 43).[50]

Activity of this kind, it seems, often devolved on women in virtue of their husbands' office; nevertheless, the experience afforded opportunities to develop rudimentary fiscal and

---

[50]Cox, p. 262, Maistres Bough and Maistres Morland (with one other), and Maister Bough and Maister Morland, each pair respectively accounting for women's and men's Hock money (Westminster, 1498); gathering of churchwardens' wives on Hock Monday (Lambeth, 1518–19). See also: Daniel, *St. John the Baptist Glastonbury*, p. 44 (1500), for money received "de Roberto Hendy de Colleccione vxoris ejus et mulierum"; above, n. 42, Peterborough, where the actual collection was organized by two women (perhaps stewards of the wives' group or guild); Weaver and Clark, *Churchwardens' Accounts*, p. 51 (1538), where, at Spelsbury, Joan Belchar was a joint keeper of the light of the Holy Trinity, evidently temporarily replacing Robert Belchar (dead in 1541), who had been churchwarden in 1526 and four times a keeper, 1526–31 (pp. 53, 41, 43, 46, 47); and *Canterbury*, pt. 1, p. 14, receipt of 6s. 8d. "de quad' mulier' dat' in denar'," suggesting a woman's collection of money from a female group (1485). For church ale receipts at St. Edmund's, Salisbury: Swayne, p. 8 (1461–62), "de diuersis jocalibus regibus & reginis hoc anno"; WRO, 1901/66/5 (1469–70 = Swayne, p. 12, incomplete transcription), under "Colleccio denar'," William Smith and Robert South's wife, John Chapman and Ralph Hayne's wife, William Harris and William Pole's wife, William Glover and William White's wife; *Boxford*, p. 18 (1535).

administrative skills. At the same time, just as on those occasions in which they took their light into the church, women were given collective visibility in public spaces (church and churchyard, street and market), often in circumstances that put them on an equal or comparable footing with men.

The end of the period dealt with here roughly corresponds with the consolidation in England of an established reformed church, soon to be faced with new challenges from dissenting groups. For Salisbury, the latter part of the sixteenth century also saw dislocation in the traditional textile industries and recurring bouts of plague, with a consequent decline in the welfare of its citizens.[51] Changing religious and economic circumstances were reflected in the relationship between women and the parish. With restrictions on the use of candles and ornaments, the work of chandlers and metal smiths (in which women had earlier been employed at Saint Edmund's) was no longer of vital importance to the parish church; in any case, Salisbury's economic downturn probably meant, as it did in Bristol during this period, that women were squeezed out of a variety of workplace opportunities in the face of what Ben-Amos characterizes as "a male demand for urban employment." Payments in churchwardens' accounts to individual women for other work within the parish church largely disappear, not only through a reduction in the need for liturgical objects but also for the number and variety of vestments and linen goods that women's skills were once called on to make, repair, or clean. Even more fundamental, the pruning of traditional feast days from the church calendar, and those of the Virgin in particular, erased ritual opportunities for women's collective celebration and visibility within the parish community.

---

[51]Paul Slack, "Poverty and Politics in Salisbury, 1597–1666," in *Crisis and Order in English Towns, 1500–1700: Essays in Urban History*, ed. Peter Clark and Paul Slack (Toronto, 1972), pp. 168–70.

The dwindling relevance (in which puritanism may have played a part) of Hocktide and dancing day similarly wiped out women's practical role in parish fund-raising. Consolidation of household ties and the enlarged authority of the male head of household, which Lawrence Stone saw as a strong factor in later sixteenth-century society, may also have played a part in minimizing women's collective rôle in the parish.[52]

By 1608, Saint Thomas's parishioners were seated throughout the church, with 168 rows of pews distributed in nave and side aisles, choir and flanking chapels: the mayor's pew, in front of his wife's, close to the pulpit; senior vestry members occupying front rows in each section, with their wives immediately behind or in the near vicinity; other women seated in most of the remaining pews in each section, with the rear row or two in each case occupied by men.[53] Thus—with the congregation ordered to reflect intertwining hierarchies of city and parish—were women now contained between men of more and lesser rank, their visibility confined to a passive presence in the pew.

---

[52]Ben-Amos, *Adolescence and Youth*, pp. 140–41—after 1600, Bristol women were channeled into domestic service or declining textile trades, while in London women were increasingly marginalized in the labor market (Caroline M. Barron, "Introduction: The Widow's World," in Barron and Sutton, *Medieval London Widows*, p. xxix); at St. Andrew's, Canterbury, in 1597, washing, cleaning, and carrying away of refuse were formally assigned to the parish clerk, who perhaps farmed the work out to women, reaping a small middleman profit (*Canterbury*, pt. 5, p. 2); above, n. 48, for Hocktide; Douglas, "'Oure Thanssynge Day,'" pp. 608–09; Stone, chap. 5, "The Reinforcement of Patriarchy," in *The Family, Sex and Marriage in England, 1500–1800* (New York, 1977), pp. 151–218.

[53]WRO, 1900/92: pp. 1–24 are ruled off to represent pews, with occupants' names written into each box so formed. Each pew (except the mayor's) was occupied by two to four people; canceled and substituted names, compared with those of men at vestry meetings, 1594–1615 (WRO, 1900/174, St. Thomas, Vestry Minute Book, 1594–1673, fols. 1r–9v) reveal the progress of men and their wives to front rows, as the former's parish status rose.

MARRIAGE

Individualism and Consensual Marriage: Some Evidence from Medieval England

Jacqueline Murray

In a letter written in September 1469, the formidable Margaret Paston described how her recalcitrant and rebellious daughter, Margery, had been summoned by the bishop of Norwich concerning her putative marriage to Richard Calle, the family's steward.[1] She wrote, in part:

> And the Bishop said to her right plainly, and put her in remembrance how she was born, what kin and friends that she had, and should have mo if she were ruled and guided after them; and if she did not, what rebuke and shame and loss it should be to her if she were not guided by them, and cause of forsaking of her for any good or help or comfort that she should have of them; and said that he had heard say that she loved such one that her friend[s] were not pleased with that she should have, and therefore he bade her be right well advised how she did, and said that he would understand the words that she had said to him, whether it made matrimony or not. And she rehearsed what she had said, and said if tho words made it not sure she said boldly that she would make it surer ere than she went

[1] I would like to thank Joseph Goering for his continuing intellectual generosity and Sherri Olson and Shannon McSheffrey for their comments. Research for this paper was supported by the Social Sciences and Humanities Research Council of Canada, Canada Research Fellowship program.

thence; for she said she thought in her conscience she was bound, whatsoever the words wern. These lewd words grieve me and her grandam as much as all the remnant. And the Bishop and the chancellor both said that there was neither I nor no friend of hers would receive her.

And then Calle was examined apart by himself, that her words and his accorded, and the time and where it should a be done. . . . and when I heard say what her demeaning was I charged my servants that she should not be received in mine house.[2]

This letter presents a fine and detailed account of the implementation of the doctrine of consensual marriage. The medieval doctrine of consent taught that the only requirement for a valid, indissoluble, and sacramental marriage was the freely-given consent, in words of the present tense, of a man and a

---

[2] *The Paston Letters: A Selection in Modern Spelling*, ed. Norman Davis (London, 1963), Letter 86, pp. 182–83. The original is found in *Paston Letters and Papers of the Fifteenth Century*, ed. Norman Davis, 2 vols. (Oxford, 1971–76), Letter 203, 1: 342–43: "And þe Bysschop seyd to here ryth pleynly, and put here in rememberawns how sche was born, wat kyn and frenddys þat sche had, and xuld haue mo yf sche were rulyd and gydyd aftyre them; and yf sche ded not, wat rebuke and schame and los yt xuld be to here yf sche were not gydyd be them, and cause of foresaky[n]g of here fore any good ore helpe ore kownfort þat sche xuld haue of hem; and seyd þat he had hard sey þat sche loued schecheon þat here frend were not plesyd wyth þat she xuld haue, and there-fore he bad here be ryth wel a-vysyd how sche ded, and seyd þat he woold wndyrstond þe worddys þat sche had seyd to hym, wheythere yt mad matramony ore not. And sche rehersyd wat sche had seyd, and seyd yf thoo worddys mad yt not suhere, sche seyd boldly þat sche wold make yt suerhere ore þan sche went thens; fore sche sayd sche thowthe in here conschens sche was bownd, wat so euere þe worddys wern. Thes leud worddys gereue me and here grandam as myche as alle þe remnawnte. And þan þe Bysschop and the schawnselere bothe seyd þat there was neythere I nere no frend of hers wold resyuere. And þan Calle was exameynd aparte be hym-sylfe, þat here worddys and hys acordyd, and the tyme and where yt xuld a be don. . . . and wan I hard sey wat here demeny[n]g was I schargyd my seruantys þat sche xuld not be reseyued in myn hows."

woman: *I take you as my wife / I take you as my husband.*[3] These words, so formulaic as to have been commonplace, surely formed the essence of the private consent exchanged by Margery and Richard.

A case like that of Margery Paston and Richard Calle was very likely not the norm in fifteenth-century England. Rather, Margery and Richard were probably anomalous in a society that valued highly the qualities of obedience and family loyalty.[4] Certainly, Margaret Paston indicated that she did not understand, much less condone, such headstrong, wilful, individualistic behavior from her daughter. Margaret had expected Margery to play her part in an overall marriage strategy designed to benefit the Paston clan, and she proved implacable when her daughter refused to co-operate. What is important about the marriage of Margery Paston and Richard Calle, however, is not whether it was a startling exception to the overall practice of marriage in medieval England. Rather, it presents a useful example of two individuals who implemented the doctrine of free consent to marriage in the face of family resistance and social and ecclesiastical pressure to conform. How was it that this couple was so certain of their legal right to marry? How did they know the correct way to marry each other? And, finally, despite the fierce opposition that greeted their union, how were they certain that the bishop of Norwich would confirm it?

---

[3]Charles Donahue, Jr., "The Policy of Alexander the Third's Consent Theory of Marriage," in *Proceedings of the Fourth International Congress of Medieval Canon Law*, ed. Stephan Kuttner (Vatican City, 1976), pp. 251–52.

[4]Natalie Zemon Davis has examined some of the strategies by which an individual, despite being embedded in familial and social systems that prescribed behavior, could exercise individual autonomy: "Boundaries and the Sense of Self in Sixteenth-Century France," in *Reconstructing Individualism: Autonomy, Individuality, and the Self in Western Thought*, ed. Thomas C. Heller, Morton Sosna, and David E. Wellbery (Stanford, Calif., 1986), pp. 53–63.

The case of Margery and Richard is a clear example of how the Church's doctrine of consensual marriage effectively challenged the very foundations of the patriarchal family and the hierarchical social structure that characterized medieval society. By dispensing with witnesses, liturgical solemnities, and dowry, in theory the individual's decision to marry could be free from the control of parents, family, and lord.[5] Once it had been disseminated across medieval English society, the consensual doctrine, when invoked, enhanced the freedom and autonomy of the individual in the crucial matter of marriage.

---

[5]Donahue, Sheehan, and many others concur that the consensual theory of marriage led to individuals exercising freedom to marry by means of clandestine exchanges of consent. This individual freedom from lord and family was the most important and enduring effect of Alexander III's decisions. The seriousness with which this evasion of parental control was seen is indicated by the attempt of the king of France to have the Council of Trent require parental consent for a valid marriage. See Charles Donahue, Jr., "The Canon Law on the Formation of Marriage and Social Practice in the Later Middle Ages," *Journal of Family History* 8 (1983): 147; idem, "Policy," pp. 256, 258–60, 268–70, and Michael M. Sheehan, "The Formation and Stability of Marriage in Fourteenth-Century England: Evidence of an Ely Register," *Mediaeval Studies* 33 (1971): 263. A. J. Finch has cautioned against reducing the very complicated issue of clandestinity to one of parental vs. individual consent: "Parental Authority and the Problem of Clandestine Marriage in the Later Middle Ages," *Law and History Review* 8 (1990): 201. Robert C. Palmer has investigated some of the complexities that could arise when the secular and ecclesiastical models of marriage collided: "Contexts of Marriage in Medieval England: Evidence from the King's Court circa 1300," *Speculum* 59 (1984): 42–67. For differing discussions of the role of the consensual theory in the formation of marriage in France, see André Burguière, "The Formation of the Couple," *Journal of Family History* 12 (1987): 39–53, and Beatrice Gottlieb, "The Meaning of Clandestine Marriage," in *Family and Sexuality in French History*, ed. Robert Wheaton and Tamara K. Hareven (Philadelphia, 1980), pp. 49–83. Various issues pertaining to marital consent and coercion in Antiquity and the Middle Ages in both the Greek and Latin worlds have been examined in Angeliki E. Laiou, ed., *Consent and Coercion to Sex and Marriage in Ancient and Medieval Societies* (Washington, D.C., 1993).

The consensual theory was refined in the course of the twelfth century.[6] Despite arguing that consummation was necessary to complete the bonds of marriage, Gratian also saw consent as essential to the formation of the union. In the *Decretum* (ca. 1140) he stated plainly, "Where they each do not consent, there is no marriage."[7] Elsewhere he argued that it was consent rather than coitus which formed the marriage bond.[8] This perspective also formed the core of Peter Lombard's theological discussion of consensual marriage in his *Sentences*. The Lombard also included the distinction between present and future consent, providing the words that would become the exemplar: I take you as my husband, I take you as my wife.[9]

---

[6]The development of the doctrine of consent to marriage has been surveyed by John T. Noonan, "The Power to Choose," *Viator* 4 (1973): 419–34, and James A. Brundage, *Law, Sex, and Christian Society in Medieval Europe* (Chicago, 1987), esp. pp. 187–90, 235–75, 332–36. As early as 866 Pope Nicholas I affirmed that the consent of the couple alone was essential for marriage. Michael M. Sheehan, "The Bishop of Rome to a Barbarian King on the Rituals of Marriage," in *In iure veritas: Studies in Canon Law in Memory of Schafer Williams*, ed. Steven B. Bowman and Blanche E. Cody (Cincinnati, 1991), pp. 187–99, and Angeliki E. Laiou, "*Consensus Facit Nuptias— Et Non*. Pope Nicholas I's *Responsa* to the Bulgarians as a Source for Byzantine Marriage Customs," *Rechtshistorisches Journal* 4 (1985): 189–201.

[7]"Ubi non est consensus utriusque, non est coniugium" (*Decretum* C.30 q.2 c.1 in *Corpus iuris canonici*, vol. 1, ed. Emil Friedberg, 2nd ed. [Leipzig, 1879]). The tension inherent in Gratian, between marriage as a free and personal act and the need to externalize and institutionalize marriage for the protection of society, is examined in Raymond Decker, "Institutional Authority versus Personal Responsibility in the Marriage Sections of Gratian's *A Concordance of Disconcordant Canons*," *The Jurist* 32 (1972): 51–65.

[8]"Matrimonium quidem non facit coitus, sed uoluntas . . ." (*Decretum* C.27 q.2 c.1). "His auctoritatibus euidenter ostenditur, quod nisi libera uoluntate nulla est copulanda alicui" (ibid., C.31 q.2 d.p.c.4).

[9]"Efficiens autem causa matrimonii est consensus, non quilibet, sed per verba expressus; nec de futuro, sed de praesenti. . . . Accipio te in virum et ego te

The doctrine received its full exposition in the marriage decrees of Pope Alexander III in the 1170s.[10] Alexander's most important pronouncements were incorporated into the Decretals of Gregory IX (1234). These included an affirmation that consent alone formed the bonds of a marriage. Furthermore, marriage was not invalidated by failure to observe local customs governing the solemnization of the union.[11] James A. Brundage has concluded that Alexander III "consistently sought to free marriages from the control of parents, families, and feudal overlords and to place the choice of marriage partners under the exclusive control of the parties themselves."[12]

The freedom to marry is part of the process by which the individual gains independence from external control.[13] John F. Benton has even suggested that this freedom is so fundamental that it is one of the tests by which to measure a society's respect for individual freedom of choice in general.[14] The consensual theory of marriage, then, accurately reflected the preoccupation with individualism that dominated the intellectual

---

in uxorem, matrimonium facit," *Sententiae* 4.27.3 (*Sententiae in IV libris distinctae*, 3rd ed., vol. 2 [Grottaferrata, 1981], pp. 422–23).

[10] Alexander's contribution to the development of the consensual theory of marriage has been studied by Donahue, "Policy," pp. 251–81.

[11] "Matrimonium solo consensu contrahitur, nec invalidatur, si consuetudo patriae non servetur" (*Liber extra* Bk. 4 t.1 c.1. in *Corpus iuris canonici*, vol. 2, ed. Emil Friedberg, 2nd ed. [Leipzig, 1879]).

[12] *Law, Sex, and Christian Society*, pp. 332–33.

[13] Colin Morris, "Individualism in Twelfth-Century Religion: Some Further Reflections," *Journal of Ecclesiastical History* 31 (1980): 202. For a discussion of the importance of group or community identification in the 12th century see Caroline Walker Bynum, "Did the Twelfth Century Discover the Individual?" ibid, pp. 1–17.

[14] "Individualism and Conformity in Medieval Western Europe," in *Individualism and Conformity in Classical Islam*, ed. Amin Banani and Speros Vryonis (Wiesbaden, 1977), p. 156.

milieu of the twelfth-century schools.[15] While individualism posed a challenge to both the feudal hierarchy and the patriarchal family, it nevertheless became increasingly important and influential throughout medieval society; consensual marriage was but one manifestation of this individualism.

Many analyses of the consensual theory of marriage focus on how it conflicted with entrenched secular values, concluding that it had little practical influence. These studies have tended to concentrate on aristocratic patrilineages that exercised rigid control of marriage as a means of forging political and economic alliances.[16] The consensual theory was universally applicable, however, and it would appear to have been more immediately relevant to medievals of modest social rank. The doctrine was disseminated throughout all levels of medieval society in a variety of ways. One of the most important means was conciliar and episcopal legislation.[17] Sermons were another and perhaps more immediate means by which the doctrine was conveyed to the laity.[18] Another source, the

---

[15]For an overview of some aspects of the development and recognition of the individual see John F. Benton, "Consciousness of Self and Perceptions of Individuality," in *Renaissance and Renewal in the Twelfth Century*, ed. Robert L. Benson and Giles Constable (Cambridge, Mass., 1982), pp. 263–95.

[16]For example, Georges Duby concerned himself only with the highest levels of French society, analyzing the marriages of kings and nobles: *Medieval Marriage: Two Models from Twelfth-Century France*, trans. Elborg Forster (Baltimore, 1978). For England see Joel T. Rosenthal, *Patriarchy and Families of Privilege in Fifteenth-Century England* (Philadelphia, 1991).

[17]Michael M. Sheehan, "Marriage Theory and Practice in the Conciliar Legislation and Diocesan Statutes of Medieval England," *Mediaeval Studies* 40 (1978): 408–60, and idem, "Marriage and Family in English Conciliar and Synodal Legislation," in *Essays in Honour of Anton Charles Pegis*, ed. J. Reginald O'Donnell (Toronto, 1974), pp. 205–14.

[18]The study of sermons about marriage or those directed specifically at married people is only in its nascent stages. See, e.g., David d'Avray, "The Gospel of the Marriage Feast of Cana and Marriage Preaching in France," in

pastoral manual or manual for confessors, is equally useful for tracing how doctrines were mediated to the parish level.[19]

Pastoral manuals were written for the express purpose of educating the parish clergy to exercise better the *cura animarum* and educate and inform their parishioners about the norms that governed a Christian mode of life.[20] Appearing in the years just prior to 1200, and with greater frequency after the Fourth Lateran Council (1215) had legislated mandatory annual confession, these manuals represent a departure from the older penitentials.[21] They stressed self-examination, emphasized

---

The Bible in the Medieval World: Essays in Memory of Beryl Smalley, ed. Katherine Walsh and Diana Wood (Oxford, 1985), pp. 207–24; David d'Avray and M. Tausche, "Marriage Sermons in *Ad Status* Collections of the Central Middle Ages," *Archives d'Histoire doctrinale et littéraire du Moyen Âge* 47 (1981): 71–119; Nicole Bériou and David L. d'Avray, "Henry of Provins, O.P.'s Comparison of the Dominican and Franciscan Orders with the 'Order' of Matrimony," *Archivum Fratrum Praedicatorum* 49 (1979): 513–17.

[19] Quite a different and significant use of pastoral manuals for the study of medieval marriage is found in P. P. A. Biller, "Marriage Patterns and Women's Lives: A Sketch of a Pastoral Geography," in *Woman Is a Worthy Wight: Women in English Society c. 1200–1500*, ed. P. J. P. Goldberg (Gloucester, 1992), pp. 60–107. Biller compares manuals from northern and southern Europe to show how they reflect their differing social contexts and the customs and values governing marriage and family in each region.

[20] Leonard E. Boyle, "The Summa for Confessors as a Genre, and Its Religious Intent," in *The Pursuit of Holiness in Late Medieval and Renaissance Religion*, ed. Charles E. Trinkaus and Heiko A. Oberman (Leiden, 1974), pp. 128–29, and Pierre Michaud-Quantin, *Sommes de casuistique et manuels de confession au moyen âge (XII–XVI siècles)* (Louvain, 1962), p. 8.

[21] For discussion of the treatment of issues pertaining to marriage and family in the penitentials see Raoul Manselli, "Vie familiale et éthique sexuelle dans les Pénitentiels," in *Famille et parenté dans l'Occident médiéval*, ed. Georges Duby and Jacques Le Goff (Rome, 1977), pp. 363–78, and "Il matrimonio nei Penitenziali," in *Il Matrimonio nella società altomedievale*, 2 vols. (Spoleto, 1977), pp. 287–315; Pierre J. Payer, *Sex and the Penitentials: The Development of a Sexual Code, 550–1150* (Toronto, 1984).

individual motivation and internal repentance, and encouraged the individual to develop an informed sense of right conduct and virtue. Pastoral manuals reflect the influence of the twelfth-century schools' preoccupation with individualism and intention.[22] They also were an important means by which the Church disseminated its reforms across Christendom.[23] They reveal how the parish clergy were expected to instruct their parishioners about how to avoid sin and cultivate virtue in daily life. Pastoral manuals, then, bring us near to the faithful and help to fill the void left by the lack of writings by the laity themselves. They also allow us to trace those ideas and teachings that the Church thought important to circulate at the parish level.

English writers in particular were active in producing pastoral manuals, manuals that we know were in the hands of the parochial clergy. For example, Alexander Stavensby, bishop of Coventry (1224–38), appended two small pastoral treatises to his Statutes of Coventry and required that every priest in the diocese have a copy of the treatises, under pain of suspension.[24]

---

[22]Colin Morris, *The Discovery of the Individual, 1050–1200* (Toronto, 1987), pp. 70–75; Benton, "Consciousness of Self," pp. 271–74.

[23]Morris, *Discovery*, p. 73, and also Leonard E. Boyle, "The Inter-Conciliar Period 1179–1215 and the Beginnings of Pastoral Manuals," in *Miscellanea, Rolando Bandinelli, Papa Alessandro III*, ed. Filippo Liotto (Siena, 1986), pp. 51–56.

[24]Article 27, Statutes of Coventry (1229x1237): "Precipimus vobis firmiter per virtutem Iesu Christi, sub interminatione anathematis et sub pena suspensionis, quatinus hec statuta serventur et scribantur simul cum sermone de septem criminalibus peccatis que ad vos mittimus, et hoc cum quodam tractatu modico de confessione. Hec serventur et scribantur sicut vultis quod ecclesie vestre non suspendantur, cum ad ecclesias vestras accesserimus vel per nos vel per nuntium nostrum" (*Councils and Synods, with Other Documents Relating to the English Church*, 2: *A.D. 1205–1313*, ed. F. M. Powicke and C. R. Cheney [Oxford, 1964], pt. 1, p. 214). It is possible that Robert Grosseteste's *Templum Dei* similarly circulated with the statutes of Lincoln.

An examination of some of the manuals, written from the late twelfth to the fifteenth centuries, reveals how quickly and widely the doctrine of consensual marriage was disseminated to the parish level.[25]

As early as the 1160s, Bartholomew, bishop of Exeter ([†]1184) wrote a penitential that highlighted Saint Paul's affirmation of the widow's freedom to choose to remarry (1 Corinthians 7: 39).[26] Given the fact that during this period the right to consent to the marriages of vassals's heirs and widows was important to the crown, for both economic and political reasons, and that it had led to coercion and the disparagement of widows, this affirmation of freedom to consent was timely.[27] Ultimately, the abuse of widows was so great that the barons insisted that King John reaffirm, in the Magna Carta, a widow's

---

See Leonard E. Boyle, "Robert Grosseteste and the Pastoral Care," *Medieval and Renaissance Studies* 8 (1979): 10; repr. in idem, *Pastoral Care, Clerical Education and Canon Law, 1200–1400* (London, 1981), Essay 1, p. 10.

[25]Michael Sheehan has already pointed out the usefulness of this type of literature for studying the dissemination of the doctrine of freedom of choice and for investigating the quality of the spousal relationship. See his "Choice of Marriage Partner in the Middle Ages: Development and Mode of Application of a Theory of Marriage," *Studies in Medieval and Renaissance History*, n.s., 1 (1978): 3–33, and "*Maritalis Affectio* Revisited," in *The Olde Daunce: Love, Friendship, Sex, and Marriage in the Medieval World*, ed. Robert R. Edwards and Stephen Spector (Albany, N.Y., 1991), pp. 32–43.

[26]See his *Penitential* C. 62 entitled "Augustinus de bono uiduitatis," which opens by stating, "De tertiis et quartis et de ultra pluribus nuptiis solent homines mouere questionem. Vnde et breuiter respondeam nec ullas nuptias audeo damnare, nec eis uerecundiam numerositatis auferre" (Adrian Morey, *Bartholomew of Exeter, Bishop and Canonist: A Study in the Twelfth Century* [Cambridge, 1937], p. 228). He also quotes Jerome as saying, "Est etiam sciendum quod omne coniugium semel legitime contractum indissolubile est," ibid., p. 229.

[27]Sidney Painter, *Studies in the History of the English Feudal Barony* (Baltimore, 1943), pp. 66–72.

right to remain unmarried.[28] By including his discussion of a widow's right to choose whether to marry, Bartholomew helped to disseminate the Church's doctrine that the individual's freedom of choice superseded both familial and feudal strategies, although this may not have been exactly what the barons intended in their objections to the royal marriage policy.

Half a century later, in his *Summa de penitentia* (1212x 1220), John of Kent extended the freedom to consent to the formation of all marriages. Relying heavily on Gratian's *Decretum*, he affirmed that coercion impedes both vows and marriage for which "the freedom of the will is required."[29] He acknowledged, however, that in practice minors who were betrothed could, at puberty, be coerced to consent to the union, if some greater good such as a peace treaty were at stake. Even so, John of Kent warned that the coercion should only be moderate, lest the outcome of the union ultimately be worse than its collapse. Coerced unions, he observed, can come to a bad end.[30]

---

[28]"No widow shall be compelled to marry so long as she wishes to live without a husand, provided that she gives security that she will not marry without our consent if she hold of us, or without the consent of the lord of whom she holds, if she holds of another" (Magna Carta, chap. 8; J. C. Holt, *Magna Carta* [London, 1969], pp. 318–21). The extent to which the Magna Carta harmonized with the contemporary canon law of marriage has been noted by Sue Sheridan Walker, "Feudal Constraint and Free Consent in the Making of Marriages in Medieval England: Widows in the King's Gift," in *Canadian Historical Society Papers* (Ottawa, 1979), pp. 97–110.

[29]"Coactio impedit matrimonium contrahendum et dirimit contractum quia in uoto et in matrimonio non solum uoluntas sed libertas exigitur uoluntatis" (*Summa de penitentia* in London, British Library, MS Royal 9.A.XIV, fol. 216r). The only comprehensive discussion of this unpublished manual is found in Joseph W. Goering, "The '*Summa de penitentia*' of John of Kent," *Bulletin of Medieval Canon Law* 18 (1988): 13–31. The author would like to thank Prof. Goering for allowing her to consult his unpublished transcription of this *summa*.

[30]"Si impuberes contrahunt sponsalia neuter poterit resilire donec peruenerint ad pubertatem. Tunc compellendi sunt ut contrahant propter bonum maius

Robert of Flamborough, a contemporary of John of Kent, wrote his *Liber poenitentialis* between 1208 and 1213. He focused on somewhat different aspects of the consensual doctrine, and his manual shows how, even by the first decade of the thirteenth century, consent and consummation had not been completely disentangled. Flamborough believed that two kinds of consent were necessary to contract a valid marriage: consent of the minds and consent of the bodies to carnal union.[31] This interpretation of consent dominates his discussion of marriage and is reiterated, for example, in his exposition of the impediments to marriage.[32]

Robert of Flamborough was also one of the earliest moralists to recognize, if grudgingly, the validity of clandestine marriages. He warned, however, that care needed to be exercised because adultery or fornication could be committed on the pretext of a clandestine union. Public perception was accorded great importance in the process of assessing the true nature of a couple's relationship. He advised,

> If, therefore, it is public rumor that there is a marriage between them, or if publicly both behaved with respect to the other, as if married, there ends, as I believe, all such evil suspicions of the

---

sequens scilicet reformacionem pacis et huiusmodi. Si autem resilire uoluerint, omnibus modis non sunt compellendi nisi condicionaliter, ut de nolente fiant uolentes cum huiusmodi coactionem soleat peior exitus sequi" (Royal 9.A.XIV, fol. 215v).

[31]"Tria exiguntur ad matrimonium: consensus animorum, consensus corporum, id est consensus in carnalem copulam, . . ." *Liber poenitentialis: A Critical Edition*, ed. J. J. Francis Firth (Toronto, 1971), 2.12, p. 64.

[32]For example: "In matrimonio contrahendo duo sunt necessaria: ut possint consentire et commisceri. Unde minores duodecim annis et castrati et frigidi non possunt contrahere matrimonium. Furiosi et adulti non capaces doli possunt commisceri, sed non consentire; unde non possunt contrahere matrimonium" (*Liber poenitentialis* 2.52, p. 86).

canons, and it will be judged by the church as a certain marriage, not presumed dubious.[33]

Flamborough's reluctance to countenance such individualistic behavior echoes in his remarks but, in the end, he affirmed the canonical position that consent is the only requirement for a valid marriage, and he even suggested that the Church should give people the benefit of the doubt in matrimonial matters.

Another contemporary moralist, Thomas of Chobham, sub-dean of Salisbury, also wrote a *Summa confessorum* (1210x 1215). This manual indicates a more subtle and less hesitant understanding of the doctrine. Chobham taught that consent of the hearts was just as necessary as verbal consent to establish an indissoluble union.[34] Furthermore, he stated, "It is clear, there-fore, that a man and a woman are able to contract marriage by themselves, without a priest and without all others, in any place, so long as they consent to a permanent way of life."[35] This is one of the earliest and most positive articulations of the consensual doctrine in English confessors' manuals. Chobham not only linked the implementation of the doctrine of consent with clandestine marriage but also reflected upon the nature of

---

[33]"In clandestinis matrimoniis non est interpretandum in melius, ut scilicet praedicentur legitima, ne sub tali praetextu adulterium et fornicatio commit-tantur. Sunt tamen matrimonia vera. Si ergo est publica fama quod matrimo-nium est inter eos, vel si publice uterque se gessit pro conjuge erga alterum, cessat, ut credo, omnis talis canonis mal suspicio, et ut de certo matrimonio judicabit ecclesia, non praesumet de incerto" (*Liber poenitentialis* 2.69, p. 96).

[34]"Sciendum est autem quod consensus in matrimonio debet esse non solum verborum sed etiam animorum" (*Thomae de Chobham, Summa confessorum*, ed. F. Broomfield [Louvain, 1968], p. 148).

[35]"Patet igitur quod vir et mulier possunt contrahere matrimonium per se sine sacerdote et sine omnibus aliis in quocumque loco, dummodo consentiant in perpetuam vite consuetudinem" (*Summa confessorum*, p. 146).

the consent. Finally, he stated that informal unions were valid, indissoluble, and sacramental.

Furthermore, Chobham placed his advice in the context of village life and indicated that free consent pertained equally to all levels of society, including serfs. Following contemporary theological opinion,[36] he affirmed that serfs had the capacity to marry without their lord's consent, although he did urge them to marry with their lord's approval. In its absence, however, a priest was fully entitled to preside at the marriage because a master could not control his serf's ability to consent.[37] In addition, Chobham moved out of the realm of the theoretical and into the practical. He advocated that priests take an active role in asserting the individual's ability to marry free from the control of his or her lord.

The principle of individual freedom of choice was developed further in the manual *Qui bene presunt* written by Richard Wetheringsett sometime between 1215 and 1222.[38] He, too, stressed that mutual consent was essential and that priests needed to enquire clearly and openly about it because consent

---

[36]Chobham drew heavily on the earlier work of his teacher, Peter the Chanter. For a discussion of the Chanter's treatment of the marriage of serfs see Michael M. Sheehan, "Theory and Practice: Marriage of the Unfree and the Poor in Medieval Society," *Mediaeval Studies* 50 (1988): 473, 478.

[37]Chobham argued that "servus et ancilla quantum ad contrahendum matrimonium bene habent libertatem proprie voluntatis. . . . Verumtamen si servus et ancilla petierint licentiam a dominis suis et domini noluerint eis dare licentiam contrahendi, tunc bene poterit sacerdos coniungere eos dominis reclamantibus, quia domini non possunt cogere servos et ancillas suas ut contineant velint nolint" (*Summa confessorum*, pp. 177–78).

[38]There is little information available for Richard Wetheringsett, and his manual remains unedited. This discussion is based on two MSS of the work: BL, Royal 9.A.XIV and Oxford, New College, MS 94. Professor Joseph Goering kindly made available his transcription of the British Library manuscript.

is the efficient cause of marriage.[39] Furthermore, Richard also advised priests to bring the consensual nature of marriage to the attention of the laity. If they wished to marry, consent in words of the present tense resulted in a full and complete union. If the couple exchanged consent in words of the future tense, subsequent sexual intercourse rendered the bond indissoluble.[40] Thus, in this manual priests are instructed, for all intents and purposes, to teach their parishioners the subtleties of the consensual doctrine, to teach the laity how to effect for themselves a valid and indissoluble, if clandestine, marriage.

Wetheringsett was equally clear in his defense of the freedom to consent. He not only counseled priests to assist people who wanted to marry in spite of opposition from either family or lord, but he also warned priests to refuse to preside at the marriages of unwilling people. He stated that under no circumstances were priests to acquiesce to threats and solemnize a union unless the couple freely consented; it was the wills of the couple that ought to be joined.[41] Wetheringsett extended the understanding of free consent and the impediment of coercion. Thus, some forty years after Alexander III had refined the consensual doctrine, the freedom to consent to marriage was entrenched firmly in canon law, though it continued to encounter resistance from secular society. By suggesting that priests themselves were being intimidated and forced to

---

[39]"Plene et aperte inquirendum est de consensu mutuo qui maxime necessarius est. Est enim causa efficiens matrimonium" (New College 94, fol. 76r).

[40]"Et sunt hec specialiter notificanda et exprimenda layitis querendo an alter utrum coniungi volentium vel per verba de presenti ubi plenum consumatum est matrimonium, vel per verba de futuro precipue si subsecuta fuerit carnalis copula" (New College 94, fol. 75v).

[41]"Nec aliquomodo propter aliquorum minas et seditiones coniungant sacerdotes nisi consencientes. Voluntaria debent esse coniugia" (New College 94, fol. 76r).

preside at coerced unions, Wetheringsett added a new dimension to the process of enforcing the doctrine of free consent.

Wetheringsett also provides evidence that by the 1220s the consensual theory was widely known, at least among the English clergy.[42] He suggests that the clergy were enforcing the prohibition against coerced marriage and were championing the individual's freedom of choice. Consequently, they themselves were becoming the victims of coercion when parents or lords had difficulty finding a priest to preside at the marriage of an unwilling person. Wetheringsett encouraged priests to remain steadfast in their support of consensual marriage and not allow themselves to be forced into a position in which they would solemnize an irregular union.

There is evidence that the advice of this early group of moralists, especially that of Chobham and Wetheringsett, began to exert an influence by the late thirteenth century, at least insofar as curbing seigniorial control of marriage. In an analysis of manor courts in Norfolk, Elaine Clark has found numerous examples of tenants resisting pressure to marry by the lord of the manor of Horsham.[43] Between 1284 and 1290 he informed a number of men and women that spouses had been chosen for

---

[42]This interpretation is supported by the fact that the great bishop and pastor Robert Grosseteste seems to have assumed the consent of the couple rather than discussing it at any length in his pastoral treatises *Deus est* (ca. 1215–30) and *Templum Dei* (1220x1230). Grosseteste discussed the couple's intentions and why they consented, rather than dwelling on the distinctions between present and future consent or public and private consent. It is possible that he believed that earlier manuals had already disseminated the Church's teaching effectively. See the discussions in Jacqueline Murray, "The Perceptions of Sexuality, Marriage, and Family in Early English Pastoral Manuals," Ph.D. thesis (Univ. of Toronto, 1987), p. 249.

[43]What follows is a summary of the evidence presented in Clark, "The Decision to Marry in Thirteenth- and Fourteenth-Century Norfolk," *Mediaeval Studies* 49 (1987): 496–516, esp. pp. 500–02.

them by a group of village elders. There was no organized protest against this order to marry, but the records indicate that individuals resisted the lord's interference in their personal lives. For example, a mother was fined because she had impeded her daughter's marriage to the man selected for her. Another man vetoed two proposed spouses and finally paid a fine for a license to marry freely. Similar patterns of vetoing selected spouses and paying fines are found at the nearby manor of Salle. Clark also suggests that the lord's authority in the marriages of his tenants was shrinking and by the end of the thirteenth century was focused solely on orphans and fatherless heirs. The stout rejection of arranged marriages by tenants, coupled with the lord's recognition that marriages had necessarily to conform to the Church's requirements, ultimately allowed tenants to circumvent imposed or unwanted unions. The dissemination of the consensual doctrine to the parish level certainly played a role in the weakening of seigniorial control and the increasing autonomy exercised by tenants in matrimony.[44]

These early pastoral manuals were among the many such writings that continued to circulate across England throughout the thirteenth, fourteenth, and fifteenth centuries, and they continued to promote the doctrine of the individual's freedom of choice in marriage. New manuals were also written and they, too, reiterated the consensual doctrine.[45] Some went

---

[44]The increasing exercise of freedom in marriage was not limited to the lower ranks. A similar weakening of the lord's control of the marriage of feudal wards has also been noted. Sue Sheridan Walker has proposed that the dissemination of the doctrine of free consent accounts for the decline, from the 12th to 13th centuries, in the number of feudal wards who needed to purchase licenses to marry freely ("Free Consent and Marriage of Feudal Wards in Medieval England," *Journal of Medieval History* 8 [1982]: 123–34).

[45]For example, after reiterating the doctrine of present consent, the anonymous *Speculum lucidum* (1281x1298) advises: "Item si per legitime ad

further and almost promoted the practice of private, clandestine unions by providing the exact words needed to form valid, indissoluble consent. For example, the most important manual written in England during the fourteenth century was William of Pagula's *Oculus sacerdotis* (1319/20x1322).[46] Pagula affirmed that marriage was contracted by consent alone given in words of the present tense, and he provided an example of the words to be used: "I take you as my wife. . . . I take you as my husband."[47] This suggests that by the early fourteenth century writers were aware of the ambiguity of language and that the courts had been faced with cases that had revolved around the exact meaning of the specific words exchanged by a couple. Pagula's manual would have lessened the confusion by providing the very phrases that formed an indissoluble marriage bond.

The promotion of the consensual doctrine was not limited to its presentation in large, learned, and comprehensive tomes like the *Oculus sacerdotis*. The anonymous pamphlet entitled *Quinque verba* (ca. 1300), which is only a few folios in length, also provided the proper form of consent: "I take you as my husband. I take you as my wife." It proceeded to stipulate that when the words were said in the future tense, betrothal, not

---

contrahendum in occulto contrahunt per verba de presenti et mutuo consensu verum est ibi matrimonium sed non salubriter quia est contra ecclesiasticam institutionem" (Cambridge, University Library, MS Gg.iv.32, fol. 109vb).

[46]For an overview of Pagula and his work see Leonard E. Boyle, "The *Oculus sacerdotis* and Some Other Works of William of Pagula," *Transactions of the Royal Historical Society*, ser. 5, 5 (1955): 81–110, repr. in idem, *Pastoral Care, Clerical Education and Canon Law*, Essay 4.

[47]"Contrahitur matrimonium solo consensu per verba de presenti ut uir dicit 'ego accipio te in meam uxorem'. Et mulier dicit 'accipio te in meum uirum uel maritum'," *Oculus sacerdotis* in Oxford, Bodleian Library, MS Rawlinson A361, fol. 138r.

marriage, was contracted.[48] This little pamphlet, written in simple Latin, would have been accessible to parish priests with even the most rudimentary education. Its contents and ideas certainly reached the parishes, and through the mediation of the priest, the laity.

By the mid-fourteenth century the problems that could result from the consensual doctrine were occupying more space in pastoral manuals. The anonymous *Memoriale presbiterorum* (1344) reflects on the problem of bigamy that could result if a private exchange of consent *de presenti* with one partner were followed by a public marriage with a different one.[49] The author presented the case of a man who married and consummated his union with a woman whom he knew had previously exchanged consent *de presenti* with another man, who was still alive.[50] Significantly, the author stipulated that both the man and the woman should receive the same penalty, presumably because they were both cognizant of the bigamous nature of their union.

The *Memoriale presbiterorum* also stands in stark contrast to many of the thirteenth-century manuals that sought to

---

[48]"Et est matrimonium viri et mulieris legitima coniunccio per hec verba de presenti: ut vir dicat mulieri: Ego te accipio in uxorem meam; et mulier statim respondeat viro: Et ego te accipio in virum meum. Quando vero sunt verba de futuro tunc sunt sponsalia et non matrimonium" (London, British Library, MS Harley 52, fol. 87v).

[49]An analysis and edition of this work is found in Michael J. Haren, "A Study of the *Memoriale presbiterorum*: A Fourteenth-Century Confessional Manual for Parish Priests," 2 vols., D.Phil Diss. (Oxford Univ., 1975).

[50]"Item siquis duxerit vel acceperit sponsam alterius cum qua contractum fuit matrimonium per verba de presenti, fidem sibi dando, sciens ipsam habere sponsum superstitem et carnaliter cognoscendo, debet penitere per quadraginta dies in pane et aqua et nichilominus septem sequentibus annis debet penitere ad arbitrium descreti confessoris et quod dicitur de sponso de presenti quia eadem pena punitur mulier contrahens in hoc casu quam et vir" (Haren, "*Memoriale presbiterorum*," 2: 122).

inculcate the doctrine of consent with all its subtleties, complications, and complexities. Rather than encouraging priests to defend the consensual doctrine at all costs, even in the face of secular hostility or sacramental ambiguity, the *Memoriale* discusses at some length the penances appropriate for both priests and laity who took part in a clandestine marriage. This discussion also indicates some refinement in the distinctions between secret exchanges of consent and the private exchanges of consent that reflect popular usage.[51] The author distinguished a clandestine marriage as taking place when a couple insisted on exchanging consent before the banns were proclaimed "in the customary manner." He condemned any priest who did not prohibit such clandestine unions in his parish or who might in some way have assisted such a union. The rather harsh penalty of three years' suspension from celebrating divine offices is prescribed, longer if the circumstances seemed to warrant it. For example, if the couple so joined were consanguines or affines, an extremely grave penance ought to be enjoined on the priest and on any others present who were aware of the impediment.[52]

---

[51]See Shannon McSheffrey's discussion in this present volume, " 'I will never have none ayenst my faders will': Consent and the Making of Marriage in the Late Medieval Diocese of London." She notes that in London private marriages were public in the sense that friends and relatives were present, but clandestine because the Church played no formal role in the proceedings. P. J. P. Goldberg makes a similar observation for York (*Women, Work, and Life Cycle in a Medieval Economy: Women in York and Yorkshire c.1300–1520* [Oxford, 1992], pp. 234–36). Goldberg characterizes the three possible types of marriage (ibid., pp. 242–43). The private exchange of consent with friends and family needs always to be distinguished from a secret or occult exchange of consent for which there were no witnesses aside from the couple themselves. Although the Church considered both "clandestine," one union was far more defensible in court than was the other.

[52]A lengthy discussion is presented under the rubric "Penitencia presbiteri et eciam laici qui interest clandestino contractu matrimoniali contra prohibicionem canonis" (Haren, "*Memoriale presbiterorum*," 2: 124–25).

It is clear that the author of the *Memoriale presbiterorum* was less interested in secret, hidden exchanges of consent by the couple alone than with those private ceremonies that might well have had witnesses but had dispensed with the ecclesiastical solemnities. The *Memoriale*, then, indicates that by the mid-fourteenth century the doctrine of consent was widely disseminated and had been incorporated into the lives of the laity, who chose to marry privately, in the presence of family and friends but without the customary ecclesiastical observances.

This conclusion is reinforced by the evidence of the *Pupilla oculi* (1385), written by John de Burgo. He remarked that the couple administered the sacrament to themselves and that the presence of a priest, though required by the Church, was in fact unnecessary.[53] This is not to suggest that de Burgo was unaware of the problems of clandestine or occult unions. He admitted that in secret marriages one spouse could easily be repudiated and denied and left without any legal recourse.[54] He also reiterated the position set out in the *Memoriale presbiterorum* and recommended a thirty-day suspension from office for those priests who did not prohibit private unions.[55] In the end, however, he affirmed that although a marriage was

---

[53]". . . quod ad collationem huius sacramenti non requiritur ministerium sacerdotis et quod illa benedictio sacerdotalis quam solet presbyter facere sive preferre super coniuges; sive alie orationes ab ipso prelate non sunt forma sacramenti nec de eius essentia; sed quoddam sacramentale ad ornatum pertinens sacramenti" (*Pupilla oculi* [London, 1516], fol. 122v). Aspects of de Burgo's discussion on the formation of marriage have been examined in Henry Ansgar Kelly, "Clandestine Marriage and Chaucer's 'Troilus,'" *Viator* 4 (1973): 435–57.

[54]"Sepe enim in matrimonio occulte contracto alter coniugum mutat propositum et dimittit reliquum probationibus destitutum et sine remedio restitutionis" (*Pupilla oculi*, fol. 127r).

[55]"Et si sacerdos parochialis tales coniunctiones prohibere contempserit ab officio per triennium diem suspendi" (*Pupilla oculi*, fol. 127r).

contracted secretly, nevertheless it was a true marriage.[56] John de Burgo, then, took a somewhat more lenient stance, reminiscent of the thirteenth-century moralists. While condemning clandestine unions, as did the author of the *Memoriale*, he nevertheless affirmed their validity. While it became increasingly problematic in practice, nevertheless, the doctrine of consensual marriage continued to be promoted in pastoral manuals. An examination of some of the fourteenth-century vernacular treatises of moral guidance confirms that this was in fact the case.

Around the middle of the fourteenth century, John Thoresby, archbishop of York, prepared a Latin manual of moral guidance that circulated through the province along with his episcopal constitutions. Thoresby asked John de Taystek to translate and expand the manual into English, under the title *Instruction for the People* or *The Lay Folks' Catechism* (1357). In order to facilitate and ensure a wide dissemination, the English version was translated into easily-memorized verse.[57]

Marriage is defined in the section devoted to the sacraments.

> The sevent sacrement is Matirmonye,
> That is, a lawefull festenyng betwix man and woman,
> At thair bother assent for to lyve samen
> Withouten ony lousyng to thair life lastes,
>
> In remedi of syn, and getyng of grace,
> If it be taken in gode attent and clennesse of lif.[58]

---

[56]". . . matrimonium rite contractum quamvis occulte; sit verum matrimonium" (*Pupilla oculi*, fol. 127).

[57]*The Lay Folks' Catechism*, ed. Thomas F. Simmons and Henry E. Nolloth, EETS, o.s., 118 (1901), pp. xii–xvii.

[58]*Lay Folks' Catechism*, p. 68. The Latin original is formulaic and echoes Gratian: "Matrimonium est viri et mulieris conjunctio individua, vitae

This is a simple definition and virtually a verbatim translation of Thoresby's original Latin. It presents in the vernacular the standard definition of marriage, originally formulated by Gratian and repeated in legal and moral texts for two centuries.[59] Thus it gave the laity access to the accepted ecclesiastical definition of marriage, resting on the notion of consent and sacrament.

John Myrc's *Instructions for Parish Priests* (pre-1450), a treatise in verse, goes much further in its discussion of consent to marriage:[60]

> ʒet teche hem a-nother thynge,
> That ys a poynt of weddynge;
> He that wole chese hym a fere,
> And seyth to hyre on thys manere,
> "Here I take the to my wedded wyf,
> And there-to I plyghte þe my trowþe
> Wyth-owten cowpulle or fleschly dede,"
> He þat wommon mote wedde nede;
> For þaghe he or ho a-nother take,
> That word wole deuors make.[61]

In these few stanzas Myrc condensed the whole of the consensual doctrine and its many subtleties. He provided a vernacular model of the binding form of consent *de presenti*. The distinctions between consent *de presenti* and unconsummated

---

retinens consuetudinem, et in isto sacramento etiam confertur gratia si puro corde et sincero animo contrahatur" (ibid.).

[59]"Sunt enim nuptiae siue matrimonium uiri mulierisque coniunctio, *indiuidu-am uitae consuetudinem retinens*" (*Decretum* C.27 q.2 dict. ante c.1 and c.3). Gratian incorporated this phrasing from Justinian's *Institutes* 1.9. It was subsequently repeated by canonists and moralists throughout the Middle Ages.

[60]*Instructions for Parish Priests*, ed. Edward Peacock, EETS, o.s., 31 (rev. ed. 1902; repr. New York, 1969).

[61]*Instructions*, pp. 6–7.

consent *de futuro* are discussed. What is significant, however, is the allusion to private marriage contained in the passage. Myrc described present consent as at once both "divorcing" the man from any previous arrangements with other women while at the same time noting that the contract is incomplete and "He þat wommon mote wedde nede." Myrc tried to suggest that the exchange of consent was a binding union but one that nevertheless required a subsequent solemnization *in faciae ecclesiae*:

> Loke also þey make non odde weddynge,
> Lest alle ben cursed in that doynge.
> Preste & clerke and other also,
> That thylke serues huydeth so;
> But do ryȝt as seyn the lawes,
> Aske the banns thre halydawes.
> Then lete hem come and wytnes brynge
> To stonde by at here weddynge;
> So openlyche at the chyrche dore
> Lete hem eyther wedde othere.[62]

In a very general fashion Myrc condemned private unions without distinguishing between occult and clandestine ones, or between an exchange of consent by the couple alone and a private wedding in the presence of family and friends. Rather, he considered any union to be irregular if it had foregone the reading of the banns or solemnization at the church door.

In terms of measuring the dissemination of the consensual doctrine to the English populace, Myrc's treatise indicates that well into the fifteenth century moralists and parish priests continued to promote present consent as the sole criterion for a valid marriage. It also provides evidence of the perceived need to control the individualistic exercise of that freedom to

---

[62]*Instructions*, p. 7.

consent. Rather than emphasizing that consent *de presenti* formed a valid and indissoluble marriage, Myrc stated that it formed an indissoluble bond that must be followed by a church wedding. Yet in the process he also provided the exact formula, in the vernacular, that formed the valid, sacramental, and indissoluble bonds of matrimony. His subtle presentation suggests an attempt by an ecclesiastic to reassert the Church's control and supervision of marriage. Thus, Myrc does not say that clandestine weddings are irregular, but valid; rather, and somewhat more rigidly, he states that those who participate in any union without the due solemnities are "cursed."

Myrc's modifications and hesitations about the freedom to consent to marriage in fact underline the successful and widespread dissemination and implementation of the consensual doctrine by the middle of the fifteenth century. Consent *de presenti* was still promoted as the only essential requirement for marriage. The correct form of the words exchanged was circulating in the vernacular and was accessible to priest and parishioners alike.[63] There is a suggestion that the exercise of individual freedom to marry was more widespread than the Church might have wished, and attempts to control and curtail its exercise had begun. Nevertheless, the Church's doctrine of consensual marriage remained fundamental and continued to be promoted in Latin pastoral manuals and in their vernacular successors and, it may be assumed, in Sunday sermons and in individual confession across England well into the later Middle Ages.

---

[63] See S. McSheffrey's essay in this volume for evidence of the degree to which common folk were aware of the canon laws governing marriage. Fourteenth-century marriage cases in the diocese of York confirm that the laity were well acquainted with the canon law governing marriage. See Frederik Pederson, "Did the Medieval Laity Know the Canon Law Rules on Marriage? Some Evidence from Fourteenth-Century York Cause Papers," *Mediaeval Studies* 56 (1994): 111–52.

This is exactly what should be expected, given that in the twelfth century, influenced by thinkers like Abelard, the Church had developed a theology that focused on individual salvation rather than on corporate redemption.[64] Within this conceptual framework, marriage was a union of two individuals, a union that could help or hinder the individual's quest for salvation.[65] Secular marriage strategies, with the accompanying risks of bigamy, incest, and adultery, could seriously imperil this quest. By emphasizing the individual's freedom of choice in marriage, the Church was fulfilling its duty to assist the individual toward salvation. The diminution of familial, feudal, and manorial authority in marriage was an essential aspect of this process.

While in matrimonial matters the Church may have promoted individual autonomy and freedom from secular and familial constraints, at the same time it expected conformity to canon law and claimed exclusive jurisdiction over marriage. The evidence suggests, however, that ecclesiastical control of the individual was no more successful or complete than control by family or lord. While throughout the period pastoral manuals and episcopal legislation stressed the necessity of due solemnization, official sanction, and parental permission to marry, they also continued to provide people with the means to escape these controls. The doctrine of consensual marriage, despite its attendant problems of clandestinity, repudiation, and

---

[64]Morris, *Discovery*, p. 152.

[65]The active role that marriage could play in helping the individual toward salvation may be understood within the context of social relationships. For example, St. Bernard spoke of the various stages of love through which the individual progressed towards God. These began with love of self, moved to carnal love, and then extended outward to love of neighbor. See the discussion in Benton, "Individualism and Conformity," p. 150.

bigamy, endured in England into the eighteenth century.[66]

And so it was that, not long after the appearance of Myrc's *Instructions*, the Paston family experienced what may have been the first example, in their family, of individualistic tendencies in matters of marriage. Twenty years before the scandal precipitated by Richard and Margery, Margaret's sister-in-law and Margery's aunt, Elizabeth Paston, had exercised her freedom to consent to marriage by refusing to marry the man selected for her by her mother, Agnes Paston. In a plaintive letter Elizabeth's cousin Elisabeth Clere described the situation to John Paston I:

> . . . for she was never in so great sorrow as she is nowadays; for she may not speak with no man, whosoever come, ne not may see ne speak with my man, ne with servants of her mother's, but that she beareth on her hand otherwise than she meaneth. And she hath sin Eastern the most part be beaten once in the week or twice, and sometime twice on o day, and her head broken in two or three places.
>
> Wherefore, cousin, she hath sent to me by Friar Newton in great counsel, and prayeth me that I would send to you a letter of her heaviness, and pray you to be her good brother, as her trust is in you. . . .
>
> Wherefore, cousin, think on this matter, for sorrow oftentime causeth women to beset them otherwise than they should do; and if she were in that case I wot well ye would be sorry.[67]

---

[66]Christopher Lasch, "The Suppression of Clandestine Marriage in England: The Marriage Act of 1753," *Salmagundi* 26 (1974): 90–109.

[67]N. Davis, *Paston Letters: A Selection*, Letter 12, pp. 24–25. The original reads: ". . . for sche was neuer in so gret sorow as sche is now-a-dayes; for sche may not speke wyth no man, ho so euer come, ne not may se ne speke wyth my man ne wyth seruauntes of hir moderys but þat sche bereth hire an hand oþerwyse þan she menyth. And sche hath son Esterne þe most part be betyn onys in þe weke or twyes, and som tyme twyes on o day, and hir hed broken in to or thre places. Whe[r]for, cosyn, sche hath sent to me be Frere Newton in gret counsell and preyeth me þat I wold send to зow a letter of hir

Elizabeth Paston's recalcitrant individualism astonished her family and brought swift and harsh retribution. But in the end Elizabeth prevailed and did not marry for another decade.[68]

Elisabeth Clere's letter suggests that while a daughter could be subject to violent and unrestrained coercion from her parents, other members of her family might legitimately be expected to offer help and support. Thus, Elizabeth Paston was able to communicate with her cousin and seek her help to secure her brother's intervention in the matter. Family members, then, could not necessarily be counted upon to provide a united front against the stubborn individual. Furthermore, the letter also suggests that the cleric Friar Newton played more than the role of passive observer in the situation. He contacted Elisabeth Clere and, we can speculate, might even have tried to reason with Agnes Paston and mitigate her harsh treatment of her daughter. Thus, the advice to priests proffered by Richard Wetheringsett some two hundred years earlier seems to have taken root among the clergy. Friar Newton, by acting as messenger, helped Elizabeth Paston to exercise her autonomy in marriage. For all her isolation and the violent treatment she received, Elizabeth Paston was not entirely alone and abandoned in her resistance to her family's marriage strategies. She was able to enlist the help of relatives and the Church's representatives, help that might in part account for her ultimate success.

---

hevynes and prey yow to be hir good brothir, as hir trost is in ȝow. . . . Wherfore, cosyn, thynk on this mateer, for sorow oftyn tyme causeth women to be-set hem oþer-wyse þan þei schuld do, and if sche where in þat case I wot weel ȝe wold be sory" (N. Davis, *Paston Letters and Papers*, Letter 446, 2: 32).

[68]The case of Elizabeth Paston and the later case of her niece Margery are discussed in Ann S. Haskell, "The Paston Women on Marriage in Fifteenth-Century England," *Viator* 4 (1973): 459–71.

Perhaps it was the example of her aunt that inspired Margery in her steadfast adherence to the validity of her secret marriage to Richard Calle. It is perhaps more startling that, having lived through the tragic treatment of her sister-in-law, Margaret Paston did not behave toward her daughter with greater leniency and compassion. After all, two subsequent marriages had left Elizabeth Paston one of the wealthiest women in England; her individualistic behavior had not, in fact, undermined the Paston's overall economic strategy and well-being.[69]

Regardless of the role that the Paston family's unique experience may have played in Margery and Richard's actions, they had plenty of opportunity to absorb the prevailing theology of marriage, a theology that was circulating across English parishes in pastoral manuals.[70] Thus, well before their interrogation by the bishop of Norwich, Richard Calle could write to Margery Paston with sadness at their separation but with confidence in the future:

> Mine own lady and mistress, and before God very true wife, I with heart full sorrowful recommend me unto you, as he that cannot be merry nor naught shall be till it be otherwise with us than it is yet; for this life that we lead now is neither pleasure to God nor to the world, *considering the great bond of matrimony that is made betwixt*

---

[69]Haskell, "Paston Women," p. 467.

[70]Nor are Richard and Margery an isolated example. Goldberg cites the 1490 case of Elena Couper, who exchanged consent in the face of parental disapproval; confronted by her angry father, she is reported to have said, "Sir, that at I have doon I will performe if the law will suffre it for I wyll have hym whosoever say nay to it. And I desire no more of your goodes but your blessyng" (*Women, Work, and Life Cycle*, p. 247). Keith Dockray has argued that 15th-century letters indicate the importance of personal preference in marriage: "Why Did Fifteenth-Century English Gentry Marry? The Pastons, Plumptons and Stonors Reconsidered," in *Gentry and Lesser Nobility in Late Medieval Europe*, ed. Michael Jones (New York, 1986), pp. 61–80.

us, and also the great love that hath be, and as I trust yet is, betwixt us, and as on my part never greater.[71]

The Pastons did everything they could to break the relationship between Margery and Richard. When they could not, they ostracized and disinherited their daughter. The bishop of Norwich reminded Margery of her familial obligations and deplored her headstrong disobedience. But for all the coercion and social disapproval, Margery and Richard remained steadfast, secure in the legitimacy and indissolubility of their union.[72] And ultimately, however grudgingly and ungraciously, both the Church and the Pastons were forced to accept it.

Social control and filial obedience may have been the norm in medieval England, a norm supported by the Church. That same Church, however, was also deeply involved in furthering the inherent dignity of each individual and advancing the cause of ecclesiastical independence from control by either family or lord. Through its insistence on consensual marriage the medieval Church gave ideological and practical support to those individuals who sought to free themselves from seigniorial,

---

[71]N. Davis, *Paston Letters: A Selection*, Letter 85, pp. 178–79 (emphasis added). The original reads: "Myn owne lady and mastres, and be-for God very trewe wyff, I wyth herte full sorrowefull recomaunde me vnto you as he that can not be mery nor nought schalbe tyll it be otherwice wyth vs thenne it is yet; for thys lyff þat we lede nough is nowther plesur to Godde nor to the worlde, concederyng the gret bonde of matrymonye þat is made be-twix vs, and also the greete loue þat hath be, and as I truste yet is, be-twix vs, and as on my parte neuer gretter" (N. Davis, *Paston Letters and Papers*, Letter 861, 2: 498).

[72]As Michael Sheehan observed, "while the controls of lordship were ephemeral in comparison to those exercised by the family, nevertheless even the latter, strong as they were, were much weakened by the insistence on the rights of the spouses" ("The European Family and Canon Law," *Continuity and Change* 6 [1991]: 356).

social, and familial constraints. This support was known and accessible at all levels of English society, in urban and rural settings, because the Church had developed effective means of communicating its doctrines to the laity. Pastoral manuals figured prominently in this process.

"I WILL NEVER HAVE NONE AYENST MY FADERS WILL": CONSENT AND THE MAKING OF MARRIAGE IN THE LATE MEDIEVAL DIOCESE OF LONDON[1]

Shannon McSheffrey

In the last several decades, scholars of medieval canon law have drawn attention to the importance of the doctrine of consent in the making of marriage in the later Middle Ages. Reacting against those who have argued that marriage choices were controlled mainly by parents who saw their children's unions as a way of increasing family income and stature, Michael M. Sheehan and others have emphasized the centrality of the exchange of consent by the principals in the late medieval sacrament of marriage.[2]

---

[1]I would like to express my appreciation to Michael Sheehan for sparking my interest in medieval marriage; to Eric Reiter and Jacqueline Murray for their comments on this paper; to Sandy Ramos for research assistance; and to the Social Sciences and Humanities Research Council of Canada and Concordia University for research funds.

[2]Sheehan, "The Formation and Stability of Marriage in Fourteenth-Century England: Evidence of an Ely Register," *Mediaeval Studies* 33 (1971): 228–63; idem, "Marriage and Family in English Conciliar and Synodal Legislation," in *Essays in Honour of Anton Charles Pegis*, ed. J. Reginald O'Donnell (Toronto, 1974), pp. 205–14; idem, "Choice of Marriage Partner in the Middle Ages: Development and Mode of Application of a Theory of

Parents could not marry off their children without any thought to their wishes, because the principals themselves had to agree in order for any marriage to be valid. Indeed, far from the parental control envisaged by C. S. Lewis and more recently by Lawrence Stone and his school,[3] Sheehan's examination of evidence from the diocese of Ely in the fourteenth century led him to argue that the Church's doctrine of consent contributed to the development of an "astonishingly individualistic" late medieval marital system.[4] Alan Macfarlane carried Sheehan's conclusions even further when he argued that after the Black Death, English people courted and married without any concern at all for the thoughts and wishes of others.[5]

In this debate over the control of marriage in the pre-modern period, historians have tended to see a rigid dichotomy between individual free choice in marriage (or marriage for love) and control of marriage choice by family (marriage for political or financial reasons). Most medieval historians have rejected the full-fledged form of the "marriage for money" argument—certainly we can no longer doubt that for the majority of the medieval population, affection, attraction, and

---

Marriage," *Studies in Medieval and Renaissance History*, n.s., 1 (1978): 3–33. For other literature on canon law and the consensual theory, see James A. Brundage, *Law, Sex, and Christian Society in Medieval Europe* (Chicago, 1987), pp. 187, 235–38, 262–69, 334–35, 414, 588, 615.

[3]Lewis, *The Allegory of Love: A Study in Medieval Tradition* (London, 1958), p. 13; Stone, *The Family, Sex and Marriage in England 1500–1800* (London, 1977), pp. 70–71, 81, 128; and Edward Shorter, *The Making of the Modern Family* (New York, 1975), pp. 54–65.

[4]"Formation and Stability," p. 263.

[5]*Marriage and Love in England: Modes of Reproduction 1300–1840* (Oxford, 1986), pp. 119–25; Macfarlane has (erroneously) read Sheehan's conclusions regarding the theory and practice of the consensual model of marriage to apply to England only.

personal choice were major considerations in making a marriage. But this need not lead us to accept the directly opposite point of view, that marriages were made without any consideration of other factors besides love and without any participation by other parties besides the principals.[6]

If, as many historians believe, late medieval England was a patriarchal[7] society in which children owed obedience and respect to their parents and other elders, how did the radical notions of free choice promoted by the consensual theory of marriage work in practice? Laypeople did not live in ignorance of the Church's teachings on the sacrament of matrimony; as marital litigation[8] from the late medieval diocese of London

---

[6]Several early-modern historians have made this point. See Diana O'Hara, "'Ruled by my friends': Aspects of Marriage in the Diocese of Canterbury, c. 1540–1570," *Continuity and Change* 6 (1991): 9–41; Miranda Chaytor, "Household and Kinship: Ryton in the Late 16th and Early 17th Centuries," *History Workshop Journal* 10 (1980): 26–29; R. M. Smith's historiographical examination of pre-modern English marriage, "Marriage Processes in the English Past: Some Continuities," in *The World We Have Gained: Histories of Population and Social Structure*, ed. Lloyd Bonfield, Richard M. Smith, and Keith Wrightson (Oxford, 1986), pp. 43–99, esp. 67–69.

[7]*Patriarchal* and *patriarchy* are used here in the sense that the model of the father-ruled household was considered ideal and that this ideal extended out of the family into society as a whole, so that men rather than women, particularly older men, were seen as the natural rulers. Patriarchy within late medieval elite families is discussed in Joel T. Rosenthal, *Patriarchy and Families of Privilege in Fifteenth-Century England* (Philadelphia, 1991), pp. 14–19 and passim. By no means was this ideal of masculine conduct unproblematic; see Lyndal Roper's discussion in *Oedipus and the Devil: Witchcraft, Sexuality, and Religion in Early Modern Europe* (London, 1994), esp. pp. 37–52, 55–56, 107–20. Gerda Lerner, *The Creation of Patriarchy* (New York, 1986), pp. 238–39, defines patriarchy in a more universal sense, but here the emphasis is on its historical specificity in late medieval England rather than its universality.

[8]For medieval ecclesiastical courts and their jurisdiction over marriage, see R. H. Helmholz, *Marriage Litigation in Medieval England* (London, 1974);

makes clear, the principals and those who helped them make their marriage vows knew the necessity of obtaining the free consent of both parties to the union.[9] The laity also understood that if there was no impediment, a man and a woman could establish a marriage by their consent alone, even if their families, employers, or lords disapproved. But while the permission of others was not required to create a valid marriage, nonetheless, late medieval women and men often consulted their parents and other "friends" when making this crucial life decision. Sometimes they even refused to make such a commitment without the consent of the important people in their lives, asserting that they would marry no one without it. Legally, only the present consent of the principals was necessary to create a binding contract of marriage; but socially, the right and wise thing to do was to marry with the advice and sometimes the consent of relatives, employers, and friends. "I will do as my fader will have me," said Margery Sheppard of East Ham in 1486, "I will never have none ayenst my faders will."[10]

This examination of the question of consent is based on a rich but as yet largely untapped source for the social history of late medieval English marriage: depositions given before the

---

L. R. Poos, "The Heavy-Handed Marriage Counsellor: Regulating Marriage in Some Later-Medieval English Local Ecclesiastical-Court Jurisdictions," *American Journal of Legal History* 39 (1995): 291–309 (my thanks to Dr. Poos for allowing me to look at this paper before publication).

[9]See, e.g., London, Greater London Record Office, MS DL/C/205, Consistory Court Deposition Book, 1467–76 (hereafter GLRO DL/C/205), fols. 4v–5v, 10r–v; and London, Guildhall Library, MS 9065, Commissary Court Deposition Book, 1489–97 (hereafter GL 9065), fols. 7r, 23r–v. For indications of how the laity was educated regarding the doctrine of consent, see Jacqueline Murray's essay in this present volume, "Individualism and Consensual Marriage: Some Evidence from Medieval England."

[10]GL 9065, fol. 20r; see below, at n. 34.

diocese of London's consistory and commissary courts in the periods 1467–76 and 1489–97.[11] Since the diocese of London included both the urban parishes of the metropolitan City itself and the more rural parishes of the counties of Essex and Middlesex and parts of Hertfordshire, the depositions allow us a glimpse of both urban and rural populations.

According to witnesses giving testimony in the several hundred marriage cases in these two deposition books, most late fifteenth-century couples from the diocese of London made no explicit reference to the consent of others when they married one another. In the majority of cases, the principals exchanged consent unconditionally ("I, John, take you, Margaret" and "I, Margaret, take you, John") in a domestic setting before witnesses. This corroborates what Sheehan and others have argued: that young people below elite social levels[12] routinely chose prospective mates for themselves through the normal course of social interaction and that the canonical requirement of consent was typically observed. But couples did

---

[11]GLRO DL/C/205 and GL 9065. See selected cases from these deposition books in *Love and Marriage in Late Medieval London*, ed. and trans. Shannon McSheffrey (Kalamazoo, 1995).

[12]Scholars generally agree that deponents and litigants in marital suits represent a socioeconomic cross-section of late medieval society, excluding the very poor and the very rich. See Sheehan, "Formation and Stability," p. 234; Helmholz, *Marriage Litigation*, pp. 160–61; Martin Ingram, "Spousals Litigation in the English Ecclesiastical Courts, c. 1350–1640," in *Marriage and Society: Studies in the Social History of Marriage*, ed. R. B. Outhwaite (New York, 1981), pp. 44–45; P. J. P. Goldberg, "Marriage, Migration, and Servanthood: The York Cause Paper Evidence," in *Woman Is a Worthy Wight: Women in English Society c. 1200–1500*, ed. Goldberg (Gloucester, 1992), p. 3. There was a heavy gender imbalance among deponents in favor of men; see L. R. Poos, *A Rural Society after the Black Death: Essex, 1350–1525* (Cambridge, 1991), p. 166; Laura Gowing, "Women, Sex and Honour: The London Church Courts, 1572–1640," Ph.D. Diss. (Univ. of London, 1993), p. 179.

not find and marry one another in a social vacuum; the people who lived around a couple, their relatives, friends, neighbors, and employers, assisted, prodded, and mediated in the making of a marriage. Most exchanged consent in the presence of family, employers, or significant others of some sort who thus indicated their tacit consent to the match. This was especially true of women and of those who were marrying young and for the first time.

Thus, for many the consent of parents or others acting in their place was implicit.[13] Less common was the practice that is the subject of this essay: making a contract of marriage explicitly conditional on the consent of family or friends. But by no means was this unusual; witnesses in about twenty-five cases in the late fifteenth-century London deposition books testified that such a condition was made. Typical of these was the response of Joan Kenryk of London, who testified that she answered William Heley's proposal of marriage in 1468 thus: "if she could acquire and have the will and consent of her great-grandfather, David Kenryk, she freely wished to consent to have him."[14] Such a condition was not necessary for all, but it was well within the range of expected behavior for young people embarking on matrimony.

Did city dwellers have more freedom of choice in their marriages than their rural counterparts? Recently P. J. P. Goldberg,

---

[13] As Beatrice Gottlieb points out, even in "love marriages" parental consent was often a necessary condition of marriage: "When parents disapproved, the usual result was that the match was broken off" ("The Meaning of Clandestine Marriage," in *Family and Sexuality in French History*, ed. Robert Wheaton and Tamara K. Hareven [Philadelphia, 1980], p. 69).

[14] GLRO DL/C/205, fol. 48r: "Willelmus Heley tractavit et communicavit plures cum ista iurata de matrimonio inter eos habendo, et ista iurata eidem respondebat quod si posset adquirere et habere voluntatem et consensum proavi sui, videlicet David Kenryk, libenter voluit consentire ipsum habere."

studying marriage and servanthood in York and Yorkshire, has argued that in the century after the Black Death both young men and women working as servants in the city of York were able to make marriage choices much more autonomously than were their country counterparts in rural Yorkshire.[15] The diocese of London in the second half of the fifteenth century does not show the same pattern: there is no measurable distinction between the urban and rural cases. This may be due to geographical differences between northern and southern England. Or, as Goldberg suggests, economic factors may be responsible. He hypothesizes that women's freedom to make marital choices was particularly linked to their economic independence; contraction of women's employment opportunities after 1450 may have eroded their matrimonial freedom.[16]

Thus while many young people continued to immigrate to London in the second half of the fifteenth century to find work, often making their first marriage while living away from their parents and other family members, they by no means made the decision to marry or not to marry on their own. Witnesses' testimony about the preliminaries to marriage in late fifteenth-century London show that even if family members were out of the picture, others would step in to make sure that this critical life decision was made sensibly.[17] Among young servants about to embark on their first marriage,

---

[15] *Women, Work, and Life Cycle in a Medieval Economy: Women in York and Yorkshire c.1300–1520* (Oxford, 1992), pp. 236, 243–55, 261–63, 273–75.

[16] For economic change see Goldberg, *Women, Work, and Life Cycle*, esp. pp. 261–63. For the diocese of London there is no measurable change between the set of depositions dating from the 1460s and 1470s and those from the 1490s.

[17] For discussion of these points for the late 16th and early 17th centuries, see O'Hara's discussion of "fictive kin" and friends in "'Ruled by my friends,'" pp. 9–41; Gowing, "Women, Sex and Honour," pp. 107, 114–15, 117.

employers were particularly important. As some cases indicate, parents often invested masters and mistresses with the responsibility of finding a suitable marriage for their children.[18]

Much more striking about the twenty-five cases in which one of the principals placed the condition of third-party consent is gender difference—about four-fifths of those who made this qualification were women.[19] Although gender differences have rarely surfaced in the debates about love or money in medieval marriages, this phenomenon should not surprise us, knowing what we do about gender and late medieval society. The depositions as a whole show that young men often acted independently in their marriage choices, while young women were more reliant on and subject to the involvement of parents and others in making this pivotal decision. These roles prefigured the relative status of wives and husbands: wives were to obey and rely upon their husbands, the main decision-makers in families.

The involvement of other parties besides the principals in the formation of a marriage, offering advice, mediating, or in fact making the marriage decision themselves through the giving or withholding of consent, indicates a number of things about the courtship process. Expectations that young people, especially women, would marry according to the advice of those older and wiser sometimes indicated a real conviction on the parts of the principals and the advisors that a good

---

[18]See, e.g., GL 9065, fols. 268v, 277v; GLRO DL/C/205, fols. 166r–168r, 172v–175r. Sometimes a woman called upon both parents and employers to give their consent (possibly because the women had to be released from service): e.g., GL 9065, fols. 52r, 182r, 188r; GLRO DL/C/205, fols. 56v–57v. Two cases show that a man's employer might be concerned that a woman was enticing his apprentice away from his work: GL 9065, fols. 72v, 113v–114r.

[19]The same held true for late 16th- and early 17th-century London. See Gowing, "Women, Sex and Honour," pp. 115–16.

marriage would result.[20] At other times, the invocation of parental approval reflected the financial or physical power some parents wielded over their young marriageable daughters or sons (the emotional and financial beatings endured by Margery Paston being a case in point[21]). But appeal to the consent of third parties could also be used as a strategy in marital negotiations, especially by women whose reactive role in courtship left them few other ways to control the process.[22] In this essay I explore the social meaning of the invocation of third-party consent and what it implies about marriage, gender, and family in late medieval English society.

Both partners sometimes used the condition of parental approval pro forma, as a courtesy that established good relations in the future between parents and the new married couple. When Maude Gyll of London was asked in 1491 if she would take Laurence Wyberd as her husband, she answered yes, but conditionally: "wyth my fadyrs leve and my moders." Her parents, who were there present, immediately replied, almost formulaically, "Thow shalt have good leve therto, and goddis blessyng and owres."[23] When Elizabeth Isaak and John Bolde of London exchanged consent in 1470, Elizabeth placed the

---

[20]Chaytor, "Household and Kinship," pp. 42–44. See also O'Hara, " 'Ruled by my friends,' " pp. 13–17; Peter Rushton, "Property, Power and Family Networks: The Problem of Disputed Marriage in Early Modern England," *Journal of Family History* 11 (1986): 205–19, esp. pp. 207, 216.

[21]*Paston Letters and Papers of the Fifteenth Century*, ed. Norman Davis, 2 vols. (Oxford, 1971–76), 1: 341–43, 541, 549; 2: 498–500.

[22]For other discussions of women's strategic use of customs that otherwise appear to restrict their choice, see Natalie Zemon Davis, "Boundaries and the Sense of Self in Sixteenth-Century France," in *Reconstructing Individualism: Autonomy, Individuality, and the Self in Western Thought*, ed. Thomas C. Heller et al. (Stanford, Calif., 1986), pp. 53–63, esp. 55, 61–63; Gowing, "Women, Sex and Honour," pp. 115–16.

[23]GL 9065, fols. 3v–5r, quotations at fol. 4r.

proviso that her twenty-year-old brother, witnessing the contract, would give his consent. He, like Maude Gyll's parents,
immediately proffered his blessing, thereby fulfilling the
condition.[24] The bride's invitations to her family to participate,
in effect, in her offer of consent to the union deflected part of
the decision-making onto a third party, so that a young woman
not socialized to be decisive might be relieved of some of that
burden. Equally important, such invocations also helped to secure the good will of the bride's parents. John Bolde said this
explicitly when later he met Elizabeth Isaak's mother, Beatrice
Isaak, and asked her approval of the match, "to this end, that
Beatrice would love John better, because he had taken Elizabeth as his wife."[25] Beatrice immediately acquiesced and gave
her blessing. In this case, John asked Elizabeth's mother's consent after the marriage was already a *fait accompli*; withholding it could not prevent or end the marriage, but the fact
that he had asked her might lead her to "love John better."

For others, appeal to the advice and consent of third parties
was more than a gesture of good will—it reflected a real
expectation that women should rely on the advice of others
before making a firm decision about marriage. Joan Bacster's
answer to Richard Parker in 1474 exemplifies the stance of
proper behavior adopted by many women: "I will have you as
my husband if my uncle Thomas Roby and his wife Ann, my
aunt, will consent to it; otherwise I will never have you as my
husband nor any other man."[26]

---

[24]GLRO DL/C/205, fols. 131v–132r.

[25]GLRO DL/C/205, fol. 132r–v, quotation at fol. 132v: ". . . ad hunc finem
quod dicta Beatrix melius diligeret dictum Johannem, pro eo quod ipse
accepit antedictam Elizabeth in eius uxorem. Et dicta Beatrix statim dedit ad
requisacionem dicti Johannis voluntatem suam."

[26]GLRO DL/C/205, fol. 277r: "Et ego volo habere vos in maritum meum si
avunculus meus Thomas Roby et Anna eius uxor avuncula mea velu<erunt>

The 1467 case of Robert Forster vs. Katherine Pekke[27] shows some of the complexities involved in a young London servant's recourse to the advice and consent of her employers in the matter of her marriage. Katherine Pekke told the court when she appeared to answer Robert Forster's suit that she had agreed to marry Robert on the condition that her master and mistress would give their approval. But when she broached the subject with John Reymonde, her master, he told her that he was not inclined to the match: Katherine was still too young and Robert was not very suitable. Besides, Reymonde later told his wife, Robert had not come in person to speak to him about the marriage as he should have. So Katherine reluctantly dismissed Robert, thanking him for his kind offer.

Soon another suitor, Thomas Goolde, sought her hand and, bolder than Robert Forster had been, he solicited and gained her master's consent. Katherine told her employer, Reymonde, that she was ready to contract formally with Goolde, and Reymonde arranged for him to come to the house to make a properly witnessed contract. But as Reymonde made preparations for this formal ceremony, his wife came to him and advised him to put Goolde off for the time being. Katherine had confided to her that perhaps she had, after all, exchanged unconditional vows of present consent with her first suitor, Robert Forster. Katherine, when consulted about the problem,

---

ad hoc consentire, sin autem nunquam volo habere vos in maritum meum neque aliquem alium." This conversation took place in Coventry. For other examples see below and GLRO DL/C/205, fols. 11v–12r, 250v; GL 9065, fols. 24v, 126r, 149v.

[27]GLRO DL/C/205, fol. 4r–v. The occasion of the suit in this case is unclear. Although most cases involved enforcement of marriage contracts, it appears that Robert Forster sued Katherine Pekke in order to establish that a marriage had not taken place, as Katherine herself claimed that she had contracted with Robert and wished to have him as her husband.

"said that she wished to be ruled by them in all things"[28] and would do whatever they thought best. Reymonde decided that Robert Forster was not such a bad match after all and invited him to come to the house. Robert and Katherine formally exchanged vows of present consent in front of Reymonde and his wife and his own master and mistress.[29]

In this case, Katherine Pekke played the role of the obedient although perhaps foolish young woman who wanted to marry appropriately and with her employers' consent. Whether her actions were in fact disingenuous is an open question—in the end she contracted with the man she had apparently wanted. But certainly her testimony and that of Reymonde and his wife indicate that she very properly appeared to desire to abide by their wishes in the important matter of her marriage.

Although women's marriage choices were clearly circumscribed by the custom of acquiring the consent of family or others to their marriages, women could sometimes employ this apparent restriction to their advantage. Some used the convention of seeking the consent or advice of important people in their lives to prevaricate when faced with a proposal of marriage they were not yet sure they wanted to accept or reject. A conditional contract of marriage provided an escape clause, serving the functions of buying time and displacing rejection to another person. Lucy Braggis of London, for instance, told Robert Pope that before she would contract with any man she wished to have the advice of her brothers. Later, when Robert pressured her to give a final answer, she responded to his ultimatum by saying that her brothers would easily provide her with another husband: there were plenty of other fish in the

---

[28]GLRO DL/C/205, fol. 7r: "Dixit dicta Katerina isti iurato et uxori sue quod voluit regi in hac re secundum eos in omnibus."

[29]GLRO DL/C/205, fols. 4r–v, 6v–7v, 10r–v.

sea.[30] William Knollys of Hornchurch, one of the few men making their contracts conditional on the consent of parents, seems to have used the condition of his mother's approval quite cynically; he confessed in court that he never in fact intended to marry Agnes Lanther but contracted conditionally with her and gave her gifts in order to "continue with her in sin."[31] In other cases the motive may have been more generous; despite the answer of Agnes Parker of Twickenham to John Pollyn's offer of marriage, "that she wished to be governed following her parents and her friends, and otherwise not," she later contracted with another man apparently without condition.[32] An answer that passed off the rejection to an amorphous group of authoritative people like "parents and friends" could leave options open and save bruised feelings.

In some cases the displacement did not work: some children expecting their parents or employers to perform the hard task of delivering a negative answer were disappointed. Joan Cardif of Walthamstow refused to give her final consent to a marriage until her mother had offered her approval; when her mother gave her blessing, however, Joan refused to go through with the marriage. Her desire to have her mother's consent may have reflected her own ambivalence about the marriage. When she had made up her own mind, though, her mother refused to co-operate and in fact testified against Joan when the man in question sued her.[33] Similarly, when Richard Tymond of East Ham asked Margery Sheppard to marry him, she contracted

---

[30]GLRO DL/C/205, fol. 36v.

[31]GLRO DL/C/205, fol. 55v: "Non tamen illa dona dedit eidem Agneti ad intencionem habendi eam in uxorem suam, sed ad complacendum et continuandum sibi in peccata."

[32]GL 9065, fols. 24v, 26r: "Dixit quod voluit gubernari secundum parentes et amicos suos et aliter non."

[33]GL 9065, fols. 22r–24r.

conditionally, saying "I will never have none ayenst my faders will." Like Joan Cardif's mother, Margery's father later consented; but despite her protestations of filial obedience, Margery balked at honoring the contract, even when her father likewise appeared in the case as the opposition's witness.[34]

Women sometimes placed the onus to seek and obtain the consent of their families or employers on the man making the offer of marriage. This could function as a proof of commitment, almost a quest before the hand of the fair maiden could be won. Joan Corvey of Rayleigh (Essex) responded to Robert Philipson's marriage proposition by saying that she would marry him if he could procure the consent of her parents and of John Pyke, her master.[35] One London woman, Alice Cawode, imposed such a condition on two different men, Gilbert Nicolson and John Wymysbury. But in her case the condition may have served only as a courtship strategy to illustrate her coy reluctance, because with both men she quickly dropped it to contract unconditionally.[36] In other cases it indicated a real necessity; when Herbert Rowland of London pressed Elizabeth Croft to marry him, she told him she would never marry anyone without the consent of Master Banks; "if that ye can get my Maisters good wil," she told him, "ye shal have myne." Later, when she did give in and married Herbert without her employer's knowledge, her actions caused considerable ire.[37]

Prevarications could cloak women's attempts to control their marital choices with an invocation or even a pretense of meek obedience to proper authority. Women's manipulation of

---

[34]GL 9065, fols. 18r–20r, quotation at fol. 20r.

[35]GL 9065, fol. 52r.

[36]GLRO DL/C/205, fols. 10v–12r.

[37]GL 9065, fols. 181v–182r, 188r–v; quotation at fol. 182r.

these customary expectations could work both in courtship and in court. Rose Langtoft of London did what many other women did when faced in a suit with a contract they did not wish to fulfill: she claimed that the contract she had made with Robert Smith had been conditional on her parent's consent. Only later did she admit that she had contracted with him freely and without condition.[38] When looking for an escape, many women seized upon a version of events that painted them as cautious, obedient, and appropriately respectful of the wishes of their parents or employers. Men's escape hatches were different but also culturally constructed: one common excuse offered by men but never by women was that they may have implied marriage in order to gain sexual favors but that they never explicitly agreed to marry and did not ever intend to.[39]

The prevarications of Rose Langtoft and others only worked because many women did indeed wish to have the advice and consent of their family, employers, and friends, and because in some cases the consequences of marrying without that advice and consent were grave. In other words, a convention can only be manipulated if it represents a normal expectation. Many depositions make clear that a couple heading for marriage and those who lived around them presumed the influence and interest of family or employers in matrimonial negotiations. John Fynk of Walthamstow assumed that Joan Munden's brother held great sway over her when he asked the brother to advise Joan to end her relationship with a certain "knave" so that John Fynk himself could marry her.[40] These interested third parties, naturally enough, often witnessed the exchange of consent. As John Gardiner said when he asked Ellen

---

[38]GLRO DL/C/205, fols. 166r–170r, 172v–177r, 182v.

[39]For instance, see GLRO DL/C/205, fols. 55v, 150r–v, 196r–v.

[40]GL 9065, fol. 149r.

Harrison and William Gilbert of London to contract marriage
again in his presence, he wanted to know for certain about the
contract precisely "because she [Ellen] is my relative."[41]

As witnesses testified, some women anticipated and feared
the disapproval of their parents. When Thomas Smyth met
Agnes Chambyrleyn in Botulph Lane and commented, "Agnes,
they tell me that you are John Holder's wife and promised to
him," she answered, "I am amazed that you know about this
matter between him and me. I beg you not to tell my parents,
because if you do, they will be angry with me."[42] John Bryan,
acting as an intermediary between William Fostar and Joan
Harries, asked Joan whether she loved William and wished to
marry him. She replied that she loved him as much as he loved
her, but she begged John Bryan not to reveal this to anyone
before she had the assent of her parents to the match.[43]

Parents and employers often played an active role in
finding and negotiating a marriage for a child. A few cases in
fact show contracts being arranged with ostensibly little participation at all by the women involved. John Mendham, for
instance, stated in his examination that he had arranged with
Elizabeth Seyve's uncle that she would marry him before he
ever approached Elizabeth about it. He later met Elizabeth in a
London tavern and asked her there if she wished to fulfill the

---

[41]GL 9065, fol. 199v: "Eo quod fuit cognata huic iurato."

[42]GLRO DL/C/205, fol. 114v: "Iste iuratus obviabat dicte Agneti, ad tunc exi-
stenti in venella vocata Botulphe lane iuxta Bylyngesgate, quam alloquebatur
iste iuratus sub ista forma: 'Agnes, dicitur michi quod vos estis uxor Johannis
Holder et eidem affidata,' que incontinenti respondebat huic iurato et dixit,
'Ego miror multum quod vos cognoscitis istam materiam inter ipsum et me.
Rogo vos ne referatis parentibus meis, quia si feceritis, culpabar ab eisdem;
sed vobis dico plane quod ipse est maritus meus et eidem sum affidata.'"

[43]GL 9065, fol. 271v.

promise of marriage made between him and her uncle.[44] Similarly, William Chowe told the court that he went to the home
of Ellen Mortymer's father in the town of Bermondsey and
told Mortymer that he had come there with the intention of
having Ellen as his wife, "yf hit plese yowe and hyr togydyr."
Mortymer and William proceeded to discuss the marriage
between them. Mortymer ended by saying, "Y maye fynde yn
my hert that ye shall have her to your wyfe"—an interesting
parallel with the phrasing commonly used by the principals in
an exchange of future consent. Ellen herself was quite literally
marginalized in the deposition; while the scribe noted her
presence at this discussion in the main body of the text, he
squeezed her own words of consent to the marriage (without
which the case had no canonical validity) into the margin.[45] In
these cases the couple may have come to a decision about their
marriage independent of and prior to the negotiations with the
woman's male relatives, but the versions the men presented to
the court pushed into the foreground their discussions with the
male relatives rather than with the women themselves.

In many cases the interests of family and the interests of
the marriageable daughter or son could coincide and the path
to marriage run smoothly. But a child who married contrary to
the wishes of the important people in his or her life could
expect repercussions ranging from displeasure to disinheritance
and disowning. Parents and employers had a number of ways
of realizing their wishes if the marital choices of their children
did not match their own. Their most effective weapon was
financial. According to his own confession, Stephan Robert, a
young Kentish gentleman, desperately wanted to marry Angela
Harewe, the stepdaughter of a London merchant, but he

---

[44] GLRO DL/C/205, fol. 53v.

[45] GL 9065, fols. 114v–115r.

steadfastly refused to contract with her without the consent of his friends. His father's will makes clear the reason for his reluctance to follow his own whims rather than the advice of his friends: the executors, no doubt the friends to which he referred, were to deliver his inheritance to him only at their discretion if he married before the age of twenty-four.[46] Dowries that parents often provided for a woman's first marriage represented an obvious means of control of marriage choice. In some cases men made their contracts conditional on the consent of the woman's parents and their delivery of a suitable gift. James Wolmer of London made the transfer of a dowry a condition of consenting to marriage with Agnes Henley.[47] John Ely of London agreed to marry Agnes Whiting-don only if her father's delivery of 5 marks was assured by a certain date.[48] Some expressed willingness to face penury for love, like Londoner Alice Seton, who confessed to another female servant that she would marry John Jenyn even if he received nothing from his uncle and she received nothing from her aunt. In the end, though, Alice Seton did not fulfill this high-minded wish and backed out of the marriage.[49]

Family members and employers had other means of making their disapproval of an unsuitable match clear and imposing their own choices. While both men and women attempted to force their will upon their children (the case of Margery Paston and her mother's intransigence again comes to mind[50]), the

---

[46]GLRO DL/C/205, fols. 37r–41r; London, Public Record Office, Prerogative Court of Canterbury Wills, Prob. 11/4, fols. 167r–169v, Will of John Roberd of Cranbrook, 1460.

[47]GLRO DL/C/205, fol. 246r.

[48]GL 9065, fols. 10r–12r.

[49]GL 9065, fol. 64r.

[50]See n. 21 above.

depositions show that fathers tended to be more successful.[51]
Men had more political and legal *savoir-faire* due to their
greater participation in public life, and some fathers used their
connections and skills in these arenas to make or break
matches. Although canon law made no provision for parental
consent, some fathers evidently felt it was their right to inter-
fere. When Richard Cordell of Enfield arranged to have banns
of forthcoming marriage issued between him and Margery
Ford, Margery's father, Hugh Ford, objected vociferously.
When he was asked in court on whose authority he did this, he
answered that it was on his own authority, and no one else's.[52]
According to a witness, Robert Bate of Saint Albans objected
when his daughter Christian made a contract with John Lorymer and was somehow able to impede church solemnization of
that marriage. Instead he moved to promote a marriage between Christian and another man, William Twygge. When both
men sued Christian in the consistory court, the witnesses for
William Twygge's case said that they testified at the request of
Christian's father, thus suggesting that he was orchestrating
Twygge's suit.[53]

It is unclear from the testimony how Christian felt about
her father's maneuvering to get her out of her contract to John
Lorymer, but some other women clearly opposed their parents'
interference. Margery Prowde of Chingford, when examined
before the court, stated that she contracted marriage with John
Brake only because she was "compelled by Thomas Mannynge
[her stepfather] and Alice Prowde, her mother." She preferred
John Penryth, with whom she had subsequently contracted

---

[51]Cf. Gowing, "Women, Sex and Honour," pp. 117–18.

[52]GLRO DL/C/205, fols. 136v–137v. Margery's mother, Alice Forde, also objected but said that she did so at Margery's request, not on her own authority.

[53]GLRO DL/C/205, fols. 209r–212r, 216r–218v, 224v–225r.

another marriage.[54] The father of Margaret Flemmyng of London arranged that Robert Walsh would contract marriage with his daughter, but Margaret herself had other ideas. According to witnesses to the case, she loved Mark Patenson and wanted to marry him; he apparently felt the same way and had given her a gold ring. Margaret's father, on discovering the ring, showed his displeasure by ripping it from her finger.[55]

Compulsion could also be exercised on men, although not in the same way as it was imposed on women: there are no cases in the deposition books of fathers (or mothers) coercing their own sons to marry a particular woman. Instead, fathers of women who had been wronged financially or sexually compelled men to marry their daughters, in medieval equivalents of shotgun weddings. Robert Rokewode of Colchester admitted that he had forced Peter Harman to contract with his daughter Alice but felt justified. Peter had sold £9 sterling worth of clothes and other ornaments that he, Robert Rokewode, had bought for the wedding.[56]

John Wellys of London, an alderman of the City,[57] used a full artillery of weapons against William Rote in forcing him to marry his daughter Agnes Wellys. William came to John Wellys's house one afternoon to drink a jug of wine with Wellys, only to be confronted with the accusation, "You have violated my daughter Agnes by knowing her carnally. Contract

---

[54]GLRO DL/C/205, fols. 266v–268r, 271r–272r, quotation at fol. 267r–v: "Ista iurata [Margery Prowde], compulsa per Thomam Mannynge et Aliciam Prowde matrem istius iurate, contraxit matrimonium cum dicto Johanne Brake."

[55]GL 9065, fols. 81r–82r.

[56]GL 9065, fol. 39v. See also ibid., fols. 221v–222r and 223v–225r.

[57]Reginald R. Sharpe, ed., *Calendar of Letter-Books Preserved among the Archives of the Corporation of the City of London at the Guidhall, Letter Books A–L* (London, 1899–1912), *Letter Book K*, pp. 1–184 passim.

marriage with her, or else I'll force you and you'll be sorry."[58] When William denied any carnal knowledge of Agnes and said that he refused to marry her, Wellys proceeded to make good his threat, taking out a dagger and lunging towards William. Wellys's blow was blocked by another man there present and William ran from the house in the ensuing scuffle. Agnes and her mother, seeing him flee, gave chase, running out after him and shouting, "Holde the thef!"[59] They soon caught him and led him back into the house, where John Wellys was waiting, still very angry:

> Wellys said to him that unless this deponent would contract marriage with his daughter Agnes, he or someone else in his name would give this deponent a sign that he would take with him to his grave. Wellys also said that he would bring this deponent before the mayor and alderman where he would be confounded by such embarrassment that the shame would compel him to contract marriage with Agnes. So, as much from fear of his body as from shame at appearing before the mayor and aldermen, this deponent contracted marriage there with Agnes.[60]

---

[58]GLRO DL/C/205, fol. 266r: "Prefatus Johannes Wellys paterfamilias allocutus est istum iuratum dicens eidem, 'Tu violasti Agnetem filiam meam, ipsam carnaliter cognoscendo. Contrahas cum illa matrimonium sin autem ego compellam te, et penitebit te.'" The rest of the case appears at fols. 253r–256r, 258v, 265v–266v, 275r–276v.

[59]GLRO DL/C/205, fol. 266r.

[60]GLRO DL/C/205, fol. 266r–v: "[Wellys] dixit quod nisi iste iuratus vellet ibidem contrahere matrimonium cum prefata Agnete filia sua quod ipse vel alius pro ipso et nomine ipsius daret huic iurato tale signum quod secum adduceret usque sepulcrum suum. Et dixit ulterius ibidem quod ipse idem Johannes vellet cum rubore adducere istum iuratum coram maiore et aldermannis ubi tali erubescencia confunderetur, quod pudor sive erubiscencia et necessitas compellerent istum iuratum ad contrahendum matrimonium cum prefata Agnete unde iste iuratus tam timore corporis sui <quam> pudore comparacionis coram maiore et Aldermannis, iste iuratus contraxit ibidem matrimonium cum prefata Agnete."

Agnes—perhaps pregnant—was clearly complicit in her father's attempts to force William Rote to marry her. She herself did not have the means to compel William to contract with her and instead relied on her father's physical and political power.

Cases of compulsion were but the most extreme examples of the involvement of families and interested others in the marriages of English people in the later fifteenth century. As we have seen, women in particular called upon the advice of others and were sometimes expected to await their consent before committing to a contract of marriage. Women could turn these conventions to their advantage. Margery Sheppard's assertion of daughterly obedience, "I will never have none ayenst my faders will," was in her case, ironically, a statement of independence and refusal to be pressured, but as medieval English social conventions required, it displaced the refusal onto an older man, perhaps remote and authoritarian. While women could use the approval of others as a bargaining chip in the emotional and economic negotiations preceding an agreement to marry, men could not use this particular ploy with much success—appearing to be dependent on the advice and consent of others was not an attractive image to present to a prospective wife or her family. But the reason that women were able to use this ploy was precisely because the stance of obedient daughter willing to be governed in all things by a wise and all-knowing father was a real expectation of female behavior. While some couples in late medieval England made their marriages taking full advantage of the freedom of choice offered to them by the consent theory of canon law, most took their marriage vows only after consulting and sometimes obtaining the permission of their families, employers, and friends.

"MARITALIS AFFECTIO":
MARITAL AFFECTION AND PROPERTY
IN FOURTEENTH-CENTURY
YORK CAUSE PAPERS[1]

©*Frederik Pedersen*

n the spring of 1357, William Aungier, a fourteen-year-old man, sought the help of the archbishop's court in York to have his marriage to Johanna Malcake, a sixteen-year-old woman, annulled. William's father, Thomas Aungier, had died around 1342 while William's mother was still pregnant. His mother had married again almost immediately and had lived with her new husband at her father's manor until the arrival of the Plague in England in 1347. William's mother, his grandfather, and his uncle (who would ordinarily have become his guardian) all succumbed to the Plague, and the guardianship of William passed to his closest surviving relative, a nephew on his mother's side called Thomas de Bekyngham. At the end of a year Thomas de Bekyngham received an offer to sell his guardianship over

---

[1]All research for this paper was carried out with the help of the generous financial assistance of the Carlsberg foundation in Copenhagen. The Carlsberg breweries were donated to the Royal Danish Society of the Sciences and Humanities in the founder's will, provided that all profits of the company were given to worthy causes, one of which has always been academic research.

175

William to Thomas Malcake, a local lord, for 10 marks. Thomas Malcake had a daughter two years older than William, called Johanna. Thomas Malcake and Thomas de Bekyngham persuaded William to exchange marriage vows with her.[2] Marriage was celebrated in the chapel of the manor of Fenwick where Thomas Malcake lived, and William, who was eight years old, and Johanna, who was ten, were put in the nuptial bed together the following night.[3] This marriage was not yet

---

[2]A witness describing himself as a neighbor of Thomas Malcake for the past 20 years says, "Et bene novit quod dictus Willelmus de Malcake, frater dicti Thome et patrinus ipsius Johanne, emit maritagium Willelmi, de quo agitur, de Thoma de Bekyngham pro decem [marcas] argentum et ipsam Johannam eidem Willelmo copulavit in matrimonio eidem Johanne, et ipsos matrimonium adinvicem compulit, induxit et excitavit contrahere quod sic contraxerunt et verba matrimonalia inter se protulerunt" (CP E 76, 1357-12, name unknown). See a calendar of the cases in David M. Smith, *Ecclesiastical Cause Papers at York: The Court of York, 1301–1399* (York, 1988). Archivists in York have referred to the cause papers (CP) in different ways. Some documents bear a Roman letter for reference; others have had an Arabic numeral assigned. Sixteen 14th-century marriage cases (CP E 159, 175, 178, 181, 186, 202, 210, 212, 213, 215, 216, 223, 238, 239, 242, 274) have no references at all. In a personal communication, Charles Donahue suggested that one refer to the documents by indicating the cause paper number and a reference to the document's previous designation (letter or numeral) if it has one. In the 16 cases where individual documents have not been numbered, I use their physical sequence in the file as the basis for a number. Numbers of individual documents do not indicate their chronological sequence, since the document that bears the highest number was almost always the document used to wrap the bundle before it was put away. Typically, documents containing depositions were the largest and therefore were used as outside wrappers. In the case of depositions, one document may contain statements from as many as 23 people. To identify the relevant section of such documents, here the name of the witness either follows the reference to the document or is included in the main body of the text.

[3]"Et presens fuit [Johannes Forester de Kilburn], ut dicit, in capella manerii de Fenwyk quodam die . . . ubi et quum vidit et audivit dictos Willelmum et

final, and according to canon law it needed to be ratified when William came of age. Only his and Johanna's consent to the marriage at an age when they were old enough to make an informed decision would make the marriage legally binding. As a member of the *familia* of William Malcake, Thomas's brother, William Aungier was sent to attend school in William Malcake's parish of Elsing in Norfolk.[4] He lived with William Malcake for six years, until the time when he was expected to ratify the marriage contract. Johanna stayed with her father in Fenwick and at the estate of the lord with whom her father served.

During this time, William Aungier saw little of Johanna: he spent a week with his future parents-in-law *causa recreationis* in the years between 1355 and 1357[5] and Johanna spent a week with William in Lincolnshire at the manor of William Malcake. Both these occasions were arranged to see if they could

---

Johannam matrimonium adinvicem contrahere in hec verba, 'ego accipio [te,] Johannam, in uxorem meam, habendam et tenendam usque ad finem vita mee' et econtra illa dicente, 'ego accipio te, Willelmum, in virum meum tenendum et habendum usque ad finem vite mee.' Et eodem die vidit matrimonium solempnizatum inter eosdem in capella predicta [in presentia] plurium amicorum utriusque partis. . . . Et eadem nocte uter[que] simul jacuerunt in lecto, nudus cum nuda, solus cum sola, sed bene scit quod carnaliter adinvicem non commiscerunt, eo quod dictus Willelmus [fuit] tunc novem annorum plene ac dicta Johanna xii annos non compleverat" (CP E 76, 1357-12).

[4] ". . . misit dictum Willelmum statim post matrimonium, ut prefertur, solempnizatum ad partes australes, videlicet ad scolas ad ecclesiam suam de Elsyn in Northfolk causa addiscendi . . ." (CP E 76, 1357-12).

[5] William appears to have suffered some lasting effects of the Plague that somewhat stunted his growth: ". . . ipse est unus miserabilis persona modica statura . . . valde parva et ut apparet ad oculum extranei qui non haberet notitiam sui ipse apparet per aspectum corporis sui nondum esse etatis ix vel decem annorum ad plus . . ." (CP E 76-12, Johannes filius Jacobi de Redness).

get along with each other.[6] But some weeks before William Aungier's fourteenth birthday, William Malcake heard the disturbing news that Johanna was no longer a virgin and that she was pregnant. While William Aungier had lived with Johanna's uncle she had had sex with several men whose names neither Johanna's uncle nor she herself knew. This made him decide to send William Aungier to Fenwick as soon as possible.[7] William stayed in Johanna's parents' house for a week, steadfastly refusing to consummate their marriage. Towards the end of the week, acting upon the unspecified "incitements" of Johanna's neighbors, William spent one night with Johanna in her bed "solus cum sola, nudus cum nuda."[8] William was not happy about this, and he discussed his predicament with his own friends. William Raynald, a witness for William Aungier, reported to the court that William Aungier had said to him,

---

[6]". . . ad explorandum an ipsi inter se mutuo poterunt diligere et an vellent ratificare matrimonium inter eos . . ." (CP E 76-12, Johannes filius Jacobi de Redness).

[7]". . . quo tempore dictus dominus Willelmus Malcake, audito quod dicta Johanna passa fuit et carnaliter cognosci a pluribus (nesciens tamen quot, sed credit quattuor) vel quinque hominibus prout fama publica laboravit, misit ipsum Willelmum ab illis partibus australibus et remotis ad villam de [Swyne]flet, [ubi] dicta Johanna tunc morabatur . . ." (CP E 76-11, unknown name).

[8]". . . et ibidem cohabitavit cum dicta Johanna per unam septimanam et hoc coactus per amicos dicte Johanne, sed de qua vi vel metu vel qui eum astrinxerunt nescit deponere. Dicit etiam interrogatus quod una nocte . . . ingressus fuit lecto dicte Johanne ad excitationem quorundam vicinorum dicte ville et sic jacuit in uno lecto cum dicta Johanna, solus cum sola et nudus cum nuda . . ." (CP E 76-11, William Raynald). The phrase *solus cum sola et nudus cum nuda* in other surviving cases implies strongly that the witness believes that the parties had intercourse. Whether William and Johanna did on this occasion was not investigated by the court. The eventual outcome of the case, a sentence in favor of William's plea to have the marriage declared null and void, indicates that the court did not think that intercourse had taken place.

"It displeases me that I ever knew her for she does not love me with an affection that holds good. And therefore, for sure, I intend never to consent to her that she be my wife, nor to cohabit with her."[9]

At the end of the week he followed his friends' advice and moved away to live alone before he initiated his case at the court of the commissary general in York.

William Aungier had explained to William Raynald that he wanted to base his marriage on "an affection that holds good," but he is the only litigant in the surviving fourteenth-century marriage cases from the archbishop's court in York who explained that he expected marriage to be based on affection. His case is unique because the choice of words reported in his statements make it clear that he had a notion of marriage which included fidelity and a lasting emotional involvement with his partner. In this paper I shall investigate the surviving matrimonial litigation preserved in fourteenth-century York cause papers, to illustrate the ambiguity of the Latin phrase *affectio maritalis* (or *affectio conjugalis*) as it was used by witnesses in the fourteenth-century York marriage cases and to demonstrate the range of its application. While the witnesses seem to have been aware of the idea of marital affection as "a loving state of mind,"[10] these two phrases maintain an element of the early Roman law ideas of marital affection as a quality of will necessary both for the establishment of a legally valid marriage and for the transfer of property.

---

[9]"Displicet michi quod uncquam novi dictam Johannam, eo quod me non diliget affectione qua tenetur. Et ideo pro certo nuncquam intendo consentire in eam quod sit uxorem meam nec cum ea coha[bi]tare" (CP E 76-11).

[10]John T. Noonan, "Marital Affection in the Canonists," *Studia Gratiana* 12 (1967): 509.

THE DEVELOPMENT OF THE NOTION OF MARITAL AFFECTION

The term *affectio maritalis* has a long history in law but was never given a clear definition. It was first used in Roman law to mean "intent to marry." The concept was used in three contexts: to establish the existence of a marriage, to distinguish marriage from concubinage, and to establish the right of offspring to inherit. When Justinian used the phrase in a *novella* in 538, he did so in order to introduce the requirement of a public registration of marriages among the upper classes in Roman society.[11] His purpose was two-fold: public registration would help enforce a prohibition on gifts between spouses and it would help distinguish legitimate from illegitimate offspring when their parents died and inheritance was distributed.[12] Although *affectio maritalis* was necessary for a legal marriage to come into being, Roman law did not require that marital affection be maintained forever between the spouses. *Affectio maritalis* indicated the will of the spouses to have each other in marriage, but the law was unconcerned with the duration of their *affectio* beyond the moment when the marriage was registered.

The meaning of *affectio* was virtually synonymous with *affectus*, indicating the will of both parties to transfer ownership of lands and goods. As such, the word was most often used to emphasize that a spouse had displayed a willingness to allow the legal effects of marriage to come into effect and thus to indicate the quality of will needed to enter into marriage.[13] The lack of emotional content in the phrase was emphasized

---

[11]*Corpus iuris civilis romani*, ed. nov., 1 vol. in 2 (Leipzig, 1720), *Novella* 74.4.2.

[12]Noonan, "Marital Affection," p. 482.

[13]Noonan, "Marital Affection," pp. 486–87.

by Ulpian's use of the words *affectio* and *affectus* in his discussion of the legal abilities of the wards and madmen: in one instance he says that members of these groups "cannot begin to possess because they do not have the will (*adfectionem*) of possession,"[14] in another he excepted the madman and the ward from the restitution of property acquired by fraud because "they lack the will (*adfectu*)" to possess things.[15] In later Roman jurisprudence the phrase acquired connotations of ties of affection and dependence. It was commonly used to signify the nature of fathers' ties with their children and the brotherly love of soldiers. By this later use the phrase acquired, in Noonan's phrase, "not simply a legal will but an emotion-colored intent not far from love."[16]

Justinian's *novella* from 538 required the written registration of marriage partners' *affectio maritalis*, and this insistence on registration of marital intent may have been the reason why the term was not further defined until the publication of Gratian's *Decretum* around 1140. Gratian emphasized the emotional content of *affectio maritalis* and underlined its importance for the legality of marriage. He insisted that marital affection was necessary for the creation of the marriage bond, and, once a marriage had been established with marital affection, nothing short of the death of a spouse could cause a marriage to fail. Like his Roman predecessors, Gratian left the exact meaning of the term unclear. In Gratian's use of the term, marital affection was separate from marital consent. To

---

[14]"Furiosus et pupillus non possunt incipere possidere quia adfectionem tenendi non habent" (Dig. 5.16.60, cited in Charlton Lewis and Charles Short, *A Latin Dictionary* [Oxford, 1987], p. 65).

[15]"Hoc edicto neque pupillum, neque furiosum teneri constat quia adfectu carent" (Dig. 43.4.1, cited in Lewis and Short, *Latin Dictionary*, p. 66).

[16]"Marital Affection," p. 488.

consent was to accept a person as a spouse, while marital
affection referred to the quality of the relationship that thus
came into being.[17] Yet, when it came to defining when a
marriage was enforceable in law, Gratian had to fall back on
external evidence that could be substantiated in court.[18] Obviously, the existence of a marriage contracted without witnesses
could not be proved or disproved by the allegations of the
plaintiff alone, but a pronouncement could be made following
the examination of witnesses who had witnessed an exchange
of vows.[19] This requirement of external proof and Gratian's
insistence on the primacy of the spoken word in the establishment of the marriage bond once again shifted attention away
from a definition of marital affection, for a further forty years.
The Decretals of Pope Alexander III (1159–81) sketched out
the meaning of the term in more detail, making marital affection not only a requirement for the establishment of marriage
but also a required part of married life. Alexander III believed
that marital affection should endure during the marriage. In his
usage, the words incorporated "an active disposition which the
spouses had a duty to cultivate," which the church courts
should not only encourage but also enforce.[20] In an elaboration
of Gratian's idea that marital consent differed from consent to
intercourse, Alexander now taught that a spouse must be
treated as more than just another bedfellow.[21]

---

[17]Michael M. Sheehan, "*Maritalis Affectio* Revisited," in *The Olde Daunce:
Love, Friendship, Sex, and Marriage in the Medieval World*, ed. Robert R.
Edwards and Stephen Spector (Albany, N.Y., 1991), pp. 36–37. Noonan,
"Marital Affection," p. 490.

[18]Noonan, "Marital Affection," pp. 498–99.

[19]*Decretum Gratiani* (Venice, 1591), *dictum post*, C.30, q.5, c.9.

[20]Noonan, "Marital Affection," p. 501.

[21]Noonan, "Marital Affection," p. 502.

A concise definition of marital affection still eluded canon lawyers. Although marriage partners were required to grant their spouses sexual intercourse on demand, it was clear that marital affection was not limited to this aspect of married life. Had that been the case, the incorporation in the Decretals of Gregory IX of Alexander III's decretal *Perveniens*,[22] which exhorted lepers' spouses to administer to them "with conjugal affection" in their illness, would not have made sense. The following decretal, *Quoniam nemini*,[23] specifically deals with the duty of a spouse to render the marital debt to the leprous partner but is otherwise virtually identical to *Perveniens*. *Quoniam nemini* could have been left out of the Decretals if marital affection only consisted in rendering the conjugal debt. Thus in the usage of Alexander III, marital affection was separated from sexual congress and acquired the meaning of an enduring quality in the marital relations of spouses during their life together.[24] Marital affection also maintained an uneasy connection with the freedom of consent required in the Church's teaching on marriage. A certain proportion of surviving medieval marriage litigation concerns the restoration of conjugal rights. Thus a wife or husband might be ordered by the Church to take back the abandoned spouse and treat him or her with marital affection.[25] In the end, canon law made no

---

[22]X 4.1.1 (= *Decretales Domini Gregorii papæ IX* [Venice, 1591], liber 4, titulus 1, capitulum 1). The Decretals, which were also known as the *Liber extra*, were first published in 1234.

[23]X 4.8.2.

[24]Sheehan, *"Maritalis Affectio* Revisited," p. 37.

[25]Noonan, "Marital Affection," pp. 503–04; Sheehan gives an example of such a command to resume cohabitation with marital affection in *"Maritalis Affectio* Revisited," p. 257; another example is found in R. H. Helmholz, *Marriage Litigation in Medieval England* (London, 1974), p. 102. As will be seen from the present study, the court in York rarely commanded litigants to live with marital affection.

attempt to define marital affection in terms that would make it possible for a court to decide whether marital affection existed. Instead the courts focused their attention on proving the existence of marriage by means of the help of witnesses. Marital affection in canon law thus has a vague quality about it that makes it difficult to define in clear terms.

A similar ambiguity in the use of the word *affeccioun* or *affection* can be found in Middle English usage. In the earliest recorded instance of its use—the discussion of the three stages of carnal desire in *Ancrene Riwle* (ca. 1230)—the word describes a desire or a wish to do something,[26] but in later texts the meaning of the word opened up to include lexical definitions as diverse as "an emotion," "love," "charity," friendship," and "love between the sexes." The Wycliffe Bible (ca. 1384), for example, translates Saint Paul's letter to the Romans as "With outen affeccioun or loue, withouten bond of pees, withouten mercy . . ." (Romans 1: 13). The meaning of the Middle English word *affect* was as ambiguous as *affeccioun* and denoted the same wide span of meaning. In fourteenth-century English usage the meaning of the word includes the same lexical definition as found in the Roman legal use meaning "capacity for willing or desiring" or simply "the will."[27]

Although the concept of affection was vague and its precise meaning both in Latin and in Middle English remained

---

[26]"Þreo degrez beoð þrin [in carnal desire] . . . þe forme is cogitatiun, þe oþer is affectiun; þe þridde is cunsence. . . . Affectiun is hwen þe þoht geað inward & delit kimeð up & te lust waxeð," *The English Text of the Ancrene Riwle*, edited from the British Museum's MS Royal C. I by A. C. Baugh, EETS, 232 (1956), p. 78b. *The Recluse: A Fourteenth Century Version of the Ancren Riwle*, ed. Joel Påhlsson (Lund, 1911), uses the Latin word *affectus* in this place.

[27]For the use of the word in these meanings, see the *Middle English Dictionary*, ed. Hans Kurath, assoc. ed. Sherman M. Kuhn (Ann Arbor, 1954–), s.v. *affeccion*.

unclear, the term *affectio maritalis* was used in surviving marriage litigation. The term was mainly used by witnesses and is rarely seen in documents intended for internal use by the courts. Though the phrase is mainly reported in documents that show what lay people said about marriage, the expression was employed as a part of an argument conducted within the parameters of canon law's understanding of marriage. Even though the term does indicate something about the nature of a marriage (and it is clear that spouses were expected to behave affectionately toward each other by witnesses and clerics alike), *affectio maritalis*—as the term is used in marriage cases preserved in York—maintained a strong connection to a specific aspect of marital consent, the consent by both partners in a marriage to joint holding of property. It thus retained a large measure of its old Roman law meaning of willing the consequences of marriage. With the exception of the example of William Aungier—who, strictly speaking, did not talk of marital affection—the phrase did not invariably indicate an emotional state required for marriage or contain information on the emotional quality of the spouses' lives together.

MARITAL AFFECTION IN THE COURTS

In this study, I concentrate on the information contained in the fourteenth-century York Cause Paper files preserved in the Borthwick Institute in York. The York Cause Papers is the name used to describe the surviving documents produced by the courts of the Northern Province, whose jurisdiction covered most of northern England, covering the dioceses of Durham, Carlisle, and York. Two hundred fifty-six cause paper files, comprising around eight hundred documents of varying lengths, survive from the fourteenth century. These files cover all aspects of court business, from procedural documents— such as libels, positions, and interrogatories—to the judgments

of the court.[28] The York files also include letters and transcripts of earlier cases from officers appointed by the court to
investigate the facts of a case in the field; and, most important,
they include a large number of depositions heard by the court.
Among the 256 cause paper files are eighty-eight files docu-
menting litigation over marriages.[29]

The documents that tell us the least about the laity are the
instruments which document the stages that the case went
through while under scrutiny by the courts. This group includes the *acta*, which listed each meeting of the court and
briefly outlined the business conducted, the appointment of
proctors for the litigants, internal memoranda, mandates to
officers of the courts, and the sentence in the case. These
documents were intended for the internal use of the courts, and
a reading of them reveals virtually nothing about the existence
of marital affection. The second group of documents includes
the plaintiff's libel, the defendant's replies to the libel, positions, articles, interrogatories, and exceptions to witnesses.[30]

---

[28] A concise explanation of the kinds of documents produced by the ecclesiastical courts can be found in Norma Adams and Charles Donahue, Jr., eds.,
*Select Cases from the Ecclesiastical Courts of the Province of Canterbury,
c.1200–1301*, Selden Society, 95 (1981), pp. 37–72.

[29] Calculating the number of marriage cases in the Borthwick Institute, I have
followed the classifications found in Smith, *Cause Papers*, which lists 87
cases as "matrimonial," "alimony," "validity of marriage," or "divorce" cases,
to which I have added CP E 108, a plea of dower transmitted from the King's
Bench. CP E 12 and CP E 14—which are listed as matrimonial—did not deal
with marriage *vows* when heard in York: CP E 12 is a plea for the payment
of a promised dowry to the *pars actrix*'s son after his wife died, while CP E 14
is a dispute over whether Thomas de Colvill had paid alimony to his wife,
Margaret Darell, who had previously obtained a *divortium a mensa et thoro*.

[30] For a discussion of the documents produced by the courts supplementing
that found in Adams and Donahue, *Select Cases*, see Helmholz, *Marriage
Litigation*, pp. 11–22.

These were usually (but not always) drawn up in consultation between a litigant and a member of the court[31] and were used to settle which issues were at stake and—more important— which contentions could be admitted as the subject of an investigation by the courts. These documents were drawn up as part of the process of eliminating issues on which the parties agreed to establish which issues were contested. Documents of this kind occasionally refer to marital affection but usually do so in a formulaic manner without any attempt to define the words. The fact that the witnesses were sometimes directly asked about marital affection, however, does suggest that the phrase was commonly known, and in some cases the silence of the witnesses about the existence of marital affection is as significant as if they had agreed that it was present in a union under investigation.

The third and final group of documents is that of the depositions admitted by the courts. Although this source is relatively silent about the meaning of the concept, the words *affectio maritalis/conjugalis* are found most frequently here. The depositions are an unusually vivid collection of narratives told to the court by the witnesses recorded by the court scribes. Among them we find descriptions of marriage negotiations, nocturnal fights over women, leisure activities, daily work, and events that occurred in the markets or in the courts. They contain stories of domestic happiness and of relationships that went sour, stories about the daily existence of paupers and rich men alike. Depositions were taken down outside the court, the witnesses being interrogated individually on the basis of written questions. The neatness, economy of phrase, and the

---

[31] A noticable proportion of litigants tried to conduct their cases on their own; e.g., Simon de Munkton, the plaintiff in CP E 248, did not employ a proctor until six months of litigation against his wife, Agnes de Huntington, had passed.

fact that they are written in Latin indicate that the depositions were not taken down at once but rather were the result of a careful distillation of the information received by the examiner during his interrogation of the witnesses, such information first being taken down as notes. The interrogation took place either in Latin or in English; the depositions often note if the questions were put to the witnesses in English, though the absence of a statement to that effect clearly cannot be taken to mean that the interrogation was conducted in Latin. The scribes who wrote up the depositions were exceedingly meticulous in their condensation of witnesses' statements. They carefully distinguished between answers given to questions asked by the court and information volunteered by the witness, signaling one with the phrase *dicit requisita/us* and the other with *dicit insuper* or *dicit etiam*. The scribes also took down the exact words of vows, paying particular attention to the distinction between formal and informal forms of address. The eighty-eight cases under investigation contain more than 580 depositions. A remarkably small number of witnesses, only eleven in all, actually used the term *affectio maritalis*, and the mere fact that it was so rarely used is suggestive. A close reading of the evidence suggests that the term was mainly used by witnesses when there was a dispute over property between the litigants.

MARITAL AFFECTION IN THE WITNESS ACCOUNTS

The meaning of the concept of marital affection remains as hazy in the witness accounts as it was in canon law, but a detailed analysis of the statements that survive suggests a number of common features in the way the phrase was used when witnesses were asked by the courts about the nature of a marital union. Apart from the libel of CP E 95, the positions of CP E 36, the articles of CP E 62 and 108, and the replications by Simon de Munkton in CP E 248, "internal" court documents do not mention "marital affection." Only in CP E 36 is it not possible to show that the litigation was connected to a dispute over property. In general, though, the words describe an on-going process in married life that followed the initial exchange of marriage vows, and most witnesses placed it in between the first exchange of vows and the later solemnization of marriage. Only one witness commented on marital affection in a case that is not demonstrably about some aspect of control over property owned by the litigants.[32] The phrase thus retained a connection with its roots in Roman law, despite its being used by only eleven witnesses in six cause paper files.[33] Each case will be analyzed below and the use of the phrase put in its context.

The earliest instance of witnesses using the phrase *marital affection* comes from CP E 12 (1313). Although the case aimed to establish whether the terms of a contract had been met, the question of whether a valid marriage existed between the litigants' children was of central importance to the outcome. The case was brought before the court by Sir Alexander Percy, who alleged that he had made an agreement concerning the marriage of his under-age son, John, to Elizabeth, daughter of Sir Robert Colvyle, seven years earlier. In accordance with the terms of their contract, Sir Alexander had immediately endowed the couple with lands in the villages of Craythorn and Berth worth 25 marks, to be held in fief. In return, Sir Robert was to pay a dowry of 124 marks within two years. John and Elizabeth had solemnized the marriage two years before the case was heard in York, but their marriage had been

---

[32] CP E 36-5, Thomas Wans, a butcher from York.

[33] Four witnesses in CP E 62, two witnesses each in CP E 12 and CP E 248. In the remaining cases, CP E 77, 95, and 108, only one witness commented on marital affection.

brief, as Elizabeth died six months later.[34] As a consequence of his daughter's death, Sir Robert tried to avoid the fulfillment of his promise. The case therefore came to revolve around the question of whether the two had cohabited and whether their cohabitation had been with marital intent. Ten witnesses were heard for Sir Alexander. Six of them described some kind of cohabitation in Sir Alexander's household, which they believed was a valid marriage.[35] Two of these witnesses, Robert de Cleveland and Thomas de Rydale, went even further. While other witnesses simply described the couple as "legally married," they volunteered the information that Sir Alexander Percy's son had lived with his wife, Elizabeth, the daughter of Sir Robert Colvyle, with marital affection before her death.[36] Robert de Cleveland mentioned marital affection in passing,[37] while Thomas de Rydale added more information: they had exchanged marriage vows "in the usual form" and had been put in a nuptial bed at the occasion of the initial contract. After this, John and Elizabeth had treated each other with marital affection and had often been seen alone in bed together:

---

[34]CP E 12-1, CP E 12-3, and CP E 12-4, Richard de Lyth and Robert de Clyveland. The witness Robert de Clyveland, who is the only witness to testify about when Sir Robert should pay the money, presumably got the details of the agreement wrong when he said the money should be paid "infra duas annos post confectionem dicte *indenture*" (my emphasis). The chronology of the case makes more sense if the money had been due two years after the solemnization of the marriage.

[35]CP E 12-4, Robert de Clyveland, Walter le Lange, Alexander Molendarius, Adam de Kyldale, Adam Fox, and Thomas de Rydale.

[36]CP E 12-4.

[37]"Vidit idem juratus, ut dicit, dictos [Johannem et] Elisabet' simul morantes apud Ormesby in manerio dicti domini Alexandri per unum dimidium annum ubi se mutuo pertractarunt affectione maritali, ipso jurato hec vidente sepius per dictum tempus . . ." (CP E 12-4).

> And for three years said John and Elizabeth lay alone together in
> their bed and they behaved with marital affection in all ways to each
> other, and the witness having seen this, as the witness says, believed
> them to be true married people until the death of said Elizabeth.[38]

Thomas de Rydale's deposition gives us a number of clues as to what he believed to be the meaning of marital affection. First of all, marital affection followed an exchange of marriage vows. Second, marital affection was described in connection with, but not necessarily as an ingredient of, sharing a bed. And third, the existence of marital affection was understood to be an integral part of the marriage, and in this case it preceded the solemnization of the marriage. It is important, too, that Robert de Cleveland and Thomas de Rydale were not asked directly about marital affection but volunteered the information, believing that the context of their evidence made their thoughts on marital affection helpful to the court.

Like the case of William Aungier, CP E 62 (1348) involved the marriage of a ward to the guardian's child. Unlike William Aungier, Constance, daughter of William de Brome, had already been married once and had two children by her first husband.[39]

---

[38]"Et vidit [iste juratus ipsos Johannem et Elisabet matrimonium contrahere] per verba consueta de quibus non recolit ad presenti. . . . [Et post matrimonium] celebratum maritali affectione pertractare aliquotiens apud Dale, Heseltoun, Rouclyf et Beverlacum in hospitio dicti domini [Roberti et aliquotiens] apud Sueton, Ormesby et Hevedoun in hospitio dicti domini Alexandri. Ipsosque Johannes et Elisabet vidit idem juratus . . . nocte sequente post dictum contractum celebratum simul in uno lecto et postquam in lecto repositi fuerant. . . . Et per tres annos multotiens jacuerunt dicti Johannes et Elisabet in unum lectum sole et maritali affectione in omnibus pertractarunt et jurato hec vidente, ut dicit, pro conjugibus legitimis habebantur usque ad mortem dicte Elisabet'" (CP E 12-4).

[39]One of the children was still alive in 1348, the other had died (CP E 62-3, Adam de Helay).

When the case was brought by William Hopton, Constance invoked a number of impediments against her alleged marriage to William, the son of Adam de Hopton: that she had married John de Rotherfield some three to five years earlier and had solemnized their marriage "in facie ecclesie"; that William was under-age at the time of the alleged contract; that there was an impediment of affinity between her and William de Hopton, since her first husband, John de Rotherfield, had been William's cousin. Finally, she alleged that she had legally married one William Boswell when John Rotherfield had been murdered a year earlier and pleaded that this marriage be upheld. Both parties in the case alleged the existence of marital affection. However, while denying that it existed in her marriage to William de Hopton, Constance argued that her marriage to John Rotherfield had included marital affection. The evidence produced in the case shows a messy mixture of a guardian's attempts to control his ward's lands, the ward's attempts to break free of her guardian's dominance, and an attempt by the guardian to regain control of his former ward's lands when the murder of her husband allowed him to prosecute the case at the court in York. Four witnesses in the case spoke of marital affection.[40] Three of these witnesses can be shown to have had a good knowledge of canon law. They were all members of a family that counted two clerics, one of whom was also a notary public, among its members.[41]

---

[40] CP E 62-3, Adam de Helay, Margaret wife of John Johnson of Danby; CP E 62-8, William de Helay; CP E 62-11, Richard de Helay. Interestingly enough, William de Helay avoided the term entirely when he was re-interrogated by the court.

[41] Adam de Helay sr., Richard de Helay, and William de Helay. A fourth male member of the Helay family, Adam de Helay jr., son of Adam de Helay sr., notarized the appointment of Constance's proctor in the case; he drew up a copy of this appointment, in which he described himself as "Adam de

The witnesses produced by Constance in the first instance to prove her marriage to John Rotherfield told the court of two exchanges of vows. Adam de Helay senior, a neighbor, said he had heard of the marriage from neighborhood rumor; Dionysia, his daughter, said the marriage had been celebrated in Adam de Helay junior's room "with a celebration of Mass" three years earlier, while two further witnesses claimed that a marriage had been celebrated in a field near Heathcliff by a stone called "Stoupandstone" five years earlier.[42] At a later meeting of the court, it became clear that Adam de Helay senior was being economical with the truth and that he had previously conspired with Adam de Hopton to force Constance to marry William Hopton despite a warning by his son William Helay, who was a cleric in York, that no good would come from their union. After the third and final production of witnesses, which took place after the collapse of William Hopton's case, the court could piece together the events of the case. The court learned that Constance had initially exchanged vows with John Rotherfield when she was fifteen years of age at the Stoupandstone in Heathcliff five years earlier, and that the marriage had been confirmed by a ceremony in Adam Helay junior's room two years later. At the time of the contract by the Stoupandstone, Constance was the ward of Adam de Hopton, John Rotherfield's uncle. Adam de Hopton had a son of nine years of age called William, whom he wanted her to marry so that he could maintain control over her land. Soon after the contract at Heathcliff, Adam de Hopton and Adam de Helay senior forced Constance against her will

---

Helay, clericus Eboracensis diocesis publicus apostolici et imperiali auctoritate notarius" (CP E 62-15).

[42] CP E 62-3, John son of John the son of Alice de Danby, and Elisabeth daughter of Clarissa de Danby.

to contract marriage with William Hopton. According to the second deposition made by William de Helay, who was present at the occasion, Constance had remained "silent and unresponsive" when Adam de Hopton had suggested the marriage. Adam de Hopton had then threatened her, that he would break her neck,

> And thus said Constance afterwards, for fear of the threats uttered by said Adam de Helay and fearing the loss of her land by said Adam de Hopton, her guardian having the deeds and possession of said lands, contracted with said William even though Adam de Hopton, the father of said William [de Helay], had previously been warned by this witness that this marriage would not come to a good end.[43]

William Hopton was not keen on the marriage, either. When Adam de Helay senior admitted that he had helped to force Constance and William to marry, he added that the parties had to be dragged to the altar "crying and resisting."[44]

Richard de Helay explained to the court that Constance and John Rotherfield had contracted marriage, had intercourse, and

---

[43]". . . et sic dicta Custantia postmodum, timore minarum eidem per dictum Adam de Helay ministratarum et amissionis terre sue dicto Ade de Hopton curatore eiusdem Custantie habente dictam terram et cartas eiusdem Custantie de eadem terra cum dicto Willelmo contraxit, prout supra deposuit, licet Adam de Hopton, pater eiusdem Willelmi, per ipsum juratum prius fuit premunitus quod illud matrimonium bonum exitum habere non posset, ut dicit . . ." (CP E 62-11).

[44]"[Adam de Hopton] una cum ipso Adam teste consensu mutuo compulerunt et cogerunt vi et metu et minis illatio ad contrahendum matrimonium predictos Willelmum et Custantiam multum renitentes et flentes, contradicente et negante dicta Custantia in tantum quod cum Adam de Helay predictus proferret verba matrimonii. Dicta Custantia noluit recitare nec recte proferre ipsa verbas matrimonii. Et dicit quod nullo tempore consensit dicto Willelmo nec alio modo nec cohabitavit cum eo nisi quatenus dictus Adam tenuit eam invita sub cura sua" (CP E 62-3, Adam de Helay).

had one surviving child. They also "lived together like man and wife with marital affection" before the alleged contract between William and Constance.[45] Margaret, wife of John Johnson of Danby, gave evidence of the marriage between Constance and John Rotherfield. For her the sequence was the same: the solemnization of marriage preceded marital affection, the birth of children followed the marriage, and the phrase was used to describe a quality of the relationship. After the solemnization of marriage she saw that

> . . . said John and Constance lived together, mixed carnally and were close with marital affection. And all these things this witness believed to be true because she often saw them live and join together in Constance's own house.[46]

For Richard de Helay and Margaret Johnson, marital affection was a visible quality of marriage and they were confident that they were able to recognize it. Their choices of verbs—*cohabito* and *adhaero* with marital affection—suggest that they intended to describe the quality of the cohabitation but that they are not necessarily making a point about the validity of the marriage contract. In contrast, Adam de Helay senior, Richard and William de Helay's father, used the verb *contraho*, commonly used to mean the making of a contract or concluding of a bargain, which suggests that he realized that the union between Constance and John Rotherfield, her first

---

[45]". . . et maritali affectione ut vir et uxor cohabitarunt ante quemcumque contractum matrimonialem habitum seu initum inter ipsam Custantiam et Willelmum . . ." (CP E 62-11).

[46]"Dicit quod dicti Johannes et Custantia cohabitarunt et carnaliter se commiscerunt adinvicem et maritali affectione sibi invicem adhererunt. Et hec omnia credit esse vera [ista jurata] quia vidit eos sepe in domo propria dicte Custantia simul habitare et comitare" (CP E 62-3).

husband, was intended to be a legally valid marriage with the implication of willing the transfer of property.[47]

The two depositions by Adam de Helay senior's son William de Helay are particularly interesting because as a cleric he would be familiar with the canon law rules of marriage. At his initial appearance before the court he was the first of six witnesses, all of whom were asked about the existence or absence of marital affection between William de Hopton and Constance. Alone among the six witnesses, William de Helay claimed that there had been marital affection.[48] Although he alleged the existence of marital affection, he almost certainly did not mean to comment on the emotional content of the marriage. He was the only witness among the six volunteering the existence of marital affection, and his statement was true if his use of the phrase *affectio conjugalis* was taken to imply the old Roman law interpretation of the phrase, "to will the consequences of marriage." There was indeed the intent to create a marriage between William de Hopton and Constance, but, as his second deposition made clear, there was no love between the two. William was a cleric and therefore conversant in Latin. He must have been aware of the meaning of the phrase *marital affection* in canon law. At first glance it therefore appears significant that he is reported as using the term *affectio conjugalis* and that the scribe carefully erased the word *maritalis* from his statement. Yet this is one instance in which

---

[47]"Dicit etiam quod sepissime vidit dictos Johannem et Custantiam cohabitare in mensa et lecto et se adinvicem utrique maritali affectione contractare ut virum et uxorem" (CP E 62-8).

[48]"Super tertio articulo requisitus dicit quod postquam Willelmus et Custantia de quibus in articulo fit mentio dicebantur precontraxisse prout in articulo continetur. Vidit eosdem per medietatem unius anni simul stare et chahabitare [*sic*, read: cohabitare] sponte ut virum et uxorem et affectione conjugali mutuo se tractare" (CP E 62-8).

the evidence of the deposition is misleading if taken alone. The articles (the document that contains the questions the examiners were to ask the witnesses) uses the words *affectio conjugalis*. He also skillfully avoided giving the court his own opinion as to whether the marriage of Constance and William de Hopton was legally binding, preferring instead to answer that he believed that her subsequent marriage to William Boswell had been entered into "legally."

The amount of property under dispute in cases where a witness mentioned marital affection ranged from several villages to about 100s., the extremes being represented by CP E 108 (1370) and CP E 77 (1357), where in each case one witness commented on marital affection. The court in York was asked to examine the validity of the marriage between John and Katherine Hiliard in CP E 108. Katherine Hiliard pleaded for the restoration of her dower on John's death, but her stepson, Peter Hiliard, refused to let her have control of it. The case was referred to the court in York from the King's Bench, where Peter Hiliard argued that his stepmother's marriage to his father had been within the forbidden degrees of consanguinity and therefore not valid. The dower in question was substantial, consisting of a third of twenty-four messuages, one mill, sixteen bulls, twenty-one bovates, five acres of meadows, pasture for three hundred sheep, and 8s. annually in rents, in the villages of Arnall, Dripole, Riston, Preston, Sutton, Hedon, and Carton.[49]

The marriage between Katherine and John Hiliard had been celebrated under suspicious circumstances in 1363 at dawn of the Monday one or two weeks before the feast of Saint Martin of Tours (30 October or 6 November) in the chapel of Riston.[50]

---

[49]CP E 108-1.

[50]CP E 108-6, Eleonora de Barton, Katherine Hiliard's sister, is the only witness to give a reasonably precise date.

Witnesses heard for Katherine all agreed that the sun had been up by the time the solemnization was celebrated. Her witness Ivo of Riston, the chaplain who celebrated the marriage, claimed that he read the banns before the ceremony[51] and that neither the guests nor the parties themselves had admitted to any impediments to marriage. Yet Peter's Hiliard's brother Thomas, who was present at the marriage ceremony, said that the church had been boarded up with linens and surplices draped across the windows, and that the door remained closed during the ceremony to prevent light from the candles escaping from the church and thus alerting the countryside to the marriage.[52]

Katherine and John cohabited for almost five years after this ceremony. Katherine's stepsister, Eleonora de Barton, said to the court that they lived

> . . . like true and legal spouses with marital affection until the death of said John . . . and they were believed and publicly reputed as true and legal spouses in the village of Riston and neighboring areas.[53]

---

[51]". . . in aurora ipsius diei postquam gallus ter cantavit venit iste juratus de villa de Arnal' ad capellam de Ristoun' una cum prefatis Johanne et Katerina, Emma Hiliard, Elienora de Bartoun, Margareta de Hedoun et Thoma Hiliard et in dicta capella ante ostium chori eiusdem capelle edidit iste juratus, ut dicit, banna publice inter personas superius nominata" (CP E 108-6).

[52]"Dicit quod ipsemet interfuit in capella de Rystoun' [una cum domino] Ivone Lardmand, capellano, Emma, matre carnali dicte Katerina, Elienore de Bartoun et Margareta de Hedoun quum Johannes Hildyard et Katarina predicta matrimonium adinvicem de facto contraxherunt et ipsum ibidem solempnizari fecerunt infra noctis tenebras ante auroram diei per spacium decem miliarum anglicorum, ostio ipsius capelle clauso et fenestris eiusdem capelle cum linthiaminibus et superpelliciis suspensis in eisdem obscuratis ne lumen candelarum ibidem accensarum exterius videretur. Et dicit in juramento suo quod numquam audivit dici vel referri quod aliqua banna fuerunt edita publice in aliqua ecclesia nec aliquid propositum publice in ecclesia super huiusmodi matrimonio contrahendo" (CP E 108-13).

[53]". . . dicit quod prefati Johannes et Katerina post huius matrimonium contractum et solemnizatum ut veri et legitimi conjuges affectione maritali

Soon after the ceremony, the couple was denounced as consanguineous to the archbishop of York by their parish priest, and, having determined that they were related within the forbidden degrees, the archbishop ordered them to cease their married cohabitation and live "as sister and brother."[54] They complied with the archbishop's command but sent a cleric, master John Estthorp, to the Apostolic See to try to procure a dispensation for them. John de Estthorp was unsuccessful, and soon after his return to England John Hiliard died, leaving Katherine with the problem of how to protect her lands.

The conjunction of the phrase *marital affection* and disputes over property is found again in CP E 77 (1357). In this case the value of the property in dispute was not large. The case is a matrimonial and divorce case in which Lucy Broun, formerly the wife William Broun, alleged that she had married William Fentryce, a farmer of Tollesby, before he had married another woman, called Alice de Normanby. Lucy Broun explained to the court that she had left William after seven years

---

adinvicem cohabitarunt usque ad mortem dicti Johannes . . . ac pro veris et legitimis conjugibus communiter habiti fuerunt et publice reputati in villa de Riston et locis vicinis" (CP E 108-6).

[54]"[John Hiliard jr.] dicit quod postquam matrimonium inter dictos Johannem et Katerinam contractum fuit denuntiatum domino archiepiscopo Ebor' qui nunc est per dominum Johannem de Hildeston, tunc rectorem ecclesie parochialis de Routhe prout iste juratus audivit quod ipsi Johannes et Katerina fuerunt consanguinei et illegitime matrimonialiter copulati. Et bene novit iste juratus quod dicti Johannes et Katerina fuerunt vocati coram domino archiepiscopo Ebor' quod comparerent coram eodem sibi super premissis et aliis articulis salutem animarum suarum concernentibus responsurum et dicit quod una vice fuit iste iuratus cum dicto Johanne, patre suo, coram domino archiepiscopo supradicto apud Thorp' juxta Ebor' et audivit a magistro Willelmo de Hornsee quod tunc per eundem dominum archiepiscopum fuit inhibitum ipsis Johanni et Katerine ne extunc adinvicem carnaliter comiscerent sed ut frater et soror se adinvicem haberent" (CP E 108-13).

of cohabitation but had returned after a couple of months to claim reinstatement into her former marital rights or at least a share of the marital home. William Fentryce, who had taken another woman into the house, refused Lucy anything for her maintenance during the case. Although William Fentryce cannot be said to have been rich, he was by no means poor. Witnesses claimed that he possessed goods worth around 100s., and one witness mentioned that he owned a plough team.

Thomas Waghcson, who was heard as a witness in this case, saw marital affection as something that followed marriage—the outward manifestation of the partners' emotional involvement in each other.

> He said that he knew well that William and Lucy . . . contracted marriage seven years ago and made it to be solemnized between them. And afterwards they behaved towards each other with marital affection, keeping company together and cohabiting for a long time. . . .[55]

Seven years later, when Lucy left William during the harvest time "without his permission," he took Alice de Normanby as his mistress. Thomas Wagheson described the new union in much more prosaic terms and carefully avoided any comment on marital affection:

> He heard it commonly said by said William's neighbors that he knew Alice carnally . . . whom this witness likewise saw twice in the last month in the house of said William. And he commonly saw her in the fields performing the work of said William and serving him. And

---

[55] ". . . dicit se bene scire quod Willelmus et Lucia . . . contraxerunt matrimonium huius a septem annis elapsis, et illud fecerunt solempnizari inter eos. Et postmodum se invicem mutuo pertractarunt affectione conjugali simul conversantes et cohabitantes per magnum tempus . . ." (CP E 77-8).

—as the witness says—one could see said Alice drive said William's plough-team during the time said William maintained her.[56]

The court rejected Lucy Broun's claims on William Fentryce, presumably because she was unable to prove that they had actually exchanged marriage vows, despite Thomas Wagheson telling the court that her cohabitation with William was characterized by marital affection and his refusal to use the same word for William Fentryce's subsequent union with Alice Normanby.

The final example of witnesses commenting on marital affection in cases involving control over property comes from CP E 248, which was brought before the court in an attempt by the husband to regain control over his wife's land.[57] The case had already started before 21 August 1345,[58] when Simon, the son of Roger de Munkton, a goldsmith of York, petitioned the archbishop of York, William de la Zouche, to be reinstated into his marital rights with Agnes, the daughter of the deceased Richard of Huntington.[59] Simon claimed that their marriage was well known and attested to in the city of York,

---

[56]"Audivit communiter dici a vicinis dicti Willelmi quod ipse carnaliter cognovit Aliciam . . . quam similiter vidit ipse testis, ut dicit, bis in domo ipsius Willelmi infra mensem proximo preterito. Et eam in campis faciente opus ipsius Willelmi et sibi deserviente vidit communiter. Et videre potest quampluries, ut dicit, ipsam Aliciam fugare carucam eiusdem Willelmi dum idem Willelmus eam tenet" (CP E 77-8).

[57]I have analyzed this case in detail in *Romeo and Juliet of Stonegate: A Medieval Marriage in Trouble* (York, 1995).

[58]A letter from the commissary general dated 30 Oct. 1345 quoting a writ of supersedeas from the archbishop dated 20 Sept. 1345 says as much: "Quia vero, sicut intelleximus, ad instantiam dicte Agnetis fecistis dictum Simonem, auctoritate nostra, ad dictam curiam nostram Eboracensis super federo matrimonii inter eos contracto coram vobis ad judicium evocari" (CP E 248-37).

[59]CP E 248-51.

since Agnes and Simon had celebrated marriage, solemnized it at the church of Saint Michael le Belfrey after the publication of banns, and had cohabited for several years. That the marriage had been consummated was evidenced by the fact that they had a child. But, Simon argued, without proper reason, "because of her inborn fear" and without the permission of the Church, Agnes had left him and was now living apart, "robbing him of his belongings due to him by marriage."[60]

Although Simon's petition to the archbishop is the earliest surviving dated document in the case, Agnes had already sued for divorce at the court of the commissary general of York some time before Simon petitioned the archbishop. At this court she had claimed that she had been in mortal danger from Simon, since he attacked her on 31 July 1345. On that day Simon and Agnes had had a row over Simon's attempt to sell some of her lands in Huntington. She had refused to consent to the sale and Simon lost his temper and attacked her, beating her over the eye "so much that blood poured out both by her nostrils and ears."[61] Simon believed her to be dead and took refuge in the cemetery of the local church, but not before he had asked a neighbor called Nicholas Franteys to go to their house to see if Agnes was still alive. She *was* still alive, but in such a bad state that, after they had washed her face at a well in the garden, Nicholas and his fellow witness William de Joveby carried her, still bleeding, to her neighbor John de Snaweshill's house. William de Joveby added that this very evening Simon expelled Agnes from their house, "vowing that she would never have any good from him nor any lands or tenements."[62]

---

[60] ". . . ipsum a possessione sua conjugale indebite spoliando" (CP E 248-51).

[61] ". . . ita quod sanguis exivit tam per nares quam aures eiusdem" (CP E 248-33).

[62] ". . . asserens quod [nuncquam] aliquod bonum ab ipse nec de terris et tenementis predictis haberet" (CP E 248-33).

Simon's reasons for bringing the case before the archbishop are uncertain. He may have hoped to avoid the usual channels of appeal and thus have a speedier decision in the case, or to avoid answering a charge of cruelty, or he may have been in a financial predicament, as is suggested by his remarks about Agnes "robbing him of his belongings due to him by marriage." He may also have hoped to obtain money by selling some of Agnes's lands, which he could not do unless she gave consent to it. One of two witnesses in this case who commented on the existence of marital affection was interrogated in connection with another attack on Agnes by Simon, who came to William de Huntington's house in Petergate in York to persuade her to resume cohabitation with him after the publication of the archbishop's command to her to resume cohabitation with Simon. Henry de Galtres, a neighbor, told the court that Agnes and Simon had not co-habited during the last six months but that they had previously lived together in Simon's father's house in York "with marital affection."[63] Simon's actions when he attacked her appeared to Henry de Galtres to be fully within the accepted norm for marital behavior:

> . . . he heard the cry of a woman, as it appeared to him at the time. Having heard this, the witness went to the window of his house in said neighborhood and saw said Agnes lying and said Simon on top of her in that neighborhood with the intention, in his estimation, that

---

[63]"Dicit super primo articulo requisitus quod infra dimidium annum proximo iam elapsum nescit deponere de aliqua cohabitatione inter Simonem et Agnetem in eodem articulo nominatos prout in eodem continet. Dicit tamen quod novit eosdem Simonem et Agnetem ante temporem dimidii anni, de quo superius deposuit simul cohabitare in domo patris dicti Simonis Ebor' maritali affectione se adinvicem pertractantes et aliter super eodem articulo deponere nescit, ut dicit" (CP E 248-54).

he might lead her as his wife to said Simon's house without causing any trouble for her.[64]

Like most of the other witness accounts investigated in this study, Henry de Galtres's deposition strongly suggests that he used the phrase *with marital affection* in the Roman law meaning of "with the intention of creating a marriage" and that marital affection occurred only when the parties were cohabiting.

Emma de Munkton, the wife of Agnes's uncle William de Huntington (and not a relative of Simon de Munkton) gave a more detailed account of the way in which Simon and Agnes had lived together. According to her deposition, marital affection followed marriage but was not necessarily the foundation on which marriage was built. To her, marital affection consisted of the inner reality of the emotion and its external expression. She described the series of events that led up to and followed the marriage of Simon and Agnes. When Agnes had moved in with Simon (in the house of his father, Roger de Munkton),

> . . . she heard said Agnes say that she had confirmed the marriage made on that account and that she would rather that said Simon had done so long before she had the twenty pounds silver [as her inheritance from her father].[65]. . . And this was said in said Roger's

---

[64]". . . audivit clamorem unius mulieris, prout sibi tunc videbatur. Quo audito idem juratus accessit ad fenestram domus sue in vico predicto et vidit dictam Agnetam jacentem et dictum Simonem super eam in eodem vico, ea intentione, reputatione sua, ut eam posset duxisse ad mansum ipsius Simonis ut uxorem suam sine aliqua molestia eidem inferenda" (CP E 248-54).

[65]Although the archbishop's probate registers prior to 1389 do not survive, Agnes's father's will is preserved in York Minster Library, Dean and Chapter Probate Register 1, fol. 14r; it was proved 14 Apr. 1333, 15 years before the case between Simon and Agnes was heard in York and seven years before she married Simon. In this will Agnes's father, Richard of Huntington, granted £20 silver to Agnes and other items to her siblings, but asked his executors to look after these until his children reached their age of discretion.

house where said Simon and Agnes lived before and cohabited as spouses joined in matrimony and engendered a son called Hamo. Later at the door of the church of Saint Michael le Belfrey in York they contracted marriage in the customary words and solemnized that marriage in said church. . . . She also says that she saw said Simon and Agnes several times after the said alleged *traductio* lie together in one bed, *nudus cum nuda* with marital affection in the house of said Roger insofar as this witness could make out.[66]

Emma de Munkton describes the marriage as a process consisting of a series of steps, from the initial *traductio* of the woman into the man's household, through the solemnization of the marriage at the church in front of witnesses, to the birth of their son. The information on marital affection —which she volunteered to the court without being asked— shows that she saw it as the external expression of an internal reality. Her use of the wording "insofar as this witness could make out" makes it clear that she was aware that she could not be sure that the external signs of affection actually covered the inner reality of the emotion. In other words, in her use of the term, marital affection consisted of two parts, an inner reality and an outer expression.

---

[66]". . . audivit eandem Agnetam dicere quod ratam habuit traductionem in hac parte factam et quod mallet quod idem Simon sic fecisset a diu antequam ipsa [de hereditate patris sue] habuisset viginti libris argentum. . . . Et hec dicta fuerunt in manso dicti Rogeri, ubi dicti Simon et Agneta moram traxerunt prius et ut coniuges matrimonialiter copulati simul cohabitarunt et unum filium nomine Hamonem inter se procrearunt. Postquam ad ostium ecclesie Sancti Michaelis de Berefrido Eboracensis matrimonium adinvicem per verba consueta contraxerunt et idem matrimonium in ecclesia predicta solempnizarunt. . . . Dicit etiam se vidisse dictos Simonem et Agnetam post dictam traductionem pretensam pluries simul jacere in uno lecto solus cum sola, nudus cum nuda infra mansum Rogeri predicti affectione conjugali, quatenus ipsa jurata perpendere potuit, ut dicit" (CP E 248-4).

The final instance of a witness using the phrase comes from CP E 36 from 1338. The sequence of events reported by the witness Thomas Wans, a butcher from York, is like the sequence of events reported by Emma de Munkton. Yet the documents of the case do not mention a dispute over property between the litigants, as might have been expected from the contexts of other statements on marital affection. The libel of the case alleged that John Page, a fuller of York, and Alice de Wethcrby had contracted and solemnized marriage fourteen years earlier, that they had cohabited, had intercourse, and behaved with marital affection for years, and that Alice had subsequently married William de Cave. Alice de Wetherby was now trying to have her marriage to William de Cave annulled because of her precontract with John Page. Thomas Wans had been present when Alice and William contracted marriage at the church of All Saints, Pavement, three years earlier. To him there was marital affection in the marriage of William de Cave and Alice de Wetherby:

> He saw said William and Alice live together in one house as man and wife for many years in the city of York with conjugal affection. Concerning any subsequent intercourse he does not know for certain, but he well believes that there was subsequent intercourse as is mentioned in the article.[67]

Thus Thomas Wans, like Emma de Munkton, described a progression from the marriage contract through cohabitation to conjugal affection. Thomas Wans also saw the cohabitation

---

[67]"[Dicit quod] matrimonium adinvicem contraxerunt et solemnizarunt in ecclesia omnium sanctorum super pavamentum. Dicit etiam quod vidit dictos Willelmum et Aliciam simul cohabitare in una domo ut vir et uxor per multos annos in civitate Ebor' affectione conjugali. De carnali copula subsequente nescit pro certo sed bene credit carnalem copulam fuisse subsequenter prout in articulo continetur" (CP E 36-5).

and marital affection as circumstantial evidence that led him to believe that William de Cave and Alice de Wetherby had sexual intercourse.

Marital affection is an elusive concept with a long history in European law. The meaning of the phrase developed over the centuries, initially meaning the willing of the (property) consequences of marriage, but developing into a phrase that encompassed the internal psychological quality of marriage. This study has examined how the notion of marital affection, as developed in Roman and canon law, was applied to the marriages of real people in the fourteenth-century court of the archbishop of York.

The scarcity of evidence on marital affection in this otherwise rich mine of information on medieval marriage, and the broad range of the use of the words *affectio maritalis*, suggests that the courts and the witnesses found the concept difficult and confusing. Only eleven of about 580 witnesses commented on marital affection; only six cases included depositions that alleged marital affection, while one more case alleged that a husband had terminated his cohabitation, withdrawing marital affection from his spouse, but did not produce any evidence to prove the prior existence of such marital affection. Given the scarcity of statements on marital affection and the original Roman law meaning of *affectio maritalis* with its implications of the transfer of property, the context of all but two of these instances of marital affection in the York cause papers suggests that the phrase continued its connection with the question of control over property.

There was a wide variation in the meaning of the phrase and no consensus among the witnesses on how to apply the term. One litigant, William Aungier, said that he was concerned that his spouse did not "choose an affection that holds good," and he terminated their relationship because she had not excluded other men from her sexual favors. The way in which witnesses like Thomas Wans and Emma de Munkton referred to spouses' marital affection suggests that they were using an understanding of the emotional aspects of marriage not far removed from its meaning in the Decretals of Alexander III. In their use of the phrase, marital affection was a necessary ingredient in marriage and indicated what appears to be a psychological and emotional aspect of the union of two people. Perhaps because of the rule that sexual congress following an exchange of vows created a valid marriage, the witnesses are reported as making separate comments on marital affection and sexual activity, but the separation of the two follows the use of the phrase suggested by Alexander III. In the case of Thomas Wans, marital affection was circumstantial evidence for sexual intercourse between the partners. Other witnesses, like William de Helay, Thomas de Rydale, and Robert de Cleveland, used the phrase in a way that has its origins in Roman law. For them the phrase appears to have described a special quality in a marriage, a willingness between spouses to admit the legal consequences of marriage. For the latter two witnesses, the phrase indicated that a marriage had been entered into and that the spouses had lived together with the intent of being a married couple accepting the legal consequences of their marriage. William de Helay's deposition gives an even sharper definition to the phrase: in his use the spouses entered marriage with the intention of allowing the transfer of control over property, but this intention was of short duration, and most certainly his use of the phrase did not admit an emotional involvement between the parties.

The ambiguity of the phrase *affectio maritalis* remains even after this analysis of its use in fourteenth-century York marriage cases. The word *affectio*, which was first used in Roman law to indicate the willingness to permit the transfer of property, in its combination with a word indicating marriage, has continued to evolve in western European thought over the centuries to the point where *affection* now has lost its initial meaning of "will" and has become the word used to describe an internalized ongoing psychological process in the emotional involvement of one person with another. Though we may never know precisely how and when this change in meaning came about, the evidence of the York cause papers suggests that the meaning of the phrase was as elusive to the ordinary litigant as it was to the academic commentator, while also suggesting that the connection between marital affection and property found in Roman law was subtly continued in the practice of the court in York.

Husband and Wife
in Criminal Proceedings
in Medieval England[1]

Margaret H. Kerr

F. W. Maitland, in describing the status of unmarried and widowed women in English law in the thirteenth century, said that in private law women had equal rights with men but that in public law they had no rights and no duties. He contrasted their situation with that of married women, who had neither private nor public rights, and he characterized the relationship between husband and wife in

[1]When Father Michael Sheehan died in August 1992, he left much unfinished work. The other contributors to this volume and I are one of the reasons he did not finish it. We, his thesis students, took up a lot of his time and energy, and our demands on him no doubt frustrated him—but I believe that he kept on giving himself to us because he knew that one day he would be able to hand his work on to us.

When I received the call for papers for this memorial volume, requesting essays on the subjects of women, marriage, and family, I was initially distressed that I had no acceptable gift to offer Fr. Sheehan; I am a legal rather than a social historian. Then I realized that I was being given a special opportunity to show my gratitude and affection. Looking through the material that I knew, I found a contribution to make to his field of the history of marriage and the family.

I hope that Fr. Sheehan would have been pleased by this book of essays, and perhaps a little proud to say of the writers, "I trained them all."

English law as one of "profitable guardianship."[2] The aspects of this guardianship included several elements. In lands that came to a wife before or during the marriage, her husband had an estate that endured for the marriage, and he could alienate this estate without his wife's consent; a wife had no power to alienate her own land without her husband's consent during the marriage. Whatever chattels a wife owned at the date of the marriage became her husband's upon marriage, and whatever chattels a husband owned could be disposed of at his discretion—except, perhaps, his wife's necessary clothes. Nor could a wife enter into a contract on her own behalf during the marriage.[3] Saint Paul's dicta that a husband and wife will become one flesh and that the husband is the head of the wife (Ephesians 5: 31 and 5: 23) seem to have been put into practice with some degree of rigor: these restrictions on the rights of a wife appear very heavy to modern men and women. Such restrictions must have seemed burdensome to the thirteenth-century English as well, for loopholes in the law certainly existed. For example, the royal courts, while not interfering in disposition of a wife's land during her husband's lifetime, nevertheless provided a standard writ to permit the widow to regain possession of the land after his death.[4] Michael Sheehan found that wives made frequent use of a

---

[2]Frederick Pollock and F. W. Maitland, *The History of English Law before the Time of Edward I*, 2nd ed., 2 vols. (Cambridge, 1968), 1: 482–85; 2: 406.

[3]Pollock and Maitland, *History of English Law*, 2: 403–05.

[4]The writ *cui in vita sua* stated that the widow claimed lands as her right and marriage portion which her husband "whom she could not contradict in his lifetime" ("cui in vita sua contradicere non potuit") had granted to the defendant (*Reading, 1248*, pleas 16, 165, 231, 283, 398, 427, 517, 590, 620, and writs a83, a195, and a196 at pp. 433 and 481; *Shropshire, 1256*, pls. 6, 305, 349). (The printed collections of primary sources upon which this study rests, and the abbreviations used to identify them, are listed in Appendix C below.)

customary right to bequeath chattels and even land.[5] A wife who carried on a trade could be sued personally in debt on her own contract in some towns.[6] It is clear that a statement of the theoretical law of husband and wife in property and contract does not entirely reflect the reality.

Maitland did not closely examine the relationship between husband and wife in the area of criminal law. If he had, he would have discovered a pattern similar to that in civil matters. Wives were legally subject to severe restrictions on their rights as accusers when a felony had been committed: practically speaking, a wife had no right to prosecute anyone for a criminal

---

[5] Sheehan, *The Will in Medieval England, from the Conversion of the Anglo-Saxons to the End of the Thirteenth Century* (Toronto, 1963), pp. 236–38; Ranulf de Glanvill, *The Treatise on the Laws and Customs of the Realm of England, Commonly Called Glanvill*, ed. G. D. G. Hall (London, 1965), p. 80: "Yet it would be truly kind and creditable in a husband were he to allow his wife a reasonable division, namely up to that third part of chattels which . . . she would have obtained had she survived her husband; many husbands in fact do this . . ."; Henry de Bracton, *Bracton on the Laws and Customs of England*, trans. and ed. S. E. Thorne, 4 vols. (Cambridge, Mass., 1968–77), 2: 179, fol. 60b: "Nevertheless, because it is only proper, she is sometimes permitted to dispose by will of that reasonable part she would have had if she had survived her husband, especially things given and granted for her personal adornment, as robes and jewels, which may be said to be her own." R. H. Helmholz, "Married Women's Wills in Later Medieval England," in *Wife and Widow in Medieval England*, ed. Sue Sheridan Walker (Ann Arbor, 1993), p. 165, concluded that by the middle of the 15th century married women's wills were rarities, perhaps because by "1450 it was more widely assumed than it had been in 1300 that married women had no independent legal interests in chattels apart from their husbands" (p. 172). There are indications in criminal records that wives owned chattels in the 13th century. In 1244, a woman who hanged herself in her husband's house had chattels valued for the court record at 5s. (*London, 1244*, pl. 141). In a case of 1286, a woman who strangled her husband in the fields with her scarf and then fled England had chattels worth 2s. (*Huntingdonshire, 1286*, 2: pl. 387).

[6] Pollock and Maitland, *History of English Law*, 2: 434–35.

offense until she was a widow, at which time she gained the right to prosecute her husband's killer, had he been slain. Wives were considered to be under their husbands' guardianship in different areas of criminal and quasi-criminal justice. Husbands could beat their wives for purposes of discipline. Husbands, but not wives, had a right to sue for damages when the wives were injured. Husbands had a cause of action against anyone who "stole" their wives, a cause of action parallel to stealing the husband's chattels. Husbands, but not wives, were punished for crimes the couple committed together, since wives were under their husbands' control. This is the theoretical law of husband and wife—but, again, it is an imperfect reflection of reality. The reality is glimpsed in the legal records, particularly those of the thirteenth century, when the nature of criminal proceedings provided much circumstantial detail.

WIVES AS THEIR HUSBANDS' PROPERTY

Husbands did have a right to use physical force on their wives, "lawful and reasonable" force for the purpose of control and punishment. This right, however, was not unlimited, for a form of writ existed in the courts to require a husband to keep the peace and not to discipline his wife excessively. Nevertheless, there were no cases in the records reviewed in which husbands were prosecuted in the royal courts for beating or assaulting their spouses.[7] Wife-beating was probably censured

---

[7]The form, in a book of royal writs, sets out a husband's duty with respect to his wife: to "treat and govern her well and honestly, and to do no injury or ill to her body other than that permitted lawfully and reasonably to a husband for the purpose of control and punishment of his wife" (Pollock and Maitland, *History of English Law*, 2: 436). Certainly some husbands needed guidance about their duty. In 1199 jurors suspected the wife of a slain man in his death, because they often fought and he used to beat her (*Lichfield, 1199*, p. 39).

and punished in the church courts under ecclesiastical law,[8] and possibly local courts also had some form of jurisdiction in wife-beating cases. R. H. Hilton, in his study of the town of Halesowen, hints at the possibility of local prosecution for intrafamilial violence; he mentions that a man was accused by a presenting jury in 1298 in the borough court of beating his sister. He also notes that there were often presentments, or charges in the court, of raising the hue and cry between husbands and wives. A fine was imposed on any individual who raised the hue "unjustly."[9]

If prosecutions for beating a wife were so rare, is this an indication that a husband had the tacit consent of the criminal

---

In 1276 Richard Scharp, wool merchant, beat his wife, Emma, so that she gave birth to a stillborn boy. He was arrested and indicted but released, and died before trial. The indictment was for the death of his son, not injury to his wife (*London, 1276*, pl. 76). In two Northumberland cases husbands beat their wives to death, in each case with a staff; they fled and were outlawed (*Northumberland, 1256*, p. 118; *Northumberland, 1279*, p. 361). In 1342 a wife died a natural death; the coroner viewed the body because it was widely said that her husband beat her unduly ("indebito") (H. E. Salter, ed., *Records of Mediaeval Oxford: Coroners' Inquests, the Walls of Oxford, etc.* [Oxford, 1912], p. 24, cited in C. I. Hammer, "Patterns of Homicide in a Medieval University Town: Fourteenth-Century Oxford," *Past and Present* 78 [1978]: 14).

[8]In the deanery of Wych, Worcs., in 1300, Thomas Louchard was whipped through the marketplace for ill-treating his wife with a rod (Harry Rothwell, ed., *English Historical Documents*, 3: *1189–1327* [London, 1975], p. 725). In the archdeacon's court, Sudbury, in 1300 Walter de Fornham had to answer a charge of mistreating his wife by beating her; he was not punished, but swore that thenceforward he would "do well" (Antonia Gransden, ed., "Some Late 13th-Century Records of the Ecclesiastical Court in the Archdeaconry of Sudbury," *Bulletin of the Institute for Historical Research* 32 [1959]: 67). The dearth of early church court records makes it impossible to know how often or how severely husbands were punished for such offenses.

[9]"Small Town Society in England before the Black Death," *Past and Present* 105 (1984): 70, 74.

justice system to treat his wife as he pleased, even to the point of killing her? Do the records provide evidence about how far his guardianship of his wife was allowed to extend? In a disturbing case reported in 1276, Roger le Tuler had killed his wife, Elicia; he was arrested and imprisoned, and he escaped, but he later appeared before the court with a royal charter testifying that Henry III (d. 1272) had pardoned him for breach of the king's peace arising from this death, on the condition that he appear to defend any private criminal action that might be brought against him for the death. No one wished to prosecute him for Elicia's death, so the court granted him "firm peace," the equivalent of a full pardon.[10] Roger le Tuler's case was, however, quite exceptional in the records reviewed. There are many cases from the beginning of the thirteenth century onward of husbands being accused by local juries of presentment or indicted by the crown for killing their wives, and the records make it clear that they were reported to the authorities and dealt with exactly as other alleged killers were.[11] Most of

---

[10]*London, 1276*, pl. 176.

[11]*Lichfield, 1199*, p. 39 (outcome unknown); *Lincoln, 1202*, pls. 579 (husband convicted, hanged), 942 (husband fled); *York, 1208*, pl. 3441 (husband suspected by jurors but passed ordeal); *York, 1218–19*, pl. 842 (husband convicted, hanged); *Worcester, 1221*, pl. 1145 (appeal against husband declared invalid, acquitted by jurors); *Shrewsbury, 1221*, pls. 775 (husband fled, abjured realm), 828 (husband fled, abjured realm), 904 (husband fled, outlawed); *Somerset, 1225*, pls. 265 (husband taken, died in prison), 275 (husband fled, outlawed); *Surrey, 1235*, pls. 540 (husband abjured realm), 434 (husband fled, outlawed); *Devon, 1238*, pl. 671 (husband burned his wife and children in their house; he fled, was outlawed); *Durham, 1242*, pls. 3 (husband arrested, escaped prison, abjured realm; his two daughters taken for consenting to the killing; they were convicted by a jury and hanged), 13 (husband acquitted by jury); *Somerset, 1242–43*, pl. 994 (wife merely "fell dead in the way," husband fled but was not guilty, could return); *London, 1244*, pl. 156 (husband fled, outlawed). For similar cases: *Reading, 1248*, pls. 934, 945; *Wiltshire, 1249*, pls. 42, 135; *Northumberland, 1256*, pp. 86, 115,

the husbands either confessed the deed and submitted to exile from England or fled from their counties and were outlawed for failing to respond to court process. Although a significant number of the husbands tried were acquitted, quite a few were convicted and promptly hanged. That husbands genuinely feared punishment for killing their wives is illustrated by a case from 1242–43. When his wife fell dead in the road for reasons having nothing to do with him, the husband fled out of fear of prosecution. When the jurors reported the matter to the court, they said that they did not suspect the husband of killing his wife; the court ordered that he might return if he wished.[12]

If husbands had no lawful right to kill their wives, and apparently no right to injure them seriously, did they, on a different level, own their wives' bodies in a sexual sense, and

---

116 (husband killed his own wife, another man's wife, and a serving maid, set fire to the house and fled; he was hanged), 118 (husband beat his wife with a staff while coming from market, so that she died immediately; husband fled, outlawed), 122; *Wiltshire, 1275–1306*, pls. 108 and 251 (husbands hanged), 760, 761, 753 (husband indicted for hiring three men to kill his wife; two of the three hit-men hanged, husband and third man apparently acquitted), 779, 780, 786 (outcomes unknown); *London, 1276*, pls. 281 (husband acquitted), 258 (husband fled, outlawed); *Northumberland, 1279*; pp. 344, 361 (husbands fled, outlawed); *Huntingdonshire, 1286*, pls. 352, 369 (husband and a woman taken and imprisoned, both died in prison), 523, 540 (husband had paid another man to kill his wife; husband fled, outlawed), 626; *Norfolk, 1307–16*, pls. 24, 53, 74 (husbands acquitted), 326, 393 (jurors' verdict was insanity; husband returned to prison to await the king's grace). Naomi D. Hurnard, *The King's Pardon for Homicide before A.D. 1307* (Oxford, 1969), cites cases in which husbands needed pardons for killing their wives: p. 76: in 1231 a jury made a presentment that a man had thrown a staff at a plough-horse but hit his wife with the iron tip so that she died—the jurors added that he had not struck his wife out of hatred but by accident; comparable material from 1236.

[12] *Somerset, 1242–43*, pl. 994.

possess a right to punish anyone who trespassed sexually?[13] The records under review show only two examples of a husband initiating a private criminal prosecution (an appeal of felony), for wife-stealing, and only one for rape of a wife. In the first wife-stealing case (1203), a husband commenced an appeal of felony against a man for robbing him of wife and goods. The defendant asked that the court record be produced to substantiate his defense that he had been previously acquitted of the charges. The record showed the acquittal, as well as a ruling that the husband had wrongfully alleged that the defendant's acts constituted felony: "in this appeal, felony does not lie," stated the court. In the second appeal (1223), the husband, who had received his wife through the gift of the king, complained that the defendant had taken her and various chattels from his house. The action was dismissed on the technical ground that the husband had not actually witnessed the abduction.[14] In the rape case in 1312, a husband appealed a

---

[13]The duty of a husband and wife to live together was enforced in the church courts on behalf of either spouse: R. H. Helmholz, *Marriage Litigation in Medieval England* (London, 1974), chap. 2. Adultery as a crime was also punished by the church courts.

[14]CRR 2: 181; CRR 11, pl. 476. In 1208 a man brought an appeal of robbery and of the abduction of *another man's* wife; one of his pledges guaranteeing that he would prosecute was the wronged husband. He did not proceed to prosecute, however (*York, 1208*, pl. 3509). In a similar case, a man appealed another of abduction of a third man's wife and of robbery. The man who brought the appeal requested trial by jury, and the jurors stated that the facts were true (*Devon, 1238*, pl. 611). 1242: a husband and wife brought an action for damages against a sheriff for imprisoning the husband for marrying the wife. The sheriff defended that the husband and nine associates had raped and then abducted his intended bride from her mother's house, and he had arrested the husband after the mother raised the hue and cry and stated her intention of prosecuting the husband. The truth was to be decided by a jury (CRR 17, pl. 53). 1302: Thomas Archur brought an action against Peter le Webbe "for goods stolen upon the abduction of Emme, Thomas's wife."

man of raping and then abducting his wife, together with goods and chattels he valued at £100. The husband did not appear in court to prosecute the defendant, who was tried at the king's suit and acquitted.[15]

These three criminal actions were almost certainly brought after the wife in question voluntarily (but not empty-handed) left the husband for another man and are closely related to a civil action for wife-stealing. Until the Statute of Westminster II in 1285, it was not a felony—that is, a crime punishable by death or mutilation—to steal a wife, but rather a trespass— a tortious wrong compensable by damages. Even after 1285 there seems to have been more interest in recovering damages from the wife-stealer than in punishing him physically. There are cases from the thirteenth and fourteenth centuries in which husbands claimed damages against people for taking their wives away from them, the earliest in 1241 and 1255.[16] From the beginning of the fourteenth century, actions for damages

---

Thomas did not prosecute his action at trial; Peter was tried at the king's suit and acquitted (*Wiltshire, 1275–1306*, pl. 369). 1412: a man was indicted for feloniously taking a man's wife and feloniously stealing goods valued at 20s. from him (*Shropshire, 1400–14*, pl. 189).

[15] *Norfolk, 1307–16*, pl. 293. In 1230 in King's Bench, John, parson of Bradewas, was required to inform Geoffrey de la Wern' and his wife Petronilla why he had brought them into court Christian in an action outside the jurisdiction of the court, being an action for damages. John replied that Geoffrey and Petronilla had brought an action against him in a lay court for rape, theft, and other infamous deeds. No details were given of the allegations of rape, so we do not know if the rape occurred before or after Petronilla's marriage. Note, however, that Petronilla herself was a party to the action (CRR 14, pl. 402).

[16] S. F. C. Milsom, "Trespass from Henry III to Edward III," Pt. I, *Law Quarterly Review* 74 (1958): 211.

based on the Statutes of Westminster of 1275 and 1285[17] were popular, and they were brought by husbands not only against men who enticed wives away but also against relatives who took in wives who had left their husbands. A substantial sum might be awarded in such an action, as in 1308 against Robert de Heydon, who had an affair with his master's wife while he was an apprentice and then later persuaded her to leave her husband for him, bringing with her goods worth £60. Robert was ordered to pay the wronged husband £60 for the goods, and the jury assessed the husband's general damages at 100 marks, a considerable sum of money.[18]

---

[17]The Statutes of Westminster I and II provided for criminal prosecution of "rape" by an individual or the king. *Rape* in the statute context is not synonymous with today's usage in common law countries but focuses on abduction and elopement rather than on nonconsensual intercourse. Westminster I (1275), c. 13, forbade the rape of a girl under age with or without her consent, or a married woman or an unmarried woman of age against her will, and provided a criminal cause of action to any individual, or to the king if no individual commenced an action within 40 days. Punishment was two years' imprisonment and a fine. Westminster II (1285), c. 34, revised these provisions and made the offense to rape a married or unmarried woman even though she consented afterwards punishable by death or mutilation, if the king rather than an individual sued. Westminster II further gave the king authority to prosecute for the goods carried off were a wife taken away with her husband's goods. It also deprived a wife who left her husband for another man of the right to claim her dower by legal action, unless her husband willingly took her back and allowed her to live with him. A statute of 1382 (6 Richard II, statute 1, c. 6) provided that if a wife or daughter were raped and consented afterwards, she and her ravisher were barred from enforcing her rights to inheritance, dower, or joint ownership of land after the death of her husband or father. The statute also gave the husband or father an appeal of rape against the ravisher, which had to be tried by jury rather than by battle.

[18]Morris S. Arnold, ed., *Select Cases of Trespass from the King's Courts, 1307–1399*, 2 vols., Selden Society, 100, 103 (1985–87), 1: xlv–xlviii and 73–93, discusses and reproduces several actions for damages for wife-stealing; Robert de Heydon's case is at pp. 73–74.

The fact that husbands were not in the habit of asserting ownership of their wives' bodies or sexuality through the criminal law does not mean, however, that wives asserted their ownership of their own bodies through the criminal law. Private criminal prosecution initiated by a wife for rape was so rare that it was an anomaly—and public prosecution by presentment or by indictment for rape of either married or unmarried women was virtually nonexistent in the thirteenth century.[19] Of 272 private prosecutions (appeals of felony) for rape found between 1194 and 1306, only five were brought by married women, and another five by widowed women.[20] The probable

---

[19] A presentment of forcible intercourse with an unmarried woman was made in 1194, but the jurors made no verdict, saying simply that they did not know if it was true: *Wiltshire, 1194*, p. 96.

[20] Appeals of rape by wives: *York 1218–19*, pls. 848, 935; *Bristol, 1221*, pl. 16 (the appellor was described as "Agnes, niece of John" rather than "wife of" and may have begun her appeal before her marriage); *Wiltshire, 1249*, pl. 207; *Northumberland, 1256*, p. 96; CRR 14, pl. 402. In a trespass action in 1276 William de Hadestok and his wife, Joan, complained that in 1269 James de Montibus went to their house, broke the door and entered, and broke Joan's finger and committed other outrages against her, to their damage of £100. The wards came and said that James and many others came with force and arms with a king's bailiff to Joan's house before her marriage, and that after he entered the house he raped Joan, throwing her to the ground and breaking her finger. James was ordered gaoled until he satisfied the plaintiffs for their damages, assessed at 100s. The action brought by William and Joan did not claim damages for the rape (*London, 1276*, pl. 519). For appeals of rape by widows: *York, 1218–19*, pl. 934; *Coventry, 1221*, pl. 902; *Somerset, 1242–43*, pl. 1237; *Wiltshire, 1249*, pl. 296; *Northumberland, 1279*, p. 316. In a King's Bench case Alice widow of Elias the cleric appealed a man of breaking into her house, lying with her ("cum ea concubuit"), wounding her, and abducting her daughter. She stated that she had complained immediately to the sheriff and had shown him her wounds and blood, and he undertook to inquire where the girl was hidden and to return her if she could be found, and to require those who had taken her to answer for the deed in the king's court at Westminster. The abductor appeared and pleaded

explanation of these odd statistics on rape is not that married women were cloistered or constantly guarded against sexual assault, but that in the late twelfth and the thirteenth centuries *rape* in the legal sense meant "rape of virginity."[21] Sexual assault that did not reduce the market value of the victim was seemingly not criminal in the early common law, although this notion soon lost currency. From the beginning of the fourteenth century there were a number of public prosecutions by indictment for rape in which the victim was a married woman.[22]

WIVES AS PROSECUTORS IN CRIMINAL ACTIONS

Women in general—not only wives—were not accorded the public legal rights of adult male "citizens" in the criminal courts. English jurists Glanvill, writing ca. 1188, and Bracton, some forty or fifty years later, were in agreement that women

---

that he had taken the daughter away with Alice's consent; he made no defense to the allegation of rape. No actual charge of rape, apparently, was before the court; it had only been included in the appeal as circumstantial evidence of the charge of abduction (CRR 7: 335).

[21] See Appendix A below, "A Note on Rape."

[22] Records from the 14th century show that rape of married women was not uncommon, but in these cases the accused were indicted rather than appealed. See *Cambridgeshire, 1332–34*, pls. 22 and 25; *Lincolnshire, 1351–54*, pls. 1 and 10*; *Lincolnshire, 1360–75*, p. 25, #61; p. 28, #76+; p. 43, #143*+; p. 208, #65+; *Gloucestershire, 1361–98*, pls. 102+, 116+, 118+, 123+, 125+, 130+, 135+, 154+. For the 15th century see *Shropshire, 1400–14*, pls. 28+, 35, 84, 100+, 185. It is best not to assume that all these cases involve what we think of as rape; those marked with an asterisk (*) were indictments for both rape and abduction—which may mean that the wife committed adultery and left her husband—and those marked with a cross (+), indictments for rape and taking of chattels—which may mean either that the accused actually raped the wife and stole goods or that she committed adultery and left her husband, and that she and the accused took goods with them from the husband's house.

had the right to prosecute criminally in only two situations: for the death of a husband—"slain within her arms," Bracton adds —or for personal injury, implicitly narrowed to rape. From about the middle of the thirteenth century women were legally permitted a third prosecution, for abortion (causing a miscarriage, usually by a beating).[23] Private criminal prosecution in the royal courts was undertaken by "appealing" the defendant of a felony; felonies included homicide, robbery, theft, arson, assault, wounding, and rape. Before 1215, trial in a woman's appeal was by ordeal; after 1215, when trial by ordeal was abolished by the Fourth Lateran Council, women's appeals were tried by jury.

---

[23]Hall, *Glanville*, pp. 173–74: Glanvill characterized the right of a woman to appeal of the death of her husband as an extension of her right to appeal of her own injuries when he noted that the former appeal is allowable because husband and wife are one flesh. Bracton, *On the Laws and Customs*, 2: 353, 419. On the appeal of causing a miscarriage see C. A. F. Meekings, ed., *Crown Pleas of the Wiltshire Eyre, 1249*, Wiltshire Record Society, 16 (1961), p. 90. Two intriguing entries in the Pipe Rolls for Henry II show women as criminal prosecutors in cases that cannot be reconciled with Glanvill's statement of the law ca. 1188. In an entry for 1155–56 a woman was being paid by the king as a "king's approver," *Pipe Rolls 2-3-4 Henry II*, ed. Joseph Hunter (London, 1844), p. 4. All other known king's approvers and ordinary approvers in the 12th and 13th centuries were men, although three women referred to in an entry in 1176–77 might have been either accused held pending trial or approvers: *Pipe Roll 23 Henry II, 1176–1177*, Pipe Roll Society, 26 (1905), p. 198. A king's approver in 1155–56 probably initiated a private criminal prosecution on behalf of the king in respect of an offense affecting the crown, e.g., forgery or breach of forest laws. Trial of an approver's appeal was by battle, but it does not seem likely that the woman approver was required to fight. Perhaps when her appeal came to trial ordeal or compurgation was employed. In the case of 1174–75 a woman and a boy "who appealed villeins who had burned [to death] their lord" were also on the royal payroll, in the same section of the record as approvers, although they themselves were not named as approvers: *Pipe Roll 21 Henry II, 1174–1175*, Pipe Roll Society, 22 (1897), p. 198.

Theoretically, the criminal records should show women without husbands and widows—other than wives prosecuting their husbands' deaths (who, for convenience here, are considered wives rather than widows)—initiating prosecutions only for rape or for causing a miscarriage. But in the records under review for the period 1194–1306, unmarried women and widows launched some 158 appeals of felony for miscellaneous offenses apart from 267 appeals of rape (only five of the rape cases involved widows). Unmarried and widowed women seem to have been active litigants, bringing appeals of the deaths of children, parents, and siblings, and occasionally of more distant relatives, of lovers, and of people not identified by relationship. They also appealed of robbery, housebreaking, burglary, assault on themselves and others, wounds, mayhem, breach of the peace, imprisonment, arson, abortion by assault, abduction, and rape of a daughter. It was unusual for an accused to raise the objection at trial that a woman had only two or three lawful appeals, although this did happen on rare occasions; whenever it did, the court immediately declared the appeal invalid.[24] It was also unusual, however, for a woman—or, indeed, for a man—to persist with any appeal right up to the trial stage. When a woman did so, the court sometimes refused to entertain her prosecution,[25] but it did not always turn a

---

[24]*Wells, 1201*, pls. 730 and 731; *Somerset, 1242–43*, pl. 929; *Shropshire, 1256*, pl. 566, and Appendix, p. lxxii; *Huntingdonshire, 1286*, 2: pl. 370. Except at Wells, in each instance where the appeal was declared invalid the case went to the jury, which either declared the appellee guilty or not guilty.

[25]*Launceston, 1201*, pls. 253 (death of her son; no determination by court), 294 (death of her son; defendants who had not fled were acquitted), 336 (death of her daughter; no determination by court); *Lincoln, 1202*, pls. 566 (housebreaking, robbery, imprisonment; no determination by court), 573 (breach of the peace; no determination by court), 589 (allegation unknown; defendant quit), 854 (robbery; no determination by court). In two cases the jury made a preliminary finding that prosecution was malicious, thus

woman litigant away. In the records that pre-date 1215, there were some unmarried and widowed women's unconventional appeals allowed to be prosecuted all the way to trial, ending either with trial by jury or trial by jury followed by the ordeal. In a number of other appeals brought by unmarried women but *not* prosecuted, the accused was tried by a jury but the ordeal was not imposed.[26] An unmarried or widowed woman's appeal therefore had the potential to operate as a form of indictment even early in the thirteenth century. This seems to have pointed the way towards treatment of women's appeals later in the century. It became common for women's unconventional appeals to be heard by a jury, and apparently all that was necessary for the woman to do was initiate the appeal.[27]

---

terminating the matter: *Lincoln, 1202*, pls. 841 (assault, beating, robbery), 909 (housebreaking, beating, robbery, rape).

[26]Prosecuted cases that went to the jury and then to the ordeal: *Wells, 1201*, pls. 742 (death of her son and her own wounds); *Lincoln, 1202*, pl. 855 (robbery in her mother's house). Prosecuted cases that went to jury only: *Launceston, 1201*, pls. 323 (breach of the peace, beating, wounds), 399 (robbery); *Northants., 1202*, pl. 72 (death of her father); *Shrewsbury, 1203*, pl. 755 (death of her son). Cases not prosecuted that went to the jury: *Wells, 1201*, pl. 735 (beating her master and killing his wife); *Launceston, 1201*, pl. 310; *Northants., 1202*, pl. 72; *Lichfield, 1203*, p. 92 (arson). For an appeal of rape tried by a jury before the ordeal was abolished see *Launceston, 1201*, pl. 337; but appeals of rape were not tried by ordeal before 1215, rather by attestation of local officials that the appellor had made an immediate complaint and had looked properly victimized (*Launceston, 1201*, pls. 342, 395; *Lincoln, 1202*, pls. 590, 916; *York, 1208*, pls. 3424, 3491). If the appellor withdrew her appeal or failed to prosecute it, the defendant was acquitted or dismissed "without a day" being set for further proceedings. In the latter case, presumably the appellor had the right to prosecute later. Following the abolition of the ordeal, trial by jury at once became the means of dealing with an appeal of rape. See *York, 1218–19*, pls. 545, 591, 594, 688, 741, 745, 763, 784, 803, 809, 818, 847, 848, 927, 932, 934, 955, 956, 957, 959, 963, 974, 976, 1074, 1082, 1095.

[27]*York, 1218–19*, pl. 737 (death of her mother); *Coventry, 1221*, pls. 734 (death of her son), 750 and 924 (death of her brother); *Shrewsbury, 1221*,

The profile that wives presented in criminal proceedings was significantly different from that of unmarried and widowed women. To begin with, overwhelmingly they brought one appeal; for the death of a husband.[28] In the records from 1194 to 1306, there are some 297 appeals brought by wives acting alone. Of these, 245 were brought for the death of a husband. Of the other fifty-two, five were for rape, twenty-

---

pl. 1242; *Worcester, 1221*, pl. 1092 (death of her son); *Surrey, 1235*, pls. 362 (robbery), 389, 390 (death of her son), 465 (breach of peace, wounds and robbery), 556; *Devon, 1238*, pls. 129 (robbery, breach of peace), 133, 140 (death of relatives), 178 (death of sister), 259 (breach of peace, housebreaking), 260, 381 (burglary of her mother's house and strangling of her mother), 525, 558 (beating, hair-cutting, robbery), 587 (beating her, threatening her son), 590 (rape of her daughter), 606 (death of a man), 614 (death of her sister), 649 and 729 (breach of peace); *Somerset, 1242–43*, pls. 760, 954 (assault), 1104 (mayhem of her shoulder), 1181, 1218 (robbery and inciting); *London, 1244*, pl. 175 (death of brother); *Reading, 1248*, pls. 810 (death of brother), 816 (beating and robbery), 857 (death of brother), 1034; *Wiltshire, 1249*, pls. 280 (housebreaking, wounding), 274 (wrongful imprisonment), 497 (burglary—defendants found guilty, hanged); *Northumberland, 1256*, pl. 108 (imprisonment); *Huntingdonshire, 1286*, 2: pls. 370 (death of her son; N.B., the county was fined, apparently because it allowed the defendant to be arrested and/or imprisoned on the appeal of a woman other than an appeal of the death of her husband, rape of virginity, or abortion of her infant), 444, 513, 549 (death of her son), 634 (death of her brother; the jurors reported that the felony had previously been pleaded before the justices itinerant, so the court refused to deal with it). There were far fewer appeals in the 14th century, but the evidence that a woman's appeal was equated to an indictment and followed by trial by jury is clear: *Norfolk, 1307–16*, pls. 45, 68, and also 463 (defendant refused jury trial and was remanded to prison *ad dietam*, i.e., to be subjected to unpleasant conditions of imprisonment until he agreed to be tried by a jury).

[28] In appeals of the death of a husband, before 1215 some defendants were tried by jury: *Bedford, 1202*, pl. 210; *Lichfield, 1199*, p. 39; *Lincoln, 1202*, pls. 693a, 738; some by ordeal: *Wells, 1201*, pl. 732; *Launceston, 1201*, pls. 265, 620; *Lincoln, 1202*, pl. 693a; *Lichfield, 1203*, p. 96. After 1215 trial was by jury. The majority of defendants fled rather than face trial.

seven for miscellaneous crimes. The remaining twenty were for assault on or wounds inflicted on the appellors' husbands.[29]

According to Bracton, no one could sue against another for felony "by attorney" as long as he himself was capable of suing. But if he were temporarily incapacitated, a kinsman or friend could sue for him, although once he recovered he had to continue the suit personally.[30] Bracton made no mention of wives acting as their husbands' attorneys in such circumstances, but the arrangement makes perfect sense, given that it was the wife, rather than a "kinsman or friend," who would

---

[29]It was less common for a husband to sue for an injury to his wife. There are six examples of such an action between 1201 and 1276: *Launceston, 1201*, pl. 408; *Lincoln, 1202*, pl. 533; *Devon, 1238*, pl. 443, and pl. 626, where a husband appealed of a beating leading to miscarriage, and of his wife's death—probably consequent upon the miscarriage and occurring after the original appeal was begun; *Somerset 1242–43*, pl. 929; *London, 1244*, pl. 84; *London, 1276*, pl. 222. In the London case of 1244 the appeal was declared invalid; the appellor's wife was still living and took no action herself. In 1276 a husband appealed a man of beating his wife so his child was stillborn. This may be an appeal of the child's death, not of the wife's beating, which puts the fact that the husband was the sole appellor in a different light. In 1201 a husband appealed of assault on himself and on his wife, and of robbery of two gold rings, 16½d., and his wife's cloak; the parties settled. In a Somerset case of 1242–43 the husband commenced the appeal for striking his wife; at trial, she appeared and also sued against the defendant, who objected that she ought not to have an appeal against him because a woman could not have an appeal against anyone except for the death of her husband or for rape; he further alleged that the suit was malicious. The jurors agreed that the action was malicious, which unfortunately prevented the court from ruling whether a woman had the right to prosecute for her own injuries. The wife, not the husband, was fined for a false appeal.

[30]Bracton, *On the Laws and Customs*, 2: 353. In 1279 a woman appealed of the beating of her brother. She appeared alone in court; the appeal was declared invalid because her brother was alive and did not appeal (*Northumberland, 1279*, p. 365).

appeal of the husband's death should his wounds prove fatal.[31] The evidence here is somewhat confused, but it appears that the appeal of a husband's wounds was essentially his own appeal before ca. 1218–19; the wife was genuinely seen as his attorney, and he was expected to take an active part in the prosecution as soon as he was able to do so. Later in the century, a wife seems to have been regarded as an independent legal person, capable of prosecuting and responsible for the consequences of failing to prosecute or of prosecuting unsuccessfully. In two appeals of a husband's wounds in 1201, the wife was the only appellor named.[32] In six cases in 1202 and 1203 the wife was the only appellor, but when she failed to prosecute, her husband and not she was fined for her default.[33] In cases in 1202 and 1238 both husband and wife were named as appellors, he apparently joining in the appeal after his recovery.[34] Yet in seven cases from 1218 to 1238 the wife was

---

[31]*Bedford 1202*, pl. 210; *Somerset 1242–43*, pls. 912, 979.

[32]*Wells, 1201*, pl. 734; *Launceston, 1201*, pl. 287.

[33]*Bedford, 1202*, pl. 254 (husband and wife both undertook to sue, therefore he was fined); *Lincoln, 1202*, pls. 587 ("his wife did not prosecute and therefore in mercy [fined]" ["non est prosecuta uxor eius et ideo in misericordia"]), 710, 747; *Northants., 1202*, pl. 15 (she "pledged her faith to follow it up if her husband would not follow it; and she has not followed it up nor has her husband"); *Lichfield, 1203*, p. 92 (the husband was fined because "he permitted his wife to come into the county court and appeal [the accused] of wounds given to her . . . he has refused to follow up the suit, when his wife had sworn to follow it up").

[34]*Bedford, 1202*, pl. 224; also pl. 254 (wife and husband both undertook to sue, although only she was named as an appellor; he was fined when she did not prosecute). *Devon, 1238*, pl. 230 (wife and husband appealed of wounds to the husband). In 1238 a wife appealed of housebreaking, beating (though of which spouse is not stated), and robbery; the jury found the defendants not guilty, and the husband, present in court, went to gaol for false appeal (*Devon, 1238*, pl. 524). It seems likely that the injured party was the husband, and the wife had brought the appeal while he was physically incapacitated.

the only appellor, and she was fined personally, or her sureties
—men guaranteeing that she would continue to prosecute to
trial—were, for failing to follow up the prosecution.[35] But in a
case in 1279, the wife was the only appellor in an appeal of
beating her husband, and the appeal was declared invalid when
the defendant asserted that the appellor wife "said nothing by
which he should be put to law," that is, had not made out a
good cause of action. She was taken into custody for an unsuccessful appeal.[36]

It was uncommon for a wife to appeal all by herself of an
offense other than death of or injury to her husband, but there
were some appeals outside these two categories, including appeals of rape, theft, robbery, assault, and the death of relatives.
Prior to 1218–19 a wife's appeal of a crime other than the
death of her husband could have only two possible outcomes.
Either the wife did not prosecute her action right up to trial, or
she did prosecute and her appeal was declared invalid at trial.[37]
But as the thirteenth century progressed, a wife's appeal, like

---

[35] *York, 1218–19*, pl. 747 (wife appealed but did not appear at trial; husband
later appealed the same defendants himself; wife's sureties were fined); *Coventry, 1221*, pls. 844 (neither the appellor wife nor her husband appeared; appellor's sureties were fined), 923 (appellor's husband had recovered from his
wounds and did not appear in court; sureties were fined); *Devon, 1238*, pls.
93 (appellor wife did not prosecute, she and her pledges were fined), 146 (a
wife, husband's two sons, and a nephew appealed of wounds to the husband;
two of the male appellors appeared but did not prosecute; they and their
pledges were fined; the appellors were taken into custody and fined for a
false appeal when the jurors said that the defendant was not guilty). Also,
pls. 364, 633.

[36] A jury trial followed, and damages were assessed at 20s. The defendant then
"complained" that the husband had assaulted him: the husband appeared and
defended the action and elected trial by jury. The jurors said he was guilty of
assault and assessed damages at ½ mark: *Northumberland, 1279*, p. 320.

[37] See Appendix B below, "A Note on Wives' Unconventional Appeals."

an unmarried woman's appeal, was often treated as an indictment and referred to a jury for a verdict.[38]

It seems that the judicial system did not attempt to prevent women, whether married or not, from initiating criminal proceedings of all kinds,[39] and generally left it up to the

---

[38]In 1218–19, Alice of Newton, wife of Simon de Mohaut, had an appeal of robbery, but she had died. The jury acquitted the defendant: *York, 1218–19*, pl. 742. In 1242–43, Matilda, wife of William de Chedeseye, appealed of breach of peace but did not prosecute; a jury found the defendant guilty: *Somerset, 1242–43*, pl. 1115. In 1249, Cecily, wife of Robert the merchant, appealed of causing a miscarriage but withdrew at trial; the case went to a jury: *Wiltshire, 1249*, pl. 562. Also in 1249, Lucy, wife of Gilbert Morin, appealed of wounding her and taking three piglets. A jury returned a verdict that the defendant had not committed felony or robbery: *Wiltshire, 1249*, pl. 169. In 1256, Emma, wife of Simon Rup' of Brumpton, together with a woman not identified as a wife, appealed of imprisonment and the death of her nursing son in gaol. A jury found the defendant guilty; he was fined a large sum for trespass: *Northumberland, 1256*, pl. 108. In 1303, Alice, wife of Richard le Reyne, appealed a man of burgling Richard's house. The appeal was heard by a jury that found the defendant a thief; he was hanged: *Wiltshire, 1275–1306*, pl. 59. At Norfolk (1310 and 1316) two criminal actions were commenced by wives for theft of sheep. Matilda, wife of Ralph Cokeman, accused a man of stealing sheep and lambs from Ralph's fold; he was acquitted by a jury. Also Mabel, wife of Thomas, accused a man of the theft of sheep; Mabel did not appear and the defendant stood trial at the king's suit (*Norfolk, 1307–16*, pls. 236, 714). In 1244, Isabel, wife of Serlo, appealed of a beating that caused her child to be stillborn. The justices ordered trial by compurgation (*London, 1244*, pl. 157). In 1238 a wife was actually encouraged to continue her appeal. Edelina, wife of Stephen the carpenter, appealed of peace and wounding. Her wound was inspected and pronounced mortal: she was told to continue her appeal until the defendant appeared or was outlawed for nonappearance: *Devon, 1238*, pl. 550.

[39]An exception to this may be found at the eyres in York, Coventry, Shrewsbury, and Worcester, 1218–21. The only recorded appeals by unmarried or widowed women were appeals of homicide: *York, 1218–19*, pls. 737, 837; *Coventry, 1221*, pls. 734, 948, 970; *Shrewsbury, 1221*, pls. 1249, 1317; *Worcester, 1221*, pls. 1131, 1138, 1227, 1230.

defendant in an appeal to complain that a woman had no standing to prosecute. The crown's unobstructive attitude towards women's appeals may have been the result of an effort to enlarge and confirm its criminal jurisdiction in the latter part of the twelfth and throughout the thirteenth centuries— partly at the expense of the sheriff, who had jurisdiction over theft in the county court, and of the lords, who had jurisdiction over beating, wounding, and brawling in their own courts. One of the first steps the crown took in this direction was the creation of a public prosecution system involving the "jury of presentment," in the Assize of Clarendon in 1166. The original mandate of this jury was to identify known or suspected robbers, murderers, and thieves; to these the Assize of Northampton (1176) added arsonists and forgers. Court records beginning in 1194 indicate that juries fulfilled their duty by reporting all appeals of felony that had been brought, supplemented by a recital of homicides, robberies, thefts, and arsons in which the offender was unknown or in which no one had come forward as prosecutor. It was apparently not part of the jury's mandate, however, to report other felonies, such as assault, wounding (of either men or women), or rape.[40] The crown, wishing to bring criminals to justice—royal justice— whenever possible, may have chosen to permit women to bring their appeals freely rather than to broaden the mandate of the presenting jury to include all assaults and interference with property. (There never seems to have been an attempt by the

---

[40] An exception was the presentment of forcible intercourse (n. 19 above). Another apparent exception, a presentment in 1208 that one man struck another, was probably a presentment of homicide, since the accused man had fled from justice—the normal reaction of a killer but not of an assailant: *York, 1208*, pl. 3480.

crown to prevent women from prosecuting a homicide.)[41] During the fourteenth century the appeal declined drastically in use and was overtaken by presentment and especially indictment, private prosecution being replaced by crown prosecution. The sex and marital status of the victim of a crime became irrelevant when the prosecutor was the king.

Wives did have alternative means of gaining access to the criminal courts, probably pre-dating acceptance of their prosecutions as a mechanism to trigger crown prosecution. This access was dependent on a husband's willingness to support his wife's appeal publicly. Husbands and wives could prosecute a criminal action jointly, probably in a manifestation of the husband's guardianship of the wife.[42] In certain joint prosecutions it seems as though the husband was the important or even essential appellor. This was especially pronounced in joint prosecutions where only the wife had suffered injury. In

---

[41]Magna Carta (1215), c. 54, forbade *arrest* or *imprisonment* on the appeal of a woman for the death of anyone but her husband. This did not forbid women to bring other appeals of death. In the eyres of 1218–21 (n. 39 above), when women may have been prevented from bringing unconventional appeals, appeals of homicide were nevertheless permitted.

[42]In a case from 1202, a husband, wife, and son appealed of peace and robbery; when no one prosecuted, the husband was fined: *Northants., 1202*, pl. 89. In 1206 a husband and wife appealed of the death of their son, drowned from a boat; the appeal was declared invalid because the appellors did not have firsthand knowledge of the death and because the jury said the defendants were not guilty: *Lincoln, 1206*, pl. 1508. In 1221 a husband and wife appealed a man of rape of their daughter. Although the jurors said that the girl had been seen by four women who said she was violated, the defendant was acquitted, probably because the victim herself did not sue: *Bristol, 1221*, pl. 15. In 1227 a husband and wife appealed of assault on both; when the court ordered the matter to proceed to trial by battle, "the appellor" withdrew, and he and his pledges were fined: *Bedford, 1227*, pl. 354. For comparable cases see *Devon, 1238*, pl. 413; *Shropshire, 1256*, pl. 577; *Wiltshire, 1275–1306*, pl. 400; *Norfolk, 1307–16*, pl. 466.

a case in 1242–43 both husband and wife appealed of wounds to the wife but did not proceed; both of them and their pledges were fined. In 1276, two husbands and their wives appealed a defendant of breaking and entering a house and beating the two wives who were there so that they both miscarried.[43] These cases, although not identified as "trespass" cases, were in line with the law of tortious trespass developing in the mid-thirteenth century. By the beginning of the fourteenth century it was the rule that a wife must sue jointly with her husband for damages for a trespass done to her. A wife could not recover damages in a trespass action, even for her own injuries, without her husband, although a husband suing alone could claim damages for injury to his wife.[44]

As a variant on joint prosecution, a husband could validate his wife's appeal by appearing with her in court. In a case from 1201, Juliana of Holworth brought an appeal of felony for the death of her son. The appeal was declared invalid against one of the defendants on the ground that her husband did not appear with her. In a 1202 case, Hawisa daughter of Turstan, wife of Robert Franctenant, appealed of the death of her father and of her own wounds. The record noted that her husband did not wish to say anything, and the appeal was therefore invalid "because she has a husband who does not appear." In another case a wife appealed of wounding (whose wounds unstated) and robbery, and the defendants defended "as against one who has a husband who does not follow the suit with his wife." The appeal was declared invalid and the

---

[43] *Somerset, 1242–43*, pl. 1219; *London, 1276*, pl. 261.

[44] *London, 1321*, 2: 125–26, 127, 128. The rule also stated that a husband ought to sue alone for a trespass done to him alone: *London, 1321*, 2: 125. For a husband and wife suing for damages for injury to the wife, see *London, 1276*, pls. 265, 519.

appellor fined; the defendants were acquitted. Similar cases appear throughout the thirteenth century.[45]

WIVES AS ACCUSED PERSONS

Did marriage provide any legal advantages to wives, such as protection from the criminal justice system? Bracton says that it did. He stated that a married woman who is under the authority of her husband may be spared criminal consequences if she is involved in a crime with him. In one passage he referred to a case heard in 1226 in which a husband was hanged for forgery. His wife was freed "because, whether or not she was privy to the crime, she was under her husband's rod ("sub virga viri sui")."[46] In another passage on the

---

[45] *Wells, 1201*, pl. 730; *Lincoln, 1202*, pl. 690; *Northants., 1202*, pl. 70. In a 1202 case a wife appealed of breach of the peace but her husband withdrew; he and the appellee fined to settle the action: *Lincoln, 1202*, pl. 798. Again in 1202, Margaret Kat appealed of a beating. Her husband said he would sue for her but he did not appear and was to be taken into custody: *Lincoln, 1202*, pl. 649. At the 1238 sitting in Devon, Sybil de Ebforde appealed of housebreaking, beating (whose not stated), and robbery. The jurors acquitted; "And William de Ebforde, Sybil's husband, who was present, is sent to gaol for a false appeal": *Devon, 1238*, pl. 524. Also in 1238, perhaps before a woman's right to an appeal of abortion was settled, two women each appealed of a beating leading to a miscarriage. Although in neither case was the husband named as an appellor, following jury acquittals both wife and husband were ordered into custody and fined: *Devon, 1238*, pls. 622, 632. In 1242–43 a wife appealed of breach of the peace, wounding, and assault on herself, and her husband appeared and sued with her at trial: both were fined for a false appeal when the appeal was declared invalid: *Somerset, 1242–43*, pl. 858. Despite the evidence of the Devon cases in 1238, husbands were not usually fined on account of their wives' unconventional appeals.

[46] Bracton, *On the Laws and Customs*, 4: 287. The expression *sub virga* is also found ca. 1130: L. J. Downer, ed. and trans., *Leges Henrici primi* (Oxford, 1972), p. 155, s. 45,3: "Likewise if a person entrusts anything to, or exchanges it with, or hands it over to, a married woman or infant boy or

criminal responsibility of married women, Bracton stated that if stolen property is found within a man's house or within his *potestas*, he will be held culpable; his wife will not, because it is not within *her potestas*. She would, however, be found culpable together with her husband if the stolen property were found in a storeroom, chest, or cupboard to which she had the keys. Generally, Bracton said, if a wife committed a crime with her husband, or gave him counsel and aid, she would be held culpable, for "though she ought to obey her husband she need not be obedient to him in heinous deeds."[47]

In the records from the first quarter of the thirteenth century, courts seem to have shown some concern about dealing with accused who were married women simply because they were married, not necessarily because they were their husbands' unwilling accomplices. In 1218–19 a wife was found guilty in an appeal of death, but she fled and the decision to outlaw her was postponed to "the great court" because she had a husband. In 1225, when a woman was accused of burglary, the jurors told the court that they knew nothing positively of her but that her husband was a lawful man. The court ordered

---

infant girl without the permission of their lord, it is not necessary for them or their lords, if they are resolved to deny responsibility, to make answer about these things while they are under authority" ("quamdiu sub virga sunt"). Cf. actions involving land claims based on the writ *cui in vita sua*, n. 4 above.

[47]Bracton, *On the Laws and Customs*, 2: 428. A woman also had a specious protection from outlawry. She could not be outlawed—because she was never "in law," for only males could be under the law in a frankpledge or tithing. However, she could be "waived" (ibid., 2: 353) "and regarded as one abandoned, for waif is that which no one claims, nor will the prince claim her or protect her when she has been properly waived, any more than he will a male who has been properly outlawed. . . . Henceforth they bear the wolf's head and in consequence perish without judicial inquiry."

the wife freed.[48] Bracton's rule does not appear in the case law until the middle of the thirteenth century, when it is explicitly mentioned in two cases in 1249. In the first, a husband and wife were accused of larceny; at trial, both were found guilty of harboring a thief, knowing him to be an outlaw. The husband was hanged. However, the jurors testified "that Agnes wife of Robert was so subjected to him that she had to obey," and she was acquitted. In the second case, Christiana Sprot was accused of the death of a merchant. The jurors said that her husband had been hanged for the death "and they say that Christiana did not take part unless by the compulsion of her husband and her fear of him." She too was acquitted.[49] More such cases followed,[50] but it seems that the presumption that a

---

[48]*York, 1218–19*, pl. 737; *Somerset, 1225*, pl. 134. In 1221 the widow of a slain man admitted that she was in the house when he was killed but denied being a party to his death. Her new husband offered 40s. to have a verdict of the jurors whether his wife was guilty or not; they said she was not (*Worcester, 1221*, pl. 1100). In 1203, Jordan and his wife Alice were found with two others who fled when the sheriff's serjeant tried to arrest them. A purse containing false coins fell, and it was unknown whether it belonged to Jordan and Alice or to the two who fled. Jordan was ordered to undergo the ordeal of cold water; Alice was not required to undergo an ordeal, probably as she was presumed an accomplice rather than a principal in the alleged crime. One cannot know, of course, whether she was not considered a principal merely because she was his wife or because of other, unrevealed circumstances. Jordan passed his ordeal but was obliged to leave England, under pain of death (he "abjured the realm"). Alice was evidently freed and not required to abjure, for she was later taken with a thief who was hanged at Lincoln. Alice seems to have led a charmed life, for she was released "out of mercy" by the justices at Lincoln (*Northants., 1202*, pl. 797).

[49]*Wiltshire, 1249*, pls. 146, 445.

[50]In 1276, Edith de Helmerton was taken with her husband, Robert Boket, for stealing sheep. Robert was hanged, but because she was pregnant she was sent to gaol to await her delivery. When a jury of 12 "sufficiently declared that she was his espoused wife," Edith was acquitted. In 1277, William Balle

wife acted under her husband's orders was not consistently applied. For example, in 1280 Denise, wife of Roger Godyng, was arrested with her husband and another woman for suspicion of burglary. The jurors said Denise was guilty, and she was hanged; her husband and the other woman were acquitted.[51] In 1329–30, Richard fitz John Byyondethebrok and his wife, Alice, were arrested for stealing oxen and cows, found guilty by a jury, and condemned to hang. Alice was spared immediate hanging only because she was pregnant, and she was remanded to gaol until she had delivered the child. A contemporary commentator on the case noted with apparent disapproval that the wife was condemned to death with her husband without any inquiry as to whether she had committed the felony in her husband's company or because he forced her to do it.[52]

In addition to the presumption that wives acted under their husbands' compulsion, there seems to have been an unwritten

---

and his wife, Isabel, were arrested and imprisoned for involvement in homicide. The jury said that William was guilty but that Isabel had acted on her husband's orders. He was hanged; she was acquitted. In 1294, John le Smyth and Edith his wife, together with Simon le Coliere, were indicted for burgling a house. The jurors found John and Simon guilty but acquitted Edith. In a 1305 case John de Ambrebury was hanged for breaking into a chest, but his wife, Isabel, was not although she was indicted for taking away the goods found within the chest. In the same year Alice, who had been the wife of William, was indicted, together with her new husband, John, for killing William. John was hanged, Alice was acquitted. See *Wiltshire, 1275–1306*, pls. 34, 112, 294, 777–78, 617 and 858 [xv].

[51] *Wiltshire 1275–1306*, pl. 159. In 1281, Ellis Sprang and Rose his wife were indicted for flaying sheep. The jury found both guilty and they were hanged (*Wiltshire, 1275–1306*, pl. 190). In 1294, Isabel Fraunceys, the wife of a confessed felon turned approver, was indicted for larceny, found guilty by a jury, and hanged (*Wiltshire, 1275–1306*, pl. 302).

[52] *Northants., 1329–30*, 1: 179.

presumption that they were their husbands' voluntary accomplices, even if only because they consented to the crime or received their husbands afterwards, both of which were felonies and capital offenses. Wives, therefore, were often accused together with their husbands and often fled from justice with their husbands. In 1256 a man immediately fled after he threw a knife at his daughter and killed her; his wife, who was present at the killing, fled after him the next day. In ensuing criminal proceedings he was said by the jurors to be guilty and was outlawed, but she was not guilty and was allowed to return if she wished. In 1276 a husband and wife were indicted for the death of a widow. They had beaten the woman earlier in the day but she had escaped from them; at nightfall the husband went to her house and stabbed her to death. The jurors were asked whether the wife was an accomplice in the death and they said that she was.[53] Of course, it was possible for husbands and wives truly to be partners in crime—witness two cases from 1242–43 in which husbands and wives fled to a church, confessed they were thieves, and, abjuring the realm, went into exile together.[54]

---

[53] *Northumberland, 1256*, p. 87; *London, 1276*, pl. 250. In 1203 when a woman appealed four men of her husband's death and they fled, the wife of one of them was also taken and accused of the death: *Lichfield, 1203*, p. 91. In 1221 a man was appealed of death, his wife and daughter accused of counseling and consenting to the offense; a jury acquitted all three: *Worcester, 1221*, pl. 1098. In 1279, a man killed another and fled; his wife also fled. He was ordered outlawed and she was ordered waived when a jury indicated that both were guilty: *Northumberland, 1279*, p. 314. See also *Wiltshire, 1275–1306*, pls. 186, 203, 295, 299, 410, 535; *Norfolk, 1307–16*, pl. 761; *Lincolnshire, 1351–54*, #3, #85, and #46; *Lincolnshire, 1360–75*, p. 44, #163, #165; p. 60, #235; p. 233, #75. On occasion, it worked the other way. In 1221 a woman slew another woman and fled with her husband; he was therefore to be exacted and outlawed: *Bristol, 1221*, pl. 22.

[54] *Somerset, 1242–43*, pls. 911 and 1008.

Wives were also charged with offenses without the record indicating that the judicial system cared whether they were married or not. This is particularly evident in the many cases in which wives were charged under regulatory statutes, especially the assizes of ale and measures, and the fourteenth-century Statute of Laborers.[55] There are cases, though, of a more serious nature, such as a 1276 case in which a wife beat a boy to death; she fled, was suspected and was to be waived (the feminine form of outlawry; see note 47 above). Her husband was required to appear in court to answer for the death, possibly as the "first finder" of the body, but the jurors did not suspect him in the death, even though he failed to appear.[56]

---

[55]*Bedford, 1202*, pls. 262, 263; *Lincolnshire, 1360–75*: Ale: p. 22, #44; p. 36, #121; p. 47, #180; p. 57, #239. Statute of Laborers: p. 6, #19; p. 36, #118 and #122; p. 38, #131 and #132; p. 46, #176; p. 47, #182; p. 81, #356; p. 92, #414. Forestalling fish: p. 100, #450.

[56]*London, 1276*, pl. 16. There are similar cases: a wife was charged with receiving her son who had been outlawed: *Northants., 1202*, pl. 42 (the wife and husband may have been separated, for the case was heard in Northamptonshire but he was described as Geoffrey of Deeping, Lincs.). A husband and wife were attached for the death of a merchant killed in their house; the husband fled, the wife appeared in court. The jurors said that the husband was not in the house at the time of the death and he was not suspected in the death, but that the wife had consented to her brothers' killing the merchant. After this verdict the wife fled, but the husband was to be allowed to return under pledges for his good behavior: *Somerset, 1225*, pl. 240. A wife was appealed of assault and battery: *Wiltshire, 1249*, pl. 47. A wife was indicted for biting a man on the finger so that he swelled up and died. She was arrested and imprisoned in Newgate but died before trial: *London, 1276*, pl. 113. A wife was charged with beating another woman to death; she fled and was to be waived: *London, 1276*, pl. 117. A woman was arrested after being pursued by the owner of an ox, stolen by a thief identified as her husband. She was taken before the court and acknowledged that she had been involved in the theft; she was hanged; *Northumberland, 1279*, p. 332. For more such cases: *Wiltshire, 1275–1306*, pls. 248, 535, 867; *Cambridgeshire, 1332–34*, pl. 24. A wife was arrested on suspicion of larceny and imprisoned to await an

Finally, there was a definitive instance where wives were liable to be at a disadvantage in criminal proceedings. This was the matter of killing a husband, which was classified as "petty treason" and was punishable by burning at the stake, as opposed to hanging for other homicides. The classification of the offense, and the vindictiveness of the penalty, might suggest that wives who killed their husbands were inexorably hunted down, tried, and condemned as threats to the social fabric. In fact, husband-slayers were treated much as other killers. While there were many women in the records of the thirteenth and fourteenth centuries who were accused of killing their husbands, only one was burned at the stake. The rest were acquitted, or fled to avoid trial, or confessed and abjured the realm, just as in any other killing.[57]

---

inquiry that was ordered following her court appearance because she had been neither indicted nor appealed. She was released when the sheriff reported nothing against her: *Cambridgeshire, 1332–34*, pls. 39, 58. A wife was charged, with a man not her husband, with killing a man; she was acquitted by a jury: *Lincolnshire, 1351–54*, pl. #1, p. 55. Several wives were indicted for thefts: *Lincolnshire, 1360–75*, p. 88, #393; p. 95, #428; p. 158, #25.

[57]*Lichfield, 1199*, p. 39: wife suspected by presenting jury; outcome unknown; CRR 5: 64: wife sent to the ordeal of hot iron to determine her guilt; she passed, for in 1211 she reappeared in the king's court, suing for her dower: CRR 6: 132; CRR 6: 306: wife burned at the stake; *Coventry, 1221*, pl. 743: wife arrested and imprisoned, escaped from gaol; CRR 13, pls. 1613 and 2091: wife was appealed of the death of her husband by the husband's sons; they did not pursue their appeal and the wife won an action she had brought against them for her dower lands; *Devon, 1238*, pls. 184: wife fled, waived; 291: wife acquitted; 579: wife fled, waived; 756: wife acquitted; *Wiltshire, 1249*, pls. 41, 164, 389; *Northumberland, 1279*, p. 347: wife fled, waived; *Wiltshire, 1275–1306*, pls. 49: wife acquitted; 65: wife acquitted; and 589, outcome unknown; *Gloucestershire, 1361–98*, Roll II, #16, pp. 86–87: outcome unknown; *Shropshire, 1400–14*, pl. 172: wife fled, waived.

In criminal law, therefore, as in the law of real and personal property, a wife's rights were in legal theory severely restricted and she was subject to her husband's "guardianship." A wife had no right to commence a criminal prosecution for harm she had suffered, with the exception of causing a miscarriage and perhaps of rape. A husband could lawfully use physical force to discipline his wife; he was responsible for crimes they committed together; he could confer on her the right to prosecute a criminal action by joining in an appeal with her, or simply by appearing with her in court.

But, just as in the law of real and personal property, the theoretical rights and restrictions pertaining to husband and wife were altered by law and custom. A husband could not use excessive force in punishing his wife, and he could not kill her without answering to the law for her death. A wife who launched an appeal of felony despite prohibition and without her husband's blessing would not be turned away from the court, especially after ca. 1221, but her appeal would be treated like an indictment and the person appealed would be subject to jury trial. Somewhat less to her advantage, as the thirteenth century passed a wife seemed to become more of an independent legal person in the eyes of the law, more likely to be held responsible for her personal and spousal criminal activities.

The theoretical restrictions on wives' rights in criminal matters, as those in property matters, probably had their ideological basis in Saint Paul's passage in Ephesians about husband and wife. But if this theory of marriage had ever been of use to the English crown in criminal matters, it certainly was no longer of use by the thirteenth century, when the crown was moving to assert its jurisdiction in criminal law by wresting control of the criminal process away from private individuals.[58]

---

[58]M. H. Kerr, "Angevin Reform of the Appeal of Felony," *Law and History Review* 13 (1995): 351.

There was no advantage to the crown in denying women a right to identify (if not to prosecute) criminal aggressors, or in permitting husbands to murder their wives with impunity; nor was there any advantage in allowing wives generous protection from punishment on the ground that their husbands must be responsible for them.[59] To a certain extent, therefore, the relationship between husband and wife in criminal matters in medieval England can be seen as a reflection of the ultimately successful effort of the crown to impose public rights and duties where none had existed before.

---

[59]Bracton's doctrine of coercion of a wife by her husband may have replaced some presumption that a married woman could not be held responsible for a crime if her husband were law-abiding. It was not intended to be applied on a blanket basis but on proof of the fact of coercion by the husband.

APPENDIX A
A NOTE ON RAPE

Roger D. Groot, "The Crime of Rape temp. Richard I and John," *Journal of Legal History* 9 (1988): 324–25, canvassed the possibility that only a virgin could bring an appeal of rape but doubted this because loss of virginity was not alleged in all cases, and because two cases in the Curia Regis rolls involved a widow and a woman with a son. Certainly the overwhelming opinion of appellors in the thirteenth century was that an appeal of rape only belonged to an *unmarried* woman, whether she was a virgin or not.

Even for the unmarried, however, it was difficult to obtain a conviction; in 272 appeals of rape there were only some thirty convictions. Bracton, *On the Laws and Customs*, 2: 416, listed the objections ("exceptions") available to the accused in an appeal of rape. They included: that the appellor was still a virgin and had not been deprived of her maidenhood; that the appellee had had the appellor as his concubine before the alleged incident; that he had her consent to intercourse; that the appellor omitted to mention her maidenhood in the appeal. In practice, appeals failed for the following reasons: (1) the appellor had been the appellee's mistress or concubine before the alleged rape: *Lincoln, 1202*, pl. 909; *Coventry, 1221*, pl. 966; *Devon, 1238*, pl. 292—although the jury reported that the appellor had refused the appellee's advances on this occasion, and that he had taken her by force; *Somerset, 1242–43*, pl. 1120; *Wiltshire, 1249*, pl. 310: the court was informed that the appellee did not "violate" the appellor because she had had intercourse with him before; however, he was convicted of an offense; (2) the appellor had consented to intercourse: *York, 1218–19*, pl. 545; *Somerset, 1242–43*, pl. 1057: the appellor failed to allege force or lack of consent; (3) the appellor failed to raise the hue and cry immediately: *Coventry, 1221*, pl. 966; see also *Surrey, 1235*, pl. 565, wherein the appellor explained carefully that the appellee caused his accomplices to sing loudly so that when she raised the hue and cry she could not be heard; *Somerset,*

1242–43, pl. 963; *Shropshire, 1256*, pl. 739 (the appellee also objected that the appellor changed the day she said the rape occurred and did not continue her appeal with the required vigor).

Sexual assault was not described only as "rape" but also as "lying with by force," "having connection with by force," and "deflowering." At Reading in 1248 the appellor and the jury made a distinction that one man (a monk) raped the appellor's virginity, and that his three accomplices then lay with her by force: *Reading, 1248*, pl. 888. However, at Durham an appellor appealed of rape but admitted that she was not a maiden: *Durham, 1242*, pl. 101. The language used to describe sexual assault in the thirteenth century is not uniform, and it is possible that the parties, the juries, and the courts did not define the terms with precision.

APPENDIX B

A NOTE ON WIVES' UNCONVENTIONAL APPEALS

The earliest reference to an unconventional appeal by a wife may be in the Pipe Roll for 1179–80. The wife did not prosecute the appeal, and her husband, who was her "pledge," or guarantor for prosecution, was fined for her failure to proceed: *Pipe Roll 26 Henry II, 1179–1180*, 29 (1908), p. 111. There are a number of other examples of unconventional appeals brought by wives in the period before 1218–19. In 1194, Tova wife of Ralph appealed of the theft of a pig, but withdrew; Matilda wife of Walter appealed of robbery of her house but withdrew; and the wife of Roger son of Wace appealed of an unspecified felony but did not prosecute: *Wiltshire, 1194*, pp. 78, 91, 112. Adelina wife of Ralph appealed two men of beating her but did not proceed. She was to be taken into custody for her failure to prosecute: *Lichfield, 1199*, p. 42. Juliana of Holworth appealed of the death of her son. The appeal was declared invalid because her husband did not participate in the appeal: *Wells, 1201*, pl. 730. Joscea wife of William de la Dune appealed of her own wounds, and the parties settled the action with the approval of the justices in eyre; William brought his own appeal of assault, mayhem, and robbery: *Launceston, 1201*, pl. 386. A wife appealed of breaching the king's peace but did not prosecute. She would have been fined for her failure but she was pardoned because she was poor; her husband also appealed the same defendants of breaching the king's peace and also did not prosecute: he was to be taken into custody as a result, and would have had to pay a fine to obtain his release: *Northants., 1202*, pl. 8. Alice wife of Geoffrey of Carlby appealed of the death of her brother but did not prosecute, and was fined; Helviva wife of Robert, son of Hugh of Croxton, appealed of the death of her son but did not prosecute; Agnes wife of William Methus appealed of robbery but did not prosecute, and was fined: *Lincoln, 1202*, pls. 560, 560a, 673, and see also pls. 847, 991, 994.

A few similar cases occurred outside this period. In 1218–19 Agnes wife of Hemer of Oglethorpe appealed of wounding her son but did not appear at the trial of the action. The appeal was declared null, the jurors found the defendant not guilty, and Agnes was fined: *York, 1218–19*, pl. 584. In 1286, Margery, wife of Nicholas Robbe of Collenne, appealed of the death of her daughter but did not prosecute; she and her pledges (including her husband) were fined: *Huntingdonshire, 1286*, pl. 407. In some cases a wife's appeal did not proceed far enough for the appellor to be fined for nonprosecution, or for the appeal to be declared invalid: *Somerset, 1242–43*, pl. 1200: Margery, wife of William of Westowe, appealed of the death of her son and the defendant was outlawed; *Northumberland, 1256*, pl. 96: Sywyna wife of John le Potir appealed of rape and breach of the peace; the defendant, however, abjured the realm because of thefts he had committed.

Note that although married women are usually identified in the records as "M. wife of N.," or by the phrase "N. and his wife M.," there are a few intriguing instances where wives are identified by surname or place-name, and in one case as a daughter and only incidentally as someone's wife: *Wells, 1201*, pl. 730 (Juliana of Holworth); *Lincoln, 1202*, pl. 649 (Margaret Kat, wife of William Burel), and pl. 690 (Hawisa, daughter of Turstan, wife of Robert Franctenant); *York, 1218–19*, pl. 742 (Alice of Newton, wife of Simon de Mohaut); *Coventry, 1221*, pl. 923 (Millicent of Long Itchington, wife of Richard son of Godfrey); *Devon, 1238*, pls. 364 (Gunnilda de Hemmeford), and 524 (Sybil de Ebforde). This raises the possibility that some women not identified in the records as wives were in fact married.

APPENDIX C
PRIMARY SOURCES

CRR

> *Curia Regis Rolls.* Vols. 1–17 for the years 1196–1237. HMSO, London, 1922–91.

Wiltshire, 1194

> F. W. Maitland, ed. *Three Rolls of the King's Court in the Reign of Richard the First, A.D. 1194–1195.* Pipe Roll Society, 14 (1891).

Norfolk, 1198

> Doris Mary Stenton, ed. *Pleas before the King or His Justices, 1198–1202.* Vol. 2. Selden Society, 68 (1952).

Lichfield, 1199

> George Wrottesley, ed. *Collections for a History of Staffordshire.* Staffordshire Record Society, 3 (1882).

Launceston, 1201

> Doris Mary Stenton, ed. *Pleas before the King or His Justices, 1198–1202.* Vol. 2. Selden Society, 68 (1952).

Wells, 1201

> Doris Mary Stenton, ed. *Pleas before the King or His Justices, 1198–1202.* Vol. 2. Selden Society, 68 (1952).

Bedford, 1202

> G. H. Fowler, ed. "Roll of the Justices in Eyre at Bedford, 1202." *Publications of the Bedfordshire Historical Record Society* 1 (1913): 215–41.

Lincoln, 1202

> Doris Mary Stenton, ed. *The Earliest Lincolnshire Assize Rolls, A.D. 1202–1209.* Lincoln Record Society, 26 (1926).

Northants., 1202

> Doris Mary Stenton, ed. *The Earliest Northamptonshire Assize Rolls, A.D. 1202 and 1203.* Northamptonshire Record Society, 5 (1930).

Lichfield, 1203
> George Wrottesley, ed. *Collections for a History of Staffordshire.* Staffordshire Record Society, 3 (1882).

Shrewsbury, 1203
> Doris Mary Stenton, ed. *Pleas before the King or His Justices, 1198–1212.* Vol. 3. Selden Society, 83 (1967).

Lincoln, 1206
> Doris Mary Stenton, ed. *The Earliest Lincolnshire Assize Rolls, A.D. 1202–1209.* Lincoln Record Society, 26 (1926).

York, 1208
> Doris Mary Stenton, ed. *Pleas before the King or His Justices, 1198–1212.* Vol. 4. Selden Society, 84 (1967).

York, 1218–19
> Doris Mary Stenton, ed. *Rolls of the Justices in Eyre, Being the Rolls of Pleas and Assizes for Yorkshire in 3 Henry III, (1218–19).* Selden Society, 56 (1937).

Bristol, 1221
> Edward J. Watson, ed. *Pleas of the Crown for the Hundred of Swineshead and the Township of Bristol . . . A.D. 1221.* Bristol, 1902.

Coventry, 1221
> Doris Mary Stenton, ed. *Rolls of the Justices in Eyre . . . for Gloucestershire, Warwickshire and Staffordshire, 1221, 1222.* Selden Society, 59 (1940).

Shrewsbury, 1221
> Doris Mary Stenton, ed. *Rolls of the Justices in Eyre . . . for Gloucestershire, Warwickshire and Staffordshire, 1221, 1222.* Selden Society, 59 (1940).

Worcester, 1221
> Doris Mary Stenton, ed. *Rolls of the Justices in Eyre . . . for Lincolnshire 1218–9 and Worcestershire 1221.* Selden Society, 53 (1934).

Somerset, 1225

C. E. H. Chadwyck Healey, ed. *Somersetshire Pleas (Civil and Criminal) from the Rolls of the Itinerant Justices*, 1: *Close of 12th Century to 41 Henry III.* Somerset Record Society, 11 (1897), pp. 28–61.

Bedford, 1227

G. H. Fowler, ed. "Roll of the Justices in Eyre at Bedford, 1227." *Publications of the Bedfordshire Historical Record Society* 3 (1916): 1–206.

Surrey, 1235

C. A. F. Meekings and David Crook, eds. *The 1235 Surrey Eyre.* 2 vols. Surrey Record Society, 31, 32 (1979–83).

Devon, 1238

Henry Summerson, ed. *Crown Pleas of the Devon Eyre of 1238.* Devon and Cornwall Record Society, n.s., 28 (1985).

Durham, 1242

K. E. Bayley, ed. "Two Thirteenth-Century Assize Rolls for the County of Durham." In *Miscellanea*, vol. 2. Surtees Society, 127 (1916).

Somerset, 1242–43

C. E. H. Chadwyck Healey, ed. *Somerset Pleas (Civil and Criminal) from the Rolls of the Itinerant Justices*, 1: *Close of 12th Century to 41 Henry III.* Somerset Record Society, 11 (1897), pp. 227–324.

London, 1244

Helena Mary Chew and Martin Weinbaum, eds. *The London Eyre of 1244.* London Record Society, 6 (1970).

Reading, 1248

M. T. Clanchy, ed. *The Roll and Writ File of the Berkshire Eyre of 1248.* Selden Society, 90 (1973).

Wiltshire, 1249

C. A. F. Meekings, ed. *Crown Pleas of the Wiltshire Eyre, 1249.* Wiltshire Record Society, 16 (1961).

Northumberland, 1256

William Page, ed. *Three Early Assize Rolls for the County of Northumberland, saec. XIII.* Surtees Society, 88 (1891), pp. 68–133.

Shropshire, 1256

Alan Harding, ed. *The Roll of the Shropshire Eyre of 1256.* Selden Society, 96 (1981).

Wiltshire, 1275–1306

R. B. Pugh, ed. *Wiltshire Gaol Delivery and Trailbaston Trials, 1275–1306.* Wiltshire Record Society, 33 (1978).

London, 1276

Martin Weinbaum, ed. *The London Eyre of 1276.* London Record Society, 12 (1976).

Northumberland, 1279

William Page, ed. *Three Early Assize Rolls for the County of Northumberland, saec. XIII.* Surtees Society, 88 (1891), pp. 312–69.

Huntingdonshire, 1286

Anne Reiber DeWindt and Edwin Brezette DeWindt, eds. *Royal Justice and the Medieval English Countryside: The Huntingdonshire Eyre of 1286, the Ramsey Abbey Banlieu Court of 1287, and the Assizes of 1287–88.* 2 vols. Toronto, 1981.

Norfolk, 1307–16

Barbara Hanawalt. *Crime in East Anglia in the Fourteenth Century: Norfolk Gaol Delivery Rolls, 1307–1316.* Norfolk Record Society, 44 (1976).

London, 1321

Helen Maud Cam, ed. *The Eyre of London, 14 Edward II, A.D. 1321.* 2 vols. Selden Society, 85, Year Books (Edward II) 26 (1968–69).

Northants., 1329–30

D. W. Sutherland, ed. *The Eyre of Northamptonshire: 3–4 Edward III, A.D. 1329–1330.* 2 vols. Selden Society 97, 98 (1983).

Cambridgeshire, 1332–34

Elisabeth G. Kimball, ed. *A Cambridgeshire Gaol Delivery Roll, 1332–1334.* Cambridge Antiquarian Records Society, 4 (1978).

Bedfordshire & Buckinghamshire, 1332–34

G. H. Fowler, ed. "Three Rolls from the . . . Sheriff of Bedfordshire and Buckinghamshire, 1332–1334." *Publications of the Bedfordshire Historical Record Society* 3 (1922).

Lincolnshire, 1351–54

E. G. Kimball, ed. *Records of Some Sessions of the Peace in Lincolnshire, 1351–1354, and the Borough of Stamford, 1351.* Lincoln Record Society, 65 (1971).

Lincolnshire, 1360–75

Rosamond Sillem, ed. *Records of Some Sessions of the Peace in Lincolnshire, 1360–1375.* Lincoln Record Society, 30 (1936).

Gloucestershire, 1361–98

Elisabeth G. Kimball, ed. *Rolls of the Gloucestershire Sessions of the Peace 1361–1398.* Transactions of the Bristol and Gloucestershire Archaeological Society, 62 (1942).

Shropshire, 1400–14

Elisabeth G. Kimball, ed. *The Shropshire Peace Roll, 1400–1414.* Shrewsbury, 1959.

FAMILY

THE CULTURAL CONSTRUCTION OF CHILDHOOD: BAPTISM, COMMUNION, AND CONFIRMATION[1]

Kathryn Ann Taglia

In the past three decades, since the publication of *Centuries of Childhood*, medieval historians have successfully refuted the so-called Ariès thesis that the medieval world failed to acknowledge that childhood was different from adulthood and that medieval people invested little emotionally in their children.[2] Because of this impressive body of research, we can now assert that medieval society did indeed have a concept of childhood and did indeed care for its youngest members. In this essay I go beyond these

---

[1] Earlier versions of this paper were presented at the 29th International Congress on Medieval Studies at Western Michigan University and at the meeting of the Canadian Society of Medievalists at the 1994 Canadian Learned Societies Conference at the University of Calgary.

[2] For Philippe Ariès's own view see *Centuries of Childhood: A Social History of Family Life*, trans. Robert Baldick (London, 1962). For more recent discussions about medieval children and childhood see Barbara Hanawalt, *Growing Up in Medieval London: The Experience of Childhood in History* (Oxford, 1993), and *The Ties That Bound: Peasant Families in Medieval England* (Oxford, 1986), pp. 171–87; David Nicholas, *The Domestic Life of a Medieval City: Women, Children, and the Family in Fourteenth-Century Ghent* (Lincoln, Neb., 1985), pp. 109–72; and Shulamith Shahar, *Childhood in the Middle Ages* (New York, 1990). For a discussion on how historians have interpreted Ariès see Linda A. Pollock, *Forgotten Children: Parent-Child Relations from 1500 to 1900* (Cambridge, 1983), pp. 1–32.

basic positive assertions and look at some medieval cultural constructions of childhood as revealed in pronouncements on baptism, confirmation, and (first) Communion drawn from northern French synodal legislation from the thirteenth through fifteenth centuries[3] and from the writings of medieval thinkers. I explore how the working out of these three sacraments reveals a discourse that placed the child in the center of several important cultural debates about identity and authority.

Let us start with a story about a baptism. Sometime in the fourteenth century a baby is born in a peasant cottage in a small Angevin village. The mother lies exhausted in her bed; the midwife and her helpers are gathered near her, anxiously inspecting the newly born girl. The baby mews softly, gasping for breath. Holding in one arm the infant, still covered with blood and mucus, the midwife dips her hand in the basin of water that was to be used to wash the infant. As she sprinkles water on the infant's head three times, the midwife says in French, "I baptize you in the name of the Father, the Son, and the Holy Spirit." She gently places the infant on the bed next to her mother; a few minutes later the child dies. In those few brief moments of

---

[3]The four ecclesiastical provinces of northern France—Rouen, Tours, Sens, and Reims—contained the dioceses of Avranches, Bayeux, Coutances, Évreux, Lisieux, and Sées (Rouen); Chartres, Meaux, Orléans, Paris, and Troyes (Sens); Angers, Le Mans, Nantes, St.-Brieuc, St.-Malo, and Tréguier (Tours); Amiens, Arras, Cambrai, Chalons-sur-Marne, Soissons, Thérouanne, and Tournai (Reims). For more on French synodal legislation and its history see Joseph Avril, "L'évolution du synode diocésain principalement dans la France du Nord du 10e au 13e siècle," in *Proceedings of the Seventh International Congress of Medieval Canon Law* (Vatican City, 1988), pp. 305–25, and Odette Pontal, *Les statuts synodaux*, Typologie des sources du Moyen Âge occidental, fasc. 11: A-III.1 (Turnhout, 1975). For the most complete list of the available printed and MS sources of French synodal legislation, see André Artonne, Louis Guizard, and Odette Pontal, eds., *Répertoire des statuts synodaux des diocèses de l'ancienne France, du XIIIe à la fin du XVIIIe siècle*, 2nd ed. rév. et augm. (Paris, 1969).

her life this infant became literally and metaphorically the body and soul of several important late medieval cultural struggles—the problem of original sin, the control and definition of the sacrament of baptism, the place of the child in the Christian community, the need to demarcate clearly the Christian from the non-Christian, and even the problem of the location of the soul. By looking at pronouncements on emergency infant baptisms, I wish to demonstrate how the body and soul of this dying infant became such an important cultural nexus.

Baptism served two closely interconnected purposes within the medieval Christian framework. It was, first of all, the initiation rite that gave the one baptized an indelible character, marking him/her as a member of the Christian community. Baptism demarcated Christians from those who had not entered into the new covenant created by Christ's coming—the pagan, the Jew, the Saracen, the "other." When Christianity had been one of the many religions of the Roman Empire, adult baptism had been the norm and the question of the member status of children was neglected. As western Europe gradually became transformed into medieval "Christendom," not to have baptized infants would have meant that the children of Christian parents would have been "others"; that a large portion of the Christian community would have been in reality not of the community. Baptism was also the rite that cleansed a human of original sin. Augustine had argued that Adam's sin, which was the sin of all humankind, tainted all people from birth, and medieval Christian thinkers concurred, arguing that even in the "innocence" of infancy, human beings still had need of God's grace to wash away the taint of this hereditary fault.[4]

---

[4]Early Christian thinkers tended to have a positive view about children born to Christian families, seeing them as innocents who, although not yet Christians, were not likely to need immediate baptism. Tertullian had argued against infant baptism: "Why should innocent infancy be in such a hurry to

Infant baptism in the later Middle Ages was then at the interstices of several important cultural problems. First of all, medieval Christian thinkers shared Augustine's distrust of the fleshly body, tainted with original sin and too imperfectly under the control of the rational soul. To many, a child before baptism was the perfect example of just such an imperfect body, irrational and corrupted with original sin—a possible polluter of sacred spaces such as the parish church and cemetery. Although by the later Middle Ages the doctrine of original sin had been softened so that the unbaptized child was doomed not to hell but rather to limbo, it was still not a doctrine that offered much comfort.[5] This is illustrated by several synodal

---

come to the forgiveness of sins? Let them come while they are maturing, while they are learning, while they are being taught what it is they are coming to. Let them be made Christians when they have been able to know Christ." See Tertullian, *De Baptismo* 18.5, CCSL 1: *Tertulliani opera, pars I*, p. 293, trans. and cited in Jaroslav Pelikan, *The Christian Tradition: A History of the Development of Doctrine*, 1: *The Emergence of the Catholic Tradition (100–600)* (Chicago, 1971), p. 290.

In the late 4th and early 5th centuries the need for infant baptism gained importance from the development of the doctrines of original sin and Christ's virgin (and sinless) birth. Augustine gave fullest utterance to the melding of these doctrines, seeing the need for infant baptism as an apt expression of just how far humanity had fallen from the ideal state represented by Christ. In Book I of *Confessions*, Augustine, although he cannot remember his infancy, has no doubt that he was a sinner even then: "Who can recall to me the sins I committed as a baby? For in your [God's] sight no man is free from sin, not even a child who has lived only one day on earth" (*Confessions*, trans. R. S. Pine-Coffin [Harmondsworth, 1961], p. 27). See also Joseph H. Lynch, *Godparents and Kinship in Early Medieval Europe* (Princeton, 1986), pp. 119–20; Pelikan, *Christian Tradition*, 1: 286–93.

As for later medieval thinkers, Innocent III, e.g., in his letter to the archbishop of Arles, asserts that baptism is absolutely necessary for the salvation of infants, as they share in original sin (X.3.42.3 in Emil Friedberg, ed., *Corpus iuris canonici*, 2nd ed., 2 vols. [Leipzig, 1879–81], 2: 644–46).

[5] In the *Inferno*, canto IV, lines 25–36, 40–42, Dante describes the limbo of the unbaptized:

statutes that consigned the unbaptized dead infant to burial beyond the cemetery. This unbaptized body was a contagion that
had to be eliminated and kept away from the cemetery in order
to protect its "cleanliness." Such a burial symbolizes all too
clearly that the child, before baptism, was not and could never
be part of the Christian community or the plan of salvation.
But the unbaptized stillborn infant was not just a danger to
him/herself and to the sacred spaces; some apparently saw this
dead child as a danger to the mother as well. Synodal legislation from Cambrai and Tournai had provisions for what to do
if both the mother and child died during the birth. If the child
died unbaptized, s/he was to be buried beyond the cemetery,
while the mother, unless she had died excommunicated, was to
be taken to the church and buried in the cemetery. Some apparently believed that the dead mother's intimate physical
contact with the dead unbaptized infant had polluted her and
thus they wanted to inter the mother outside the cemetery with
her infant; however, the legislation objects, stating, "We ought
not to turn her pain into a fault."[6]

> . . . Here, so far as I could tell by listening, was no lamentation more
> than sighs which kept the air forever trembling; these came from
> grief without torments that was borne by the crowds, which were
> vast, of men and women and little children.
>
> The good Master said to me: "Dost thou not ask what spirits are
> these thou seest? I would have thee know, then, before thou goest
> farther, that they did not sin; but though they have merits it is not
> enough, for they had not baptism, which is the gateway of the faith
> thou holdest. . . . For such defects, and not for any guilt, we are lost,
> and only so far afflicted that without hope we live in desire."

Dante Alighieri, *The Divine Comedy*, trans. John D. Sinclair, vol. 1, *Inferno*
(New York, 1939), pp. 59, 61.

[6]Cambrai synod, before 1260, P. C. Boeren, ed., "Les plus ancien statuts du
diocèse de Cambrai (13e siècle)," *Revue de droit canonique* (de Strasbourg) 3
(1953): 133: "Si autem [infans] mortuus reperiatur, extra cymiterium tumuletur. . . . Si mater mortua fuerit in partu, non negentur ei aliqua jura

A second cultural problem was that infant baptism was figured as the normal means of entry into the Christian community, and ecclesiastical authorities, not surprisingly, were interested in keeping this membership gateway under their supervision and control. Baptism, however, was the one sacrament in the Middle Ages that could be performed by anyone—cleric or lay person, man or woman, Christian or not. The validity of the sacrament rested in the correct saying of the formula and the sprinkling/pouring of water upon the child (or the immersion of the child in water).[7] The prerequisite was merely

---

christianitatis, sed in ecclesia deferatur et in cymiterio tumuletur, nisi aliud obstiterit, et poenam non debemus ei vertere in culpam."

Similar legislation is found in Cambrai synod, 1287 or 1288, Boeren, ed., "Les plus ancien statuts," *Revue de droit canonique* 4 (1954): 133; Cambrai synod, ca. 1300–07, Dom Edmond Martène and Ursin Durand, eds., *Veterum scriptorum et monumentorum historicorum, dogmaticorum, moralium, amplissima collectio*, 9 vols. (Paris, 1724–33; repr. New York, 1968), 7: 1293; Tournai synod, 1366, Jacques Le Groux, ed., *Summa statutorum synodalium cum praevia synopsi vitae episcoporum tornacensium. . .* (1726), p. 4.

Peter Lombard in his *Sentences* argues, "Et sicut parvuli qui sine baptismo moriuntur numero infidelium adscribuntur, ita qui baptizantur fideles vocantur. Quia a fidelium consortio non separantur cum orat Ecclesia pro fidelibus defunctis." *Sententiae in IV libris distinctae* 4.4.4, 3rd ed., 2 vols. in 3 (Rome, 1981), 2: 259.

[7]Pope Nicholas I in his letter to the Bulgarians stated that all baptized in the name of the Trinity or in Christ's name (as stated in Acts) were baptized whether the baptism was performed by a Jew, Christian, or pagan. See Gratian, *Decretum*, De Con. 4.24, in Friedberg, *Corpus*, 1: 1368. (The complete text of the letter is in Giovanni Domenico Mansi, ed., *Sacrorum conciliorum nova, et amplissima collectio*, 31 vols. [Florence, 1759–98], 15: 32.) Peter Lombard concurred, saying that if a heretic performs a baptism following "forma a Christo tradita, verum baptismum dat" (*Sententiae* 4.6.2, 2: 268–69).

Alexander III in a canon cited in the *Liber extra* delineated the two necessary phrases of the baptismal formula as "[e]go baptizo te" and "in nomine Patris, et Filii et Spiritus sancti, amen" (X.3.42.1 in Friedberg, *Corpus*, 2: 644). Lateran IV in its first canon confirmed that "the sacrament of

that the form handed down from the time of Christ be used. For the late medieval church the normal and natural baptismal ceremony was one publicly enacted before witnesses (in front of and inside the parish church), complete with exorcisms and anointings, as well as the baptism proper, all of which was done by the parish priest. An emergency baptism done by a lay person—midwife, neighbor, or parent[8]—bypassed ecclesiastical attempts to control entry into the Christian community, turning the baptism into a private, hurried, "unnatural" ceremony, managed by a non-cleric. Still, a priest could not always be there when a birthing suddenly began to go wrong, or if a child was born too weak to survive for more than a few moments.[9] If the French synodal legislation contains anything

---

Baptism, which by invocation of each Person of the Trinity, namely, of the Father, Son, and Holy Ghost, is effected in water, [and when] duly conferred on children and adults in the form prescribed by the Church by anyone whatsoever, leads to salvation" (H. J. Schroeder, ed. and trans., *Disciplinary Decrees of the General Councils: Text, Translation, and Commentary* [St. Louis, 1937], p. 239).

[8]Under normal circumstances a parent was not to baptize his/her child (nor to stand as a godparent), as this would set the parent in an incestuous spiritual kinship with the other parent. In the *Decretum*, Gratian tells the story of a father who, because of dire necessity, baptized his son. The need for the baptism outweighed the incestuous relation the father had accidently caused between himself and his wife, and so the couple did not have to separate (*Decretum* 2.30.1.7 in Friedberg, *Corpus*, 1: 1098–99). On parents not being allowed to stand as godparents see Lynch, *Godparents and Kinship*, pp. 277–81.

[9]Synodal legislation from Chartres (ca. 1355–68) and Tréguier (ca. 1334) contains statutes insisting that priests should without delay go to baptize a baby (the Chartres statute adds "nisi causa racionabili"). See Chartres, ca. 1355–68, Maurice Jusselin, ed., "Statuts synodaux et constitutions synodales du diocèse de Chartres au XIVe siècle," *Revue historique de droit francais et étranger*, 4e sér., 8 (1929): 80; Tréguier, ca. 1334, Dom Edmond Martène and Ursin Durand, eds., *Thesaurus novus anecdotorum*, 5 vols. (Paris, 1717; repr. New York, 1968), 4: 1097.

about children, it is almost always instructions that the priest should teach the laity, both men and women, the correct baptismal formula in their native language (whether French or Breton).[10] Many of the statutes from various synods remind the priest to instruct the laity also to sprinkle or pour water upon the child during the saying of the baptismal formula.[11]

The emphasis in the synodal legislation shows that not only men but also women were to learn what to do in a baptismal emergency; however, the ecclesiastical hierarchy was even more hesitant about allowing laywomen to baptize than laymen. Both Robert Pulleyn and Thomas Aquinas were uncomfortable with women baptizing, but they allowed it in extreme necessity.[12] Yet by the late Middle Ages the bishops in northern France through their synodal legislation were urging parish priests to

---

[10]See, e.g.: Paris, ca. 1196–1208, Odette Pontal, ed. and trans., *Les statuts synodaux français du XIIIe siècle*, 1: *Les statuts de Paris et le synodal de l'ouest* (Paris, 1971), p. 54; Rouen, ca. 1231–35, Guillaume Bessin, ed. *Concilia Rotomagensis provinciae*, 2 vols. (Rouen, 1717), 2: 53–54; Coutances, n.d. (13th c.), Mansi, *Sacrorum conciliorum*, 25: 30–31; Bayeux, 1300, Mansi, *Sacrorum conciliorum*, 25: 61; Orléans, n.d. (before 1314), Martène and Durand, *Veterum scriptorum*, 7: 1274; Reims, ca. 1328–30, Thomas Marie Joseph Gousset, ed., *Les actes de la province ecclésiastique de Reims*, 4 vols. (Reims, 1842–44), 2: 539; Tréguier, ca. 1334, Martène and Durand, *Thesaurus novus*, 4: 1097–98; Meaux, n.d. (ca. 1346), Martène and Durand, *Thesaurus novus*, 4: 892; Chartres, n.d. (ca. 1355–68), Jusselin, "Statuts synodaux," p. 80.

[11]Paris, after 1311, Fr. de Harlay, ed., *Synodicon ecclesiae Parisiensis auctoritate* (Paris, 1674), p. 33; St.-Brieuc, 1421, B. Pocquet du Haut-Jussé, "Les statuts synodaux d'Alain de la Rue, évêque de Saint-Brieuc," *Bulletin et Mémoires de la Société archéologique du département d'Île-et-Vilaine* 47 (1920): 22–23.

[12]Robert Pulleyn, *De caeremoniis, sacramentis, officiis et observationibus ecclesiasticis* 1.13, PL 177: 389, and Thomas Aquinas, *Summa theologica* 3a.67.4, in *Baptism and Confirmation*, ed. and trans. James J. Cunningham, O.P., 57 (New York, 1975), pp. 62–65.

teach this basic baptismal ceremony to certain women ahead of everyone else in the parish. These women were the local midwives, who could be expected to attend many of the births in the community and who would be able to judge the chances of a baby's survival. The first legislation mentioning midwives specifically is from a 1311 Paris synod; it states that in every vill there should be skilled midwives sworn to perform emergency baptism.[13] Legislation from a 1365 Meaux synod declares that because of the perils of birth, a midwife or two should be found in each parish. Such midwives, carefully chosen, were to be sent to the bishop's court for an examination and oath-taking in order to obtain a "certificate" of approval. The parish rector was to keep records on these midwives.[14] The Reims council of 1408 provides a checklist of concerns for a visiting diocesan official to use when he toured the parishes. One matter on this list was to make sure that the local midwives understood the correct way to perform a baptism.[15] By placing midwives under semi-official supervision and insisting that parish priests instruct all their parishioners on how to perform an emergency baptism, ecclesiastical authorities were attempting to make sure that even the most hastily performed baptism still followed the correct formula and that the passage of all infants into Christian membership remained somewhat under their control. That ecclesiastical officials were uneasy about the laity overstepping the carefully laid rules about emergency baptism is certain; diocesan statutes from the

---

[13]Harlay, *Synodicon*, p. 33.

[14]Meaux, 1365, Martène and Durand, *Thesaurus novus*, 4: 929.

[15]Council of Reims, 1408, Mansi, *Sacrorum conciliorum*, 26: 1070. For other legislation on midwives see Arras, n.d. (15th c.), Johann Friedrich Schannat and Joseph Hartzheim, eds., *Concilia germaniae*, 11 vols. (Cologne, 1759–90; repr. Aalen, 1970–96), 8: 246; Tournai, 1481, Le Groux, *Summa statutorum*, pp. 82–83.

mid-fourteenth-century synods of Chartres and Meaux firmly reminded parents that they were only allowed to perform a baptism in "greatest necessity."[16]

What if the baby did not die immediately after a lay baptism? How could the Church regain power from this disruption in the "natural" order of baptism and normalize the baby's non-normal passage into the Christian community? The synodal legislation does provide some answers to these problems, which further display the ecclesiastical hierarchy's uneasiness about and even hostility towards the laity baptizing infants.

After a lay baptism, if the baby should survive, the parents were to present the child to the parish priest. The priest was to question discreetly the person who had performed the ceremony (and any witnesses) about what was done and said. If all seemed correct, then the priest was to approve the lay baptism. Most of the synodal legislation then insists that the priest should complete the ceremony.[17] The Synodal de l'Ouest, Angers's great diocesan collection from the early thirteenth century, speaks about the priest "supply[ing] what is lacking, namely the bit of salt and the touching of the ear with saliva. . . . [After this is done, he should perform] over the

---

[16]Chartres, ca. 1355–68, Jusselin, "Statuts synodaux," p. 80: "Ut pater vel mater non baptisent pueros suos nisi in summa neccessitate." Meaux, ca. 1346, Martène and Durand, *Thesaurus novus*, 4: 892: "Doceant etiam sacerdotes patrem et matrem posse baptizare in maxima et summa necessitate, aliter autem non."

[17]See, e.g., Synod of Paris, in Pontal, *Les statuts synodaux français*, 1: 56, and PL 212: 59; Orléans, ca. 1314, Martène and Durand, *Veterum scriptorum*, 7: 1272–75; Meaux, ca. 1346, Martène and Durand, *Thesaurus novus*, 4: 842; Cambrai, before 1260, Boeren, "Les plus ancien statuts," 3: 133; Cambrai, 1287 or 1288, Boeren, "Les plus ancien statuts," 4: 132–33; Cambrai, ca. 1300–07, Martène and Durand, *Veterum scriptorum*, 7: 1292, and Paris, Bibliothèque Nationale, MS lat. 1592, fol. 55, col. 1; and Tournai, 1366, Le Groux, *Summa statutorum*, pp. 3–4.

font, without the immersion, the rest of [the baptismal] ceremony."[18] Synodal statutes from Arras (ca. 1270–90), Tréguier
(ca. 1334), and Chartres (ca. 1355–68) mention that the priest
was to sign the lay-baptized child with chrism.[19] All this was
to be done not because the lay baptism failed to wash the child
clean of original sin or to bring him/her safely across the
border of death into the new life of Christianity, but to "aug-
ment the virtue" of the lay ceremony.[20]

Various synods from northwestern France provide an interesting proscription against the laity naming the baby, in an
effort to emphasize ecclesiastical control over baptism and
even over the identity of the infant. By 1220 a synod from
Angers had issued a statute which ruled that in an emergency
baptism the lay person, performing the baptism, was not to
name the child. This statute was also added to a synodal
collection from Rouen (ca. 1231–35), while the legislators of
the 1247 LeMans synodal collection expanded on this judgment, decreeing that the nameless, lay-baptized child was to be
brought to the parish priest, who was to name the infant before
the church door and then take the infant inside the church to
"complete" the baptism.[21]

---

[18]"[S]uppleatur quod deest, scilicet pabulum salis et aurium linitio cum
salvia. . . . et super fontes, sine immersione omnia fiant, que solent fieri"
(Synodal de l'Ouest, in Pontal, *Les statuts synodaux français*, 1: 140, 142).

[19]Arras, ca. 1270–90, Antoine Alexandre Gosse, *Histoire de l'abbaye et de
l'ancienne congrégation des chanoines réguliers d'Arrouaise, avec des notes
critiques, historiques et diplomatiques* (Lille, 1786; repr. Arras, 1972), p. 581;
Tréguier, ca. 1334, Martène and Durand, *Thesaurus novus*, 4: 1097–98;
Chartres, ca. 1355–68, Jusselin, "Statuts synodaux," p. 80.

[20]"[N]on quantum ad salutem, sed quoad augmentum virtutum," Coutances,
n.d. (13th c.), Mansi, *Sacrorum conciliorum*, 25: 30–31.

[21]Synodal de l'Ouest, in Pontal, *Les statuts synodaux français*, 1: 140;
Rouen, ca. 1231–35, Bessin, *Concilia Rotomagensis*, 2: 53–54; Le Mans,
1247, Martène and Durand, *Veterum scriptorum*, 7: 1371.

Having the priest "complete" the baptismal ceremony in the parish church was a way of eliding the perceived threat of lay baptism to the ecclesiastical hierarchy's twin desires to control the sacrament of baptism and the child's entry into the Christian community. While the actual baptism could be done by anyone, the insistence that the supporting baptismal rituals be performed publicly by the parish priest to complete and add to the virtue of the actual baptism allowed the ecclesiastical authorities to integrate a correctly accomplished lay baptism into their conception of a "normal" baptism and the child into their conception of a "normal" Christian.

What if the priest had doubts about whether the lay person had performed the baptism correctly, or what if the child was a foundling and his/her baptismal status was unknown, or what if the child had been baptized "partially born," when he or she had only a limb outside of the birth canal? No one could be baptized twice—a repeated baptismal ceremony would create uncertainty about the child's identity (in which ceremony was the child's Christian identity marked?) and blur the boundaries of membership in the Christian community (exactly when did the child become part of the Christian community?). Yet, in such situations of unknown baptismal status how could one be sure that the first baptism had counted (or had even occurred)? Sometime during the Carolingian period the conditional baptismal formula ("If you are baptized, I do not baptize you, but, if you are not yet baptized, I baptize you, etc.") was developed as a response to such problematical situations. There is no indication in any of the Carolingian legislation that this formula was seen by the ecclesiastical hierarchy as a recent innovation; rather, it was seen as long-standing and acceptable practice. Alexander III confirmed the acceptability of the conditional formula in a text that was gathered in the decretal collection of

Gregory IX.[22] Most of the northern French synodal legislation giving priests directions about the conditional baptism simply states that if there is any doubt about the efficacy of the lay baptism, or if the child's baptismal status is unknown, then the priest should do the complete baptismal ceremony and recite at the font the conditional formula, thus clarifying the infant's status in the community.[23] In two synodal texts it is mentioned that the priest was to speak the conditional formula out loud and in French so that the laity present at the ceremony would understand that no one can be baptized twice.[24]

In the fifteenth century, the legislators of Saint-Brieuc showed open doubt about whether any lay baptism could possibly be valid. In the priest's manual from the 1421 synod the opening statement on baptism is strictly conventional, decreeing that all that is needed for a proper baptism is the correct saying of the baptismal formula and a three-fold pouring of water upon the infant's head. This pronouncement, however, is

---

[22] X.3.42.2, Friedberg, *Corpus*, 2: 644: "De quibus dubium est, an baptizati fuerint, baptizantur his verbis praemissis: Si baptizatus es, non te baptizo, sed, si nondum baptizatus es, ego te baptizo, etc."

[23] Synodal de l'Ouest, in Pontal, *Les statuts synodaux français*, 1: 140, 142; Rouen, ca. 1231–35, Bessin, *Concilia Rotomagensis*, 2: 54; LeMans, 1247, Martène and Durand, *Veterum scriptorum*, 7: 1371–72; Cambrai, before 1260, Boeren, "Les plus ancien statuts," 3: 133; Cambrai, ca. 1300–07, Martène and Durand, *Veterum scriptorum*, 7: 1292–93; Bayeux, 1300, Mansi, *Sacrorum conciliorum*, 25: 61; Paris, after 1311, Harlay, *Synodicon*, pp. 33–34; Reims, ca. 1328–30, Gousset, *Les actes*, 2: 539; Orléans, ca. 1314, Martène and Durand, *Veterum scriptorum*, 7: 1274–75; Tréguier, ca. 1334, Martène and Durand, *Thesaurus novus*, 4: 1097–98; Meaux, ca. 1346, Martène and Durand, *Thesaurus novus*, 4: 892–93; Chartres, ca. 1355–68, Jusselin, "Statuts synodaux," p. 80; Tournai, 1366, Le Groux, *Summa statutorum*, pp. 3–4. On foundlings see Coutances, n.d. (13th c.), Mansi, *Sacrorum conciliorum*, 25: 30–31.

[24] Chartres, ca. 1355–68, Jusselin, "Statuts synodaux," p. 80; Reims, ca. 1328–30, Gousset, *Les actes*, 2: 539.

undercut later in the same chapter, since, unlike all other legislators who, when speaking about lay baptism, allow one properly performed to stand, the Saint-Brieuc legislators insist that the priest conditionally baptize an infant already baptized in such a ceremony. They did not believe that the "rudeness and ignorance of the laity" could be easily overcome by the priests' teaching of the correct words; the stress of the moment, they felt, was all too likely to overcome any remembrance of what to do. This skepticism about the validity of lay baptism and the uneasiness about the physical and spiritual status of a child thus baptized was further reflected in the insistence that pre-baptismal exorcisms be said over such a child, "because it often occurs that a malignant spirit is expelled from a baptized one through an exorcism."[25] Most of the legislation and writers examined did not see the need for newly baptized infant to be exorcised, even if the baptismal ceremony had been performed by the laity.[26] Even so, one wonders how many lay baptisms were accepted by parish priests—did many priests, as the synodal legislation from Saint-Brieuc suggests, automatically assume that the "rudeness

---

[25]Saint-Brieuc, 17 Oct. 1421, Pocquet, "Les statuts synodaux d'Alain de la Rue," p. 24: "In casu quo debilis infans viveret, defferendus est ad ecclesiam et omnes solemnitates precedentes sunt faciende, eciam exorcismi quia bene contingerit spiritum malignum a baptizato per exorcismos expelli, et verba baptismi reiteranda sub condicione dicendo: si tu es baptizatus, non te baptizo, sed si tu non est baptizatus ego baptizo te in nomine Patris, etc. . . . Non enim potuit cetum est quod forma baptismi fuerit debite observata propter ruditatem et ignoranciam laicorum, et propter turbacionem assistancium ex dolore matris et timore mortis infantis." In a regular church baptism the child is exorcised before the baptism proper.

[26]Reims, ca. 1328–30, Gousset, Les actes, 2: 539, is the only other synodal collection in which I found a statute demanding that a lay-baptized child be exorcised before being allowed entry into a church for the completion of the baptism.

and the ignorance of the laity" prevented the laity from ever baptizing correctly?

It may seem that in this struggle to control baptism the infant has been lost, pushed to the margins of the discussion. Paradoxically, the infant was once again returned to the center of debate if something went wrong (such as a breech birth) and there was doubt that the child would come completely out of the birth canal alive. Should/could a "partially" born infant be baptized? This was clearly a troubling case about the boundaries and definitions of human existence. Gratian states that if a woman was baptized during her pregnancy, the fetus still in her womb was not baptized at the same time "because one who is not yet born like Adam can not be reborn with Christ."[27] While a fetus still in the womb could not be baptized and a living child totally birthed must be baptized, the infant still part-way in the birth canal was in a dangerous liminal position. This confusion of borders is seen clearly in the lack of consensus in the texts. Thomas Aquinas disapproved of a baptism being done in this case, especially if the baptism was performed with the water sprinkled on some body part other than the head. If the child should survive the trauma of the birth, then he felt a conditional baptism should be performed. Other theologians considered an emergency baptism done on a partially born infant valid, no matter where the water was sprinkled (or poured) on the infant.[28] Most of the

---

[27]Gratian, *Decretum* 3.4.115, Friedberg, *Corpus*, 1: 1397: "quia qui natus adhuc secundum Adam non est, regenerari secundum Christum non potest." See also Peter Lombard, *Sententiae* 4.6.3, 2: 270–72.

[28]Thomas Aquinas, *Summa theologica* 3a.68.11, in Cunningham, *Baptism and Confirmation*, pp. 114–17: "[Q]uod expectanda est totalis egressio pueri ex utero ad baptismum, nisi mors immineat. Si tamen primo caput egrediatur, in quo fundatur sensus, debet baptizari, periculo imminente: et non est postea rebaptizandus, si eum perfecte nasci contigerit. Et videtur idem faciendum

synodal legislation dealing with this problem does allow for emergency baptisms. Like the theologians, the legislators were divided over whether a second conditional baptism would be needed if the child should survive the trauma of the birth. Legislation from a thirteenth-century Soissons synod and from various other synods held in northeastern France from the mid-thirteenth to the fifteenth century discuss the possibility of baptizing a partially born infant if the head is visible. During a difficult birth where the infant's survival was of concern, if the infant's head was free from the birth canal, then an emergency baptism could be performed. The Soissons legislation goes on to discuss the partially born infant, who might have only a limb (for instance, an arm) extending from the birth canal. If necessary, a baptism should be performed on the protruding limb, because "it piously ought to be believed that the highest priest, God, will make up the defect; still, however, [the child] is not to be buried in a consecrated place [if s/he should not survive]." If the infant did survive, then s/he was to be baptized with the conditional formula in a church ceremony.[29]

---

quaecumque alia pars egrediatur, periculo imminente. Qui tamen in nulla partium exteriorum integritas ita consistit sicut in capite, videtur quibusdam quod, propter dubium, quicumque alia parte corporis abluta, puer post perfectum nativitatem sit baptizandus sub hac forma." For Aquinas's reasons about why the head should be privileged over other parts of the body see *Summa theologica* 3a.66.7 (Cunningham, pp. 32–33). For other theologians' positions see Jules Corblet, *Histoire dogmatique, liturgique et archéologique du sacrament de baptême*, 2 vols. (Paris, 1881–82), 1: 261; Sylvie Laurent, *Naitre au Moyen Âge: de la conception à la naissance: la grossesse et l'accouchement XIIe–XVe siècle* (Paris, 1989), p. 226.

[29] Soissons, n.d. (13th c.), Martène and Durand, *Veterum scriptorum*, 8: 1538: "[S]i sit caput quod appareat, aqua aspergatur cum verbis debitis ad baptismum, et baptizatus est. Si vero alia pars, utpote manus vel pes appareat solum, similiter aspergenda est, et pie credendum est, quod summus sacerdos Deus supplet defectum; sed tamen non est in terra sancta inhumandus."

A final text takes us back to northwest France, this time to Saint-Brieuc and the synod held there in 1421.[30] A baptism when only the infant's head was outside the birth canal, even if performed by the child's father, was apparently thought to be valid. In addition, Alain de la Rue, bishop of Saint-Brieuc, and his legislative helpers found a baptism done when the water was poured on any other appendage to be valid as well:

> The whole soul is in all [of the body] and it is wholly in whatever body part . . . , [and so] it is not suitable to baptize [conditionally] an infant who is completely born since when he was baptized, a certain rebirth underlay the uterine birth.[31]

This seems to be an argument against the need for a conditional baptism, which runs counter to even the Soissons legislation, and certainly counter to other statutes from this same synodal gathering that insist that an infant who had been baptized by a lay person needed to be exorcised and baptized

---

See also Cambrai, before 1260, Boeren, "Les plus ancien statuts," 3: 133; Cambrai, 1287 or 1288, Boeren, "Les plus ancien statuts," 4: 133; Cambrai, ca. 1300–07, Martène and Durand, *Veterum scriptorum*, 7: 1292–93; Tournai, 1366, Le Groux, *Summa statutorum*, p. 4; Arras, n.d. (mid-15th c.?), Schannat and Hartzheim, *Concilia germaniae*, 8: 246. (It is unclear whether this section of the legislation on baptism was promulgated in the mid-15th century or is from a much later date; the editorial note mentions that this statute on partial births and baptism is not in an "ancient edition," but not when it was included in the Arras synodal book.)

[30]Unfortunately, Pocquet, editor of the 1421 synodal statutes, had difficulty transcribing the MS at this point, so some speculation is necessary.

[31]Saint-Brieuc, 17 Oct. 1421, Pocquet, "Les statuts synodaux d'Alain de la Rue," pp. 23–24: "[A]nima est tota in toto et tota est in qualibet parte corporis . . . , sed infantem qui totus est infra matris uterum non est conveniens baptizare quia cum baptismus sit quedam regeneracio, nativitatem ex utero supponit."

conditionally by a priest.[32] What is it about the emergency baptism of a partially born infant that causes Alain de la Rue and his legislative helpers to see a second baptism in this circumstance, even a conditional second baptism, as being an invalid re-baptism? Certainly the legislation's striking statement that "a certain rebirth underlay the uterine birth" grants to this type of baptism a powerful symbolic imagery that might have overcome doubts about the efficacy of this type of baptism and concerns over "malignant spirits."

If the infant's body was the focus of attention in problems we have examined for baptism, it was concerns over Christ's Body (and Blood) that caused ecclesiastical authorities gradually to withhold Communion from the child until the "age of discretion." First Communion had been part of the infant initiation ceremony in the ancient church and in the western medieval church until at least the eleventh century. As well, the canon law collections of Regino of Prüm, Burchard of Worms, and Ivo of Chartres all contained the same instructions that all who were dangerously ill, including infants, were to receive

---

[32]The legislation from northeastern France does not assert that the infant was not to be named during this emergency ceremony, but this is implied by starting the baptismal formula with "Infans." In a second statute from the 17 Oct. 1421 St.-Brieuc legislation, clear directions are given that a partially born infant is not to be named: "Sed si fetus sit in utero et pars extra, si baptizetur, nullum nomen debet imponi nominando expresse dum baptizatur nec sexus distingui, sed per hoc pronomen 'te' indicari substania debet, dicendo: ego baptizo te et cetera" (Pocquet, "Les statuts synodaux d'Alain de la Rue," p. 25). Clearly, naming, sex, and gender were related, and if the sex and name were gotten wrong, then the infant could be endangered and the validity of the sacrament cast into doubt. In legislation from Nantes at the end of the 15th century that Pontal has examined, the actual act of baptism was gendered. Immersion was to be done if the one to be baptized was female, while infusion was to be performed on male infants (*Les statuts synodaux français*, 1: 141 n. 7).

Communion.[33] Infants and young children, while perhaps not being viewed as the ordinary recipients of the Eucharist, were allowed to partake of it when it was deemed necessary or fitting. In the eleventh century, the eucharistic controversy brought to the forefront of Christian thinkers' minds what it meant to say, that the Eucharist was the *real* body and blood of Christ, that it was the sacrament that perfectly recreated Christ's living sacrifice. "This sacrifice was instituted by the Lord not only to be offered, but also to be eaten," the late twelfth-century thinker Baldwin of Ford declared.[34] Such an insistence, focusing sharply on the faithful consuming the historical body of Christ, clashed directly with the physical reality of infancy—babies cannot chew and they often slaver and drool. As a way of avoiding the possibility of an infant spitting out the eucharistic wafer, Robert Pulleyn recommended that the baby could communicate under one species only—the Blood of Christ. The priest was to dip his finger into the chalice and then place it in the newly baptized infant's mouth.[35] This solution was short-lived, however, for by the thirteenth century the chalice generally was being withheld from all the laity and babies were being effectively shut out of

---

[33]Regino of Prüm, *Libri duo de synodalibus causis et disciplinis ecclesiasticis* 1.69, PL 132: 205; Burchard of Worms, *Decreta* 5.10, PL 140: 754; and Ivo of Chartres, *Decreta* 2.20, PL 161: 165.

[34]*Le sacrement de l'autel* 2.2.2., ed. J. Morson, O.C.S.O., in *Sources chrétiennes* 93: 226, cited and trans. Jaroslav Pelikan, *Christian Tradition*, 3: *The Growth of Medieval Theology (600–1300)* (Chicago, 1978), p. 188.

[35]*De officiis eccl.* 1.20, PL 177: 392: "Pueris recens natis idem sacramentum in specie sanguinis est ministrandum digito sacerdotis, quia tales naturaliter sugere possunt." Others who mention that children should be allowed to communicate under one species when necessary are Paschal II, Ep. 85, PL 163: 442; William of Champeaux, *De sacramento altaris*, PL 163: 1039; and Radulph Ardens, Hom. 51, *In die sancto Paschae*, PL 155: 1850.

Communion.[36] Another solution was that of giving the child a wafer that had been simply blessed, not consecrated. *Pain bénit*'s physical resemblance to its consecrated cousin made many ecclesiastical officials uneasy; although the 1255 synod of Bordeaux permitted this practice, the synod of Paris (ca. 1196–1208) and synods from Cambrai and Tournai frowned upon it—stating that no one should receive an unconsecrated wafer, not even a child.[37] In the synodal legislation from northwestern France, however, where *pain bénit* and the consecrated wafer were one and the same thing, unconsecrated hosts could be given to a child in place of blessed bread on Easter Day. It was important, however, that the child eat the unconsecrated host immediately and not carry it outside the church.[38] Clearly, there was worry that the child would play with the host, whether it was unconsecrated or just blessed, and not

---

[36]In Milan, Amiens, and Augsburg infants apparently were still admitted to Communion in the later Middle Ages, but J. D. C. Fisher argues that this is because "[these] Churches [were] no doubt jealous of their ancient traditions, and sufficiently eminent to be able to maintain them in spite of what was happening elsewhere" (*Christian Initiation: Baptism in the Medieval West; A Study in the Disintegration of the Primitive Rite of Initiation* [London, 1965], pp. 106–07). The Council of Trent formally abolished the practice of infant Communion, ruling that baptized infants had no need of Communion (Trent, session 21, 16 July 1562, chap. 4 in Norman P. Tanner, S.J., ed., *Decrees of the Ecumenical Councils*, 2 vols. [London, 1990], 2: 727).

[37]For the synod of Bordeaux see Fisher, *Christian Initiation*, p. 105. Paris, ca. 1196–1208, in Pontal, *Les statuts synodaux français*, 1: 56; Cambrai, ca. 1238–40, Boeren, "Les plus ancien statuts," 3: 145; Cambrai, before 1260, Boeren, "Les plus ancien statuts," 3: 145; Cambrai, ca. 1287–88, Boeren, "Les plus ancien statuts," 4: 141; Cambrai, ca. 1300–07, BN lat. 1592, fol. 4v, col. 1; Tournai, 1366, Le Groux, *Summa statutorum*, pp. 22–23.

[38]Angers, ca. 1220, in Pontal, *Les statuts synodaux français*, 1: 150; Le Mans, 1247, Martène and Durand, *Veterum scriptorum*, 7: 1383; Tours, n.d. (before 1396), Étienne Fougeron, "Statuts synodaux de Tours," *Mémoires de la Société archéologique de Touraine* 23 (1873), 2nd fasc.: 62.

treat it respectfully. The Cambrai and Tournai legislators were also concerned that the handing out of unconsecrated wafers to any of the laity, even children, would lessen the sacredness of the Eucharist.

The doctrine of the real presence demanded more than that a baby not spit up the Eucharist—it demanded that the person receiving the Eucharist show true reverence, that s/he comprehend (in some way) that what s/he was consuming was the actual body and blood of Christ.[39] Lateran IV gave expression to this requirement for respectful devotion and understanding when it linked Communion (along with penance) to the age of discretion, ordering all people who reached this age to communicate (and confess) at Easter.[40] Synodal legislators tried to make Lateran IV's pronouncement on Communion more concrete by suggesting that children reach the age of discretion around their seventh or tenth year and this is when they could communicate.[41] Just as baptism came to represent the infant's first step into the Christian community, Communion came to symbolize the child's entry into the world of adult spirituality.

---

[39] The legislation mentions other ways in which proper reverence for the Eucharist was to be expressed. Before the priest carried the Eucharist to the sick, "[f]requenter moneantur laici et etiam pueri, ut ubicumque viderint deferri sanctum Corpus domini statim genua flectant, tamquam Domino et Creatori suo, et junctis manibus quousque transierit orent," Rouen, ca. 1231–35, Bessin, *Concilia Rotomagensis*, 2: 63.

[40] Lateran IV, canon 21, in Schroeder, *Disciplinary Decrees*, pp. 259–60.

[41] For the seventh year: Tours, ca. 1216–17, Joseph Avril, *Les conciles de la province de Tours/Conciliae provinciae turonensis (saec. XIII–XV)* (Paris, 1987), p. 120; Rouen, ca. 1231–35, Bessin, *Concilia Rotomagensis*, 2: 55; Bayeux (1300), Mansi, *Sacrorum conciliorum*, 25: 63. For the tenth year: Cambrai, ca. 1238–40, Boeren, "Les plus ancien statuts," 3: 145; Cambrai, 1287 or 1288, Boeren, "Les plus ancien statuts," 4: 141; Cambrai, ca. 1300–07, Martène and Durand, *Veterum scriptorum*, 7: 1301; Tournai, 1366, Le Groux, *Summa statutorum*, pp. 22–23.

A child who was allowed to communicate was a reasoning being, no longer shielded by baptismal innocence.[42]

Like first Communion, confirmation—the post-baptismal episcopal anointing and imposition of the hands—had been part of the initiation ceremony of the early church. For the Fathers, such as Ambrose and Leo the Great, this episcopal act sealed and completed the baptism.[43] As Christianity spread beyond the urban areas of the Mediterranean world into the thinly populated regions of northwestern Europe, it became impossible for bishops to preside personally over every initiation ceremony, and priests became the ordinary baptismal celebrants. It is during this period that we observe a developing confusion about confirmation, its authority, and its relation to baptism; however, from this confusion confirmation gradually emerged as a distinct sacrament administered by the bishop alone. It is interesting to note that the western church did not follow the strategy of the eastern church, which kept confirmation as part of its initiation ceremony (thus allowing it to

---

[42]Interestingly enough, the synodal legislation did not link penance and Communion together the way the Lateran IV canon did. The legislation generally urged priests to warn their flock to confess annually; however, this message was especially for those members who were 14 years and older. This seems to have been influenced in part by the fact that children under the age of 14 were viewed as too young to fast (often used as a type of penance). See, e.g., Cambrai, 1287 or 1288, Boeren, "Les plus ancien statuts," 4: 134; Angers, Pentecost, 1295, *Les statuts synodaux français du XIIIe siècle*, 3: *Les statuts synodaux angevins de la seconde moitié du XIIIe siècle: précédés d'une étude sur la législation synodale angevine*, ed. and trans. Joseph Avril (Paris, 1988), p. 183. There are also gradations of penance in some of the legislation—where the seriousness of the deed (and who is to administer the penance) is determined by the age and gender of the penitent. See, e.g., Cambrai, 1277, Boeren, "Les plus ancien statuts," 3: 402, and Cambrai 1287 or 1288, Boeren, "Les plus ancien statuts," 4: 155–57.

[43]See Fisher, *Christian Initiation*, pp. 142–44.

be administered by priests). Western ecclesiastical authorities, however, did not desire confirmation to wither away.

In fifth-century southern Gaul, one of the first areas in Western Europe where the rite of initiation divided into the two ceremonies of baptism and confirmation, Faustus of Riez offered a new metaphor to describe confirmation as a now distinct rite. Confirmation no longer just sealed and completed a baptism; it strengthened the one baptized, enabling this new Christian to "[hold] fast to the new being taken on in baptism" by increasing the natural capacity of his/her moral power.[44] Faustus in his Pentecost homily on confirmation used a military analogy to describe this strengthening:

> Because those who are to live in this world all their days have to walk among invisible foes and perils, in baptism we are reborn to life, after baptism we are strengthened, and if the benefits of regeneration suffice for those who immediately after birth pass from this life, nevertheless for those who are to live on in this world the graces of confirmation are necessary. Regeneration by itself saves those who are to be received into the peace of the age of bliss, whereas confirmation arms and equips those who are to be kept for the struggles and battles of this world.[45]

---

[44]Peter Cramer, *Baptism and Change in the Early Middle Ages, c. 200– c. 1150* (Cambridge, 1993), p. 182; Faustus of Riez, *Homilia de Pentecosten*, in L. A. van Buchem, *L'homélie pseudo-Eusébienne de Pentecôte. L'origine de la 'confirmatio' en Gaule Méridionale et l'interprétation de ce rite par Fauste de Riez* (Nijmegen, 1967), p. 41.

[45]Faustus of Riez, *Homilia de Pentecosten*, p. 41: "[Q]uia in hoc mundo tota aetate victuris inter invisibiles hostes et pericula gradiendum est. In baptismo regeneramur ad vitam, post baptismum confirmamur ad pugnam. In baptismo abluimur post baptismum roboramur.

"Ac sic continuo transituris sufficiunt regenerationis beneficia, victuris autem necessaria sunt confirmationis auxilia. Regeneratio per se saluat mox in pace beati saeculi recipiendos, confirmatio armat et instruit ad agones mundi huius et proelia reservandos. Qui autem post baptismum cum adquista

In the Carolingian period, the composer of the Pseudo-Isidorian decretals took up Faustus's Pentecost homily on confirmation and attributed it to a Pope Melchiades.[46] In addition, the Pseudo-Isidore gathered other writings on confirmation stressing its importance for those who survived infancy, along with writings on the exclusive right of the bishop to perform this ceremony.[47] These false decretals were used to uphold the authority of the bishop. Confirmation, as delineated by the arguments found in this collection, not only became a display of episcopal authority but also an exhibition of the bishop's pivotal position in the Christian Church. Without the bishop one could not be confirmed; without confirmation one could not be a "true" Christian. Only the confirmed Christian, enlisted under the bishop's leadership and fully equipped by the bishop, could successfully undertake the struggle towards a Christian life.[48]

---

innocentia immaculatus pervenit ad mortem, confirmatur morte, quia iam potest peccare post mortem." (Trans. Fisher, *Christian Initiation*, p. 126.)

[46]Paul Hinschius, ed., *Decretales pseudo-Isidorianae, et Capitula Angilramni* (Leipzig, 1863), p. 245.

[47]Two other passages discuss confirmation and the bishop's role. The first passage, in Hinschius, *Decretales pseudo-Isidorianae*, pp. 63–64, is attributed to Clement of Rome (but is in truth an invented text): "Omnibus ergo festinandum est sine mora renasci deo et demum consignari ab episcopo, id est septiformem gratiam spiritus sancti percipere, quia incertus est uniuscuiusque exitus vitae. Cum autem regeneratus fuerit per aquam et postmodum septiformis spiritus gratia ab episcopo, ut christianus nequaquam poterit, nec sedem habere inter perfectos si non necessitate, sed incuria aut voluntate remanserit, ut a beato Petro apostolo accepimus ut ceteri sancti apostoli praecipiente domino docuerunt, et demum ex operibus bonis ostendat in se similitudinem eius, qui eum genuit patris." The second, in Hinschius, ibid., p. 146, is attributed to Urban I (but really is from the 836 Council of Aix-la-Chapelle): "Omnes enim fideles per manus impositionem episcoporum spiritum sanctum post baptismum accipere debent, ut plene christiani inveniantur; quia, cum spiritus sanctus infunditur, cor fidele ad prudentiam et constantiam dilcitatur."

[48]Cramer argues that for the Carolingians confirmation operated as a mirror, reflecting the person in the world whether or not s/he was still wearing the

While confirmation's definitional shift proved to be useful for reinforcing episcopal authority, it did not allow that confirmation was necessary for salvation. As confirmation became detached from baptism and developed into a separate sacrament, the foundations of its own authority became ever more unstable, as they—unlike those of baptism—did not rest upon clear dominical grounds. This instability is reflected in the writings of such authorities as Peter of Poiters and Hugh of Saint Victor, who tried to argue that confirmation was close to indispensable for salvation, while not denying salvation to those infants who died having only received baptism. These arguments, however, could only be arguments that confirmation was nearly essential to salvation or arguments that good Christians would not neglect to be confirmed.[49] That the practice of confirmation was separated in time from baptism and could only be performed when the bishop was readily accessible to one who needed the ceremony—an infrequent occurrence in the lives of many people living in the distant

---

"right/rite" clothes. The mirror metaphor represents confirmation not as a set of moral principles that the Christian would use to structure her/his life but as the *ordering* of these principles. For Carolingians this "[moral] norm was physically represented by the bishop who promulgated the laws and gave 'ordo.'" Thus confirmation was intimately tied to the bishop and his authority (*Baptism and Change*, p. 183).

[49]Hugh of St. Victor, *De sacramentis* 2.7.3, PL 176: 461, and Peter of Poiters, *Sententiae* 5.3 and 5.9, PL 211: 1229, 1243. Peter of Poiters in his discussion about whether confirmation is "dignius" than baptism compares baptism to water and confirmation to wine and concludes that "aqua utilior vino, sed vinum dignius et excellentius est" (PL 211: 1243). Other theologians, following Rabanus Maurus, argued that the grace received in confirmation, although it differed from baptismal grace, was a supplement to baptismal grace. The subleties of this line of reasoning, which also drew upon the idea of confirmation as strengthening, still could not grant confirmation an essential nature. See Fisher, *Christian Initiation*, pp. 62–65, 128–29.

rural reaches of the dioceses of northern France—further heightened tensions about the necessity of confirmation and who was to receive it and when.

In response to these tensions, confirmation became not the moment of completion and consummation in the initiation rite but a statement of public affirmation to the bishop of one's standing in the Christian community and of one's movement towards having a proper comprehension of what it was to be Christian. Reiterating Faustus's metaphor, a statute from a thirteenth-century Coutances synodal book stressed: "[Confirmation] aids the increase of grace by which the Holy Spirit is poured onto the baptized. The Christian is armed by this sacrament and is instructed on the tribulations of this world and against the devil."[50] Thomas Aquinas echoed this, adding that "the one confirmed receives the power publicly and, as it were, *ex officio*, to profess faith in Christ in his speech" and that "in confirmation man receives a maturity in the life of the spirit."[51] Infants are obviously poor candidates for confirmation thus defined. By the end of the thirteenth century, synodal legislators began to insist that only children seven years and older be taken to the bishop for confirmation.[52] In two north-

---

[50]Coutances, n.d. (13th c.), Mansi, *Sacrorum conciliorum*, 25: 31: "[Q]uod Sacramentum praestat augmentum ad gratiam; per quod Spiritus Sanctus infunditur in baptizato; quo Sacramento armatur Christianus, et instruitur ad agones hujus mundi et contra diabolum."

[51]Thomas Aquinas, *Summa theologica* 3.a.72.5 (Cunningham, *Baptism and Confirmation*, pp. 204–05): "ita confirmatus accipit potestaem publice fidem Christi verbis profitendi, quasi ex officio"; and *Summa theologica* 3a, 72.1 (pp. 188–89): "[i]n confirmatione autem homo accipit quasi quandam aetatem perfectam spiritualis vitae." (Trans. Cunningham.)

[52]Cambrai legislation from before 1260 orders priest to tell parents to take their baptized children to the bishop for confirmation; however, the instructions on preparing for confirmation are directed towards children seven years old and up. See Boeren, "Les plus ancien statuts," 3: 134. The later

eastern French synodal collections from the end of the fifteenth century, statutes state that those to be confirmed had not only to be at least seven, but they also had to know some basic Christian texts—the Creed, the Lord's Prayer, the Ave Maria.[53] Confirmation was developing from a sacramental adjunct to baptism into an initiation rite for the maturing child, who could rationally affirm his/her faith and explicate the basic tenets of church teaching.

This evolution of confirmation into an autonomous sacrament reveals also a working out of a strategy to deal with other important cultural anxieties centered on the corporate assembly of believers. Given the conception of the whole of Christian society as the body of Christ, the dispersal of this society into scattered communities, directed often by poorly educated priests, led to concerns that the limbs, as it were, were not submitting to the proper dictates of the head. The insistence that the members of the community come before the bishop to be confirmed articulated the Church's perceived need

---

Cambrai synods legislation orders people to take their children seven years or older to be confirmed; there is no mention of younger children needing confirmation (see Cambrai, 1287 or 1288, Boeren, "Les plus ancien statuts," 4: 134; Cambrai, ca. 1300–07, Martène and Durand, *Veterum scriptorum*, 7: 1293–94). Legislation from St.-Brieuc, 17 Oct. 1421, and Arras, n.d. (second half 15th c.), forbids confirmation of anyone under the age of seven years (Pocquet, "Les statuts synodaux d'Alain de la Rue," pp. 26–27; Schannat and Hartzheim, *Concilia germaniae*, 8: 247). See also Soissons, n.d. (13th c.), Martène and Durand, *Veterum scriptorum*, 8: 1539; Arras, 16 Oct. 1291, Gosse, *Histoire de l'abbaye*, pp. 603–04; Reims, ca. 1328–30, Gousset, *Les actes*, 2: 539–40. William of Melitona saw the failure to confirm children at infancy not as a rereading of the sacrament's purpose but as a simple problem of parental laziness (*De sacramento confirmationis*, ed. Kilian F. Lynch, in *The Sacrament of Confirmation in the Early-Middle Scholastic Period*, 1: *Texts* [St. Bonaventure, N.Y., 1957], p. 113).

[53] Arras, n.d. (15th c.), Schannat and Hartzheim, *Concilia germaniae*, 8: 247; Tournai, 4 Oct. 1481, Le Groux, *Summa statutorum*, pp. 95–96.

for a centralized (and centralizing) authority. This episcopal authority had to do, in part, with correct instruction and the dissemination of church doctrine. This control of doctrine related to an anxiety also at the heart of baptism and Communion—the identification of who is a true member of the body of Christians. Did the faithful really understand what made them Christians and not "other"? The rôle of confirmation evolved from a completion of baptism to a public profession of faith that had the individual submit to the bishop. This transmutation of confirmation indicates a peculiar double function: confirmation is an indoctrination and yet it involves an individual choosing independently and freely to submit to the bishop's authority.

The tensions and instabilities over where confirmation's authority was sited spilled over into everyday life and troubled this ideal that the individual profess and submit to the bishop. There was a fair degree of indifference by both the laity and their parish priests to the bishop's authority to confirm, were we to judge from the frequency with which synods reiterated the importance of this authority in their legislation. Statute after statute sternly asserts that priests were frequently to warn the people to have themselves and/or their children confirmed.[54] Neither priests nor flock were to wait for the bishop to come to them; instead, when the bishop was nearby, the

---

[54]Soissons, n.d. (13th c.), Martène and Durand, *Veterum scriptorum*, 8: 1539; Synod of Paris (ca. 1196–1208), in Pontal, *Les statuts synodaux français*, 1: 56; Chartres, ca. 1355–68, Jusselin, "Statuts synodaux," p. 81. While some of this legislation still discussed infant confirmation, it also contained instructions for youths and adults who had not yet been confirmed, thus pragmatically acknowledging that confirmation was moving out of the realm of infancy and losing all connection to baptism. See, e.g., the three above-noted statutes and those from Orléans, n.d. (before 1314), Martène and Durand, *Veterum scriptorum*, 7: 1275, and Meaux, ca. 1346, Martène and Durand, *Thesaurus novus*, 4: 893.

priests (or their clerics or chaplains) were to spread the word personally about the bishop's coming and make arrangements for a procession from the parish to the bishop. The parish priest, with a cross preceding, was to lead this group, which was to include all those who needed to be confirmed or had need of the bishop's advice.[55] If the sacrament of confirmation was thus both a locus of episcopal authority and the rite expressing the Church's desire for a free profession from those over the age of discretion, the local clergy and laity nonetheless appeared to have maintained a certain skepticism toward this sacrament, and perhaps toward the ecclesiastical hierarchy in general.[56]

---

[55] See, e.g., Paris, ca. 1196–1208, in Pontal, *Les statuts synodaux français*, 1: 56; Orléans, n.d. (before 1314), Martène and Durand, *Veterum scriptorum*, 7: 1275; Meaux, ca. 1346, Martène and Durand, *Thesaurus novus*, 4: 893; Chartres, ca. 1355–68, Jusselin, "Statuts synodaux," p. 81; Rouen, ca. 1231–35, Bessin, *Concilia Rotomagensis*, 2: 54; Bayeux, 1300, Mansi, *Sacrorum conciliorum*, 25: 61; Soissons, n.d. (13th c.), Martène and Durand, *Veterum scriptorum*, 8: 1539; Angers, ca. 1220, in Pontal, *Les statuts synodaux français*, 1: 142; Le Mans, ca. 1247, Martène and Durand, *Veterum scriptorum*, 7: 1372.

[56] Although I could not locate any statutes about meting out punishments for the failure to confirm in the synodal legislation I investigated, there is evidence from English councils and synods, as well as an example from the 1351 *Constitutions* of Lucca. Some English 13th-century councils set age limits for children and penalties for parents who failed to take their children for confirmation by these ages. For example, the council of Exeter ordered that if the bishop was accessible, parents should have their children confirmed before the age of three. If the parents should fail to do this, then they were to fast every Friday until they had rectified the situation. In 1281, Archbishop Peckham at the Council of Lambeth expressed concern that there were many who had never been confirmed. Sanctions were ordered against those who had not been confirmed and had not been reasonably impeded from confirmation. They were not to receive Communion (except on their deathbeds) until they received the sacrament of confirmation. This canon was integrated into the *Sarum Manual* and the 1662 *Book of Common Prayer*. The Lucca statute threatens prelates and rectors with excommunication if they do not tell

As even this short examination of infant baptism, (first) Communion, and confirmation reveals, the medieval church was indeed interested in children and their place in the Christian community. This interest took many forms, centering on the child's body and soul as the contested sites of concern. The Church's role in saving and fashioning that body and soul displays that, for the Church, childhood was to be constructed in relation to these three sacraments. This interest in children also reveals important debates over how ecclesiastical authority was to be maintained and reinforced through the administration of these sacraments.

While the ecclesiastical hierarchy acknowledged that the importance of guaranteeing an infant salvation made it imperative that laity learn how to baptize correctly, this acknowledgment clashed directly with the equally important desire to keep this sacrament under ecclesiastical control. Already there had been a diffusion of baptism as priests replaced bishops as the ordinary baptisands.[57] To prevent the further diffusion of

---

their people once a month that they and/or their children are to be confirmed. The need for such punishment reinforces both the importance of what was at stake for the bishops and the problems they had in maintaining control. For more see Fisher, *Christian Initiation*, pp. 122–24.

[57]Under the Roman ritual the proper times for baptism were during the holy seasons of Easter and Pentecost (the Gallican rite permitted baptism also during Epiphany). The desire to encompass baptism within the sacred temporality of Easter and Pentecost ran up against the fear of an infant dying unbaptized. The uncertainty created from the difficulties of balancing these two opposing needs was expressed throughout the early and High Middle Ages in various legislative acts that preferred Paschal and Pentecostal baptisms *except* if death threatened. By the 13th century the fear of a child dying unbaptized triumphed over the ecclesiastical desire to keep baptism within the precincts of the holy seasons. This loss of connection between baptism and the two important holy seasons on the church calendar also contributed to the diffusion of baptism. For examples of synodal legislation demanding that infants be baptized without delay see above. For discussions on the

"sacredness," the church hierachy fought a rearguard action, trying as much as possible to keep baptism under the precinct of the parish priests. While not denying that anyone could perform a baptism, measures were put in place to try to prevent the laity from rashly usurping this power. The priests were to teach the laity the correct procedure of words and water, but they were also to emphasize that this was an emergency measure to be done only *in extremis*. Midwives were to be licensed by the bishop, and priests were not to dawdle if called to a birthing. The conditional formula was to be used after all dubious baptismal ceremonies, and the rest of the ecclesiastical ceremony performed to complete a lay baptism. The extent of ecclesiastical officials' distrust of lay baptism, however, was perhaps most fully displayed in the extreme demand from Saint-Brieuc and Reims that priests perform exorcisms on the lay-baptized child. All these measures illustrate the Church's anxiety about keeping baptism firmly under its control.

A second problem was that only a child who had been baptized could be fully integrated into the Christian community; however, baptism, unlike circumcision, does not leave a visible mark on its recipient. How did the Christian community recognize those who were properly baptized and therefore its members, if some were baptized in rushed, private, "nonnatural" ceremonies? A lay baptism might have been valid, but it lacked the proper performance of a church baptism, which attempted to move the community of worshipers from the particulars of the event into the eternity of the divine present. This public presentation served as a visible marker, pointing out to those witnessing that the sacred/the invisible was

---

historical separation of baptism from the Paschal and Pentecostal seasons, see Fisher, *Christian Initiation*, pp. 28–29, 45–47, 57, 82, 86–87, 109–19, and Cramer, *Baptism and Change*, pp. 137–38, 140, 155–56, 282.

present among them. The infant's body was the locus of this moment, for the visible and audible performance of the baptism reflected the invisible and silent struggle for the child's soul. It is not surprising that much of the legislation reveals an uneasiness about accepting a simple emergency baptism done by a lay person. This ceremony lacked the full theater of a church baptism which, with its exorcisms, effluvia, and pre- and post-baptismal anointing, more fully reflected the anthropology that the medieval church wished to be displayed. Childhood began in these first moments, when the infant, saved from Adam's sin by God's grace, moved from the world of death into the world of Christianity.

These perceived instabilities in ecclesiastical authority and the child's spiritual status created by emergency lay baptism were further exacerbated by an uneasiness over the possible corrupting forces of the unbaptized or lay-baptized infant body. The body of the unbaptized dead infant could possibly contaminate the cemetery and even create an uncertainty over the possible polluted status of the baptized mother who died with her child. For the legislators of the 1421 Saint-Brieuc synod and the ca. 1328–30 Reims synod, an infant body baptized by the laity was by definition a suspect site that demanded an exorcism.

The next steps into the world of Christianity, (first) Communion and confirmation, had at one time been part of the process of infant initiation; however, by the late Middle Ages they were separate rites that traced the movement towards adulthood and proper understanding of Christian doctrine. A correct attitude towards the Eucharist, the real body of Christ, demanded both the physical ability to chew and swallow the wafer and the mental acuity to express proper reverence, both skills beyond an infant. The restricting of Communion to those of the "age of discretion" was in addition a part of the general trend that moved the communion chalice away from the laity

and elevated the blessing of the host (both literally and figuratively) to the moment of the Mass. As for confirmation, although it was the most poorly defined of the three sacraments
examined here, it was in the process of evolving into the
sacrament in which, having reached the "age of discretion,"
one rationally affirmed one's faith publicly and enrolled one's
self fully in the Christian body under the leadership of the
bishop. The very fluidity of confirmation and the repeated
urgings that all should be confirmed display the ecclesiastical
hierarchy's struggle to impose its authority upon Christian
communities; however, the laity did seem to agree that the
Church did have authority over the child and that the Church's
construction of childhood had validity when it came to the
sacraments of baptism and Communion.

"QUE NOS IN INFANCIA LACTAUIT": THE IMPACT OF CHILDHOOD CARE-GIVERS ON PLANTAGENET FAMILY RELATIONSHIPS IN THE THIRTEENTH AND EARLY FOURTEENTH CENTURIES

John Carmi Parsons

As with so much surrounding the royal houses of the Middle Ages, their child-rearing practices have been little studied save by popular writers. This is especially true for England, whose monarchy has long supported a cottage industry in sentimental accounts of royal lives past and present. The anecdotal style characteristic of such writing may explain scholarly reluctance to approach the wealth of detailed records that survive from the later medieval English royal households—a regrettable aversion, given what the material might add to our knowledge. Perceptive use has been made of the notably scantier records that survive for child-rearing in other royal houses, for example, France. But English royal child-rearing has been studied only for the late eleventh and twelfth centuries, and the few details that survive for that period allow only bare outlines to be suggested: we are told that royal sons were raised apart from their parents until they were old enough to serve some political purpose, while royal parents paid even less attention to daughters before marrying them off at an early age.[1] Such arguments are often justified by citing the infamously bad relationships among King Henry II and his sons. It is quite possible, however, that the turbulent history of that family circle after Henry's sons were grown has colored interpretations of the scant evidence we possess for his sons' early years. And it may well be that only a lack of pertinent evidence for twelfth-century Angevin domestic life precludes a more nuanced account. Eleanor of Aquitaine's gift of land to her son John's nurse, for example, implies that she was grateful for the woman's service, while Alexander Neckham's boast that his mother nursed Richard I suggests that such appointments served the interests of the nurses' families as well; perhaps Neckham owed his education to such royal favors.[2]

Questions about many aspects of royal child-rearing remain. Fostering, for example, is often represented as defining noble or royal upbringing. But does it really prove parental disinterest, or avoidance of bonding with young children who might soon die? To the contrary, Nicholas Orme contends that

---

[1] Ralph V. Turner, "Eleanor of Aquitaine and Her Children: An Inquiry into Medieval Family Attachment," *Journal of Medieval History* 14 (1988): 321–35, and "The Children of Anglo-Norman Royalty and Their Upbringing," *Medieval Prosopography* 11/2 (Autumn 1990): 17–52. Turner's views are critiqued by Lois L. Huneycutt, "Public Lives, Private Ties: The Responsibilities of Queenship and the Success of Royal Mothers in England and Scotland, c. 1070–1204," pp. 293–310, and Kimberley LoPrete, "Adela of Blois as Mother and Countess," pp. 311–32, both in *Medieval Mothering,* ed. J. C. Parsons and Bonnie Wheeler (New York, 1996). For France, E. A. R. Brown, "The Prince Is Father to the King: The Character and Childhood of Philip the Fair of France," *Mediaeval Studies* 49 (1987): 282–384.

[2] R. Turner, "Eleanor of Aquitaine and Her Children," pp. 325–26; Mary G. Cheney, "Mr Geoffrey de Lucy, an Early Chancellor of the University of Oxford," *English Historical Review* 82 (1967): 750–63.

the use of foster parents need not imply that parents took no part in rearing their children, and it has been shown that much of what is said about English medieval parents' disinterest in children rests upon the account of a late medieval Italian traveler, who misrepresented much of what his informants told him. With growing frequency, historians argue that medieval parents did value their children, though not necessarily for purely emotional reasons; aristocratic parents, for example, could regard their children as political or diplomatic assets, as valuable to them as peasant children were to their parents as economic resources.[3] Friction between noble fathers and sons, moreover, has recently been attributed not to parental disinterest but to inheritance customs that generated rivalry among aging fathers, restive heirs, and jealous younger sons—a more convincing theory for the behavior of Henry II's sons, with their ambitions for a vast inheritance, than appeals to supposedly bleak but perhaps only poorly-documented childhoods.

---

[3]For fostering as avoidance of parental involvement with children, Lawrence Stone, *The Family, Sex and Marriage in England 1500–1800* (London, 1977), pp. 83–84. Cf. David Herlihy, *Medieval Households* (Cambridge, Mass., 1985), p. 158; Alan Macfarlane, *Marriage and Love in England: Modes of Reproduction, 1300–1840* (Oxford, 1986), esp. "The Value of Children," pp. 51–116; see also Nicholas Orme, *From Childhood to Chivalry: The Education of the English Kings and Aristocracy, 1066–1530* (London, 1984), pp. 16–17. The Italian text is *A Relation, or Rather a True Account, of the Island of England, with Sundry Particulars of the Customs of These People . . . about the Year 1500*, trans. Charlotte A. Sneyd, Camden Society (1847), pp. 24–29; see comments by Lorraine Attreed, "From *Pearl* Maiden to Tower Princes: Towards a New History of Medieval Childhood," *Journal of Medieval History* 9 (1983): 43–48, esp. p. 47, and Barbara A. Hanawalt, "Networks for Fostering Lady Lisle's Daughters," in Parsons and Wheeler, *Medieval Mothering*, pp. 239–58, esp. 239–42.

Royal daughters, moreover, were by no means as neglected by their parents as has been generally thought.[4]

A look at the outlines of thirteenth-century English royal child-rearing may revise aspects of that dismal view of medieval childhood offered by long-term surveys such as those of Philippe Ariès and Lloyd DeMause, in contrast to the more positive picture produced by surveys of shorter periods of time.[5] Indeed, between the early Angevins and their thirteenth-century heirs, whose family relationships are held to have been warm and tranquil[6]—so much so that Edward I's bad relations with his heir are a notable exception—there is a contrast that begs for attention. But the only previous study of thirteenth-

---

[4]Jane Beitscher, "'As the Twig Is Bent . . .': Children and Their Parents in an Aristocratic Society," *Journal of Medieval History* 2 (1976): 181–91. See also Huneycutt, "Public Lives, Private Ties," and J. C. Parsons, "Mothers, Daughters, Marriage, Power: Some Plantagenet Evidence, 1150–1500," in *Medieval Queenship*, ed. Parsons (New York, 1993), pp. 63–78.

[5]Current discussion of medieval childhood depends from Ariès, *L'enfant et la vie familiale sous l'Ancient Régime* (Paris, 1960), trans. Robert Baldick as *Centuries of Childhood: A Social History of Family Life* (New York, 1962). The extreme view of abusive medieval childhood is DeMause, "The Evolution of Childhood," introduction to *The History of Childhood*, ed. DeMause (New York, 1974), pp. 1–74. Linda A. Pollock, *Forgotten Children: Parent-Child Relations from 1500 to 1900* (Cambridge, 1983), pp. 1–12, notes that studies dealing with limited spans of time tend to produce less horrific visions of pre-modern childhood than do the sweeping studies cited above. Cf. Attreed, "*Pearl* Maiden to Tower Princes," pp. 43–58.

[6]Hilda Johnstone, *Edward of Carnarvon, 1284–1307* (Manchester, 1946), pp. 128–29; Michael Prestwich, *Edward I* (Berkeley, Calif., 1988), pp. 122–29; J. C. Parsons, *Eleanor of Castile: Queen and Society in Thirteenth-Century England* (New York, 1995), pp. 38–39. Margaret Howell, *Eleanor of Provence: Queenship in Thirteenth-Century England* (Oxford, 1997), passim, adds many helpful details on the upbringing of Henry III's children.

century English royal children, published in 1923, was chiefly concerned with household finance and administration, not family relationships.[7] This approach was dictated by the administrative and financial nature of the extant sources for medieval English royal households, but a new look may offer fresh answers to questions left by that early effort.

As a first point, for example, it is clear that the use of wet nurses and other care-givers for the kings' children cannot be adequately explained by reductive appeals to parental preferences for maintaining distance from the children. The practicalities of raising a king's children were a major factor. Kingship in thirteenth-century England was as much an itinerant affair as it had been in the twelfth; the king and his wife traveled around the realm almost uninterruptedly, and very young children could not tolerate such peregrinations. In a royal household, moreover, wet nurses were no mere affectation—there were many demands on a queen's time, and she was rarely able to nurse the children she was expected to bear, but not necessarily to raise.[8] More subtle considerations were

---

[7]Hilda Johnstone, "The Wardrobe and Household of Henry, Son of Edward I," *Bulletin of the John Rylands Library* 7 (1923): 384–420; eadem, *Edward of Carnarvon*, is also chiefly administrative in scope.

[8]David Herlihy, "The Natural History of Medieval Women," *Natural History* 87 (1975): 56–67, esp. p. 65; the births of Eleanor of Castile's children parallel those of Blanche of Castile on which Herlihy bases his ideas (J. C. Parsons, "The Year of Eleanor of Castile's Birth and Her Children by Edward I," *Mediaeval Studies* 46 [1984]: 245–65). As it was believed a nursing mother would not conceive, wet nurses freed a queen to resume childbearing (R. Turner, "Eleanor of Aquitaine and Her Children," pp. 325–26, and "Children of Anglo-Norman Royalty," pp. 23–24; Christiane Klapisch-Zuber, "Blood Parents and Milk Parents: Wet Nursing in Florence, 1300–1530," in eadem, *Women, Family, and Ritual in Renaissance Italy*, trans. L. G. Cochrane [Chicago, 1985], pp. 132–64, esp. 158–59).

introduced by the expansion of royal power from the twelfth century and a growing reliance on ceremonial that underscored the majesty of kingship, widening the distance between king and people. The growth of reverence for the king had its impact on his family; children of Henry III and Edward I were accorded the honorific *dominus* and *domina* from an early age if not from birth, and Edward's eldest son was most likely deemed armigerous even in childhood.[9] Exaltation of the king's family meant that there was now no household within the realm of sufficient dignity to shelter his children save his own, and the risks of sending them to foreign courts were so obvious as to need no comment.[10] The only other option was

---

[9]The honorific was accorded even before birth (see n. 13 below). Edward's daughter Berengaria, who died in her second year, is "domina" in a June 1277 wardrobe entry (London, Public Record Office [PRO], E 101/350/24, m. 2). His son Henry (1268–74) and daughter Eleanor (1269–98) are "dominus" and "domina" in 1273–74 (Johnstone, "Wardrobe and Household of Henry," pp. 400–20 passim, with reference at 419 to their brother "dominus" John, who died at age five; on Henry, see also Geoffrey de Piccheford's letter quoted below). Cf. *Annales monasterii de Oseneia (A.D. 1016–1347)*, in *Annales monastici*, ed. H. R. Luard, 4 vols., Rolls Series (RS), 36 (London, 1864–69), 4: 245. Sons of Edward I's brother Edmund of Lancaster (grandsons of Henry III) were not so designated (Johnstone, *Edward of Carnarvon*, p. 28). For the arms attributed in a roll of ca. 1270–80 to Edward I's son Alphonso (1273–84), who was never knighted, Noel Denholm-Young, *History and Heraldry, 1254 to 1310: A Study of the Historical Value of the Rolls of Arms* (Oxford, 1965), pp. 62–63. A shield of England with the eldest son's label appears on the Beatus page of a psalter illuminated in 1284 in anticipation of Alphonso's marriage to the count of Holland's daughter (London, British Library, Add. 24686, fol. 11r).

[10]Edward I's daughter Joan was fostered 1274–78 by his mother-in-law, the dowager queen of Castile, but that lady then resided in her French county of Ponthieu (J. C. Parsons, *The Court and Household of Eleanor of Castile in 1290* [Toronto, 1977], p. 39 n. 146).

to settle the children in a household subordinate to the king's but with its own income and accounting office,[11] quartered at royal manors and staffed with wet nurses, governors, governesses, and other sundry care-givers. It is on that amalgam of household and nursery, and specifically on the care-givers most intimately associated with the kings' children, that this essay concentrates.

The children's household was not immobile, but it changed location less often than did those of the king and queen. In their earliest years, the children spent most of their time near London, with Windsor Castle a favored location. This did not mean that the children rarely saw their parents, who visited the children's residences as often as they did any other royal manor. The children joined their parents for such special occasions as the 1274 coronation and translations of saints' relics, and customarily resided with them whenever the court was stationary for some time—as, for example, the extended residences, often at Westminster, that coincided with the great feasts of the Church when parliaments were held. The children began to travel with their parents when they were about seven years of age, but for several years thereafter they often returned to their household for periods of time to recuperate from itinerant royal life.[12]

That both children and care-givers thus stayed well within the parents' purview allowed the latter to monitor the children's welfare closely, and it is clear that the Plantagenets were not indifferent parents. Edward I made offerings for at least one of his unborn children, already individualized and named; practiced midwives were valued when royal women

---

[11]First instituted by Henry III for his son Edward; T. F. Tout, *Chapters in the Administrative History of Mediaeval England*, 6 vols. (Manchester, 1920–33), 1: 256 and 2: 5–6.

[12]Parsons, *Eleanor of Castile*, p. 38 n. 106 (at p. 270).

were confined. Unavoidable separations between parents and children required some way for the king and queen to maintain a presence in their children's lives, and their early training offered such means. Eleanor of Castile's favored Dominican friars, for example, were installed in her children's household and probably saw to their education, as brothers of that order may well have done for Eleanor herself in childhood, and in 1290 she sent one of her scribes to dwell at Woodstock, where her young son was then living.[13] When parents were apart from their offspring, letters were regularly exchanged with those responsible for the children. The care-givers were keenly aware of the obligation to protect as well as provide:[14]

---

[13]Edward I in 1306 offered for "Lord Richard, the child now in the queen's womb" (Pierre Chaplais, "Some Personal Letters of Edward I," *English Historical Review* 77 [1962]: 79–86, esp. p. 81 n. 3). For the midwife who attended Henry III's womenfolk, see discussion of Sybil Giffard below. For the friars, J. C. Parsons, "Piety, Power, and the Reputations of Two Thirteenth-Century English Queens," in *Queens, Regents and Potentates*, ed. Theresa M. Vann (Cambridge, 1993), pp. 107–23, esp. 122; on Eleanor of Castile's education, Parsons, *Eleanor of Castile*, p. 9, and "Of Queens, Courts, and Books: Reflections on the Literary Patronage of Thirteenth-Century English Queens," in *The Cultural Patronage of Medieval Women*, ed. June Hall McCash (Athens, Ga., 1996), pp. 175–201, esp. 177–78; for the scribe in 1290, Parsons, *Court and Household*, p. 96.

[14]Letters on Edward I's children are noted in Parsons, *Eleanor of Castile*, pp. 31, 38. The letter quoted is PRO, SC 1/7/179 (s.d., author's trans.; given names expanded and the words in brackets supply a damaged passage), ca. 1 Aug. 1273 when an order issued for the bucks from Odiham (*CCIR 1272–1279*, p. 25). As constable of Windsor, Piccheford was responsible for the children's safety (Johnstone, "Wardrobe and Household of Henry," pp. 387–88). John de London' served both Eleanor of Provence and Eleanor of Castile (Parsons, *Eleanor of Castile*, p. 97).

Abbreviations for London, PRO publications of rolls and calendars of rolls: *CChR = Calendars of Charter Rolls*, 6 vols. (1903–27); *CCIR =*

To their reverend and discreet Lord Walter de Merton, chancellor of the lord king of England, Geoffrey de Piccheford and John de London' send greeting with increase of reverence and honor. As we have heard that certain malevolent enemies of the lord king and their fellows have lately conspired to the disturbance of the tranquility and peace of the king, gathering their followers with force and arms in the counties of Essex and Leicester and elsewhere, we ask, pondering, that your discretion will be pleased to advise us what is behooves us to do . . . [in this matter as regards] the care we are undertaking of the children of the lord king. Touching which, may it please you to write to Sir Robert de Insula, constable of Odiham, that he allow Robert de Say yeoman of the Lord Henry son of the lord king to take two bucks in the park of Odiham to [Henry's] use, for he greatly desires venison. May you prosper in the Lord.

The most personal testimony for parental feelings among the thirteenth-century Plantagenets is offered by letters from the royal parents themselves, such as a well-known missive from the widowed Eleanor of Provence asking her son Edward I to allow the mother of a minor in wardship to visit the child: "I know how great is the longing of a mother to see a child from whom she has long been parted."[15] Several of Edward I's letters testify to his vivid interest in the young children of his second marriage. These letters are of surprising impact, originating as they did with a king then in his sixties, much preoccupied with affairs of state and notoriously bad-tempered.

Calendars of Close Rolls, 9 vols. for reigns of Edward I and Edward II (1892–1908); *CFR = Calendar of Fine Rolls*, 3 vols. for Edward I and Edward II (1911–13); *CIPM = Calendars of Inquisitions Post Mortem*, 6 vols. for Henry III, Edward I, Edward II (1904–08); *CLR = Calendars of Liberate Rolls*, 6 vols. for Henry III (1917–64); *ClR = Close Rolls*, 15 vols. for Henry III (1902–75); *CPR = Calendars of Patent Rolls*, 15 vols. for Henry III, Edward I, Edward II (1898–1910).

[15]PRO, SC 1/16/151; see Johnstone, *Edward of Carnarvon*, p. 23.

Yet Edward sends detailed instructions for his sons' devotions on the feast of the Nativity of the Virgin in September 1302 (when the boys were aged two and one) and wishes to be informed of their behavior on that occasion. He writes them of his pleasure at their recovery from illness and issues orders, doubtless really meant to be carried out by the adults around them, that the boys were to supervise preparations for his arrival at Kennington. These letters support other indications in the evidence discussed here of an awareness of childhood as a distinct stage of earthly existence—an observant note is struck, for example, by Edward's order that his sons should reach Saint Radegund's Abbey before him, so they will have time to get used to the place before he arrives. Surely the most remarkable of the letters is Edward's reproachful September 1306 missive to the woman in charge of the children. This is not the message of a detached father; it reveals a king's lively concern for the welfare of children whose extreme youth—his daughter was four months old—must presuppose his indifference, were the idea unreservedly accepted that noble parents were disinterested in young children who might soon die. (By 1306, Edward had buried eleven of his first wife's children.)[16]

> [The king] to his well beloved Margerie de Hausted', greeting. Know that we are greatly astonished that among others who have sent us news of the state of our children dwelling at Northampton, you have as yet sent us no news of their state nor how it seems to you with them. For we would have more faith in your report than anyone else's, and we will hold as more certain the news you send us of them than any news that others send us. Wherefore we pray that you yourself look well to their state and how they are growing and if at play they are lively and cheerful and well behaved, and certify us

---

[16]Chaplais, "Personal Letters of Edward I," p. 86 (my trans.); I must thank Prof. Brian Merrilees of Victoria University for advice.

fully by your letters by the bearer and other messengers, and cause us to know how it seems to you with them. And above all else we pray that you look well to Eleanor our young daughter, and cause us to know fully how it seems to you with her. At Wellhouse, the twenty-first of September.

Edward's letter adds to what is already known of the woman to whom it is addressed. Margerie de Haustede had long served Eleanor of Castile, of whose jewels she had had custody, and clearly she was regarded as an exceptionally trustworthy woman. Edward's letter manifests his confidence in her, and in 1316 his son-in-law the earl of Essex named Margerie and her husband guardians of his son Eneas de Bohun (Edward I's grandson), should the earl die before Eneas came of age.[17] Margerie's case argues that care-givers for the king's children were chosen with great care, another point in favor of the position that Plantagenet parents were attentive to their children's upbringing even if they could not be with them all the time. As Lorraine Attreed emphasizes, we need new ways of looking for medieval children, and a closer look at the care-givers is thus in order; their careers may offer new insights into the dynamics of child-rearing from the standpoint of their young charges as well as that of the parents. A starting point is found in a list of the householders of Edward I's children who received robes at Pentecost 1273. These included

---

[17]Margerie was one of the few women to carry oral commands from the queen to the Wardrobe (Parsons, *Court and Household*, pp. 35–37, 84, 90, 102, 106, 117, 119). The earl of Essex wed Edward I's daughter Elizabeth in 1302; Eneas was their fifth son (Thomas Turner, "The Will of Humphrey de Bohun, Earl of Hereford and Essex, with Extracts from the Inventory of his Effects, 1319–1322," *Archaeological Journal* 2 [1846]: 346). The name of Margerie's son Humphrey, born ca. 1270 (see n. 37), suggests long-standing Haustede-Bohun ties.

five women who can be identified as wet nurses, and the careers of three of them reward attention: Alice de Luton, Cecily de la More, and Alice de la Grave (or Leygrave).[18]

That Alice de Luton's name heads the 1273 list reflects her impressive seniority within the children's household; she had nursed King Edward himself in his infancy. As with most of these women, Alice's parentage is obscure; she was the wife of a knight, John de Luton, to whom she apparently bore a son in 1238, which would have put her in an excellent position to nurse Edward, born in June 1239.[19] After Edward no longer required her services, she entered the household of his mother, Eleanor of Provence, and Henry III showed her many favors. By 1262 she was attending Edward's wife, Eleanor of Castile, perhaps to care for her children; and for her services to Eleanor, Alice was granted land near Windsor Castle in 1267.[20] Before May 1268, Henry III gave Alice the Norfolk lands of John de Sanes, a Norman; these she sold to William Gerberge of Yarmouth in May 1269, after she acquired manors

---

[18]Attreed, "From *Pearl* Maiden to Tower Princes." The 1273 list is PRO, C 47/3/21/44, m. 2. Of the others it names, Amicia de Derneford nursed Edward's son Henry (1268–74). She was granted a wardship in Feb. 1275 and Edward protected her right there (*CPR 1272–1281*, p. 79; *CClR 1279–1288*, p. 520 [PRO, E 13/4, m. 7, has an action in Michaelmas term 1290 by Edward and Amicia against John Dauueler's widow, who detained £5 that John owed the king but which was demanded from Amicia, who held the wardship]). Joan la Neyre perhaps nursed one of the children who died before 1273 (for whom, Parsons, "Year of Eleanor of Castile's Birth," pp. 257–59).

[19]*ClR 1254–1256*, p. 57; *ClR 1268–1272*, pp. 119–20. Her son was said to be aged 56 in the autumn of 1294 (*CIPM* 3, no. 171).

[20]*ClR 1256–1259*, pp. 2–3; *CLR* 5: 120; *ClR 1261–1264*, pp. 329, 357. She went to Gascony with Eleanor of Provence, 1254 (*CPR 1247–1258*, p. 376), and to France with Eleanor of Castile, 1262 (*CPR 1258–1266*, p. 220); for the 1267 grant where she is Alice "la Norice," *CChR* 2: 84.

at Hartwell and Little Hampden (Buckinghamshire) from William de Hertewelle by reason of his debts to the Jewry, which Eleanor of Castile may have given Alice. (It was perhaps the Luton tenure at Hartwell that led a herald in 1566, in apparent ignorance of the 1269 purchase, to make Alice a Hertewelle daughter on the assumption that she had entered these manors by inheritance.)[21] Edward I in 1280 exempted Alice for life from the suit she owed at the king's honor court at Adstock and 8s. she owed yearly for view of frankpledge. She died in September 1294.[22]

Of Alice's children, William was studying at Oxford in 1256 and occurs as a chancery clerk from 1263; in February 1264 Henry III presented him to the church of Longborough (Gloucestershire).[23] As he married, William must have been in minor orders which (like other royal clerks) he later re-nounced.[24] When he did so is not clear; debts to him were

---

[21] For the Sanes lands, *ClR 1264–1268*, p. 499; *ClR 1268–1272*, pp. 119–20; *CChR* 2: 123; for Hartwell and Hampden, *CChR* 2: 117. Henry III's Apr. 1268 grant of the Hertewelle debts to Eleanor of Castile is *ClR 1264–1268*, p. 449. Perhaps the herald sought to extend the lineage of Alice's descendants (who held Hartwell into the 20th century); perhaps the descendants assumed or claimed the filiation. If Alice was a Hertewelle, the vendor of 1269 was likely a nephew (*Victoria County History, Buckinghamshire* 2: 296, where Hertewelle's debts do not appear). No contemporary proof of Alice's alleged Hertewelle filiation has been found.

[22] *CPR 1272–1281*, p. 418 (expanded Nov. 1289: *CClR 1288–1296*, pp. 27–28); for her death, *CFR* 1: 347 and *CIPM* 3, no. 171.

[23] *ClR 1256–1259*, pp. 2–3; *ClR 1261–1264*, pp. 329, 357; *CPR 1258–1266*, pp. 381, 382.

[24] The church of Longborough was in the king's gift in 1264 through the minority of the heir of John de Gatesden, once Eleanor of Provence's clerk, who to Matthew Paris's disgust had married in 1244. See *CPR 1258–1266*, p. 382; Matthew Paris, *Chronica majora*, ed. H. R. Luard, 7 vols., RS, 57

acknowledged by Gloucestershire debtors as late as 1269, which implies that he still had interests there possibly connected with Longborough; but Eleanor of Castile's clerk William de Yattenden' died as rector of Longborough in November 1270.[25] William de Luton did well as a royal clerk, and in 1267 he secured a manor at Garthorpe (Leicestershire) by reason of Alice de Garthorpe's debts to the Jewry, which he perhaps acquired through administrative contacts. He was a knight by February 1291 and, barely outliving his mother, died in the spring of 1295, leaving a widow, Beatrice, and a son, Thomas, fifteen.[26]

Alice de Luton also had a daughter, Grace (wife of Henry de Middelton), Eleanor of Castile's damsel in 1279 when she received a Devonshire wardship. Grace's daughter, Margaret de Middelton, had royal letters asking the abbess and convent of Romsey to admit her in February 1294; she was a nun of that house in 1298 when, doubtless because of her links to the

---

(London, 1872–84), 4: 403; I. J. Sanders, *English Baronies: A Study of Their Origin and Descent, 1086–1327* (Oxford, 1960), p. 128; *CIPM* 1, no. 454.

[25] *ClR 1264–1268*, p. 88; *ClR 1268–1272*, p. 103; *CLR* 5: 131, 145; *The Register of Walter Giffard, Lord Archbishop of York, 1266–1279*, ed. William Brown, Surtees Society, 109 (1904), p. 101; *CPR 1266–1272*, p. 480; *Select Cases from the Ecclesiastical Courts of the Province of Canterbury, c.1200–1301*, ed. Norma Adams and Charles Donahue, Jr., Selden Society, 95 (1981), pp. 236–64; *Register of Bishop Godfrey Giffard, September 23rd, 1268, to August 15th, 1301*, ed. J. W. Willis Bund (Worcester, 1898), p. 83 (Adams and Donahue, *Select Cases*, p. 245, assume this letter was to Eleanor of Provence, but cf. Parsons, *Eleanor of Castile*, p. 97).

[26] *ClR 1264–1268*, p. 254; *ClR 1268–1272*, p. 412; *CCIR 1279–1288*, pp. 120, 346 (it is unclear if all these debts involved the Jewry); on Garthorpe, *ClR 1264–1268*, p. 364. See also *CCIR 1288–1296*, p. 190; *CIPM* 3, no. 237; *CCIR 1288–1296*, p. 462; *CIPM* 4, no. 51. Perhaps the acquisition of Garthorpe marks William's abandonment of his orders.

court, she was sent to seek Edward I's license to elect a new abbess. (Henry III had sent a tun of wine for the 1263 profession at Wherwell Abbey of Alice de Luton's kinswoman Alice "de la Chaumbre.")[27] An Alice de Middelton was in the train of Edward I's daughter Joan in 1293, and possibly this family also produced Robert de Middelton, Eleanor of Castile's secondary wardrobe clerk in the late 1280s.[28]

The Cecily de la More named in the 1273 list of robes also occurs as Cecily de Cleware, and she appears to have been the wife of John de la More of Bray and Clewer (Berkshire); certainly she was a sister of Geoffrey and Nicholas de Bochurst, implicated in a trespass in the king's park at Windsor around 1281. Cecily nursed Edward's eldest daughter, Eleanor (1269–98), and his third daughter, Margaret (1275–ca. 1333); in 1284 she took charge of the infant Edward of Caernarfon's household, though she was not his nurse.[29] John de la More

---

[27]For the wardship, *CPR 1272–1281*, p. 310; *CIPM* 2, no. 505. Was Grace's husband kin to William de Middelton, royal clerk and bishop of Norwich, who came of a Norfolk family? The Sanes lands Alice held in the 1260s would have given her Norfolk connections around the time Grace might be expected to have married. See Thomas Madox, *The History and Antiquities of the Exchequer of the Kings of England* (London, 1711), pp. 165–66, 743; *Rôles Gascons*, ed. M. Francisque Michel and Charles Bémont, 3 vols. (Paris, 1896–1906), 3: xlviii. On Margaret de Middelton, *CClR 1288–1296*, p. 382; *CPR 1292–1301*, p. 342. For Alice "de la Chaumbre," *CLR* 5: 120.

[28]For Alice, *CPR 1292–1301*, p. 28; for Robert, Parsons, *Eleanor of Castile*, pp. 92, 100.

[29]Johnstone, "Wardrobe and Household of Henry," p. 390 and n. 2. PRO, SC 1/18/89 (to Edward I from Hamo Hauteyn, s.d.), identifies Cecily de la More, "une dame ke est entendaunt a la garde ma dame vostre fille," as sister of the Bochursts who with Cecily's son Robert broke into the king's park after gathering at Geoffrey's house (cf. *CClR 1279–1288*, p. 99). The child in Cecily's care was Margaret (*CClR 1272–1279*, p. 296 [June 1276]); as she

was chamberlain to Edward I's eldest daughter in 1290, when Edward of Caernarfon's household included a yeoman called "Cliwar'," perhaps Cecily's son.[30]

Alice de Leygrave nursed Edward of Caernarfon (born 1284), though she was in the children's household as early as 1273 as *berceresse* (rocker) to his brother Henry (1268–74). Around 1288 Edward I gave Alice the wardship of Frank de Scoland, who married Alice's daughter of the same name.[31] In 1311–14, Alice and her daughter Cecily attended Queen

---

would not have needed a wet nurse by 1281, the letter suggests that royal wet nurses might care for their charges after weaning. PRO, E 101/350/12, m. 3, shows Eleanor of Castile's squire sent to Windsor to fetch Cecily de la More in May 1284, just after Edward of Caernarfon's birth in Apr. and possibly when his nurse Mariota Maunsel fell ill (Johnstone, *Edward of Carnarvon*, p. 9). See also *CPR 1292–1301*, pp. 97, 229; *VCH Berks*. 3: 105 n. 82.

[30]John de la More was a knight by 1285 when he was sued for £20 by the executors of Nicholas Syfrewast of Clewer (PRO, E 13/12, m. 2d); he occurs as young Eleanor's chamberlain in May 1290 (E 101/352/12, fol. 16). "Cliwar'" occurs in Edward of Caernarfon's household, June–Aug. 1290 (C 47/3/22, m. 1). The letter cited above names Cecily's son Robert, but *VCH Berks*. 3: 105 n. 82 names John de la More's son and heir, Nicholas (d. ca. 1334).

[31]Johnstone, "Wardrobe and Household of Henry," p. 390 and n. 4, and *Edward of Carnarvon*, p. 9 and nn. 6–8. For gifts and grants, Parsons, *Court and Household*, p. 107; *CPR 1307–1313*, pp. 264 (*CIPM* 5, no. 234, suggests this was ineffective as the heir was of age), 341, 510, 581; *CPR 1313–1317*, pp. 86, 480, 517; *CPR 1317–1321*, p. 251. For her place at court in Edward II's reign, *The Household Book of Queen Isabella of England, for the Fifth Regnal Year of Edward II, 8th July 1311 to 7th July 1312*, ed. F. D. Blackley and Gustave Hermansen (Edmonton, 1971), index 247 s.v. "Legrave"; Pierre Chaplais, *Piers Gaveston: Edward II's Adoptive Brother* (Oxford, 1994), pp. 8–9. On the Scoland wardship, *CIPM* 4, no. 53; *CPR 1307–1313*, p. 180; *CPR 1317–1321*, p. 141; *CPR 1324–1327*, p. 87; Charles Moor, *Knights of Edward I*, 5 vols., Harleian Society, 80–84 (1929–32), 4: 228. On Cecily de Chaucombe, *CClR 1318–1323*, p. 174.

Isabella; by 1318, Cecily had married a Hampshire knight, John de Chaucombe (died 1330). Edward II in 1313 sought a corrody at Saint Mary's, Winchester, for Juliana, *neptis* of Alice de Leygrave "who suckled us in infancy" ("que nos in infancia lactauit"), and in 1318 failed to obtain a corrody at Barking Abbey for Alice's daughter Ellen.[32]

Felicia de Shortefeud, who nursed Edward I's third son, Alphonso, is not named in the 1273 list, as Alphonso was born in November 1273. Felicia was the daughter and heir of Robert de la Wike, who held of the king in the manor of Cookham, a Windsor Castle dependency; her husband, William de Shortefeud, tenant in another Windsor dependency, at Bray, was at least the second of his family to hold office as clerk of the works at the castle. After Alphonso died in 1284, Edward I granted Felicia the ward of lands in Somerset, but she encountered difficulties there and appealed to Edward's eldest daughter, who responded,[33]

> Eleanor, daughter of our lord the king of England, to her dear in God Sir William de Hamelton, greeting. We pray you, dear sir, for Lady

---

[32]Respectively, *CClR 1307–1313*, pp. 581–82 (original Latin quoted in Johnstone, "Wardrobe and Household of Henry," p. 390 n. 4); *CClR 1313–1318*, p. 611.

[33]*CChR* 2: 189–90 *bis*; *CPR 1266–1272*, p. 434 (where "Robert" de Shortefeud is an error for William), p. 463; *CClR 1279–1288*, p. 447; *VCH Berks.* 3: 107. On the Meriet wardship, *CClR 1279–1288*, p. 324; *CPR 1281–1292*, p. 173 (the letter is PRO, SC 1/25/94, s.d. [author's trans.; words in brackets supplied for clarity]). On Windsor tenants in the households, J. C. Parsons, "Toward a Social History of the English Royal Court: The Senches of London, 1246–1349," *Medieval Prosopography* 9/2 (Autumn 1988): 51–71, esp. pp. 55–56; cf. lands near Windsor granted Alice de Luton as above, and lands there held by others in the households noted in Parsons, *Eleanor of Castile*, p. 97 and notes.

Felicia who was the nurse of Lord Alphonso our brother, to whom the lord king our father not long since gave a wardship in the manor of Meriet in Somerset until the full age of the heir of Sir John Meriet; but there is a knight named Sir Roger Basset who has married the widow of that Sir John, who by reason of the dower the lady has in that manor causes Lady Felicia and her husband William de Shortefeud much grievance and trouble as we understand from them, and as the said William himself can show you. [We pray] that for love of us you shall make and be willing to grant such remedy from Chancery as will be of use to them and suitable in such case. And do so that we may thank you for them. Farewell.

Notes on other members of the Plantagenet children's household will demonstrate the prevalence of such long-term ties among the households, ties assured by marriage and family. The Margerie de Haustede of Edward I's letter of September 1306 was the wife of Robert de Haustede senior, of Kegworth (Leicestershire).[34] The Haustedes apparently came to royal notice in 1266 when, at Eleanor of Castile's instance, Henry III pardoned William de Haustede for trespasses during the recent troubles; two years later, again at Eleanor's request, William's son Robert was pardoned half his debts at the Exchequer and allowed to pay the balance by installments.[35] Robert and Margerie married by 1270 and were in Eleanor of Castile's household by 1280. Robert was knighted at Christmas 1289, when their son Robert junior was sent at Edward I's orders to dwell with Edward of Caernarfon. After Queen

---

[34]G. E. Cokayne, *The Complete Peerage* (GEC), new ed., rev. ed. Vicary Gibbs et al., 13 vols. in 14 (London, 1910–40), 6: 402; Moor, *Knights*, 2: 202–04; Margerie's parentage is unknown.

[35]Ultimately Robert was pardoned everything he owed at the Exchequer (*CPR 1258–1266*, pp. 567–68; *CIR 1264–1268*, pp. 466–67; *CIR 1268–1272*, p. 305; *CPR 1272–1281*, pp. 253, 438).

Eleanor died in 1290, Margerie entered the household of the king's daughters; in 1295 she was associated with that of young Edward, and as noted earlier she was afterward responsible for the king's children by Queen Margaret. Robert de Haustede senior died in 1321, Margerie early in 1338.[36] Of their children, William and Humphrey were ordained priests in 1295 and 1296, respectively; they were presented to churches by Edward I and Edward II, and William was made keeper of the king's Exchange in London. Under Edward II, Robert de Haustede junior served as steward of the New Forest. John, the youngest Haustede brother, had the most eminent career of the four, as Edward II and Edward III's steward in Gascony. Joan de Haustede, damsel to Edward I's daughters in 1290, wed John de Mereworth soon thereafter and continued to serve the king's daughter Countess Elizabeth of Essex (1282–1316).[37]

Such examples could be multiplied almost indefinitely. Margerie Biset, probably a granddaughter of Henry II's steward Manasser Biset, cared for King John's daughter Isabella and then attended Eleanor of Provence; Henry III trusted her enough to send her to meet privately with his imprisoned cousin Eleanor of Brittany. Matthew Paris praised Margerie's piety in no uncertain terms: she customarily rose several times

---

[36]The year of their marriage is inferred from their sons' ordinations (following note). See also Parsons, *Court and Household*, pp. 35–37; *Book of Prests of the King's Wardrobe for 1294–5*, ed. E. B. Fryde (Oxford, 1962), p. 105; *CIPM* 6, no. 316, and 8, no. 150.

[37]I treat this family more fully in an article now in preparation. On William and Humphrey, *Registrum Roberti Winchelsey Cantuariensis Archiepiscopi A. D. 1294–1313*, ed. Rose Graham, 2 vols. (Oxford, 1952–56), 2: 712–13, 909, 913; *The Rolls and Register of Bishop Oliver Sutton, 1280–1299*, ed. Rosalind M. T. Hill, 8 vols., Lincolnshire Record Society (1948–), 2: 136 and 7: 82, 88, 98. The suggestion in Parsons, *Court and Household*, p. 83 n. 106, that Joan de Mereworth was Eleanor of Castile's laundress is withdrawn.

each night to read the psalter, and while doing so one September night in 1238, heard an intruder who had entered the king's chamber to kill him and had the man apprehended, for which she enjoyed royal favor to the end of her days.[38] Sybil de Cormeilles assisted Eleanor of Provence at Edward's birth in 1239 and helped other royal ladies in childbirth; her husband, Hugh Giffard, was Edward's boyhood *custos*, their sons Archbishop Walter of York and Bishop Godfrey of Worcester were close to the king's family, and a granddaughter, Sybil de Mandeville, was among Eleanor of Castile's damsels.[39] Guy Ferré senior became Edward of Caernarfon's *magister* after decades of service to Henry III, Eleanor of Provence, and Edward I; his brother was Eleanor of Castile's steward John Ferré and a nephew was her knight Guy Ferré junior. John

---

[38]Sanders, *English Baronies*, pp. 5–6; William Dugdale, *Monasticon anglicanum*, 2nd ed., 6 vols. in 8 (London, 1846), 6: 643–45. On Margerie (d. 1242), *Dictionary of National Biography*, s.v. "Isabella (1214–1241)"; *CPR 1232–1247*, pp. 103, 282, 286, 330–31; *ClR 1234–1237*, pp. 91, 224, 492; *ClR 1237–1242*, pp. 111, 146, 259, 424; *ClR 1247–1251*, p. 173; Matthew Paris, *Chronica majora*, 4: 200 and 3: 497–98. Cf. *Flores historiarum per Matthaeum Westmonasteriensem collecti*, ed. H. R. Luard, 3 vols., RS, 95 (London, 1890), 2: 228; *Annales Londonienses*, in *Chronicles of the Reigns of Edward I and Edward II*, ed. William Stubbs, 2 vols., RS, 76 (London, 1882–83), 1: 33–36 (wrongly in 1236).

[39]Helen Maud Cam, *Liberties and Communities in Medieval England, Collected Studies in Local Administration and Topography* (Cambridge, 1944), p. 130; Sanders, *English Baronies*, pp. 86–87. On Sybil, *CLR* 1: 418, 456, 498; *CPR 1232–1247*, p. 247; *ClR 1247–1251*, p. 247; *ClR 1259–1261*, p. 343; *CLR* 5: 177. On Hugh Giffard, *CLR* 1: 15, 65; *CPR 1232–1247*, pp. 487, 495. For their son Walter, *Register of Walter Giffard*, ed. Brown, p. 101; on Godfrey, *Register of Bishop Godfrey Giffard*, ed. Bund, p. 224; *Annales Prioratus de Wigornia*, in Luard, *Annales monastici*, 4: 500; Parsons, "Piety, Power," p. 113. On Sybil de Mandeville, Parsons, *Court and Household*, p. 155.

Ferré's wife, Joan, and possibly Guy junior's first wife, Margerie, were among Eleanor of Castile's ladies; John's son Otelin was Edward of Caernarfon's yeoman. Edeline Popiot, *magistrissa* of Edward I's daughter Joan, accompanied the girl when she came to England from Ponthieu in 1278; Edeline's husband, Philip, had served Eleanor of Castile's mother and became a knight in her household. Joan de Ingham or Hengham, in Joan's household in the 1280s, was the wife of John de Ingham, knight of the queen's household, and their son Oliver was in Edward of Caernarfon's household in 1290.[40]

It is not surprising that these long-standing ties to the king's family generated such strong bonds of loyalty as are suggested by the letter on behalf of Felicia de Shortefeud quoted earlier. The atmosphere was evidently a cordial one in which individuals were genuinely interested in each other's welfare, as is shown by the case of Elena de Gorges. Her husband's family had a long history in the royal households, and Elena superintended that of Edward I's teenaged daughters before their marriages. At some point between May 1286 and August 1289, Elena's son became involved in a lengthy legal dispute, to her evident distress, and two of the king's daughters intervened on his behalf, apparently more than once:[41]

---

[40]For these families see, respectively, Parsons, *Court and Household*, pp. 32–34, 38–39, and 155 n. 3.

[41]GEC 6: 14–15; the letter quoted is PRO, SC 1/10/133, undated; cf. M. A. E. Green, *Lives of the Princesses of England, from the Norman Conquest*, 6 vols. (London, 1849–55), 2: 300. On the Gorges and Eleanor of Provence, *CLR* 4: 320, 412; *ClR 1256–1259*, p. 456; *ClR 1242–1247*, p. 153; *CLR* 3: 75–76 (the Roberga of this entry occurs as a Gorges in Eleanor of Provence's jewel account, PRO, E 101/349/13, m. 1). On Ralph, *CChR* 2: 227; *Calendar of Pleas in the Exchequer of the Jews*, various eds. for the Jewish Historical Society of England, 4 vols. (1920–), 4: 130–31. Elena visited Edward I's daughter Mary at Amesbury, June 1288 (L. Guilloreau, "Marie de

To the honorable father in God, my lord John by the grace of God bishop of Ely, Eleanor and Joan daughters of the king of England send greeting and good love. Dear sir, forasmuch as we understand that peace is not yet made among Sir Hugh Despenser and Sir John Lovel the heir, and Sir Ralph Gorges and Sir John Lovel the bastard, for whom we have besought you aforetime, we again pray and require you as much as we can that if you please, you shall be willing to take pain to bring accord among them. And forasmuch as we see that our dear friend the Lady de Gorges is still sick at heart, we have great pity for her and we would be more at ease if she were relieved of the great pain of heart that she has at the contest that is among them. And therefore, dearest sir, we pray if it please you that you shall be willing to take pain that good peace shall be made and that the matter be brought to a good end. . . . Dear sir, may God keep you, body and soul.

A few points may be distilled from the evidence described above. There are strong indications here of considerable care in the choice of care-givers for the king's children, appreciation for the care the children received, and of the grown children's esteem for their childhood attendants. There are echoes of this pattern in a well-known story about Edward I's son Thomas of Brotherton, who rejected a French nurse's milk but throve when an Englishwoman replaced her; while every detail of the story cannot be verified, Thomas's nurses certainly were changed in his infancy and a physician was called

---

Woodstock, une fille d'Édouard I moniale à Amesbury," *Revue Mabillon* 9 [1914]: 341–59, esp. p. 342 n. 3). She had a loan of £6 13s. 4d. from the king's wardrobe, 7 Jan. 1290 (PRO, E 101/352/12, fol. 15), was paid her son's fee as the king's household knight, 27 May 1290 (PRO, C 47/4/5, fol. 34v), and in Aug. 1290 had money for the offerings of the children's household at Mass (C 47/3/22, m. 2). Elena was living on 5 Feb. 1291, when for her service to the king's children her son John was granted a suitable marriage; she had died by 8 Feb. 1292 (*CPR 1281–1292*, p. 422; *CFR* 1: 304).

to examine the new nurse and pronounce on the quality of her milk.[42] The women who served as wet nurses gained for their families many opportunities for advancement, as shown by William de Luton's Oxford studies and his years in Chancery, and perhaps in an earlier generation by the career of Alexander Neckham, son of Richard I's nurse. These unassuming families were suitably but not extravagantly rewarded by their charges' parents, an echo of the chary attitude toward patronage shown by Edward I and Eleanor of Castile.[43] Daughters and female relatives married well or were settled in aristocratic convents, where at least one of them evidently based a certain distinction on her royal connections. Women's place in the royal households requires emphasis; just as it was through them that their kinfolk gravitated into the households or other areas of royal service, family ties between one establishment and another were reckoned through them, and they are encountered far more frequently than their husbands in the queens' and the children's household records.[44] Finally, attention must be drawn to the prevalence of families within and among the households, clearly encouraged by the king and queen (especially Eleanor of Castile). This profile of a court kept in order by family relationships recalls the idea that emotional ties within medieval families were more diffuse than in the modern nuclear family; the young Plantagenets grew up in a vast surrogate family

---

[42]Prestwich, *Edward I*, p. 131.

[43]Prestwich, *Edward I*, p. 562; Parsons, *Eleanor of Castile*, pp. 34, 61–63.

[44]Parsons, "Mothers, Daughters, Marriage, Power," p. 72, and *Eleanor of Castile*, pp. 88–90. Note that the letter quoted above calls Felicia de Shortefeud "lady," though her husband is not called a knight. Were the wet nurses accorded this distinction, as the queen's women of the bedchamber today are "Honourable" for life whether or not they are so entitled by birth or marriage (Andrew Duncan, *The Reality of Monarchy* [London, 1970], p. 152)?

whose vertical generational and lateral kindred ties made of it an inherited affinity, with many people available to serve as emotional centers.[45]

These are just the sort of details we lack for Plantagenet childhoods in the twelfth century, when the same familial order may well have prevailed but cannot be documented. If households so ordered generated positive relations within the king's family in the thirteenth century, there is no reason to insist that they could not have done so in the twelfth, a point which favors the inheritance custom theory over that of neglected childhoods to explain the conflicts among Henry II and his sons. Even for the thirteenth century, this raises many questions about the means by which royal offspring bonded with their parents once they began to take their places in the life of the realm. The children's adjustments are not easily judged, as they left no explicit accounts of their experiences, but some outlines can be surmised.

We may doubt that royal care-givers would have been so bold as to try to alienate their charges' affections from their true parents, but problems might well have arisen as the surrogates passively became the children's early emotional foci.[46] The favors that adult Plantagenets showed former care-givers

---

[45]Parsons, *Eleanor of Castile*, pp. 33–35, 88–91. On diffuse emotional ties in medieval families, Michael Mitterauer and Reinhard Sieder, *The European Family: Patriarchy to Partnership from the Middle Ages to the Present*, trans. K. Oosterveen, M. Hörzinger (Oxford, 1982), pp. 61–63; cf. R. Turner, "Children of Anglo-Norman Royalty," p. 23.

[46]Charles de la Roncière, "Tuscan Notables on the Eve of the Renaissance," in *A History of Private Life*, 2: *Revelations of the Medieval World*, ed. Georges Duby, trans. Arthur Goldhammer (Cambridge, Mass., 1988), pp. 157–309, esp. 220. Some royal nursemaids have evolved intense attachments to their charges, with appalling results; e.g., Frances Lonsdale Donaldson, *Edward VIII* (London, 1974), p. 10.

and their kin suggest that the children did bond with their care-givers and that such bonds remained strong. The histories of some of Edward I's children hint at complications, as they had to displace early care-givers and transfer loyalties to their natural parents when they began to spend more time in the latter's company.[47] When Edward and his wife left England on crusade in 1270, their children, including young Eleanor (1269–98), were left in the care of Edward's uncle Richard of Cornwall; but after Richard and Henry III died in 1272, the children's care was assumed by the widowed Eleanor of Provence until the new king and queen returned to England in 1274. During this period, young Eleanor seems to have formed strong bonds with her grandmother, which were important enough for her parents to take notice of them later.[48] When the girl first began to travel with the king and queen in the 1270s and was periodically sent from court to rest from her travels, she did not return to the children's household but instead went to stay with her grandmother; during the Welsh campaign of 1282–84, Edward and his wife took the second daughter, Joan, to Wales, but young Eleanor again lived with the dowager. Close bonds between grandmother and grandchild may also be seen in the circumstances of young Henry's last illness in October 1274, when he was attended not by the mother whom he had met for the first time in his memory only weeks earlier

---

[47]James Bruce Ross, "The Middle-Class Child in Urban Italy," in DeMause, *History of Childhood*, p. 202, thinks that between the ages of two and seven the child "must have known most closely the mother's care and developed its first emotional bond with her," precisely the years in which late 13th-century Plantagenet children were not consistently in their parents' presence.

[48]Ross, "Middle-Class Child," pp. 196–97, supposes that a child returned from a rural wet nurse to an urban household might have problems "finding" its birth mother in a large establishment and might initially bond with an older family member.

but instead by the grandmother he knew well. A similar profile emerges for Edward's second daughter, Joan (1272–1307), raised from 1274 to 1278 by her maternal grandmother. Joan's life after she came to England offers several incidents suggestive of an independent and assertive—not to say defiant— attitude toward her parents, which it is tempting to link to the years she spent apart from them before she first made their acquaintance at the age of six.[49]

Ultimately, however, there are strong indications that in adulthood Edward's daughters were devoted to him. Given the difficulties sketched above for two of them, it may be wondered how this came about, and a closer look is in order at the period in which the children first began to encounter their parents. There was some parental awareness that this breaking-in period was a sensitive time: the children were often returned to their household for periods of time (or young Eleanor's bonding with her grandmother was respected), and Edward ordered that his young sons have time to accustom themselves to a new residence before he arrived. Again, these are adult sensibilities; the children's experience is less readily documented but must be considered here as well. Within their household's dignified obscurity, the young Plantagenets were likely accorded some deference, and care-givers probably did their best to instill in them proper respect and loyalty for their absent parents. For the most part, however, the children probably first grasped their distinctiveness as members of the king's family when they began to travel with their parents and witnessed the reverence accorded them, and as they shared in that deference by participating in the splendid ceremonies that surrounded the couple. Such events surely impressed on them the special nature of their relationship to their parents.

---

[49]Details and further examples in Parsons, *Eleanor of Castile*, pp. 39–41.

Returning them to the company of the humbler companions in their household might be supposed to have furthered their socialization by allowing them to realize their new-found eminence as they interacted with inferiors. Long-standing intimate relationships with care-givers and their families would presumably preclude arrogance as the children assimilated a new awareness of their rank, would encourage the frankness and *debonnaireté* toward others esteemed in the well-born and so clearly witnessed in the letters quoted here.

Although the degree of success was bound to vary from one individual to another, this system seems to have worked well for Henry III's children and for Edward I's daughters. This, however, only highlights the misfiring of relations between Edward and his heir. It has been surmised that this came about largely because young Edward was denied even the earliest contact with his parents. Born in April 1284, he never saw them while they were in Gascony between May 1286 and August 1289. In this regard it should be borne in mind that the two sisters similarly cut off from their parents for roughly the same length of time, and at roughly the same point in their lives, later had difficulties in establishing relationships with them. At the age of five-and-a-half, the boy met for what was surely the first time in his memory a father and mother aged fifty and forty-eight. Eleanor of Castile was already fatally ill; she died fifteen months later, and her son probably had very few memories of her. Her death in November 1290, followed seven months later by that of Eleanor of Provence, led to the almost complete dissolution of Edward I's intimate circle, which was reconstituted only after his second marriage in 1299. These losses, combined with the king's absence on Scottish and Flemish campaigns in the 1290s, left young Edward to grow up in rural isolation at King's Langley, where he most likely evolved that liking for ditching and swimming for which he was later widely mocked. Edward II's inadequacies have been traced to a consequent lack of ease and confidence in his relationship with a formidable and irascible father.[50]

Much about this account is persuasive, but it offers easy resolution to only some questions. An anonymous chronicler writing a year after Edward I's death, and claiming to speak from personal observation, said that Edward was fond of talking about his children, which seems not out of character in a man who had enjoyed a close-knit family circle in his own childhood.[51] His lively interest in his children by Queen Margaret has been noted, and he was undoubtedly very fond of his daughters by Eleanor of Castile; Elizabeth (1282–1316), who grew up beside young Edward, became very close to the king, indeed was probably his favorite child, whom he kept with him much of the time in his later years as his relationship with his heir worsened. Mary (1279–1332), dedicated in the convent at Amesbury in 1285, was often indulged with gifts and money by the king, who visited her convent and brought her to court. She could write, some years later,[52]

> To the very high and very noble prince, her dearest and most beloved lord and father, my lord Edward by the grace of God king of

---

[50]Johnstone, *Edward of Carnarvon*, pp. 23–25, 29–30, 100, 128–31.

[51]*Opus chronicorum*, in *Johannis de Trokelowe, et Henrici de Blaneford . . . Chronica et annales*, ed. H. T. Riley, RS, 28.3 (London, 1866), p. 48; Johnstone, *Edward of Carnarvon*, p. 128.

[52]On Elizabeth, Prestwich, *Edward I*, pp. 127–29. It was she whom young Edward asked for help when he was in disgrace with the king in 1305; *Letters of Edward Prince of Wales, 1304–1305*, ed. Hilda Johnstone (Cambridge, 1931), pp. 70, 75, 115. Mary's letter is PRO, SC 1/19/111, s.d. (my trans.; words in brackets supplied for clarity), written in or after June 1292, as Mary became a "nun of the convent of Amesbury" only late in 1291 (Parsons, "Year of Eleanor of Castile's Birth," p. 264). The letter probably dates from one of Edward I's Scottish campaigns.

England, Mary his devoted daughter, humble nun of the convent of Amesbury, sends greeting and all reverence, with her desire for his blessing. Dearest father, by the very great desire I have to hear good news of you, I now write you and pray you and humbly require you that for the ease of my heart it may be your pleasure to send me by every messenger [news of] your state, which may God of his grace ever preserve in good prosperity as my heart desires. I commend you, dearest Father, to Jesus Christ, and may He give you long life and good. Written at Woodstock the Sunday next after Saint Bartholomew.

Kings could be at greater ease with their daughters than with their sons,[53] but it was in these same years, when he was still occupied with Scottish affairs, that Edward I was showing such interest in the young sons of his second marriage. The evidence thus throws into even sharper relief Edward's poor relationship with his heir and thus requires a new approach.

It is suggested here that the young man was under a cloud almost from birth. A royal family is intimately linked to sovereign power, and its personal histories, tragedies as well as triumphs, are played out on a commensurate scale. Of the ten children in Edward I's family by Eleanor of Castile who died young, the only one to live long enough to give his parents some sense of a developing personality was Alphonso (1273–84), whose death in August 1284, at the time of the king's greatest military success and only four months after young Edward's birth, was clearly a devastating blow to both parents. Archbishop Pecham's moving letter to the king on this occasion leaves no doubt of the loss Edward I sustained, and of all her children who died young, Eleanor of Castile had only Alphonso's heart reserved for burial with her own.[54] Of

---

[53]Parsons, "Mothers, Daughters, Marriage, Power," pp. 68–69.

[54]Parsons, *Eleanor of Castile*, p. 39. On parental grief at the loss of children, Attreed, "*Pearl* Maiden to Tower Princes," p. 46; Margaret L. King, *The*

course, Alphonso's death had far weightier implications than those of his six infant sisters. From October 1274 until his death, he was heir to the throne; his parents were used to thinking of him as such, and were probably rather more focused on him than on their other children. After evidently only a short time to anticipate his death,[55] they had to admit the infant Edward, an unknown quantity, into exactly the same place Alphonso had occupied—if not in their hearts, certainly in their thinking and planning. The king might have found it difficult to do so; he might have resented the boy who now took the place of the much-regretted Alphonso. At forty-five, Edward I could no longer expect that within a few years a well-trained son could begin to assume some administrative burdens. It would be years before he could look to the new heir for support, and, given the king's age, there was the troubling prospect that young Edward might succeed as a minor. By 1284 Queen Eleanor was well into her forties; hopes for more sons were slight, and the king, who had already buried four sons, had to confront the infinitely disturbing possibility

---

Death of the Child Valerio Marcello (Chicago, 1994). Of the six daughters of Edward I and Eleanor who died, one was in her second year, the others only months old. Of the sons other than Alphonso, John died at age five while his parents were on crusade; Henry, two when they left on crusade, died 10 weeks after their return to England. A fourth son, name unknown, died soon after birth. See Parsons, "Year of Eleanor of Castile's Birth," pp. 257–65.

[55] In late Apr. 1284 Alphonso offered the Welsh regalia at Westminster (*Flores historiarum*, ed. Luard, 3: 61), and he arrived at Canterbury on pilgrimage on 1 May (continuator of Gervase of Canterbury, in *The Historical Works of Gervase of Canterbury*, ed. William Stubbs, 2 vols., RS, 73 [London, 1879–80], 2: 292); clasps he offered at Canterbury were noted in the king's jewel account, PRO, E 101/372/11, m. 1. He was ill long enough before he died on 19 Aug. for the news to reach Fontevrault Abbey in Poitou, to the nuns' visceral distress (PRO, SC 1/47/113, prioress Gila to Edward I, s.d.).

that he might be left with a daughter as his heir.[56] The infant
Edward could have become for his father the embodiment of
these sad and dangerous prospects, and this could have strengthened any aversion to the child. The boy who represented such
ominous complexities also may have grown up in unknowing
competition with a dead brother whose virtues could have been
inversely elaborated as the heir's perceived failings multiplied.
By the time father and son began to come into regular contact
with each other in the later years of the reign, young Edward
was well into his teens and, whatever the true nature of his
relationship with Piers Gaveston, he was already leading an
untidy life to which his father clearly took exception.[57]

Speculation on such matters after seven centuries is risky.
It is seductively easy to suppose that paternal rejection alone
explains Edward II's susceptibility to male favorites. But his
reaction to such neglect could account for the testing nature of
his behavior toward his father in Edward I's last years—his
insolence to the king's favored minister Walter Langton in
1305, and his provocative 1307 demand that Gaveston receive

---

[56]His daughters' rights were clearly of concern to Edward I in the next years;
Thomas Rymer, ed., *Foedera, Conventiones, Litterae*, rev. ed., 4 vols.
(London, 1816–69), 1: 742.

[57]F. D. Blackley, "Adam, Bastard Son of Edward II," *Bulletin of The Institute of Historical Research* 37 (1964): 76–77; cf. Johnstone, *Edward of Carnarvon*, p. 100. In correspondence with the author dated 14 Aug. 1996,
J. R. S. Phillipps modified his views on Edward II's sexuality as expressed,
e.g., in his review in *American Historical Review* 95 (1990): 1180–81, of
Jeffrey S. Hamilton, *Piers Gaveston, Earl of Cornwall 1307–1312: Politics
and Patronage in the Reign of Edward II* (Detroit, 1988); Phillipps now finds
the evidence "so ambiguous that I regard this conclusion [that Edward II was
homosexual] as far from certain." Chaplais, *Piers Gaveston*, finds no contemporary evidence for a sexual relationship between Edward and Gaveston, nor
any contemporary suspicions of such a liaison.

the county of Ponthieu or the earldom of Cornwall, a request that reportedly led the king to tear out his son's hair. This was not, however, the rebellious conduct of the Young King, nor is it even mildly reminiscent of the Lord Edward's flirtation with the opposition to Henry III. In 1307, young Edward held a good deal of land as prince of Wales, earl of Chester, and duke of Aquitaine and did not seek more for himself, only for his favorite; his rupture with the king in 1305 was followed by the pathetic spectacle of the heir trailing after his father's household in the ensuing period of disgrace, during which his letters reveal him daily hoping to regain favor.[58]

In that crisis, young Edward turned to his stepmother, Queen Margaret, and his sister Elizabeth to smooth things over and to obtain small favors from the king.[59] Among those favors in 1305 was the return of four yeomen he wanted with him, first among them John de Haustede and John de Weston. The former we have met as a son of that Margerie de Haustede who stood so high in Edward I's estimation. John de Weston's credentials were scarcely less respectable: son of Sir John de Weston, household knight and steward to Eleanor of Castile, later paymaster to Edward I's army in Scotland, and by 1305 steward to Queen Margaret's children. Sir John's wife, Christiana, had been a lady of Queen Eleanor's household. Sir John himself had grown up in the household of Edward I's children in the 1270s and was probably the son of an earlier John de Weston, Eleanor of Castile's steward in the 1260s, by one Hawise who was Eleanor of Provence's damsel. The

---

[58]Prestwich, *Edward I*, pp. 127, 130, 549–50, 552; Johnstone, *Edward of Carnarvon*, pp. 70–71, 97–102, 123–24. I owe to E. A. R. Brown the observation in this context on young Edward's trailing after the king in 1305.

[59]Johnstone, *Edward of Carnarvon*, pp. 100–01; Margaret again came to her stepson's assistance in 1306 (ibid., pp. 115–16).

second pair of yeomen whom young Edward wanted restored to him were his nephew Gilbert de Clare (Joan's son) and Piers Gaveston.[60] The presence of that inherited affinity, that extended surrogate family which dominated his early years, is obvious in young Edward's thinking, and there seems to be a calculated sequence among the yeomen he sought: the first two with their generational links to the royal households meant to reassure the king that his son was well-disposed to the approved circle, Gilbert de Clare to manifest his loyalty to his blood kin. The heir may even have hoped that his request for John de Haustede and John de Weston might enlist the much-esteemed Margerie de Haustede and the well-established Westons as advocates on his behalf. When he had, with the help of his stepmother and sister, allayed any worries on the king's part about his loyalty, young Edward's request to have Gaveston rejoin him might be the less jolting. The households

---

[60]The letter thanking Elizabeth for asking the king to allow Haustede and Weston to return, and requesting that she now ask for Clare and Gaveston, is Johnstone, *Letters of Edward Prince of Wales*, p. 70; Joan's 1305 support of her brother (ibid., pp. 60–61) may explain the request for her son to rejoin his household. Moor, *Knights*, 5: 181–82, confuses the three Westons. For the first, who fl. 1262–70 and may have died on the crusade of 1270, *CPR 1258–1266*, p. 325; *ClR 1264–1268*, pp. 8, 505; *CPR 1266–1272*, p. 727; *CChR* 2: 86; *CPR 1266–1272*, p. 382. On Hawise, *CPR 1258–1266*, p. 678. For the second John (fl. 1273, d. 1323), Johnstone, "Wardrobe and House-hold of Henry," p. 390. He was queen's squire, 1278 (PRO, C 47/4/1, fol. 40) and a knight by Jan. 1282 (S. Lysons, "Copy of a Roll of the Expenses of King Edward the First at Rhuddlan Castle in the Tenth and Eleventh Years of His Reign," *Archaeologia* 16 [1812]: 32–79, esp. p. 49). See also *CChR* 2: 256, 267; *CPR 1281–1292*, pp. 8, 239, 417, and Michael Prestwich, *War, Politics, and Finance under Edward I* (London, 1972), p. 160. On Christiana, *CChR* 2: 234, and Parsons, *Court and Household*, p. 156; the queen's order to the constable of Dover to assure Christiana's passage to France is PRO, SC 1/30/52 (Westminster, 7 June s.a.).

had, then, instilled and supported the heir's loyalty to his father and given him an affinity to whom he could turn in adversity. Unfortunately, the households could do nothing to help him negotiate his personal relationship with his father.

It is not to be denied that we are dealing here with special cases, but some points can be extrapolated from Plantagenet experience to suggest refined approaches to the history of the medieval family in general. To deal specifically with evidence presented here, two points can be made. First, confiding a young child to surrogate care-givers for a time might pose obstacles to the evolution of strong parent-child relationships, but such impediments need not, in optimum conditions, have been insurmountable. (The question, of course, is whether, or when, optimum conditions prevailed.) Second, evidence concerning those among Edward I's daughters who were separated from their parents in childhood suggests that in estimating the effects of resorting to care-givers, the impact on the children themselves may have been undervalued. For one thing, adults who employed care-givers could remember their children when they were absent, but children who grew up in the care of surrogates could not well recall the parents who were occasional presences in their young lives. The children could well suffer conflicts as they balanced their feelings for their care-givers with those they were expected to develop for their parents. If the role of surrogates is to be brought to bear on histories of familial strife, perhaps less attention should be given to alleged adult disinterest in children than to the mechanisms by which children were integrated into their birth families, and the problems they experienced in the process.

That Plantagenet power, privilege, wealth, and patronage could guarantee excellent care for the king's children suggests reference to the links theorized among the quality of child-care, the worth attached to the individual, and the evolving sense of self in the medieval period.[61] The obstacles Edward I's daughter Joan encountered in bonding with her parents notwithstanding, it cannot be doubted that her care-givers in Ponthieu and in England were attentive, and that as an adult Joan gave evidence of a vigorous sense of self in her defiant support of Edward of Caernarfon in 1305, as well as her reportedly quite spirited defense of her clandestine second marriage in 1297.[62] It is, of course, unwarranted to argue that the Plantagenet evidence entirely confirms a coupling of quality child-care to the individual's sense of self, but Joan's case can contribute to the discussion, and further investigation of the household records may well turn up additional evidence.

Finally, the sources reviewed here suggest that in a society whose order largely depended on blood ties, the very importance attached to such ties left them exposed and vulnerable to events whose effects might linger for decades. The loss of a promising son was likely as hard for a merchant or peasant family as for a noble house; we have in Edward II's case an especially powerful example that suggests we need more nuanced ways of evaluating the impact of such events. The implication that affinal relationships might be more stable, given

---

[61]DeMause, "Evolution of Childhood," p. 51; Attreed, "*Pearl* Maiden to Tower Princes," p. 48; John F. Benton, "Individualism and Conformity in Medieval Western Europe," in *Individualism and Conformity in Classical Islam*, ed. Amin Banani and Speros Vryonis (Wiesbaden, 1977), pp. 145–68, and Benton, "Consciousness of Self and Perceptions of Individuality," in *Renaissance and Renewal in the Twelfth Century*, ed. Robert L. Benson and Giles Constable (Cambridge, Mass., 1982), pp. 263–95.

[62]For Joan's second marriage and her justification of it, Parsons, "Mothers, Daughters, Marriage, Power," pp. 76–78. P. D. Johnson, "*Mulier et Monialis*: The Medieval Nun's Self-Image," *Thought* 64 (1989): 242–53, considers a certain self-confidence as inherent in medieval aristocratic women but does not theorize a connection to child-rearing practices.

the vulnerability of blood relationships, is not earth-shattering in itself. But Edward of Caernarfon's manipulation of his yeomen's affiliations in 1305 suggests that new insights may emerge when attention is turned to that grey area where blood and affinity overlap, where tensions between them are most visible and the individual's engagement with them is most easily discerned.

KINSHIP TIES, BEHAVIORAL NORMS, AND FAMILY COUNSELING IN THE PONTIFICATE OF INNOCENT III

Constance M. Rousseau

oth the medieval family and the Catholic Church provided their members with extremely valuable and beneficial services. The family tried to fulfill basic biological and emotional needs and attempted to secure the future of its members. The Church offered spiritual guidance and the only means to eternal salvation. Although the Church was concerned with its otherworldly mission, both it and the family were involved in temporal affairs, and each possessed its own set of interests. Sometimes these concerns conflicted; at other times they intertwined in creating the fabric of a Christian society.[1]

---

[1] In addition to standard scholarly abbreviations, the following will be used: *Cal.*—Christopher R. Cheney and Mary G. Cheney, eds., *The Letters of Pope Innocent III (1198–1216) Concerning England and Wales: A Calendar with an Appendix of Texts* (Oxford, 1967); DBC—Heinrich Singer, ed., *Die Dekretalensammlung des Bernardus Compostellanus Antiquus*, Bd. 171 Abh. ii (Vienna, 1914); Pott.—August Potthast, ed., *Regesta pontificum romanorum inde ab anno Christum natum MCXCVIII ad annum MCCCIV*, 2 vols. (Berlin, 1874–75); *Register*—Othmar Hageneder and A. Haidacher, eds., *Die Register Innocenz' III*, Bd. 1: *Pontifikatsjahr, 1198/1199* (Graz, 1964), O. Hageneder, Werner Maleczek, and A. A. Strnad, eds., Bd. 2: *Pontifikatsjahr, 1199/1200* (Rome, 1979). RNI—Friedrich Kempf, ed., *Regestum*

In recent scholarly discussions there has been a discernible trend toward emphasizing opposition and tension between the family and the Catholic Church. John Boswell, in his study of homosexuality, cited numerous New Testament passages where Jesus seemingly repudiated the family's important position in Jewish culture and Mosaic law.[2] In a 1978 article on marriage Michael M. Sheehan noted, "It has been said in jest, though not without a serious overtone, that Christianity destroyed the family."[3] The unnamed observer to whom Sheehan referred (the ethicist Paul Ramsey) made such an assertion because of the Church's insistence upon consensual marriage, which weakened the family's control over the couple. The emphasis of conjugality over consanguinity has also been argued by Charles Donahue, Jr., and Jack Goody.[4] Goody further contends that the Church attempted to regulate strictly the family's marital

---

Innocentii III papae super negotio Romani imperii (Rome, 1947); Theiner—Augustin Theiner, ed., *Vetera monumenta Slavorum meridionalium historiam illustrantia*, 1 (Rome, 1863).

[2] *Christianity, Social Tolerance, and Homosexuality: Gay People in Western Europe from the Beginning of the Christian Era to the Fourteenth Century* (Chicago, 1980), p. 114. See Mt 8: 21–22; Mt 10: 35–37; Mt 12: 46–50; Mt 19: 29; Lk 9: 57–60; Lk 14: 26–27. For discussion of marriage and family life in the New Testament and patristic sources see Willy Rordorf, "Marriage in the New Testament and in the Early Church," *Journal of Ecclesiastical History* 20 (1969): 193–210, and Elizabeth A. Clark, "Antifamilial Tendencies in Ancient Christianity," *Journal of the History of Sexuality* 5 (1995): 356–80.

[3] "Choice of Marriage Partner in the Middle Ages: Development and Mode of Application of a Theory of Marriage," *Studies in Medieval and Renaissance History*, n.s., 1 (1978): 6.

[4] Donahue, "The Policy of Alexander III's Consent Theory of Marriage," *Proceedings of the Fourth International Congress of Medieval Canon Law*, ed. Stephan Kuttner (Vatican City, 1976), p. 259; Goody, *The Development of the Family and Marriage in Europe* (Cambridge, 1983), p. 156.

and inheritance strategies because of the clergy's desire to accumulate vast amounts of property alienated from members of kin groups, which were then used to advance ecclesiastical interests.[5] After studying the lives of many urban saints, David Herlihy generalized that since kin ties and obligations were synonymous with worldly cares that competed with an individual's duty to God, "the medieval Church saw no absolute value in close and emotional family attachments."[6]

Despite these scholarly evaluations, the general assessment of the tension or outright antagonism between the Church and the family put forth by recent scholars must be considerably nuanced. There are other aspects of family-Church relations that must be considered before any conclusions can be drawn. A fruitful way of analyzing the Church's attitudes toward family ties and behavior is to focus on the perspective of one of the most dynamic popes of the Middle Ages, Innocent III (1198–1216).[7] By examining his correspondence, found primarily in the Vatican Registers,[8] we will find that this pope, while counseling people concerning their behavior in some specific and highly visible situations, emphasized literal family ties and gave an extended interpretation of family expectations, along with a broader definition of what comprised actual

---

[5]*Family and Marriage*, pp. 83–102, 103–56, 221.

[6]*Medieval Households* (Cambridge, Mass., 1985), p. 114.

[7]For discussions of Innocent III see Brenda Bolton, *Innocent III: Studies on Papal Authority and Pastoral Care* (Aldershot, 1995); C. R. Cheney, *Pope Innocent III and England* (Stuttgart, 1976); Raymonde Foreville, *Le pape Innocent III et la France* (Stuttgart, 1992); Michele Maccarrone, *Studi su Innocenzo III* (Padua, 1972); Helene Tillmann, *Pope Innocent III*, trans. Walter Sax (Amsterdam, 1980).

[8]See *Cal.*, pp. ix–xxiv, for discussion of registers, editions of letters, etc. *Registra Vaticana*, 4–7, 7A, 8, and 8A in the Archivio Segreto Vaticano, contain the correspondence from Innocent's pontificate.

kinship.[9] Thus, through an analysis of Innocent's letters we can begin to arrive at a fuller understanding of the relationship between the medieval Church and the family.

Scholars who study Innocent III have often utilized his papal registers to analyze politics or ecclesiastical matters but have not considered what the letters reveal about his view of families and their kin relations. The language used by Innocent to describe familial behavior offers us a window into various aspects of his ideology of family relations as well as into the family as an institution. A key element in this ideology was his consideration of the conduct of relatives. When these actions were beneficial to the Church, the pope employed the family and its members as a model of behavior that he encouraged and counseled other kin to emulate.

Papal recommendations of this kind are found in several letters in the registers. In one instance, Innocent commanded Philip Augustus of France to follow in the footsteps of his *father* ("patris tui vestigia") in his devotion and assistance to the Church. In turn, the pope would extend Rome's benevolence and goodwill to the king.[10] In another letter the pope

---

[9]While there has been little study of the pope as family counselor, there has been extensive research done on the papacy's intervention in marital matters. See, e.g., James A. Brundage, *Law, Sex and Christian Society in Medieval Europe* (Chicago, 1987); Donahue, "Policy," pp. 251–81; Charles Duggan, "Equity and Compassion in Papal Marriage Decretals to England," in *Love and Marriage in the Twelfth Century*, ed. Willy van Hoecke and Andries Welkenhuysen (Louvain, 1981), pp. 59–87; Constance M. Rousseau, "The Spousal Relationship: Marital Society and Sexuality in the Letters of Pope Innocent III," *Mediaeval Studies* 56 (1994): 89–109; Michael M. Sheehan, "Sexuality, Marriage, Celibacy and the Family in Central and Northern Italy: Christian Legal and Moral Guides in the Early Middle Ages," in *The Family in Italy from Antiquity to the Present*, ed. David I. Kertzer and Richard P. Saller (New Haven, 1991), pp. 168–83.

[10]*Register* 1: 5–6, no. 2; PL 214: 2–3 (9 Jan. 1198).

similarly invoked the memory and crusading valor of Count Raymond of Toulouse's *grandfather* in an attempt to persuade Raymond to emulate his example and reconcile himself with the Church.[11] In a letter of 1212 granting apostolic protection, Rome exhorted Alfonso II, king of Portugal, that his *grandfather*, a diligent defender of the Catholic faith, was an example to be imitated.[12] In turn, Alfonso II, following in the footsteps of his *progenitors* ("progenitorum tuorum vestigiis inhaerendo") would pay annual tribute to Rome for her protection.[13]

Besides direct papal intervention to encourage a relative to mold his conduct on that of kin, other letters reveal the pope's deep-seated assumption that family members would naturally follow their relatives without any direct pressure from Rome. This opinion is indicated in a letter of 1206 to the prelates and princes of Hungary ordering them to swear fidelity to the soon-to-be-born heir of King Andrew II (1205–35), as their

---

[11]*Register* 1: 595–97, no. 397; PL 214: 374–75, (4 Nov. 1198). See also RNI, pp. 97–101; PL 216: 1034–35 (1 Mar. 1201), where the pope invoked a similar familial model of devotion to the Church to Otto during the dispute over the imperial throne. Sometimes an individual would follow a familial model that was not beneficial to the Church or others. Innocent noted how Philip of Swabia, following in the footsteps of his progenitors, intended to oppress Milan. Refer to RNI, p. 234; PL 216: 1094–95 (20 July 1203). See a similar statement in RNI, p. 244; PL 216: 1099 (11 Dec. 1203), where Innocent said that Philip of Swabia wished to take Sicily away from his nephew Frederick and the Church.

[12]PL 216: 562–63 (16 Apr. 1212).

[13]PL 216: 562–63 and *Register* 1: 613–16, no. 410; PL 214: 387–88 (mid-Nov. 1198), where Innocent exhorted Empress Constance, queen of Sicily, to imitate the obedience and support of the Church given by previous rulers, her father, brother, and nephew. Papal advice to follow in a relative's footsteps or papal confirmation of a person already doing this is also found, respectively, in *Register* 1: 671–72, no. 448; PL 214: 424–25 (9 Dec. 1198), and PL 216: 171 (12 Jan. 1210).

monarch commanded.[14] In his letter Innocent asserted that according to a legal understanding a father and his son comprised the same person, and hence there was a high probability that the son would and ought to favor those persons whom his father cherished. The Hungarian ruler had been beneficent in his governance, and it was presumed that his offspring would imitate these paternal actions and moral strengths.[15] The pope therefore implied that the child would not only learn proper administration from his father but also moral principles and social behavior.[16]

This papal theory is similarly expressed in a later letter celebrating the arrival of the Hungarian royal heir, the future Bela IV.[17] Extending his congratulations to the baby's uncle, the bishop of Bamberg, Innocent expressed his hope that the child would succeed to the throne and, like his progenitors, be devout and faithful to the Church. The pope concluded, "By the grace of God, let him be an excellent imitator."[18]

---

[14]PL 215: 895 (7 June 1206).

[15]PL 215: 895, "Cum pater et filius interpretatione iuris eadem persona fingantur, satis probabiliter subinfertur, quia quos pater retinet in visceribus charitatis, eosdem filius et deligere debeat et fovere. Charissimus siquidem in Christo filius noster . . . illustris rex Hungarorum, quam circumspecta provisione incoeperit disponere regnum suum, regnique principes quanta dilectionis exibitione studeat honorare, vos ipsi eo certius nostis, quo frequentius vobis et vestris munificentiae suae subsidia benignius impendit per quod est verisimiliter praesumendum, quod soboles, quae, divina disponente clementia, subcrescet ex ipso, quoad strenuitatem morum et regendi sollicitudinem, paternam debeat providentiam imitari."

[16]PL 215: 895.

[17]Jean Baptiste Pitra, ed., *Analecta novissima spicilegii Solesmensis*, 1 (Paris, 1885; repr. Farnborough, 1967), pp. 520–21 (29 Nov. 1206).

[18]Note that Pitra, *Analecta*, pp. 520–21, has "primogenitoribus"; however, *Reg. Vat.* 7, fol. 123r [lib. 9, no. 186], has "progenitoribus": "Noverit igitur tuae fraternitatis discretio, quod felix ista nativitas usque adeo exhilaravit cor

An objection could be made that the pope was only attempting to ensure the continuity of policies and attitudes advantageous to the Church and was not expressing an actual concept of a *familial model* of conduct. Furthermore, it could be claimed that Innocent mentioned family members only because they had been the previous holders of positions of power that their successors now held. Yet his choice of phrases demonstrates that in addition to ensuring continuity, a familial model of behavior indeed underlay Innocent's directives.

The pope invoked the ideal of "following in the footsteps of another" in two different senses in his letters. He advised individuals to emulate either their predecessors or their progenitors in various instances. In the latter case, a specific relative, such as grandfather or father, would be named.

Predecessores signified those persons who had lived before an individual. Innocent employed the phrase "follow in the footsteps of one's predecessors" in cases where there was no familial or kinship bond between an individual and those who had held the position before him. For example, in June 1206 the pontiff ordered the bishop of Pavia to institute monastic reform in his diocese and noted that the bishop, following in the footsteps of his *predecessors* ("praedecessorum tuorum in haerens vestigiis") regarded the papacy and Church with faith and devotion.[19] The pope thus praised or confirmed the

---

nostrum cum speremus quod filius nutu divino progenitus, sicut suis *progeni-toribus* est successurus in regni solio, sic devotionis et fidei quam ad sacro-sanctam Romanam Ecclesiam semper habuisse noscuntur, sit Dante Domino, eximius imitator . . . " (my emphasis). The pontiff advised this emulation of a familial model for not only legitimate but also illegitimate members of a kin group, as seen in another letter, to Geoffrey, archbishop of York and bastard son of Henry II, who is told to imitate his ancestors' deeds. Refer to RNI, pp. 313–14; PL 216: 1131 (17 Feb. 1206).

[19] PL 215: 913 (19 June 1206). An earlier letter (1198) confirmed the bishop of Durham's institution of prebends and other ecclesiastical dignities made in

continuity of policy established by the predecessor that was being carried out by the present holder of power.

Progenitores signified not only those who came before but also those who were ancestors. In the introduction of an epistle to Andrew of Hungary in 1205, concerning a dispute with the archiepiscopal seat of Esztergom, Innocent expressed the hope that Andrew would follow in the footsteps of his *progenitors* in his devotion and support of the Roman Church.[20] Another letter to Andrew concerning the postulation of an episcopal candidate noted how the "progenitores" *and* "praedecessores" of the addressee had been of great service to the Church.[21] Hence, Innocent's distinction of terms indicated that although all progenitors were predecessors, not all predecessors were necessarily progenitors.

If the pope had desired to ensure merely the continuity of an established policy, he could have used the term *predecessores* even in cases where relatives had held positions of power to which subsequent kin succeeded. The pope did not choose to use this terminology, however, and employed the term *progenitores* or named a specific relative because he desired to emphasize not only continuity of a policy beneficial to the

---

this church in which the prelate followed the example of his predecessor. See *Register* 1: 692, no. 470; PL 214: 437 (16 Dec. 1198): "Ex caritatis siquidem, sicut credimus, fonte processit, *quod bone memorie predecessor* tuus et *tu post eum ipsius exempla secutus* in ecclesia de Denluton prebendas et personatus provide statuistis, ut in eo honorabilius de cetero Domino serviatur et ecclesia ipsa . . . melius providere" (my emphasis).

[20] PL 215: 661–62 (24 June 1205). See also Pitra, *Analecta*, p. 500 (1205). Here Innocent praised the marquis of Montefeltro for following his progenitors in his devotion to the Church.

[21] PL 215: 675 (26 June 1205). In PL 216: 433–34 (7 June 1211) the pope noted that in executing a crusade a ruler would be following the footsteps of his *progenitors*.

Church but *also* the emulation of a particular mode of good conduct that had been established by an individual's ancestors.

We have previously analyzed how the family itself sometimes provided a model of behavior for its members to imitate. In addition to these guidelines, Innocent III constructed a Christian ideology for familial relationships by setting forth his own behavioral norms for the family, which often advanced its interests and those of the Church. The registers reveal several instances of papal intervention in matters involving either interfamilial strife or extrafamilial threats. These cases give valuable insights into the papal position pertaining to the proper conduct of relatives, the obligations and responsibilities inherent in kinship ties, and even rare glimpses into the emotional bonds of the family.

The struggle for the Hungarian throne in 1197 between King Imre and his brother, Andrew, the sons of the deceased Bela III, provided the pope with an opportunity to emphasize the inherent obligations and expectations attached to filial and fraternal ties in this case of interfamilial conflict. Although James R. Sweeney has argued that the pope's intervention on behalf of Imre was strictly political,[22] the evidence demonstrates that Innocent was also concerned with the quality and workings of family relationships.

In a decretal of January 1198 to Duke Andrew, Innocent first employed an argument based on filial devotion and respect to ameliorate the civil strife and to cause the parties to recognize their kin obligations. The pope noted that on his deathbed King Bela, under the pain of a curse ("sub interminatione maledictionis"), had commissioned his son Andrew to

---

[22]"Papal-Hungarian Relations during the Pontificate of Innocent III, 1198–1216," Ph.D thesis, Cornell University, 1971 (Ann Arbor, 1980), p. 29, n. 9; pp. 30–31.

execute a paternal crusading vow.[23] Andrew had promised to
fulfill his parent's will without delay; however, he was now
warring against his brother, King Imre. Innocent therefore
ordered Andrew to discharge this vow before the feast of the
Exaltation of the Cross (14 September) for the sake of peace
and his own salvation. The pope further declared that if
Andrew failed to perform his father's command, he would render himself unworthy of the paternal succession, be deprived
of his inheritance, be subject to anathema, and be denied the
right of royal succession should Imre die without heirs.[24]

As supreme judge of Christendom, Innocent held within his
purview vows and their lack of execution.[25] In addition to the
question of vows, the text exhibits the pontiff's concern for an
heir's appreciation of the responsibilities and obligations attached to his inheritance. Failure to discharge the testamentary
wishes of his benefactor/father meant the loss of the bequest.
This legal precept was based on Roman law's doctrine of
inheritance, which had influenced the pope.[26]

---

[23]*Register* 1: 17–18, no. 10; PL 214: 8; X.3.34.6 (29 Jan. 1198).

[24]*Register* 1: 17–18, no. 10; PL 214: 8; X.3.34.6: ". . . ne, si onus tibi a patre
iniunctum et a te sponte susceptum occasione qualibet detrectaris, paterna te
reddas successione indignum et hereditatis emolumento priveris, cuius recusa-
veris onera supportare. Sciturus extunc anathematis te vinculo subiacere et
iure, quod tibi, si dictus rex sine prole decederet, in regno Ungarie compe-
tebat ordine geniture, privandum et regnum ipsum ad minorem fratrem tuum
appellatione postposita devolvendum."

[25]See X.3.34.

[26]Othmar Hageneder, "Exkommunikation und Thronfolgerverlust bei Innocenz III," *Römische Historische Mitteilungen* 2 (1957/58): 14–15. According
to James A. Brundage, *Medieval Canon Law and the Crusader* (Madison,
1969), p. 78, n. 40, although the inheritance of a vow was new in canon law
it was certainly stated in the Roman law Dig. 50.12.2.2: "Voti enim
obligationem ad heredem transire constat." Roman inscriptions also indicate
that heirs frequently fulfilled the vows of the deceased. Brundage, p. 78,

In his letter to Duke Andrew, Innocent also gave equal weight to both the fulfillment of a vow and the point that this enterprise had been delegated by Andrew's father under the penalty of a paternal curse.[27] Thus, not only was there recognition of the heir's responsibilities but also there was the implicit papal emphasis on filial piety and devotion.

This interpretation concerning the obligations and duties inherent in a father-son relationship is confirmed by more explicit evidence. In a letter of 5 November 1203 to Andrew, Innocent asserted that from the beginning of his youth Andrew had promised to go on crusade *both* because of the command of his father *and* because of his own vow.[28] Filial obedience was likewise emphasized in a letter of 1203 to Imre, where the pope noted that although Andrew was bound by filial devotion to execute both the vow of his father and the paternal mandate, he failed to do so because of the conflict between the brothers.[29] Thus, in addition to the moral obligation to fulfill

---

argues that Innocent established that "an unfulfilled crusade votive obligation of a person could be transferred to his heir and the heir's execution could be enforced by the sequestration of the inherited estate."

Innocent justified his intervention in the Hungarian succession and the question of the suitability of a royal candidate not on the basis of feudal ties but because of the traditional ties of *devotio* that earlier monarchs had established with Rome. See Karl Jordan, "Das Eindringen des Lehnswesens in das Rechtsleben der römischen Kurie," *Archiv für Urkundenforschung* 12 (1931/32): 96–97; Sweeney, "Papal-Hungarian Relations," pp. 35–36.

[27]*Register* 1: 17–18, no. 10; PL 214: 8; X.3.34.6.

[28]PL 215: 170 (5 Nov. 1203): "Cum inter tuae primordia iuventutis tam ex mandato paterno, quam voto proprio, militiae tuae primitias voveris Jesu Christo. . . ."

[29]PL 215: 169–70 (5 Nov. 1203): "Licet autem ipse in votis habuerit exsequi votum patris, et mandatum ejus filiali devotione complere, quia tamen inter serenitatem tuam, et ipsum, peccatis exigentibus, dissensionis scrupulus intervenit, nondum est quod proposuerat exsecutus praesertim cum ab hoc eum defectus retraxerit expensarum."

the vow and the duty of an heir to honor a legator's wishes, filial obedience and respect arising from the blood tie was an equally important reason for a son to execute the wishes of his parent. Innocent probably realized that if Duke Andrew did embark on a crusade in 1198, his departure would assist in the papacy's plan to recapture the Holy Land and end the fraternal strife in Hungary. Despite papal exhortations, warfare between Andrew and Imre continued, with Andrew allying himself with the Austrian duke Leopold VI.[30]

In his efforts to settle the dispute Innocent simultaneously utilizes another line of argument, which emphasizes the *fraternal* bonds between Duke Andrew and Imre.[31] Employing biological imagery in a letter of 15 June 1198, Innocent urged Andrew to exhibit honor and reverence to King Imre so as to end the civil war and thus "may the *affection of mutual charity* unite you as it united the paternal blood and the maternal womb" (my emphasis). The pope strictly forbade Andrew to incite sedition against Imre. Moreover, he warned that Andrew's allies might desert him, since they would not trust him if he violated natural and fraternal bonds. Hence, the pope ordered the archbishops of Esztergom and Kalocsa and their suffragans to excommunicate Andrew and to put his lands under interdict if he should move against Imre.[32] Through his letter Innocent

---

[30]*Continuatio Garstensis*, in MGH SS 9: 595; *Continuatio Lambacensis*, in MGH SS 9: 556; Sweeney, "Papal-Hungarian Relations," p. 37.

[31]*Register* 1: 374–75, no. 271; PL 214: 227–28 (15 June 1198).

[32]*Register* 1: 374–75, no. 271; PL 214: 227–28: ". . . mandamus, quatinus taliter de cetero in fidelitate ipsius ac devotione persistas, ut ferventis ac fidelis servitii novitas aboleat offense preterite vetustatem et *sic vos adinvicem mutuus uniat caritatis affectus, sicut sanguis paternus et uterus maternus univit. Ad hec tibi districtius inhibemus, ne in regem vel regnum arma movere presumas vel seditionem aliquam suscitare, ne forsan amici te deserant, si fratrem habueris inimicum, et de fide tua desperare cogantur, si fraterne ac naturalis pacis federa te senserint violare . . .* " (my emphasis).

thus invokes blood ties not only to instruct against interfamilial struggles and to enjoin the duty of kin to establish peace for the family and the state but also to encourage and restore a form of familial affection between the parties.

Hostilities between the brothers nevertheless persisted until March 1200, when the apostolic legate sent to reconcile the brothers negotiated an acceptable truce. With peace temporarily restored, Innocent continued to press for Hungarian participation in the Fourth Crusade to Palestine;[33] it was not forthcoming because of hostilities between Hungary and Bosnia. A further impediment was Duke Andrew's renewal of the conflict with Imre late in 1203, after Andrew had rebuilt his support among the Hungarian nobility. In the ensuing struggle Andrew was captured and imprisoned. The papal exhortation for the discharge of familial duty and Hungarian participation in the Holy Land did not come to fruition, since King Imre died on 30 November 1204. The governing of the kingdom fell then to Duke Andrew, the most suitable member of the Arpád dynasty, who seized the throne from the heir, Imre's five-year-old son, Lászlo.[34]

Innocent intervened in a second case in which a relative actively attempted to deny another family member his rights and failed to recognize kin responsibility. Geoffrey, archbishop of York and illegitimate son of Henry II, had complained to the pope, charging that Richard of England had deprived him of his archiepiscopal temporalities, this resulting in his banishment and beggary.[35] As a response Innocent sent a letter to

---

[33]Theiner, p. 59, no. 114.

[34]Sweeney, "Papal-Hungarian Relations," pp. 56–62, 64–65.

[35]*Register* 2: 102–04, nos. 55(57, 58); C. R. Cheney and W. H. Semple, eds. and trans., *Selected Letters of Pope Innocent III Concerning England (1198–1216)* (London, 1953), pp. 10–14; PL 214: 595–97 (28 Apr. 1199). See also Cheney, *Pope Innocent III and England*, pp. 280–81.

Richard in 1199, declaring that his actions had caused shame to the king, the prelate's *brother*, and that the churchman deserved better treatment.[36] Papal emphasis of the fraternal, albeit illegitimate, bond between king and ecclesiastic is further seen when Innocent exhorted Richard not to be indifferent to his brother's banishment, to receive the archbishop fully into his royal favor, and to *love him as a brother.*[37]

In these letters Innocent's use of fraternal language is neither mere formulaic rhetoric nor a metaphorical expression of the spiritual brotherhood of all men in Christ. Rather, the pope employs such terminology to emphasize the actual and widely recognized biological kin ties between Geoffrey and Richard and the obligations that flowed from this relationship. This interpretation is confirmed when we compare the language found in papal letters concerning other disputes between royal and episcopal powers with that describing Geoffrey's dilemma. Although the letters express spiritual brotherhood between prelate and pontiff, using such conventional terms of address as "fratris nostri," there is no mention of either a

---

[36]*Register* 2: 102–04, nos. 55(57, 58); Cheney and Semple, *Selected Letters*, pp. 10–14; PL 214: 595–97: ". . . et tuam etiam, ut prosequamur verum, verecundiam cuius est frater. . . ."

[37]*Register* 2: 102–04, nos. 55(57, 58); Cheney and Semple, *Selected Letters*, pp. 10–14; PL 214: 595–97: "Attendas igitur, quanta nos infamia, quanta te detractio sequeretur, si vel iusta petitio exulis non introiret in aures nostras, *vel te fratris exilium non moveret*; et eundem archiepiscopum ob reverentiam apostolice sedis, *que te tamquam filium diligit specialem* et in hoc et maioribus de celsitudinis tue sinceritate confidit, in plenitudinem gratie regalis admittas et *diligas sicut fratrem* et velut Christi ministrum honores, ut in uno et eodem negotio Deum tibi reddas propicium, consulas apostolice sedis honori, tue saluti provideas et *fratri subvenias exulanti*" (my emphasis). This letter failed to reach its addressee, as Richard had already been dead three weeks when it was composed. See Cheney, *Pope Innocent III and England*, p. 281.

spiritual or kin relationship between monarch and prelate.[38] Granted, no familial bond existed between these churchmen and king; however, the pope, who could have expressed a spiritual bond between these parties, did not. Hence, Innocent's use of fraternal terminology to describe the relationship of Geoffrey and Richard indicates actual family ties, not spiritual ones. In the case of Geoffrey, there is indeed the injustice of the despoiling of a prelate; but there is the further injustice of a kin member maltreating his relative.

Innocent's discussion of Geoffrey of York's plight not only gives specific instructions on proper treatment of kin but also hints at the need for fraternal affection. The papal assumption that some form of familial affection should be present among kin, either illegitimate as in the case of Geoffrey or legitimate, is further confirmed by a letter of 1203[39] involving a different case altogether.

Besides some suggestions of family affection, Innocent's letter concerning Geoffrey of York indicates a somewhat

---

[38]See PL 215: 484–86 (13 Dec. 1204). This letter exhorted John of England to receive and bring back John, archbishop of Dublin, from a seven-year exile and to make royal restitution for his despoliation. In PL 215: 1406–08 (27 May 1208), the pope called Stephen Langton, archbishop of Canterbury, "fratrem nostrum" but not "brother" to the king in either a spiritual or biological sense. PL 215: 1455–57 (22 Aug. 1208) named John as the pope's "son in Christ," a common form of address using kinship terms in a figurative spiritual manner; no fraternal bond in either a natural or spiritual sense was described between John and Langton.

[39]In PL 215: 198 (9 Dec. 1203), the pope exhorted Philip Augustus of France to treat his spouse, Ingeborg, with marital affection and render the conjugal debt, since the woman had left her brothers and sisters to wed the French king and she would receive no recompense for all she had given up if Philip refused to perform his sexual duty. The text hints at some notion of familial affection and ties between Ingeborg and her siblings that had been lost and should be replaced by conjugal affection.

sympathetic papal attitude toward bastardy. The English common law considered an illegitimate child a *nullius filius*, or son of no one, who possessed neither inheritance rights nor heirs except those of his own body. Despite this secular theory, these papal letters give the contrasting impression that a bastard, even with his irregular birth, still stood within the system of kinship, either immediate or extended. The pope recognized at least the existence of a blood, if not a legal, relationship between the bastard and his natural family, and this tie required proper treatment of the bastard relative.[40]

This recognition of such a blood relationship was further implied in the pope's letter to Archbishop Geoffrey, which discussed the descent of Geoffrey from the royal family. The prelate was told that if he investigated the praiseworthy deeds of his ancestors that extended the fame of the royal house and imitated them, he would be confirmed as their follower, for "the tree is known by its fruit and illustrious works demonstrate an illustrious succession."[41]

---

[40]For bastardy in England refer to Norma Adams, "*Nullius Filius*: A Study of the Exception of Bastardy in the Law Courts of Medieval England," *University of Toronto Law Journal* 6 (1945–46): 361, who also sees growing opposition to the succession of bastards in the secular realm, discussed in R. H. Helmholz, "Bastardy Litigation in Medieval England," *American Journal of Legal History* 13 (1969): 360–83, and J. L. Barton, "Nullity of Marriage and Illegitimacy in the England of the Middle Ages," in *Legal History Studies 1972: Papers Presented to the Legal History Conference*, ed. Dafydd Jenkins (Cardiff, 1975), pp. 28–49.

[41]RNI, pp. 313–14, PL 216: 1131 (17 Feb. 1206): "Si eximia facta progenitorum tuorum, quibus multimode laudis titulo renitebant, sedula meditatione discutias si, qualiter per insignia gesta suam dilatauerint famam et regie domus ampliauerint decus, subtiliter perscruteris, ad imitandum eos totis te conuenit uiribus laborare, ut per ostensionem operum sectator ipsorum merito comproberis. Nam arbor a fructu cognoscitur, et clarum heredem opera clara depingunt."

Thus, Innocent broadly defined kinship ties and emphasized them in order to restore interfamilial peace. He likewise used them as the reason for the family to assist its members in struggles against extrafamilial threats. The dispute over the imperial throne between Philip of Swabia and Otto of Brunswick offered Innocent an opportunity to counsel on proper family relations and assistance.

After the death of Henry VI, Holy Roman Emperor in 1197, the Staufen faction in the following year elected Philip, duke of Swabia and brother of the deceased emperor as king of the Romans. Three months later, another group of electors chose Otto of Brunswick, son of Duke Henry the Lion of Saxony and Bavaria and Matilda, elder sister of Richard and John of England. This political situation was further complicated by the support of Kings Philip Augustus of France and Richard of England to Philip and Otto, respectively.[42]

At first, Innocent did not support either imperial candidate. Fear of imperial encirclement caused the pope to open negotiations with Philip; when these broke down, Innocent cautiously waited, ready to aid Otto when there was evidence of his success. Finally, on 1 March 1201 the papacy publicly accepted Otto of Brunswick as the imperial successor.[43]

After Innocent identified Otto as significant to papal policy and ecclesiastical interests, a series of letters was sent to King John of England, Otto's uncle, in order to elicit assistance for his relative and to emphasize the obligations inherent in kinship ties. At first, Innocent simply mentioned the familial

---

[42]Tillmann, *Pope Innocent III*, pp. 103–10; Cheney, *Pope Innocent III and England*, p. 283. For discussion of relations between Innocent and Philip Augustus and John, see Bolton, "Philip Augustus and John: Two Sons in Innocent III's Vineyard?" in *Innocent III* (n. 7 above).

[43]RNI, pp. 74–91; Tillmann, *Pope Innocent III* pp. 103–04, 110; Cheney, *Pope Innocent III and England*, p. 283.

relationship between John and Otto. The pope scolded the king, who had failed to pay his *nephew* Otto the legacy bequeathed by Richard the Lion-Hearted in his testament, the terms of which John was obligated by oath to fulfill.[44] As judge, Innocent could intervene, since John was failing to execute his vow; however, the letter also implied a moral obligation for John because of the familial tie of uncle-nephew. The papal assertion of the bond of uncle-nephew, noted in several other letters,[45] was more precisely defined when Innocent called John the *avunculus* or maternal uncle of Otto.[46]

Was the pope's mention of kinship ties in the preceding letters merely stating a fact, or was there another motive involved? Clearly, kinship bonds were noted because the pope desired John to recognize his family obligation to Otto. This is revealed in the pope's explicit assertion in a letter of 1201 that John should support Otto because of their kinship ties. The pope argued that Otto descended from the English royal family, was therefore directly related to John by consanguinity; there was no kinsman more closely related to John. Hence, John should aid him by delivering the legacy and supplying troops; these acts would glorify his family. In a much later letter (1206), the pope continued to tell the king that his aid of Otto's cause would enable him to glorify his stock (*genus*) and

---

[44] RNI, pp. 73–74; PL 216: 1024 (?Aug. x Sept. 1200 in *Cal.*, Dec. 1200 in Pott.).

[45] DBC, p. 80, 3.20.1 (?Nov. 1201 in *Cal.*, Oct.–Nov. 1201 in Pott.); RNI, pp. 134–35; PL 216: 1050–51 (1 Mar. 1201); Theiner, p. 61, no. 192; PL 214: 1175 (20 Feb. 1203); Cheney and Semple, *Selected Letters*, p. 48, and RNI, p. 310; PL 216: 1129 (23 Sept. 1205), which all mention kinship ties.

[46] RNI, pp. 161–62; PL 216: 1062. (2 Nov. 1201 in Pott., 1 Mar. 1201? in *Cal.*, beginning of Nov. 1202 in RNI) John was the brother of Otto's mother, Mathilda. See esp., in RNI, pp. 134–35; PL 216: 1050–51, where Innocent mistakenly called John the *patruus* or paternal uncle of Otto.

extend the memory of his name by and through Otto. John and Otto shared the honor of the same name, and therefore the king should help his relative.[47]

But a complication in executing the papal command had arisen. Earlier in May 1200, John had signed the Treaty of Le Goulet with Philip Augustus, whereby the English king swore that neither he, nor his kin, nor others would assist Otto financially or militarily except with the assent of Philip Augustus.[48] According to Roger of Hovedene, John's excuse for withholding payment of the legacy was based on this clause in the treaty.[49] In his letter to John, Innocent pointed out that Philip could not release John from the obligation ("debito") by which he was bound to his nephew Otto.[50] This *debito* could either signify the familial duty of John as uncle to aid his nephew or an actual debt owed to Otto, in this case possibly the legacy that had been bequeathed by Richard. Basing his argument on Scripture, the pope ruled that John's oath to Philip Augustus was illicit and ordered him to help Otto in his struggle for the

---

[47]RNI, pp. 134–35; PL 216: 1050–51. In RNI, pp. 313–14; PL 216: 1131 (17 Feb. 1206), Innocent also designated the blood relationship between Otto and Geoffrey, archbishop of York, as uncle-nephew and stated that Otto lacked the prelate's support and that of other blood relatives: "Cum itaque carissimus in Christo filius noster illustris rex Otto, nepos tuus, tuo et aliorum consanguineorum suorum amminiculo presens indigeat. . . ."

[48]RNI, pp. 161–62; PL 216: 1062. For the complete text of the Treaty of Le Goulet see A. Teulet, *Layettes du Trésor des Chartes*, vol. 1 (Paris, 1863), no. 578, col. 218b: "In conventionibus istis domino regi Francie habemus conventionem, quod nos nepoti nostro Othoni nullum auxilium faciemus nec per pecuniam, nec per milites, nec per gentem, nec per nos, nec per alium, nisi per consilium et assensum domini regis Francie."

[49]William Stubbs, ed., *Chronica Magistri Rogeri Houedene*, 4 vols., Rolls Ser., 51 (London, 1868–71), 4: 116.

[50]RNI, pp. 161–62; PL 216: 1062.

throne since "reason dictated and nature demanded that an uncle help his nephew."[51]

Continuing this theme of nature in another letter of November 1201, the pope gave a colorful description of the biological and organic reality of kinship that obliged the king to aid his relative. The pope exhorted John, saying:

> . . . let the abundance of your riches water the twig [Otto] which sprouted from your tree since it is bone from your bones and flesh from your flesh; lest through a lack of moisture, its verdancy should wither in some way. . . .[52]

Innocent continued to exhort John to pay the legacy and provide men and supplies to Otto in a letter of 1202. But he also noted that other people (probably Philip Augustus and his allies) were opposing Otto, because of Otto's familial ties to King John, their enemy.[53] This statement implied that since

---

[51]RNI, pp. 161–62; PL 216: 1062: ". . . cum et ratio dictet et natura deposcat ut auunculus debeat subuenire nepoti. . . ." According to Cheney in *Pope Innocent III and England*, pp. 283, when Richard died King John had written warmly in Otto's support and in Apr. 1199 he took over a large debt that Richard had incurred on behalf of Otto. But after the Treaty of Le Goulet in 1200, which John used as a pretext to stop aid, Otto objected, and hence Innocent intervened.

[52]Theiner, p. 61, no. 192; DBC, p. 80, 3.20.1: ". . . ut sic plantam, in quam tui germinis arbor pullulavit, cum sit os ex ossibus tuis et caro de carne tua, divitiarum tuarum copia irrigaret, nec per humorum defectum langueret in aliquo viror eius. . . ." See also a later letter in RNI, p. 311; PL 216: 1129–30 (17 Feb. 1206), where Innocent stated that John was bound to assist his nephew Otto not only by reason of *flesh and blood* but also for reasons of opportunity and honor: "Cum karissimo in Christo filio nostro illustri regi Ottoni, nepoti tuo, tenearis magnifice subuenire, non solum ratione carnis et sanguinis, uerum etiam consideratione commodi et honoris. . . ."

[53]RNI, pp. 193–94; PL 216: 1075 (28 Mar. 1202): ". . . ut nouimus, aliquos contra eum non in odium persone, sed sanguinis grauiter commoueri non tam ipsum quam te in eo, vel ipsum pro te ledere cupientes."

these dynastic blood ties were detrimental to Otto, John should assist his nephew so that these ties could become advantageous. A later letter (ca. September 1205) similarly urged John to take action "lest the fact that he [Otto] was related to you by the nearest line of consanguinity becomes a burden rather than an honor."[54]

There is evidence that by at least 17 February 1206 John had finally begun to heed papal persuasion and supported Otto's cause, since at this time the pope was requesting *more* aid than the small amount given thus far.[55] The last of these exhortatory epistles dated between 15 July and early August 1208 continued to request immediate support.[56] In the end, Philip of Swabia was assassinated on 21 June 1208 and Otto IV was unanimously elected and crowned emperor on 11 November 1208.[57]

---

[54]RNI, pp. 307–08; PL 216: 1128 (22 Sept. 1205): "Ne igitur ad onus sit ei potius quam honorem, quod te proxima linea consanguinitatis attingit. . . ."

[55]RNI, p. 310; PL 216: 1129 (17 Feb. 1206). This small amount of aid clearly did not mean that John had paid the legacy bequeathed to his nephew, since the pope was still requesting payment of the legacy in RNI, p. 311; PL 216: 1129–30 (17 Feb. 1206).

[56]RNI, p. 359; PL 216: 1150 (15 July x early Aug. 1208 in *Cal.*, init. Aug. 1208 in Pott.). Innocent also encouraged and exhorted Otto's brother, Henry, Count Palatine of the Rhine, to aid him in the imperial struggle and noted the fraternal affection of Henry for Otto, which Otto should likewise demonstrate to Henry as his brother. These ties presumably could be mutually advantageous: Henry's aid to Otto and Otto's advancement of Henry upon attaining the throne. See RNI, pp. 120–21; PL 216: 1044–45 (1 Mar. 1202).

Innocent's counsel that the family should assist and protect its members was further demonstrated in his intervention to elicit the support of Canute, the Danish king and brother of Queen Ingeborg, to assist his sister in her defense in the divorce suit initiated by Philip Augustus, king of France. Refer to Theiner, p. 50, no. 126 (July 1200), and PL 214: 883–84 (22 Oct. 1200).

[57]Tillmann, *Pope Innocent III*, pp. 137–38.

In contrast to the behavior of King John of England, sometimes relatives without papal counsel recognized their duty to aid their kin. The pope encouraged this behavior. Geoffrey Fitzpeter, justiciar of England, had asked the pope for a three-year deferment of a pilgrimage vow in return for the establishment of a hospital and monetary aid to the Holy Land. As one of his reasons for postponement Fitzpeter alleged that powerful enemies wished to disinherit his young heirs. These enemies had already seized a large portion of his sons' inheritance and would be able to obtain the remainder were he to leave England. In response the pope sent two mandates, dated 7 July and 16 December 1205, to the bishop of Lincoln, and he granted Fitzpeter's petition so that he not only could remain with the king who needed his counsel but also so that the inheritance of the justiciar's sons would be protected ("ei praesidium filiorum").[58]

Through his many letters to the faithful of Christendom, Innocent attempted to construct an ideology of familial conduct that we can see as being overwhelmingly supportive and positive toward the importance of kinship ties, affective bonds, and familial responsibilities. Real biological kinship was a serious matter for this pope, who did not seem to place much emphasis on kinship in a metaphorical sense in the letters we have analyzed.

Papal instruction in the letters stressed an increased sense of familial solidarity. Innocent exhorted kin to emulate their own family's model of exemplary conduct as previously set forth by living and deceased relatives. He also counseled kin and regulated their conduct by encouraging norms of proper Christian familial behavior and the right treatment of all

---

[58]*Cal.*, p. 105, Vatican Archives, AA Arm. I–XVIII, no. 4098 (7 July 1205), and PL 215: 745–46 (16 Dec. 1205).

relatives (immediate, extended, legitimate, or illegitimate) that resulted from these kinship and emotional relationships. If the family failed to recognize these responsibilities, the pope intervened, not only to protect individuals from their kin but also to ensure that the relatives would fulfill their familial duty. Thus, Innocent did not possess a suspicious and negative attitude toward close family attachments in secular matters.[59] In his family counseling he broadly defined and interpreted kinship, its expectations, and its obligations in order to benefit the Church and to strengthen the medieval Christian family.

---

[59]He was less sympathetic towards clergy and religious whose close family attachments caused them to pursue private familial interests that were detrimental to the Church. See my article "Pope Innocent III and the Familial Relationships of Clergy and Religious," *Studies in Medieval and Renaissance History* (Sept. 1993): 105–48.

THE CURTEYS WOMEN IN CHANCERY:
THE LEGACY OF HENRY AND RYE BROWNE

Timothy S. Haskett

The present volume is a most fitting one in which to offer this small *inventio et expositio*, for it proceeds directly from research begun some fourteen years ago under the guidance of Father Michael Sheehan. That this essay pertains to social history, to the family in particular, and that it is grounded in part in wills is unsurprising. Less usual, perhaps, is that it involves an area of Father Sheehan's research and teaching that is sometimes overlooked: the history of law and legal institutions. Two such institutions are involved in the case under scrutiny: the probate jurisdiction of the archbishop of Canterbury and the court of the chancellor of England. The law at issue is, for Canterbury, the canon law; for the Chancery it is the dictates of conscience, drawn from the civil law, and the canon law and its moral base, manifested through the royal prerogative and the king's obligation to do justice and exercised through the king's chief officer. The instruments through which we can see both of these legal fora invoked are the testaments of Henry Browne and his wife, Rye, and, subsequent to their probate, a bill initiating a case in the Court of Chancery. All three are edited and presented here for the first time.

The proving of a will usually rested with the ecclesiastical ordinary, or his delegates, in whose area of jurisdiction the

349

testator resided; intestate administration also was to be had at this diocesan level. The probate jurisdiction exercised by the archbishop of Canterbury was, however, unique in a number of ways. There was, of course, a basic diocesan element, under which were proved the wills of laymen and clerics of the city and diocese of Canterbury, although normally the archdeacon's court rather than the archbishop's would act in such cases; also from this diocesan authority came the wills from the exempt parishes within the archbishop's collation and from his peculiars.[1] But the metropolitan authority of Canterbury brought many other wills before the archbishop or his officials, under his prerogative jurisdiction. Often with the probate annotation "de prerogativa" or "ratione prerogative ecclesie sue Cantuariensis" came the wills of testators who died during a metropolitical visitation, as well as wills proved while a suffragan see was vacant.[2] In addition, the Canterbury prerogative claimed the proof of wills wherein the deceased person had possessed *bona notabilia*, that is, goods of value greater than £10 dispersed throughout different dioceses of the province.[3] The claim of the right to prove such wills was an attempt by Canterbury to simplify administration where several diocesan jurisdictions might be involved due to the extent of the wealth of some testators.

The two testaments that are the subject of this essay, however, are in a Canterbury register because of a completely

---

[1] E. F. Jacob, ed., *The Register of Henry Chichele, Archbishop of Canterbury, 1414–1443*, 4 vols. (Oxford, 1943–47), 2: x.

[2] Jacob, *Register*, 2: ix.

[3] Jacob, *Register*, 2: x. Also, Irene J. Churchill, *Canterbury Administration: The Administrative Machinery of the Archbishop of Canterbury, Illustrated from Original Records*, 2 vols. (London, 1933), 1: 380–423; the records from which the wills that are the subject of this study are taken are discussed at 1: 419–23.

different, and more irregular, prerogative reason: the testators were residents of the English continental outpost of Calais. In 1379, Pope Urban VI had granted the archbishop of Canterbury authority in spiritual matters in the region in and around Calais, as well as in parts of Picardy. Ostensibly, this was done to protect the faithful there from schismatic and heretical opinions, and to help them as the French-English wars made recourse to their diocesans impossible. The more pragmatic reason was to reward Archbishop Simon Sudbury and Richard II for their support against the French-backed anti-pope, Clement VII.[4] The exercise of testamentary jurisdiction was, of course, part of this authority, and is explicit in several commissions to commissaries in the fifteenth century.[5] The jurisdiction was abandoned after the Treaty of Troyes in 1420 but was resumed by 1440, and it continued to be exercised until Calais was lost to the English in Mary's reign.[6]

The activity of the medieval English Court of Chancery is not nearly as well studied as the work of its contemporary ecclesiastical courts; there remains debate as to the nature of its jurisprudence, and its utility and importance in late medieval English society is only now being appreciated. Yet a few brief remarks may be offered. The jurisdiction grew not from the Chancery's own departmental work as the central writing office of the government but from the jurisdiction of the king's Council to deal with bills of complaint. In the second half of the fourteenth century such bills, addressed to the king in Council, came to be passed to the chancellor; before 1400 most petitioners had begun to address their pleas to him directly. While in the thirteenth century the chancellor, in response to a

---

[4]Churchill, *Canterbury Administration*, 1: 508–09.

[5]Churchill, *Canterbury Administration*, 1: 509–14.

[6]Churchill, *Canterbury Administration*, 1: 514–19.

petition, might have allowed a new form of original writ to effect remedy, once the writ categories were closed—and this by the mid-fourteenth century—the only general remedy was to refer the bill to Parliament, in the hope of legislation. But the chancellor, the most powerful individual in the kingdom after the king himself and wielding prerogative authority, could treat the matter ad hoc and grant specific remedy by decree, a decree that bound only the parties to the suit.[7]

Why was this activity necessary? Basically, the common law was increasingly unable to help people in a variety of areas. Procedure in the common law courts of King's Bench and Common Pleas was fully circumscribed by the writ system, and mesne process made it dependent upon the good will of the sheriffs. Forms of pleading, rules of evidence, and the uncertainties of jury trial further constrained common law process, and there were many possibilities for mechanical failure. The very strength of the substantive law could produce injustice, because judges preferred to suffer mischiefs to individuals rather than make exceptions to clear rules. The usual example given is the debtor who did not ensure that his sealed bond was canceled once he had paid. His payment was no defense, for the law regarded the bond as incontrovertible evidence of the debt and the debtor suffered the hardship of having to make a second payment. The mischief was deemed to result from his own foolishness, and as one writer has said, "the law did not bend to protect fools."[8] In similar fashion, one who made an oral contract where the law required writing would

---

[7]See Timothy S. Haskett, "The Medieval English Court of Chancery," *Law and History Review* 14 (1996): 245–313, for a complete assessment of the study of the court and new directions in research. This particular recitation is taken from John H. Baker, *An Introduction to English Legal History*, 3rd ed. (London, 1990), p. 117.

[8]Baker, *Introduction*, p. 118.

have no remedy, and land granted on trust that certain wishes be carried out would in the view of the law belong absolutely to the grantee, who could not be compelled to obey the instructions of the grantor. It was not that the common law held that a debt should be repaid twice, or that a promise or trust could be broken. Nonetheless, these would be the results if the strict rules of evidence were observed, and while these rules might exclude the merits of the case from consideration, they could not be relaxed without destroying certainty and condoning carelessness.[9] It was undoubtedly wrong for a person to take advantage of such conditions, but this failing was a matter for his or her conscience, not for the common law.

The chancellor, however, was not a common law judge and thus was not bound by common law procedural formalities and customs. Process in his court—the Court of Chancery—began by bill of complaint, not original writ; pleading was relatively informal, there was no jury, and evidence could be taken both from witnesses and the parties themselves. Chancery was always open, and the court could sit anywhere. Such advantages led to swift and inexpensive justice. The chancellor could deal with the exceptional case, he could enforce the dictates of conscience and protect the foolish, he could order bonds canceled where they served unjust ends or order discovery of documents needed to enforce legal rights, or order parol contracts to be performed and fiduciary obligations to be carried out. In an insightful statement describing the essence of the court, John Baker has remarked that "[The chancellor's] court was a court of conscience, in which defendants could be coerced into doing whatever conscience required in the full circumstances of the case."[10] There was, at least until the sixteenth century,

---

[9]Baker, *Introduction*, p. 119.

[10]*Introduction*, p. 118.

little if any conflict with the common lawyers and judges, for this activity in Chancery interfered not at all with the general rules of the common law courts: each Chancery case was seen to turn on its own facts alone, and Chancery decrees operated *in personam*, binding the parties in the case, but they were not judgments of record that bound anyone else.

The two jurisdictions—the ecclesiastical court and the Court of Chancery—are related to one another in a way that is especially important for the present case. When I began the first systematic study of the medieval Court of Chancery—the *Early Court of Chancery in England Project (ECCE), 1417–1532*—it was hoped and expected that some matters relating to the activity of the church courts would be found there, and in this we have not been disappointed.[11] The list of ecclesiastical persons appearing in Chancery is extensive and includes abbesses, abbots, archbishops, archdeacons, bishops, canons, cardinals, cellarers, chanters, chantry priests, chapel priests, chaplains, churchwardens, clerks, commissaries, confessors, curates, deans, friars, holywater clerks, incumbents of parish churches, monks, parish clerks, parish priests, parochial chaplains, parsons, petty canons, prebendaries, priests, priors, prioresses, provincials, rectors, and vicars. While the presence of such people does not mean that all of them were pursuing, or being pursued, concerning church matters, it is clear that Chancery was a venue in which much was argued by churchmen and -women. Certain substantive matters pertaining to the Church have also been found, as fruits, mortuaries, offerings, pluralities, and tithes are present, if in a limited number of cases. Matters that denote both ecclesiastical and secular

---

[11]A full description of the ECCE Project can be found in Haskett, "Medieval English Court of Chancery," pp. 281–85; the following information is found in pp. 285–309. The database for the project includes information gathered from nearly 7,000 cases.

concerns appear as well, such as parsonages, patronage, presentations, and resignations. Some of the specific ecclesiastical objects of Chancery cases include abbeys, advowsons, benefices, chantries, chapels, churches, convents, parsonages, prebends, priories, rectories, and vicarages. Again, these are only those overtly related to the Church, and many others of a more general nature also pertain to ecclesiastical concerns. Even some few moral offenses, usually within the purview of the church courts, are found in Chancery, offenses such as adultery, desertion of spouse, fornication, and enticement.

Yet there is another type of Chancery case that comes closest to the concerns of this essay. One of the features of ecclesiastical probate records in the Middle Ages is that the amount of litigation stemming from the administration of wills after probate is very small indeed. This might leave the impression that, contrary to our expectations, there were few if any disputes over legacies, no misappropriation of moveables or real property by executors, no difficulties of any kind arising either from duplicity or honest error on the part of anyone involved with the estates of the deceased. Yet if such details are sparse in the ecclesiastical records, they abound in the records of the Court of Chancery. We have found here the regular appearance of many people involved in probate matters: administrators, executors, legatees, and testators. In addition, beneficiaries and others with interests in the disposal of the property of *defuncti* regularly appear, and on both sides of the issues. But here, as in other areas, the line between ecclesiastical and secular matters is blurred, even if jurisdictional divisions are clear. While the church courts had undoubted authority to prove wills, the contents of those wills could involve many interests and several jurisdictions before all of a testator's bequests and directions were fulfilled. But the trust put in the executor to administer faithfully the will entrusted to him was something the Court of Chancery would enforce. As we shall see, fiduciary arrangements contained in a will, or even adjunct to it, also found in this court a forum for their defense.

A comprehensive study of testamentary matters in Chancery is under way, but the case that is the subject of this essay is indicative of the value of linking the activity of the Chancery Court with the records of other jurisdictions. It was found as the result of a quick check of the ECCE Project Database for any correlations with a group of English language testators that had been assembled for another study.[12] Indeed, the single match that resulted was almost overlooked, as that other study was to be closed at the year 1450 and the case found relates to testaments written and proved nearly a decade later. The match was even more fortuitous because the find was not a single instrument but a pair, written by a husband and wife who died within a very short time of one another. Their testaments are found in the *Stokton* volume of the Prerogative Court of Canterbury probate registers in the Public Record Office, London, on consecutive folios: that of Henry Browne is on folio 124r–v, while Rye Browne's is on folio 125r–v.[13] Housed in the same repository—a closeness never imagined by those who originally made the records—the Chancery case, from the tenure of Chancellor George Neville, bishop of Exeter, is found in class C 1 *Early Chancery Proceedings*, Bundle 28, number 53.[14] The three documents together provide what for the moment, at least, is a unique case that allows us to see in broader scope than usual the activities of the families involved both before and after the deaths of the principals. The

---

[12]Timothy S. Haskett, " 'I have ordeyned and make my testament and last wylle in this forme': English as a Testamentary Language, 1387–1450," *Mediaeval Studies* 58 (1996): 149–206.

[13]Public Record Office, London, PROB 11/4 (*Register Stokton*), fols. 124r–v, 125r–v.

[14]PRO, London, C 1/28, no. 53.

activities are mundane and for the most part regular, and neither the probates nor the Chancery case would have been of any particular importance to those outside of the families involved and some of their closest associates; yet for that very reason they may be assigned a greater significance for the researcher, as they give expression to normality.

Henry Browne seems to have done quite well for himself, a burgess of Calais, with a career as a chandler. While the bequests in his testament written on 17 October 1458 are not lavish, they do indicate a degree of prosperity, such that allowed him to make generous provisions for his widow, his family, and his servants. In common with many testators, Henry probably had his will written at a time of uncertainty as to his own health, for only about six months elapsed between composition and probate—an average figure for the time, even if there could be a considerable lapse between death and probate[15] —and this seems to imply some pressing worry that demanded he make provision both for his material goods and for the well-being of his soul, the two concerns that a testament had to address. Rye Browne ordered her affairs on 1 February 1459, only three-and-a-half months after her husband, who had died by the time she composed her instrument: she describes herself explicitly as his widow; she notes that her burial location is to be beside her husband, not beside where he had directed he be entombed; she provides for prayers for the both of them. She also makes several references to the proper execution of Henry's testament—the content of which she clearly knows—so indicating that his probate is still pending. Indeed, Henry's testament would not be proved until two

---

[15]See Jacob, *Register*, 2: lx, App. B, for a table illustrating speed in the granting of probate. As noted below, Henry was dead by the time his wife's testament was written on 1 Feb. 1459; the date of his probate is 9 Apr. of that year, so at least two months and some days—probably rather longer— had passed between his death and the proving of his testament.

months after Rye composed her own. While Canterbury jurisdiction over these testaments came from their principals' residency in Calais, probate was not handled by the archbishop's commissary there but by the archbishop or his delegate at Lambeth. Henry's testament was proved by Thomas Wymark, one of his named executors, who, *nota bene*, was also the respondent in the Chancery case, Rye's through a proctor for her nominated executors. The two instruments were proved at about the same time, presumably when a sailing to England and the parties involved were available, and thus they arrived if not together, then at least close enough to be part of the same probate sitting of the court.

The two testaments are very similar in form and formulae and also in their variances: both shift back and forth in bequests in a manner which, while generally systematic, nonetheless shows modification and afterthought as the testators recite their various provisions. Perhaps most noteworthy, though, is the division of concerns and types of bequests that the two display. While the division is by no means unexpected, close comparison of the testaments shows clearly the areas of responsibility that this husband and wife each had in the management of their household resources. The evident closeness in form, formulae, order, substance, and style indicates that the same scribe wrote them, probably a legal and business writer used regularly by the family, and possibly Geoffrey Poynnaunt, the notary named in Henry's testament as a witness.

The testaments begin in similar fashion in their invocations and in the initial commendation of the testators' souls to God, the Blessed Virgin, and the whole heavenly company, with their bodies to be buried in the south aisle of Our Lady's Church in Calais.[16] The Carmelite Friars in Calais were clearly

---

[16]This church, Notre Dame, remains the main church of the town, situated at its old center.

favorites of the Brownes, and the order was in all likelihood responsible for this church dedicated to the Blessed Virgin: both Henry and Rye provide 20s. for their exequies to be undertaken by the Carmelites.[17] Henry further allows funds for a priest to sing for him for a half year, while Rye, having survived her husband, directs that a priest sing Masses for them both for a whole year. Henry's briefer allowance is supplemented by an additional provision for remembrance on his anniversary. Emphasizing that Our Lady's was their parish church, both Henry and Rye provide a sum to make amends for offerings they had neglected—Henry gives twice as much as Rye, but we cannot assume that this means he was the more negligent; Rye also mentions forgotten tithes—and both provide for the fabric of the church, Rye with a sizable money gift and Henry with a supply of lead; to this Henry adds one piece of real property and the revenues from another.

The Brownes's involvement with other churches in or near Calais is evident in identical provisions from each for the fabric of the church at Marck, some ten kilometers east of Calais, Rye's bequest to the church of Coulogne, a mere two kilometers' distance to the south, and Henry's gifts to Saint Nicholas's (for the fabric and for the Saint Thomas chapel) and Saint Peter's—both apparently in Calais—and to the church at Guînes, ten kilometers south of the town. A closer study of the devotional practices attached to these various churches might yield some reasons behind these particular targets for legacies and tell something about local spirituality and perhaps the guild structures of mid-fifteenth-century Calais, but this is beyond the scope of this essay. There is

---

[17]The Carmelites were closely associated with Marian devotion, making their vows to God and Our Lady, so their association with Our Lady's Church is sensible. See J. Smet, "Carmelites," in *New Catholic Encyclopedia*, 18 vols. (New York, 1967–88), 3: 118–21.

nonetheless some direct insight into the devotional life of Henry and Rye. Each leaves sums to several "brotherhoods," the confraternities of the town. For Henry the most important of these is the Brotherhood of the Trinity Table at Our Lady's Church.[18] The priest he directs to have sing for him is to do so at the Trinity Altar, and one of his largest church bequests is of 6s. 8d., to be given toward the Table's almsgiving every year. The sum is to be taken in perpetuity from a rented Calais tenement and rendered twice a year by the wardens of the Table, at the Annunciation and at Michaelmas. If this almsgiving ever ceases, the sum is still to be collected, then divided among the poor directly. Henry also provides for the poor by bequeathing bedchamber items—a feather bed, a bolster, a pair of sheets and a coverlet, and these are the only goods that he disburses in the entire testament—to the *maison Dieu*, whose location he does not specify; it, too, might well be based at Our Lady's.[19] He provides a one-time gift to the Brotherhood of Saint Barbara at Our Lady's, and an even smaller amount to the Brotherhood of the Resurrection at Saint Michael's. It is with these last two bequests that Henry's and Rye's testaments meet once more, and this indicates that these confraternities either allowed membership to both men and women or (at least) provided an outlet for the devotional energies of both sexes. While she allows only half the amount of his gift to the Brotherhood of Saint Barbara, Rye provides for the Brotherhood of the Resurrection not only well over twice the sum Henry allows but adds the directive that the two

---

[18]The Carmelites established confraternities attached to their churches, esp. Marian confraternities. This Trinity Table brotherhood was probably one, and the Brotherhood of St. Barbara, mentioned below, also operated in their church. See Smet, "Carmelites."

[19]The position of this bequest in the testament—never a certain basis from which to derive additional information—is wholly unhelpful in this instance.

of them be prayed for daily. In addition, Rye provides a small sum for the Brotherhood of Saint Anne "in the Fieres" and a large bequest for the Brotherhood of Our Lady's Gate; both of these confraternities may also have been at Our Lady's, given the placement of the bequests in her testament and the title of the latter.

Thus far the two testaments have shown close similarities both in form and formulae, and in religious obligations and devotional interests. At this point, however, appears one of the two major distinctions between them: Henry's testament includes a brief mention of real property, while Rye's does not. While there is no reason that women could not own, possess, or control such property, especially in the urban setting, for the Brownes it was clearly the case that he managed this side of their affairs. As we shall see, Rye had the governance of almost everything else. Henry's real holdings were not extensive. We have noted already the use of one Calais property to provide revenue for the work of the Trinity Altar at Our Lady's; save for two caveats, he gives all his other lands and tenements within and without Calais to the two men he later names as executors. This provision turned out to be the crucial one for the subsequent case in the Court of Chancery, as we shall see. There is no specification of the extent of these holdings, but it is unlikely to have been large. It is possible that the earlier bequests to churches at Marck, Guînes, and Coulogne, all within ten kilometers of Calais, indicate the locations of Henry's extramural property. The purpose of the bequest is that the property be used to support Rye in her widowhood, which would turn out to be but a brief period. After her death, almost all is to be disposed of for the good of Henry's and Rye's souls; two houses are exempted from this general directive, to go instead to Henry's two nephews.

The two testaments converge in their content once more as both Henry and Rye move on to bequests to family members, servants, friends, and those to be involved in the administration of the testaments; Henry also has a single bequest to a business associate. Yet at the same time the second major—and again, not unexpected—distinction between the instruments is evident: if Rye has nothing at all to say concerning real property, her personal bequests of goods and chattels are far more extensive than those of Henry, and even the money she distributes is a sizable sum. At this point, a clear mapping of the relationships involved may be helpful. There are two main families, the Brownes and the Bakerses:

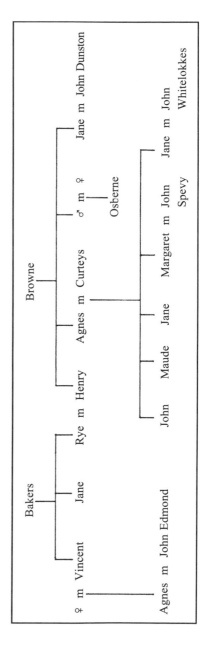

Rye provides legacies for nearly twice as many people as does her husband (twenty-six to his sixteen).[20] She mentions eleven separate family members to Henry's five (and to Henry's five Rye also leaves something). Henry makes provision for a greater number of servants (four to Rye's two), and it is he alone who mentions a business associate (his apprentice). Both make allowances for executors (Rye's two to Henry's three, plus Henry names an overseer). It does seem that Rye had more friends than her husband, as she provides for nine such people, while Henry names but two; only one is common to them both. All of Henry's legacies to individuals are in money, and in sum amount to £32 17s. 8d. In contrast, Rye's bequests are for the most part comprised of plate and household utensils, bedding, and clothing. Nonetheless, she does disburse two substantial amounts of money: one of Henry's sisters, Jane Dunston, is to receive 7 nobles (£2 6s. 8d.), and she, along with Rye's sister and brother and the children of Henry's other sister, Agnes Curteys, are to share in £40.[21] This latter provision is by itself more than the total of all Henry's money bequests to individuals, so clearly Rye was a woman of some capital resources, at least in her widowhood.[22] When we

---

[20]Included in this tally are gifts to executors, overseers, and witnesses: Rye includes these as part of her general bequests; Henry reserves them, more regularly, for the closing section of his testament, where executors and overseers are named. Rye is included, named by Henry as his principal executor, but it would seem unlikely that he intended that she receive the same gift as the other executors. Also, Rye's single undifferentiated bequest to Agnes Curteys's children is not included, as each of them is a beneficiary singly elsewhere in her testament.

[21]Rye also bequeaths Jane Dunston 20d. for the redemption of pawned jewelry.

[22]These might have been drawn from her dowry and thus out of her control while Henry lived. It is to be noted that the £40 is to be taken from her estate only after her debts have been paid and both her testament and Henry's have been fulfilled. Should these requirements exceed her expectations, the sum

consider the total amount of money that Rye disperses, compared with her husband, and remember that such money bequests form but a small proportion of her disbursements, the suggestion that she controlled considerable moveable wealth becomes even stronger.[23]

	Henry	Rye
Exequies	£2 0s. 0d.	£1 0s. 0d.
Churches	£2 13s. 4d.	£0 16s. 8d.
Confraternities	£0 16s. 8d.	£0 18s. 4d.
Family	£13 0s. 0d.	£42 8s. 4d.
Servants	£6 17s. 4d.	
Friends	£7 0s. 0d.	
Executors/Overseer	£2 0s. 0d.	
Business Associate	£4 0s. 0d.	
TOTAL	£38 7s. 4d.	£45 3s. 4d.

It is not possible to ascribe a monetary value to the goods and chattels that Rye disposes, but it is evident that, once they are included, the total value of her dispositions is much greater than her husband's. Granted, he has provided for some annual revenues and over time these would increase the amount of his gifts, and he does manage the disposal of real property of undetermined value, but in all else Rye plays the major role in directing the family's resources.

There are some evident distinctions in the way Rye manages her bequests. Her two executors are rewarded each with a single silver vessel. Servants receive clothing only. Family and

---

might well be reduced. That Rye uses her own resources to make sure that both of their obligations are satisfied is a mark of both affection and moral obligation, which are by no means exclusive.

[23]For the various categories in the following table, see Appendix A, the parallel lists of "Bequests and Directions," below.

friends are usually allotted a mixture of clothing or bedding and vessels or utensils. While her sister and brother and her sister-in-law Jane Dunston probably receive the most valuable legacies, due to the large money division and portions of the residue of her estate, the single greatest number of items is to go to the unnamed daughter of Jane Elmynes, a friend: she is to receive items of clothing, a bed and linens, and vessels. The distribution of Rye's bequests among family members is interesting. John and Maude Curteys, Jane Dunston, Agnes Edmond, and Margaret Spevy, all of whom receive monetary legacies from Henry, also do very well by Rye. Of these five, four are from Henry's family, the exception being Agnes Edmond. Indeed, this emphasis on Henry's family is a feature of the whole of Rye's familial bequests, as save for Agnes Edmond, Jane Bakers, and Vincent Bakers and his wife all of Rye's family bequests are to members of the Browne clan. There is no evidence whatsoever in the two testaments that Rye and Henry had children of their own—indeed, no evidence of any that had died in infancy or youth[24]—and turning to their wider family in their testamentary instructions is thus to be expected. Also, Rye's family seems much less extended than does Henry's, with but a brother, a sister, and a niece, while on Henry's side a brother had married, producing a son, a sister more prolifically generated four girls and a boy, and a second sister had married. Having provided for every member of her side of the family, Rye also makes bequests for every living member of Henry's. His sister Agnes is omitted, and as Henry similarly did not mention her it is likely that she had died by the time the testaments were written.[25] Similarly,

---

[24]This is corroborated by the Chancery bill, where the petitioners note that Henry died without issue.

[25]Certainly she was dead by the time the Chancery case was brought; the bill specifically mentions her as deceased.

Henry's brother and his wife are not to be found in either testament, and they, too, had probably died.

In Rye, then, we find a woman who appears to have been both mindful of her obligations and affections for her own kin, and comfortably integrated into her husband's family, so much so in the latter case that she takes considerable care to ensure that every one of them is remembered. Her specific allocation of legacies may be seen in the testament itself (Appendix C below) and in the list of Bequests and Directions provided in Appendix A below, but the cumulative extent of her wealth in goods and chattels may be noted here. In all, Rye disposes of the following: eight girdles (six women's, two men's), three kirtles (women's), eight gowns (five women's and three men's), one doublet, one bodice; two beds, four pillows, four pairs of sheets, two boardcloths, one washing towel, six napkins, one basin and laver; three mazers (one covered, one gilt, one broken), five silver cups (two with gilt feet), nine silver goblets (two covered and one of these gilt), sixteen spoons (ten of them silver), four salt cellars (two round, one covered), five pieces of silver plate, five other pieces of plate (three pounced), one chafer, six vessels with two chargers, one silver powder box; the instruments and equipment pertaining to the craft of one of Henry's nephews. The list is in keeping with the household furnishings of a moderately prosperous urban craftsman's family, and they are divided in detail and with evident care. As is common in testaments, distribution of the household is completed by provision for goods and chattels not bequeathed to specific individuals or institutions: Rye directs that her sister, Jane, and Vincent Cherkesson, a friend, divide half of such items, and that Henry's sister Jane Dunston and the Curteys children each have a quarter. Finally, Rye notes that her debts are to be paid and directs that anything left over after her instructions are carried out be administered by her executors as they see fit.

As noted, Henry's fifteen bequests to individuals are all in money, and several carry conditions. Four are directed towards providing dowries, one to a family member and another to a servant, while the remaining two are his sole bequests to friends. The first and fourth of these—to Maude Curteys and Agnes Strale—are unencumbered, but the second and third—to Jane Climyn and Elsabeth Cornelys—which are the largest at 100s. apiece, carry the common provision that the girls are to have the money only if they govern themselves well, presumably that they conduct themselves morally and marry properly. Henry's largest legacy to a family member, his nephew John Curteys, stipulates that he was to benefit only if he would be governed by Rye. It was suggested earlier that Agnes Curteys, John's mother, had died by the time Henry made his will, and it is probable as well that her husband, John's father, had also died. John would then be the sole male child and heir in that line of the Curteys family, and Rye's guidance might well have been envisioned as an important, moderating influence on him. In addition, Rye's bequest to him of all the instruments and equipment that pertain to his craft might well indicate that as one of only two male heirs on Henry's side of the family—and possibly the eldest—John is to have the material resources, including perhaps his house and workshop, necessary to carry on Henry's business as a chandler.[26] If such is the case, then Rye's governance of him becomes even more important. It could further be suggested that this is connected with Henry's single bequest relating to his business activities: he provides the substantial sum of £4 to his apprentice, but only if he finishes his term. This would certainly have to be under the tutelage of another of the chandlers' guild, and it is

---

[26]John Curteys is to receive a house after Rye's death, yet even this might not prejudice this suggestion.

possible that John Curteys, as Henry's successor, would fill that role. Henry concludes his bequests in normal fashion, with the direction of any residue to Rye for the payment of his debts; anything remaining afterwards is to be disposed of by her and her co-executors.

The two testaments close with the nomination of executors. For Henry, Rye is to be the principal, along with Thomas Wymark and William Fythian; Thomas Wardon, alderman of Calais, is asked to oversee execution. Rye selects one of these men, Thomas Wardon, along with Henry Durham. She mentions two others of Henry's executors—Wymark and Fythian— as witnesses, along with the chaplain, Robert Abraham. Henry names men hitherto not found in the document—the notary Geoffrey Poynnaunt, John Brightwyne, and Henry Merreman— as witnesses to his testament. So here once more is indicated closeness and commonality in the drawing of the two instruments: three of these crucial functionaries are common to both Henry and Rye, indicating familial trust in them to carry out their wishes after they had died.

Probate of Henry's testament took place at Lambeth on Monday, 9 April 1459, and administration was given to Thomas Wymark, one of the nominated executors, although the court reserved the right to commit the charge also to William Fythian, when he appeared. Rye was nowhere mentioned; by this time she, too, had died. Wymark was ordered to render an inventory before the Assumption, 15 August. The following Sunday, 15 April, Rye's testament was proved, also at Lambeth. Neither executor was present, but administration was assigned to them through their proctor, Master John Alysaunder.[27] They

---

[27]The appearance of a proctor and of but one of Henry's executors is perhaps not unusual, given the difficulties of travel between Calais and England. As we shall see, the petitioners in the Chancery case note that the excursion is not an easy one.

were given a little longer to produce their inventory, which the court required by Michaelmas, 29 September.

These average testaments of two average people, neither very wealthy nor prominent, and valuable just because of such ordinariness, would usually be like so many others of their type, the sole witnesses to their principals' lives. Perhaps local guild or municipal records might show some traces of their activities, but by and large being copied into an episcopal probate register constitutes the extent of the record and the historian's resources. Yet with the Brownes we are fortunate—although the family perhaps was not—in that, while there is no evidence that the execution of Rye's testament caused difficulties, Henry's real property legacy did lead to some trouble. Between July 1460 and March 1465—and given the probate dates, more likely very early in that span[28]—the Brownes, or at least some of Henry's heirs and one of his executors, emerge once more in the record, this time in the Court of Chancery. The case was formally submitted in a bill sent to the chancellor—in reality, handed in at the Chancery—by eight people. Despite the considerable size of this group, the right claimed rested in the five women petitioners, as the bill itself later admits: Maude Curteys, Jane Curteys, Margaret Spevy (formerly Curteys), Jane Whitelokkes (formerly Curteys), and Agnes Edmond (formerly Bakers). The husbands of the latter three—John Spevy, John Whitelokkes, and John Edmond—do appear initially in the bill as petitioners along with their wives, but the right that the bill champions lies undoubtedly with the women, all clearly described as daughters and heirs of Agnes Curteys, who, they claim, was herself sister and heir of Henry

---

[28]It is not possible to be more precise as to the date of the case. Chancery bills are usually only datable by the tenure of the chancellor to whom they are addressed. In this case, Bishop George Neville of Exeter took up the office on 25 July 1460; he was provided to York on 15 Mar. 1465.

Browne.[29] There is an evident problem, then, in this description of Agnes Edmond.[30] It is clearly stated in the bill that she is a daughter of Agnes Curteys, yet in Henry's testament it is just as certain that she is Rye's niece, the daughter not of Agnes Curteys but of Vincent Bakers, Rye's brother.[31] Henry is insistent on this: he describes three of Agnes Curteys's children—John, Maude, and Margaret—as his nephew and nieces, and Agnes Edmond definitively as not of his, but Rye's, family. So, while Agnes Curteys's children certainly would have been Rye's nephew and nieces by marriage, Henry takes pains to distinguish the two sides of the family, and the Edmonds are undoubtedly on the Bakers's side. Chancery bill presentation, while in general accurate—for the court would not support faulty or false accounts[32]—was susceptible to honest error, or even to the occasional misrepresentation in order to strengthen the petitioner's case. Henry's testament, in comparison, is a close familial document, composed by one who knew well the relationships involved; it is to be trusted over the bill in this respect.

Like the testaments of Henry and Rye, the bill is unremarkable save in one aspect, to which we shall turn later. Its form and formulae are standard, and the core of its subject—an enfeoffment to use which, it is claimed, has gone awry—is shared with thousands of other Chancery suits of the fifteenth

---

[29]Agnes, we are told, is dead by the time the bill is brought.

[30]See the family tree above.

[31]*Cousin* is the term used in the documents, and can describe a variety of relationships, especially extended ones. The precise relationship can usually be determined from the context.

[32]See T. S. Haskett, "The Presentation of Cases in Medieval Chancery Bills," in *Legal History in the Making, Proceedings of the Ninth British Legal History Conference*, ed. William M. Gordon and T. D. Fergus (London, 1991), pp. 11–28.

century. Again, like most other Chancery cases, the bill is the sole documentation of the case: there are no writs, returns, interrogatories, or depositions to flesh out the substance or process of the case. It would be a rather ordinary complaint, were it not for the additional presence of the testaments and our resulting knowledge of the family involved. The petitioners—the Curteys women—claim that Henry Browne had purchased three messuages and a cottage in Calais, and that he had done so lately. The recentness of the acquisition might be critical to their case, for this would make it possible—although the argument would by no means be a strong one—for them to propose that it postdated the testament and therefore was intended to fall, and should be considered, outside the purview of the provisions Henry made for his real property. At the very least, they would need to argue that Henry intended this to be the case. We make here the reasonable assumption that the petitioners knew the contents of Henry's testament. They describe how Henry took joint possession of the messuages and cottage with Thomas Wymark who, it will be recalled, is one of his executors and the one who is given administration at probate; he is also one of Rye's witnesses. This arrangement was made, we are told, "of grete trust" which Henry had in Thomas, and although the phrase is highly formulaic, it had nonetheless necessarily to be a true contention if the bill were to succeed: the breach of trust was the central element of most Chancery cases, and especially so in ones such as this.

The arrangement the petitioners have described is a variant of what is commonly termed an *enfeoffment to use*, or simply a *use*. Here, Thomas is enfeoffed jointly with Henry to Henry's use; Henry's directions will, therefore, govern the disposition of the holding, and Thomas's joint enfeoffment is designed solely to make it easier—and in some circumstances, simply possible—for Henry to dispose of it, because Thomas already has a legal capacity to act with respect to the property, and will have the more once Henry is dead. The use was regularly employed in England from at least the late fourteenth century to evade the common law bar on conditional enfeoffments and especially the devolution of real property by last will or testament. Its employment as a customary evasion only came to an end when in the sixteenth century the Crown sought, for fiscal reasons, to end the practice and restore the old incidents of feudal tenure.[33] Until that time it was the Court of Chancery that upheld the unwritten promise central to the use, which would coerce the feoffee to do as his feoffor had instructed. While the common law did not recognize the trust that this promise represented, the chancellor did, and he enforced the maxim that promises ought to be kept, especially where the arrangement was clear and the promise was clothed. The clothing in the present case, as in most other use cases, was the accrued benefit to a third party, and this was expressed in terms of the intention that governed the use: the petitioners here describe how it was agreed that if Henry predeceased Thomas, then Thomas should enfeoff Henry's heirs in fee when so required. The petitioners note that Henry died without issue and that they, as daughters of Henry's sister Agnes, are his right heirs.

Their claim does raise the question of the rôle of the rest of the family with respect to this matter. What has happened to John Curteys, Agnes's sole son and one of Henry's two nephews on his side of the family? Further, while it seems certain that their mother, Agnes, is dead, there is no reason to believe that Henry's other sister, Jane Dunston, has died, and

---

[33]Baker, *Introduction*, pp. 283–95. The Statute of Uses (1536) abolished completely the power to devise, and was a financial success. Nonetheless, widespread opposition produced both the search for loopholes and demands for repeal, and in 1540 the Statute of Wills conferred for the first time on landowners the legal power to dispose of freeholds by will.

she would surely have as great a claim to being Henry's heir
as would the Curteys women. And what of Osberne Browne,
Henry's other nephew? His parents, too, are not associated
with the bill, although as they are named in neither testament
it is likely that they have died. So there are at least three other
people who have not just as good as, but better, claim to be
heirs of Henry Browne than do the petitioners in this bill.
What has apparently happened is that a section of the family—
here, Agnes Curteys's children along with Agnes Edmond,
who is masquerading as one of them—has taken action alone
on the pretext of a use constructed, they might claim, after
Henry had composed his testament and which, they must
claim, the feoffee Thomas Wymark has abrogated. If we
compare this claimed arrangement with Henry's real property
bequest in his testament, it is noteworthy that Wymark is there
nominated, along with William Fythian, to take charge of all
Henry's lands and tenements in and around Calais. Together,
they are instructed to use it first of all to support Rye, and
after her death to dispose of it for the good of the souls of
Henry and Rye, save for houses to go to John Curteys and
Osberne Browne who, it should be remembered, are not parties
to the Chancery case. Save for them, the Church of Our Lady,
and the Brotherhood of the Resurrection Table, there is no
provision whatsoever in Henry's testament for real property to
go anywhere other than to help Rye and himself. And further,
the five true petitioners are all well rewarded by one or both of
the testators, but like almost all the other beneficiaries, not in
real property. There is no apparent reason why Wymark and
Fythian should not have followed Henry's written instructions
encompassing all his real property, and this should, apparently,
have included the three messuages and cottage named in the
bill—unless, of course, Henry had made Wymark promise as
the bill relates, but there is, it would seem, no way of testing
this directly. Someone, as in every good detective story, is not

telling the whole truth; at the very least, someone has miscon-
strued or been misinformed. But who?

The petitioners, as expected, claim that they as right heirs
have often asked Wymark to enfeoff them, and this "according
to the said entente and last wyll" of Henry Browne. Again, the
phrase is both formulaic and absolutely necessary: the respondent is accused of failing repeatedly to grant their legitimate
request, which they state is in accord with Henry's intention as
expressed at the time the use was established. The mention of
Henry's last will ought not to deceive. It is a common phrase
and, unless there is unambiguous evidence to the contrary it
must not be taken to refer to a written testament or last will.
The present documents show this clearly: we have the testament,
and its provisions governing real property are fully at odds
with what the petitioners claim, so this cannot be the directive
to which they refer. Rather, they seek to emphasize that the
viva voce arrangements Henry made when he established the
use were never changed, and thus they represent the last and
therefore the valid expression of his will in this matter alone.
But the argument could not have ended here; at least, it should
not have, if the petitioners had any serious expectation of success, for there is one provision in Henry's testament that could
support rather than prejudice their case. It was noted above
that they emphasize the recentness of Henry's purchase of the
property in question, and it was suggested that they might try
to argue that this placed the use beyond the purview of the
testamentary direction. This was, nonetheless, noted as a weak
argument, especially if the purchase and use postdated the testament, in which case the testament's real property provisions
ought to supersede it. Yet if it did not, if Henry acquired the
property and established the use before his testament was written—and, it will be recalled, there was very little time between
its composition and his death in which he might have undertaken all this—then the petitioners ought to have cited the

instrument in support of their contention. For near the close of his testament, after the residue and remainder provisions, Henry insists strongly that his testamentary bequests in both real property and moveables "for barre not my bequestes before."

Now, this need not—and in the present case certainly should not—be taken to refer to an earlier written testament or last will. Were this so, such an instrument would appear at probate. Instead, the purpose is to exempt any distribution or arrangement already made at the time this testament was written. Here is where the petitioners should have rested one part of their case, inasmuch as Henry's testamentary disposition of real property would have to be addressed in their plea: Henry made the purchase and established the use before he made his testament, and it is this use—perhaps along with other dispositions—that is specifically referred to in this exemption. This by no means, of course, demonstrates that their description of the details of the use is true, or that the use even existed, but it does make it possible for their contentions to stand against the testament.

Having outlined their complaint, the petitioners, like all others in Chancery, have to ask for assistance, and as a preface to this, they here state that they have no remedy at common law. Once more, this is a required statement and one that must necessarily be true if a Chancery case were to proceed, let alone succeed: if there was a common law remedy and access to it was not blocked by poverty or by the power of an adversary, then Chancery would not take the case. This statement in place, the bill then moves to its prayer, where the petitioners ask specifically for help. Sometimes this is left in very general form, and only the chancellor's aid or succor is invoked. But here the prayer is more complex and is the one unusual element of the bill. The petitioners ask for a *subpoena*—the instrument that put most Chancery cases in motion—to compel the examination of Thomas Wymark before the king in Chancery.

This much again is stock and central: success in any Chancery case depended upon the parties telling their stories under oath before the court, so this powerful summons to the respondent was what petitioners most desired. The respondent might well appear, but certainly the king would not be present; rather, a Chancery master or other clerk would hear and record his sworn interrogation, although it was by no means impossible that the chancellor himself might hear the case. If the respondent could not come, or if some circumstance demanded investigation locally, arrangements would be made to take sworn depositions on site, and these would be returned into Chancery for determination. Here, such a request is made, but it is of irregular and intriguing form. It hinges on the petitioners, if not the respondent, being in Calais. At the very end of the bill they ask the chancellor to consider how difficult it is to travel between Calais and England, noting "the Inberdens auenture and passage ouer the see." Because of this, they have asked him for a second writ, a *dedimus potestatem*, which is to be sent to Calais and by force of which the parties to the case are to be examined. This raises one query: the previous and standard request for the subpoena asked to have Wymark examined in Chancery, yet the *dedimus potestatem* appears to be based on the expectation that all the parties—petitioners and respondent, and perhaps even witnesses—are in Calais. It could be argued that if the bill was presented as soon as possible after the 9 April 1459 probate of Henry's will, when Wymark might still have been present near Lambeth, the petitioners may have expected that there was a good possibility that he could be summoned into Chancery before returning to Calais. In such a hope they would not have been misled. In cases where writs have survived it is evident that Chancery did move swiftly, and in some instances the appearance of respondents is very soon after the submission of the bill. Even the specifics of some bill prayers show that petitioners assumed it was possible for their adversaries to be brought into Chancery within a very few weeks, even days, of submitting their bills.[34] Nonetheless, this bill is addressed to the bishop of Exeter, which means that by the time it was submitted at least fifteen months had passed since the probate of Henry's testament.[35]

Surely Wymark would not have been detained so long simply to deal with the matter; he was—although executors could be slow about it—to have returned an inventory to the court by the middle of August 1459. Of course, it is possible that Wymark was a resident of England and therefore accessible to the Chancery regularly, but his appearance as a witness to Rye's testament and his role in the disposition of Henry's real property and residue argue against this. It would seem that Wymark was indeed a resident of Calais, and that while the petitioners follow regular form in asking for a subpoena to bring him into Chancery, they expect that he will be examined in situ, in Calais. They do ask that the *dedimus potestatem* be granted "vppon" the subpoena, perhaps indicating a progression from the regular to the necessary in the circumstances of their case, but one way or the other the petitioners wanted to ensure the sworn examination of their adversary.

---

[34] A few examples may be noted, these coming from C 1 Bundle 9. The case in nos. 1–2 saw the bill submitted on 2 Nov. 1438, with the Chancery examination of the respondent 15 days later. Once a writ was issued, examination upon it could be very swift (nos. 87–88: writ 10 Oct. 1436, examination 12 Nov.), or take a little longer (nos. 4–6: writ 2 Feb. 1443, examination 3 May). When composing their bills, petitioners seem to have expected the court to act quickly. While an instance may be cited where almost instantaneous response was asked for (no. 28), where a week was deemed to be sufficient (no. 151), or rather longer—eight months—was expected (no. 3b), average expectation in the few bills that specify a date for the examination of the respondent was about three months (nos. 74, 161, 162, 204).

[35] Recall that probate was in Apr. 1459; the bishop of Exeter took up the chancellorship in July 1460.

A *dedimus potestatem* could not be issued undirected: it had to be addressed to someone, or at least to some office. In this provision the bill demonstrates an interesting history, for it was altered, most probably after its initial submission. When it was first written, the petitioners asked for the writ to be directed to William Claxton and Lowes Lyman, presumably residents of Calais. Neither is given occupation, rank, or title, which raises the possibility that they were named as men sympathetic to the petitioners' case, although this can but be suggested. On review, however, these men were deemed to be either insufficient to the task, or perhaps suspect as nominees of only one of the parties to the case. The matter at issue was a serious one, and either those advising the petitioners, or more probably the court itself, sought to make proper arrangement for the taking of important testimony, which had to be fair and reliable both in its gathering and in its transmission, and added interlinearly two other people. An official was needed, and so the mayor of Calais, either the one at the time the writ was to be drawn or whoever might occupy the office when the writ arrived, was included. This "whoever" clause was a common and effective one, for if only the incumbent were named and he should leave office or die before the instrument arrived, process could come to a halt while a new writ was sought in the name of the new official, whereas in the present case the mayor, whoever he might be, was to act. A second name was also added, John Byngham. Who he was we are not told, but he, the mayor, and the two previously-mentioned men were deemed to be an appropriate panel by whom the parties to the case were to be examined: the Curteys women with the one impostor, Wymark if he had not been in Chancery already, and possible witnesses or others who might claim an interest in the matter.

Later in the bill it is asked that the panel certify its examinations "with all other concernyng the premyssez" into the

Chancery, and that this be done either jointly or severally.[36] This is to be expected, as the court in using the *dedimus potestatem* is seeking information upon which it might base its judgment, and thus usually the writ requires simply the return of that information. Yet there is the mention of "all other," and the explanation seems to lie in a short phrase just before the requirement of the sealing, for the work of the panel was not to end with the interrogations: "And aftyr all suche examynacioun doon and had[,] to doo and execute that trouthe and conscience will require in that behalfe." The petitioners are seeking authority for the panel not just to examine; once the facts of the case are before them they want the mayor, Claxton, Byngham, and Lyman to make a decision based upon truth and conscience. These determining principles are standard to Chancery cases, and conscience especially is the motivating element in all of the activity of the court. But it is rare to see the suggestion that an examining panel, containing no court officers or clerks, be charged to make a determination. Even for the mayor this would be an irregular assignment, despite his familiarity with the contracts and trusts of urban and mercantile law. Perhaps this was an attempt by the petitioners to see the case removed entirely to Calais, something that would be especially important for them if Wymark were resident, even temporarily, in England. It is followed immediately by the sealing request—presumably now to include both facts and judgment, either for Chancery's use or its approval[37]—and then

---

[36]This seems to be the meaning of the phrase "vnder their sealez or ich of theyre seales," of which the last five words are interlined to bring the request in line with the earlier emendation that added the two new names. Perhaps this is due to the mayor now being involved, as his seal of office would carry a distinct and greater weight than the personal seals of the others.

[37]This is a crucial point. Chancery was not a court of record; it judged each case on its own merits on the basis of conscience and therefore did not need

by the request for the chancellor's consideration of the difficulties of travel. Of the case and its principals, and of the Brownes and Bakerses, for the present we know nothing further.

What, then, do these three instruments offer the researcher? First and foremost, they provide context for one another, allowing us to build a more detailed family structure for the people involved than is usual. From this we can assess patterns of familial responsibility, and perhaps even affection, and see the methods of managing family resources employed over generations. The two testaments, like all of their kind, are especially useful in this regard, more so coming as they do from a husband and wife. But it is the Chancery bill that permits us to see beyond the simple provisions of the testators and the structure of their family. The pursuit of the bill perhaps raises more questions than it answers, but it does cast new light upon the activity of Thomas Wymark, a trusted friend of both Henry and Rye Browne, a man who was to manage Henry's real property in support of his widow and to dispose of his residue in concert with her as executrix, who became Henry's executor and administrator, who was a beneficiary of and witness for Rye, yet whom, if the petitioners are right, Henry ought not to have

---

—indeed, could not have—a permanent record of its activities to serve as precedent. The only reason that the bills and other ancillary documents survive is the tendency of bureaucracies not to sort and dispose of material. Normally, then, information taken pursuant to a *dedimus potestatem* was returned to the court to be used in the hearing of the case, and then—if the historian is fortunate—thrown in a bin with the bill to await the unexpected sorting and classification by H. C. Maxwell-Lyte's associates in the PRO only at the turn of the present century; the alternative fate of the instrument was destruction, purposefully or by neglect. So, in the present case the sealed return upon the writ would not have been for record purposes, and thus ratification of the panel's judgment, were Chancery to allow these petitioners' very irregular request, or the rendering of judgment by Chancery as the usual course, would be intended.

trusted to fulfill the promise he made as a feoffee to use. We
are also shown that while Rye and Henry were at pains to provide something, however small, for most if not all of their living
family members on both sides, this did not preclude division
and perhaps even conniving on the part of at least one group.

The Curteys women—real and supposed—form a distinct
subgroup within the larger family, probably by their own
design and certainly by their exclusion from any real property
bequests. If this is so, it is intriguing that what amounts to one
of the smallest sections in Henry's testament was, by omitting
them as beneficiaries in real property, the cause of the Chancery case. And even with such an exclusion these women had
not done badly by Henry and Rye: Maude Curteys and Agnes
Edmond each received 40s. from Henry and silver from Rye;
Margaret Spevy also received 40s. from Henry, and both silver
and clothing from Rye; Jane Whitelokkes and Jane Curteys
each received silver from Rye. Interestingly enough, the three
husbands who appear at the opening of the bill—John Spevy,
John Whitelokkes, and John Edmond—themselves had received
nothing from either Henry or Rye. The suggestion might, then,
be made that this case is the result of scheming by disappointed or opportunistic in-laws, here nephews-in-law, and that
while the right claimed in the bill rests with the Curteys
women as Henry's heirs, it was perhaps their husbands who
launched the case in the hope of securing for themselves a
small portion of the real property that had been Henry's. It
may be simple coincidence that there are three husbands and
three messuages at issue in the bill; the presence of the cottage
might be the cause of some debate, should the case ever prove
successful. But it must be remembered that the bill does ask for
examination of all the parties, the women included, and one
must ask whether they would perjure themselves in support of
a false claim, or even be willing to accede to the abrogation of
their uncle's intentions. Did they even know at this point that

the case had been submitted? By this point, however, we are deeply into the speculative. In the end, it must be said that while much reliable information is provided by these two testaments and the Chancery bill, if one wishes to come to some conclusion concerning the action of the Curteys women, of their menfolk, and of the trustworthiness of Thomas Wymark, the answers can but be subjective, even if they are informed. To judge by Henry's and Rye's trust of and reliance upon Thomas Wymark, it is hard to conclude that they misjudged as badly as the promoters of the Chancery bill would suggest.

Yet the best of relationships can sour or break down under the temptation of personal gain; executors have been known to look first to their own interests; and feoffees to uses are, as the mass of Court of Chancery litigation attests, constantly being brought to task for misfeasance. This writer would like to think that in this case the stronger temptation was found on the side of some of those Henry and Rye left behind, and if the Curteys women are not to be accounted avaricious, their husbands might well be. Whether or not Michael Sheehan would have been able to shed some light upon these matters cannot be known, but certainly his wise counsel would have been sought in the exploration of these many questions. After all, it must be admitted that it is largely owing to his legacy that they have been asked in the first place.

APPENDIX A

BEQUESTS AND DIRECTIONS OF HENRY BROWNE	*BEQUESTS AND DIRECTIONS OF RYE BROWNE*
BURGESS AND CHANDLER OF CALAIS	WIDOW OF HENRY BROWNE

PLACE AND DATE

(Made at Calais, 17 October 1458)

PLACE AND DATE

(Made at Calais, 1 February 1459)
(MS *1458*)

SOUL AND BODY

His soul: to God, the Blessed Virgin, and all the heavenly company

His body: to be buried in the south side of Our Lady's Church

SOUL AND BODY

Her soul: to God her former and maker, the Blessed Virgin, and all the heavenly company

Her body: to be buried in the south aisle of Our Lady's Church, beside Henry

EXEQUIES

The Carmelite Friars [at Our Lady's]: 20s., obit

A priest [Carmelite?]: to sing for him for a half year at the Trinity Altar [at Our Lady's]

Anniversary: 20s., at his burial and thereafter every year

EXEQUIES

The Carmelite Friars [at Our Lady's]: 20s., obit

A priest [Carmelite?]: after her debts are paid, to sing for her and Harry for one year [at Our Lady's]

CHURCHES

CHURCHES

The church at Coulogne (MS *Colne*): 3s. 4d., churchwork

The church at Guînes (MS *Guynes*): 6s. 8d., churchwork

The church at Marck (MS *Mark*): 3s. 4d., churchwork

The church of St. Nicholas [Calais?]: 6s. 8d., to the Chapel of St. Thomas; 6s. 8d., churchwork

The church at Marck (MS *Mark*): 3s. 4d., churchwork

The church of Our Lady [Calais]: 6s. 8d., to the high altar for neglected offerings; 10s., from a parcel [of real property] that the church holds from him [a grant with retention of revenue?]; lead, piece of, to churchwork, approximately 7 hundredweight; "Brooke" [a real property], his parcel therein, which the church holds from him [originally a grant with retention of revenue?]

The church of St. Peter [Calais?]: 13s. 4d., churchwork

The church of Our Lady [Calais]: 3s. 4d., to the high altar for neglected tithes and offerings; 6s. 8d., churchwork

CONFRATERNITIES

The Brotherhood of St. Barbara, at Our Lady's (MS *seint Mary chirch*), Calais: 6s. 8d.

The maison Dieu (MS *mesyndewe*) [Calais?]: feather bed; bolster; sheets, 1 pair; coverlet

The [Brotherhood of the] Resurrection at St. Michael's Church, [Calais]: 3s. 4d.

The [Brotherhood of the] Trinity Table at Our Lady's (MS *St. Mary's Church*), Calais: 6s. 8d. per year, for the Alms of the Table, to be taken from a rented Calais tenement, and collected at every Annunciation and Michaelmas by Nicholas of the Mynte,

CONFRATERNITIES

The Brotherhood of St. Anne "in the Fieres" [at Our Lady's?]: 3s. 4d.

The Brotherhood of St. Barbara, at Our Lady's: 3s. 4d.

The Brotherhood of Our Lady Gate [at Our Lady's?]: 20d.

The Brotherhood of the Resurrection [at St. Michael's church, Calais]: 10s., for Rye and Harry to be prayed for daily*

[*They are to "besett in the Resurreccioun table" to be prayed for daily—perhaps either a daily remembrance at the confraternity's table for distributing charity or enrollment in its record of members and benefactors. In the latter case,

Roger Morecroft, and Alderman Richard Feny, present wardens of the table, and their successors forever; if the Table's almsgiving ceases, the sum is to be divided among the poor

REAL PROPERTY

Land and tenements both in and outside of Calais:

given to *Thomas Wymark* and *William Fythian* for support of *Rye*; after her death, disposal of for *his and Rye's souls*

exceptions: after Rye's death, to *Osberne Browne*, his cousin [nephew], one house (now occupied by Laynard Barbour); to *John Curteys*, his cousin [nephew], one house (formerly owned by John Sought, on the street leading to St. Peter's)

FAMILY

remembrance on one's anniversary might be more usual than a daily regimen.]

FAMILY

Jane Bakers, her sister: £10, ¼ share of £40 remaining after debts paid and her and Henry's testaments fulfilled (shared with brother Vincent Bakers, Jane Dunston, and Jane Dunston's sister's children); girdle, blue fringed; mazer, little covered; household goods not bequeathed, portion of ½ (shared with Vincent Cherkesson)

Vincent [Bakers], her brother: £10, ¼ share of £40 remaining after debts paid and her and Henry's testaments fulfilled (shared with sister Jane Bakers, Jane Dunston, and Jane Dunston's sister's children); girdle, plain blue man's

Vincent [Bakers] *and Jane Bakers*: cups, 2 standing silver with no covers, one with a gilt foot; goblets, 2 silver; spoons, 4 silver

Vincent's [Bakers's] *wife* [her sister-in-law]: girdle, plain red

Osberne Browne [Henry's cousin (nephew)]: salt cellars, 2 round silver covered; piece, little pounced

Jane Curteys [Henry's cousin (niece)]: cup, silver standing covered, with a hart above; salt cellar, silver; goblet, silver covered; spoons, 6

John Curteys, his cousin [nephew]: 100s., if he will be governed and ruled by Rye

John Curteys [Henry's cousin (nephew)]: instruments and equipment that belong to his craft; gown, murrey furred with ficheux, with a scarlet hood; girdle, harnessed, with a white band; bed, the great; pillows, 2; sheets, 2 pairs

Maude [Curteys], his cousin [niece]: 40s., for her marriage

Maude Curteys [Henry's cousin (niece)]: piece, flat; goblet, silver; spoon, silver

Jane Dunston, his sister: 40s.

Jane Dunston (also MS *Dunstons, Donston*) [Henry's sister]: £10, ¼ share of £40 remaining after debts paid and her and Henry's testaments fulfilled (shared with Jane Bakers, Vincent Bakers, and her sister's children); 7 nobles*; 20d., for the redemption of pawned jewelry; gown, musterdevillers with gray fur; kirtle, little red; silver, new flat piece of; goblet, silver covered; spoons, 2 silver; house-

[*The equivalency generally given for one noble is 6s. 8d., thus here £2 6s. 8d.]

hold goods not bequeathed, ¼ (shared with her sister's children)
Jane Dunston's sister's children [Henry's "cousins" (nephews/ nieces), e.g., Agnes Curteys's children]: £10, ¼ share of £40 remaining after debts paid and her and Henry's testaments fulfilled (shared with sister Jane Bakers, Vincent Bakers, and Jane Dunston); household goods not bequeathed, ¼ (shared with Jane Dunston)
John Dunston (MS *Donston*) [Henry's brother-in-law]: gown, musterdevillers furred with beaver; doublet, Henry's best

Agnes Edmond (MS *Edmonde*), Rye's cousin [niece]: 40s.

Agnes Edmond [her cousin (niece)]: cup, silver standing with a gilt foot; goblet, silver; spoon, silver

Margaret Spevy, his cousin [niece]: 40s.

Margaret Spevy, (also MS *Spevies wife*) [Henry's cousin (niece)]: gown, sanguine; kirtle, sanguine; cup, silver standing; goblet; spoon, silver
Jane Whitelokkes [Henry's cousin (niece)]: piece, flat with a bell in the covering; goblet, silver; spoon, silver

SERVANTS

Jane Climyn, his servant: 100s., for her marriage if she governs herself well
Fuller, his servant: 6s. 8d.
John Nokys, his servant: 6s. 8d.

SERVANTS

Thomasina, her servant: gown, furred with black sheepskin; kirtle, red

Nicholas Trippe, his servant; 20s.

Clays Trippe, her servant: gown, musterdevillers lined with frise

FRIENDS
(NO SPECIFIED RELATIONSHIP)

FRIENDS
(NO SPECIFIED RELATIONSHIP)

Henry Cherkisson: silver, flat piece

Vincent Cherkesson: gown, russet furred with ficheux; household goods not bequeathed, portion of ½ (shared with Jane Bakers)

Elsabeth Cornelys: 100s., for her marriage if she governs herself well

Jane Durham (MS *Dourham*): girdle, little blue

Jane Elmynes and *Elizabeth More-mannes*: bodice, best coral

Jane Elmynes's daughter: gown, best; girdle, best; bed, blue hanging, with couch; sheets, 2 pairs; pillows, 2; boardcloths, 2; washing towel; napkins, 6; basin and laver; chafer; silver, flat piece; vessels, 6, with 2 chargers

Elizabeth Moremannes: piece, pounced

Katherine Moremannes: girdle, sanguine fringed; silver, flat piece

Bartholomew Pressour's wife: girdle, plain blue; piece, pounced; mazer, with a gilt band

Agnes Strale, daughter of Nicholas Strale: 40s., for her marriage

Agnes Strale: powder box, silver

BUSINESS ASSOCIATE
Daniel Damkynson of the Wale, his apprentice: £4, if he serves out his apprenticeship

PEOPLE ASSOCIATED
WITH THE TESTAMENT
Henry Durham (also MS *Dourham*)
(executor): salt cellar, silver
covered
William Fythian (MS *Fydian, Fyd-
yan*) (witness): silver, flat piece
Thomas Wardon (executor): mazer,
large broken gilt
Thomas Wymark (witness): goblet,
gilt covered standing

DEBTS
To be paid

RESIDUE

RESIDUE

To Rye for payment of debts
Remainder disposed of by Rye with
advice of Thomas Wymark and
William Fythian

Administration as seems best to
executors

CAVEAT
All the preceding bequests are not to
prejudice arrangements already made.

EXECUTORS
(13s. 4d. to each)
Rye (principal)

EXECUTORS

Thomas Wymark

Thomas Wardon

William Fythian

Henry Durham

OVERSEER
(13s. 4d.)
Thomas   Wardon,   alderman   [of
Calais]

WITNESSES

John Brightwyne

Henry Merreman
Geoffrey Poynnaunt, notary

Others, not named

PROBATE
9 April 1459, at Lambeth
Administration granted to Thomas
Wymark

Inventory before the Assumption
next
Reservation of committal to William
Fythian, when he comes

WITNESSES
Robert Abraham, chaplain

William Fythian (MS *Fidyan*)

Thomas Wymark
Others, not named

PROBATE
15 April 1459, at Lambeth
Administration granted to the named
executors *per* Master John Alysaunder, proctor
Inventory before Michaelmas next

APPENDIX B

Testament of Henry Browne[38]

PRO, London, PROB 11/4 (*Reg. Stokton*), fol. 124r–v

In the name of God Amen the xvij day of October, the yere of our lord God M^l CCCC lviij^{ty} I Herry Browne Chaundeler and burgeis of Caleis devise this my present testament and last wil in this wise. First I commende my soule to almyghty God and our blissid Lady seint Mary and to alle the blissid company of hevin. And my body to be buried in the south side of oure Lady Chirch Item I bequeth to the High Auter for myne offeringes for gotyn vj s. viij d. Item I bequeth to the Chirch werk of our Lady a pece of lede, vij^C or there abowte And also all the parcell of Brooke that canne be founde due to me of the said Chirch and x s. of money of the parcell of the Chirch þat is owing me. Also I geve and bequeth vnto Nicholas of the Mynte Roger Morecroft and Richard Feny Alderman wardeyns of the Trinite table in seint Marys Chirch of Caleys a yerely Rent of vj s. viij d. to be takynne and levyed by the said wardeyns nowe being, and that for the tyme shulbe of myne heires and assignees of and oute of a tenement callid the Trane wherein dwellith nowe Gerard Goldsmyth at ij termes of the yer that is to say at the fest of the Annunciacioun of our lady, And at the fest of Seint Michell the Archanigill, To haue and to hold the said yerely rent of vj s. viij d. to the said Nicholas of the Mynte Roger Morecroft and Richard Feny nowe wardeyns and to theim that in tyme to come shalbe wardeins foreuermore in sustentacioun and Releving of the Almes of the said Trinite table yerely during the vppeholding of the said Almesse And if so be that the said Almes faille that thenne the said Annuell Rent to be devidid vnto pouer people for euermore. Item I bequeth to the frere[39] Carmes of the said towne of Caleis to bringe me to the Erthe xx s. Item I bequeth to the mesyndewe a Fethirbed a bolster a pair shetis and a couerlit. Item I bequeth vnto the Resurreccioun at seint Michaels

---

[38]In the editions no modern punctuation has been added, and the MS orthography and morphology have been maintained.

[39]Interlined.

Chirch[40] iij s. iiij d. Item I bequeth vnto the Chapell of seint Thomas at seint Nicholas Chirch[41] to be levied of suche duetees as the seid Chirch oueth me vj s. viij d. Item I bequeth to the chirch werk of seint Nicholas vj s. viij d. Item I bequeth to the chirch werk of seint Peters[42] xiij s. iiij d. Item I bequeth to the chirch werk of Mark[43] iij s. iiij d. Item I bequeth to the chirch werk of Guynes[44] vj s. viij d. Item I bequeth to the brethered of seint Barbara of seint Mary chirch vj s. viij d. Item I bequeth to Agnes my wifes Cousin the wife of John Edmonde xl s. Item to Margaret Spevy my Cousin xl s. Item I bequeth to my Suster Jane Dunston xl s. Item I bequeth to John Curteys my Cousin C s. with that he be of goode gouernaunce and wele Rewlid to my wife. Item I bequeth to Mawde my cousin to hir mariage xl s. Item I bequeth to Jane Climyn my seruaunt toward hir mariage and she goueren hir wele C s. Item I bequeth to Elsabeth Cornelys mariage and she gouern hir wele 100 s. Item I bequeth to Agnes the doughter of Nicholas Strale to hir mariage xl s. Item I bequeth to my seruaunt Nicholas Trippe xx s. Item I bequeth to my seruaunt John Nokys vj s. viij d. Item I bequeth to my seruaunt Fuller vj s. viij d. Item I bequeth to Dnayell[45] [fol. 124v] Damkyn-son of the Wale my preyntis iiij li. with that he serve out his termes. Item I wol that there be ordeyned a prest to singe for me for half yere atte the Trinite Auter. Item I wol that there be ordeyned for me at my burying moneth mynde and tweluemonth mynde at euery tyme xx s. Item I bequeth all my landes and tenementes with all ther ap-portenaunces Lying within the towne of Caleys and without vnto

---

[40]Again, presumably in Calais but not found. There is a rue Saint-Michel in the old city, near Notre Dame.

[41]A church presumably in Calais, but not identified.

[42]Once more, presumably in Calais, but not positively identified. There is a Church of St. Pierre in the modern suburb of Saint-Pierre-lès-Calais, which was built in the mid-19th century. Whether an earlier church of the same dedication is referred to here, or another of the same name in the old city, is uncertain.

[43]Marck, a village about 10 km east of Calais, on the road to Dunkerque.

[44]Guînes, a town 10 km south of Calais.

[45]*Recte* Danyell.

Thomas Wymark and William Rythian,[46] and they for to se that Rye
my wife haue the Revenues and profittes thereof terme of hir life.
And aftre the deceasse of my saide wife to be disposid for me and
hir as the said Thomas and William shall seme best. Except I will
þat Osberne Browne my Cousin haue the hows that Laynard Barbour
dwellith nowe in, to him and to his heyres aftre the deceasse of Rye
my wife, foreuermor. Item I bequeth to John Curteys my Cousin a
hows with theapportenaunce lying in the way toward seint Petris
sumtyme longing to John Sought to him and to his heires aftre the
deceasse of Rye my wife. The Residue of all my other goodes meve-
able and vnmeveable whereso euer that they be founde I geve and
bequeth vnto Rye my wife to se that my dettes be fully paied and to
dispose the Remenaunt as she shall seme best by thaduise of the said
Thomas Wymark and William Fythian shall seme best. Prouided
allway that this gift and bequeth of my forsaid londes and tenementes, and my moveable goodes as is befor rehersid for barre not
my bequestes before And of this my present testament and last will I
make and ordeyne Rye my wife principall executrix, and with hir
Thomas Wymark and William Fythian Executours. And Thomas
Wardon Alderman overseer And I bequeth to eueriche of theim for
ther labour xiij s. iiij d. Wytnes Gefferey Poynnaunt Notarye John
Brightwyne Herry Merreman and other.

Probatum fuit suprascriptum testamentum apud Lamebith', Nono die
mensis Aprilis Anno domini Millesimo quadringentesimo quinquagesimo nono, ac approbatum etc. Et commissa sunt administracio etc.
Thome Wymark vni executori etc. de bene et fideliter administrando
etc. Ac de pleno et fideli Inuentario etc. citra festum Assumpcionis
beate Marie virginis etc. Necnon de fideli compoto calculo etc. in
debita iuris forma iuratis. Reservata potestate committendi etc.
Willelmo Fythian alteri executori cum venerit etc. Approbacione et
insinuacione presens per quemcunque Iudicem etc.

---

[46]*Recte* Fythian.

APPENDIX C

Testament of Rye Browne

PRO, London, PROB 11/4 (*Reg. Stokton*), fol. 125r–v

In the name of God Amen, the first day of the moneth of Feverer, the yere of our lord God M^l CCCC Lviij I Rye Browne the vidue of Herry Browne Burgeis of the Towne of Caleis, being in good mynde make ordeyne and devise my present testament and last will in this maner and forme. First I bequeth my soule to God Almyghti my fourmore and my maker and till his moder seint Mary and to alle the holy company of hevin, my body to be buried in the south Ile of our lady Chirch beside my housbond. Item I bequeth to the high Auter of the said chirch for my tithes forgoten and offeringes necligently iij s. iiij d. Item I bequeth to the Chirch werk of the said Chirch vj s. viij d. Item to the Brotherede of seint Barbara in the same chirch iij s. iiij d. Item I bequeth to the Frere Carmys to be at myn obite and termentes xx s. Item to the brethered of seint Anne in the Fieres iij s. iiij d. Item to the brethered of the Resurreccioun vndir this condicioun that my housband Herry Browne and I besett in the Resurreccioun table to be daily prayed fore x s. Item to the brethered of our Lady Gate xx d. Item to the Chirch werk of Mark iij s. iiij d. Item to the Chirch werk of Colne[47] iij s. iiij d. Item I bequeth to Jane Elmynes doughter my best gowne and my best girdill an hanging bed of blewe with the couche as it standith ij paire of shetis, ij pillowes ij bordclothes and a wasshingtowell vj Napkins a basin and a Lavour a Chafer a Flat pece of siluer a half dosin vessell with ij chargeours Item I bequeth to Jane Donston a mustred villers gowne firrd with gray and a litill kirtill of Red vij nobles and xx d. for certayne Jowell that Lyen to wedde for the said Jane Dunston Item I bequeth to Spevies wife a sangueyn gowne and a sangwein kyrtyll. Item I wol that John Curteys haue all the instrumentes and habilementes that arn longing to his Crauft bothe for wax and white light. Item to the said John Curteys a murrey gowne furrid with Fichux and a Skarlet hoode and the grete bed that stondith a boue with ij pelowes and ij pair of Shetis a herneysid girdill with a white coors Item I

---

[47]Coulogne, a village less than 2 km south of Calais.

bequeth to Thomasin my seruaunt a gowne furred with blak bouge
and a Red kirtill Item to John Donston a gowne of musterdevilers
furred with bever and his[48] best doubelet Item to Clays Trippe my
seruaunt a musterdevilers gowne Lyned with Frise Item to Vincent
Cherkesson a Russett gowne furred with Ficheuux Item to my suster
Jane Bakers my blewe frengid girdill. Item to Vincent my brother
and to Jane my suster ij standing cuppis of siluer vncouered, the one
with a gilt fote. Item to the said Johanne[49] Bakers a Lytill Couered
maser. Item to Vincent and to the said Jane ij Goblettis of siluer.
Item to the said Vincent and to the said Jane iiij siluer spones Item I
bequeth to Katerine Moremannes my Sangweyn girdill frengid and a
flat piece of siluer Item I bequeth to Elizabeth hir doughter a
pounced pece. Item I bequeth to Vincentys wyfe my playne red
girdill. Item to Bartholomewe Pressours wife a playn blewe girdill a
pounced pece and a maser with a gilt bonde Item to Vincent my
brother a playne blewe mannys girdill. Item I bequeth to Johanne
Dourham a Litill blewe girdill Item to Henry Dourham a salt saler of
siluer Couered Item to Jane Elmynes and Elizabeth Moremannes my
best corall bodys Item to Agnes Edmond a standing cuppe of siluer
with a gilt fote a gobelett of siluer and a siluer spone. Item to
Margaret Spevy a standing cuppe of siluer a gobelett and a spone of
siluer. Item I bequeth to Jane Whitelokkes a Flat pece couered with
a bell in the Coueryng a gobelett of siluer and a siluer spoone. Item
I bequeth to Johanne Curteys a Standing Cuppe of siluer couered
with an hert a boven a salt salier of siluer couered a gobelett of
siluer and vj spones. Item to Jane Donston a newe Flat pece of siluer
a gobelett of siluer couered and ij siluer spones Item to Maude
Curteys a Flat pece and a gobelett of siluer and a siluer spone. Item
to Herry Cherkisson a Flat pece of siluer. Item to Thomas Wardon a
grete maser gilt and brokin. Item to Thomas Wymark a standing
gobelett couered and gilt. Item to William Fydian a Flat pece of
siluer. Item to Agnes Strale a powder boxe of siluer. Item to Osberne
Browne ij Rounde salt salers of siluer couered and a litill pounced
pece Item I will that aftre my dettes been paied that ther be a prest

---

[48]Presumably, Henry's.

[49]*Read* Jane.

founde synging for my housband and for me a yer during. Item all stuffe of houshold vnbequethin the oon half to be devided vnto Vincent Cherkesson and to Jane my Suster And the other half eqally to be devided to Jane Dunstons and to hir[50] sustir Childern by the advice [fol. 125v] of myn Executours. Item I will that the summe of xl li. sterling aftre my dettes paied and bequestes and all thinges fulfillid aftre the tenure of my husbandes testament and myne That thenne þe said summe of xl li. sterling shall eqally be devidid by twix my brothir Vincent and Jane my suster and Jane Dunstons and hir susters Childern by thadvice of my said executours. The residue of alle my goodes mcvcable and vnmeveable I wol that myne executours haue the administracioun therof, And that they dispose it for me as for my husband as it shall seme theim best. And to this my last wil and testament I make and ordeyne myn executours Thomas Wardon and Herry Durham. In witnes and testamonies of this my present testament and last will being present sir Robert Abraham Chapeleyn Thomas Wymark William Fidyan and other moo. Made and yevin at Caleis the yere and the day abouesaid.

Probatum fuit suprascriptum testamentum apud Lamebith' quintodecimo die mensis Aprilis Anno domini Millesimo quadringentesimo quinquagesimo nono. Et commissa fuit administracio etc. executoribus in dicto testamento nominatis in persona magistri Johannis Alysaunder procuratoris etc. De bene et fideliter administrando etc. Ac de pleno et fideli Iuentario etc. citra festum sancti Michaelis Archangeli proximum exhibendo necnon de fideli compoto calculo siue Raciocinio etc. in debita Iuris forma iuratis. Approbacione et insinuacione etc. Reprobatis cassatis et annullatis etc.

---

[50]Given the following direction of a portion of £40 to the same persons, it appears that it is Jane Dunston's sister's children who are the intended beneficiaries here.

APPENDIX D

Spevy, Spevy, Edmond, Edmond, Whitelokkes, Whitelokkes, Curteys,
Curteys v Wymark
PRO, London, C 1/28, no. 53

To the right reuerent Fader in God the Bysshop of Excestr' and
Chaunceler of Englond

Mekely besechyn youre good and gracious lordship John Spevy and
Margaret his wyf John Edmond and Agnes his wyf John Whitlok and
Jane his wyf Jane Curteys and Maud Curteys Cosyns and heirez vn
to on Henry Broune late of Cales chaundeler for asmoche as the said
Henry Broune late purchased thre mesuages and a cotage with
thappurtenaunce in the said Tovne of Cales and the [said][51] Henry
Broune of grete trust toke astate of the said thre mesuages and
cotage to hym and to on Thomas Wymark of Cales ioyntly to theym
and to their heirez in fee for euer to that entente that yef the said[52]
Henry died and the said Thomas Wymark ouerlyvyd that thenne the
said Thomas shuld of and in the said thre mesuages and cotage after
the descesse of the said Henry enfeoffe the said heirez of the said
Henry in fee for euer whenne he wer therto by them requyryd and
the said Henry dyed withoute issue of his body begotyn after whos
decesse your said besechers as Cosyns and heirez vn to the said
Henry That is to say the said Margaret wyf of the said John Spevy
Agnes the wyf of the said John Edmond Jane the wyf of the said
John Whitlok Jane Curteys and Maud Curteys a foresaid as
doughters to oon Agnes Curteys nowe dede late Sustir and heir vn to
the said Henry Broune haue ofte tymes requyred the said Thomas
Wymark to enfeffe your said suppliauntez in fee accordyng to the
said entente and last wyll of the said Henry Broune of and in the
said thre mesuages and Cotage withappurtenaunce and that to do he
vtterly refusyth Wherefor please it youre said good and gracious
lordship thes premyssez to consider and þat your said besechers may

---

[51]MS torn.

[52]Interlined.

haue noon remedy by the cours of the Comen lawe of this lond to graunt a writt sub pena to be directyd vn to the said Thomas Wymark comaundyng hym to appere by fore the kyng oure soueraigne lord in his Chauncery[53] atte a certeyn day by you to be lymytted, and there to be examyned in the premyssez And theruppon that your said lordship will graunte a writte of dedimus potestatem vppon the said wrytt of sub pena to be directed vn to the mayre of Caleys that now is or for the terme shalbe[54] William Claxton John Byngham[55] and Lowes Lyman and to eueriche of theym[56] they to call by fore them the said parties ther to examyn them and eueryche of them in the said mater as it is aforc rchersyd And aftyr all suche examynacioun doon and had to doo and execute that trouthe and conscience will require in that behalfe And thenne the said mayre William John Byngham and Lowes[57] to certyfye in to the said Chauncerye the said examynacioun with all other concernyng the premyssez vnder their sealez or ich of theyre sealez[58] consyderyng gracious lord the Inberdens auenture and passage ouer the see fro the said Tovne of Cales in to Englond and thedir a gayn And your said besechers shall pray to God for you.

Plegii de prosequendo   Johannes Methelay ⎤
                                                              ⎥ de London' Gentilmen
                         Johannes Toller   ⎦

---

[53]Followed by filler over erasure.

[54]*the mayre . . . shalbe* interlined.

[55]*John Byngham* interlined.

[56]*and to . . . theym* interlined.

[57]*mayre, John Byngham* interlined.

[58]*or . . . seales* interlined.

INDEX

abbesses, 24n. 11; in the *Ecclesias-*
tical History of the English
People, 26–27, 28, 29, 30, 36. *See*
also Æbbe; Ælfflæd; Æthelburh of
Barking; Æthelhild; Æthelthryth;
Anna; Hild; power
Abelard, 146
abortion, 223, 226n. 27
adhaero, 195
Adstock, 301
adultery, 218, 218n. 13, 222n. 22,
355
Æbbe (abbess), 30
Ælfflæd (abbess), 26, 29, 29n. 24,
45, 45n. 76
Æthelberht of Kent (king), 27n. 19,
40, 40n. 59
Æthelburh, daughter of Anna,
27n. 19
Æthelburh of Barking (abbess)(saint),
24, 24n. 13, 27, 27n. 19, 30, 43;
disempowered by Bede, 36–37
Æthelburh Tate, 27n. 19, 40n. 59
Æthelhild (abbess), 42, 42n. 65
Æthelthryth (Audrey)(abbess), 27,
30, 30n. 25, 37–38, 44
Ætla (bishop), 43n. 69
affeccioun (affection), 184, 209
affectio (*affectus*), 180–81, 208–09
affectio conjugalis, 196, 196n. 48,
197, 198, 200n. 55, 205, 205n. 66,
206; defined, 179, 187. *See also*
marital affection

affectio maritalis ("maritalis
affectio"), 179, 180, 181, 184,
185, 187, 188, 207, 208, 209; confusion as to, 207; in court depositions, 187, 188; and property
disputes, 199, 207; in witness
accounts, 189, 191n. 38, 195,
195nn. 45, 46, 196, 196n. 48. *See*
also marital affection
Alexander III (pope), 124n. 5, 126,
135, 182, 183, 208; on baptism,
260n. 7, 266
Alfonso II (king of Portugal), 329
Alhflæd of Northumbria, 40n. 59
Alphonse of Pecha (bishop), 56, 65
Alphonso, son of Edward I, 294n. 9,
305–06, 317–18, 318n. 55
Alvastra monastery, 63
Alysaunder, Master John, 368, 390
Ambrose (saint), 276
Amesbury convent, 309n. 41, 316,
316n. 52, 317
Amiens, 274n. 36
Ancrene Riwle, 184
Andrew II, of Hungary (duke; king):
and a crusade as vow fulfillment,
334, 335, 336–37; and Inno-
cent III's succession intercession,
329–30, 332–34, 334n. 24,
335–36, 335–36n. 26, 337
Angela of Foligno, 60
Angers, 264, 265